THE DUTY TO OBEY THE LAW

Selected Philosophical Readings

Edited by
WILLIAM A. EDMUNDSON

ROWMAN & LITTLEFIELD PUBLISHERS, INC.
Lanham • Boulder • New York • Oxford

ROWMAN & LITTLEFIELD PUBLISHERS, INC.

Published in the United States of America
by Rowman & Littlefield Publishers, Inc.
4720 Boston Way, Lanham, Maryland 20706

12 Hid's Copse Road
Cumnor Hill, Oxford OX2 9JJ, England

British Library Catloguing in Publication Information Available

Library of Congress Cataloging-in-Publication Data

The duty to obey the law : selected philosophical readings / edited by
William A. Edmundson
    p. cm.
    Includes bibliographical references and index.
    ISBN 0-8476-9254-X (cloth : alk. paper). — ISBN 0-8476-9255-8
(paper : alk. paper)
    1. Obedience (Law) 2. Political obligation. I. Edmundson,
William A (William Atkins), 1948– .
  K256.D88 1999
  340'.115—dc21
                                             98-37982
                                            CIP

Printed in the United States of America

∞ ™ The paper used in this publication meets the minimum requirements of
American National Standard for Information Sciences—Permanence of Paper
for Printed Library Materials, ANSI Z39.48–1984.

*for David
and Isabella*

CONTENTS

Acknowledgments   ix

Introduction   1
    William A. Edmundson

1 The Obligation to Obey the Law   17
    Richard A. Wasserstrom

2 The Justification of Civil Disobedience   49
    John Rawls

3 The Conflict between Authority and Autonomy   63
    Robert Paul Wolff

4 Is There a Prima Facie Obligation to Obey the Law?   75
    M. B. E. Smith

5 The Principle of Fair Play   107
    A. John Simmons

6 Political Authority and Political Obligation   143
    Rolf Sartorius

7 The Obligation to Obey: Revision and Tradition   159
    Joseph Raz

8 Legitimate Authority and the Duty to Obey   177
    Kent Greenawalt

9 Presumptive Benefit, Fairness, and Political
    Obligation   193
    George Klosko

10 Legal Theory and the Claim of Authority   *213*
      Philip Soper

11 Freedom, Recognition, and Obligation: A Feminist
      Approach to Political Theory   *243*
      Nancy J. Hirschmann

12 Special Ties and Natural Duties   *271*
      Jeremy Waldron

13 Who Believes in Political Obligation?   *301*
      Leslie Green

14 Surrender of Judgment and the Consent Theory of
      Political Authority   *319*
      Mark C. Murphy

Index   *347*
About the Contributors   *351*

ACKNOWLEDGMENTS

The editor wishes to acknowledge the assistance of the members of his fall 1997 jurisprudence seminar at Georgia State University, and the generous research support of the College of Law.

Chapter 1 by Richard A. Wasserstrom was originally published in 10 *UCLA Law Review* 780. Copyright 1963, The Regents of the University of California. All rights reserved.

Chapter 2 by John Rawls is reprinted by permission of the author from *Civil Disobedience,* Hugo Bedau, ed. (New York: Pegasus, 1969), pages 240–255.

Chapter 3 by Robert Paul Wolff is reprinted by permission of the author from *In Defense of Anarchism* by Robert Paul Wolff (Harper & Row, 1971), pages 3–19.

Chapter 4 by M. B. E. Smith is reprinted by permission of The Yale Law Journal Company and Fred B. Rothman & Company from *The Yale Law Journal,* vol. 82, pages 950–976.

Chapter 5 by A. John Simmons is reprinted from *Moral Principles and Political Obligations* by John Simmons, pages 101–108, 114–142. Copyright © 1979 by Princeton University Press. Reprinted by permission.

Chapter 6 by Rolf Sartorius is reprinted from the *Virginia Law Review,* vol. 67 (1981), no. 3. Reprinted by permission.

Chapter 7 by Joseph Raz was previously published in the *Notre Dame Journal of Law, Ethics & Public Policy,* vol. 1 (1984), pages 139–155.

Chapter 8 by Kent Greenawalt is reprinted from *Conflicts of Law and Morality* by Kent Greenawalt, pages 47–61. Copyright © 1987 by Oxford University Press, Inc. Used by permission of Oxford University Press, Inc.

Chapter 9 by George Klosko is reprinted from *Philosophy & Public Affairs,* vol. 16, pages 241–259. Copyright © 1987 by Princeton University Press. Reprinted by permission.

Chapter 10 by Philip Soper is reprinted from *Philosophy & Public Affairs,* vol. 18, pages 209–237. Copyright © 1989 by Princeton University Press. Reprinted by permission.

Chapter 11 by Nancy J. Hirschmann is reprinted with permission by the American Political Science Association from *American Political Science Review,* vol. 83 (1989), pages 1227–1244.

Chapter 12 by Jeremy Waldron is reprinted from *Philosophy & Public Affairs,* vol. 22, pages 3–30. Copyright © 1993 by Princeton University Press. Reprinted by permission.

Chapter 13 by Leslie Green is reprinted from *For and Against the State,* J. Narveson and J. T. Sanders, eds. (Lanham, Md.: Rowman & Littlefield, 1996), pages 1–17.

Chapter 14 by Mark C. Murphy was previously published in *Law and Philosophy,* vol. 16 (1997), no. 2, pages 115–143. Reprinted with kind permission from Kluwer Academic Publishers.

INTRODUCTION

William A. Edmundson

The question "Why should I obey the law?" introduces a puzzle as old as antiquity. The puzzle is especially troublesome if we think of cases in which breaking the law is not *otherwise* wrongful, and in which the chances of getting caught are negligible. Philosophers from Socrates to H. L. A. Hart have struggled to give reasoned support to the thought that we do have a general moral duty to obey the law but, more recently, the greater number of learned voices has expressed doubt that there is any such duty, at least as traditionally conceived. The controversy today is as vigorous as ever, and involves scholars and students in the diverse fields of philosophy, law, government, political science, and sociology. This anthology is intended to make available the best of the recent work on this subject. The order is chronological, in order to reveal the unfolding of issues in the course of the dialectic.

THE CONTRIBUTIONS

The first chapter is Richard Wasserstrom's "The Obligation to Obey the Law," published in 1963, when the Freedom Rides in the American South made the justifiability of civil disobedience an intensely debated topic. As Wasserstrom points out, many of the greatest historical writers on the subject—including John Locke, David Hume, and John Austin—viewed the problem of "political obligation" (as it is often called) as identical to the question, When does a government become so abusive

1

that its subjects are justified in rebelling against it, with its overthrow as their object? As interesting as this latter question is, it obscures the former, which seizes our interest when a generally just regime, or a regime not bad enough to justify outright rebellion, demands obedience to particular laws that the actor finds abhorrent.

Wasserstrom introduces a distinction that all subsequent discussion takes note of. By *a duty to obey the law*, we may mean any of three things. We may mean an absolute duty, which no set of circumstances may override, or we may mean a *prima facie duty*, in the terminology of British philosopher David Ross. A prima facie duty may in circumstances be overridden without, however, ceasing to count as an invariably important and relevant factor in moral deliberation—a factor that is normally conclusive as to the question, What is our duty all things considered? Third, by asserting that there is a duty to obey the law we may mean that what the law requires on a given question is often but perhaps not always worth considering in deciding what one morally ought to do. This third interpretation is the weakest of all.

Wasserstrom's chapter focuses on the question whether there is a duty to obey the law in the absolute sense, assuming that the government issuing the law is generally just. This brings to the fore the issue whether there is a duty to obey a *bad* law promulgated by an otherwise *good* state. One conceptual argument for an absolute duty would hold that "immoral" is part of the meaning of "illegal" and that therefore whatever conduct is counted as illegal is ipso facto immoral, i.e., contrary to what morality requires. This conceptual argument, as Wasserstrom points out, is associated with the "natural law" tradition. But, for reasons given in the essay, Wasserstrom does not credit this argument, nor does he find persuasive the thought that what is *really* illegal must often be determined by extensive moral reflection. Therefore, Wasserstrom must directly confront the possible existence of valid law, promulgated by a reasonably just state, that nonetheless fails to bind in the absolute sense. He concludes that such laws may exist.

John Rawls is unquestionably the preeminent political philosopher of our day. He has addressed the problem of political obligation in several writings, one of which is included here. In his first essay on the subject, "Legal Obligation and the Duty of Fair Play" (1964), he made explicit two assumptions: (1) that citizens of an at least nearly just state do have a prima facie moral obligation to obey its laws, and (2) that this obligation rests upon some more general moral principle, rather than some special principle of its own. He then set out to show that the principle of fair play is the general moral principle of which the duty to obey the law is but a special case. Rawls's principle of fair play states, roughly, that our voluntary acceptance of the benefits of the cooperative sacrifices of others imposes upon us a duty not to take advantage by avoiding similar sacrifices when our turn comes. The principle was first defended by H. L. A. Hart and is the subject of the contributions of John Simmons and George Klosko in this volume.

In "The Justification of Civil Disobedience," the 1969 article that is included here, Rawls adheres to the main lines of his earlier essay, but focuses on the justification of disobedience rather than the derivation of the prima facie duty of obedience. Rawls explains how unjust laws can arise within a generally just institutional framework and then defends the position that civil disobedience in such conditions is justifiable only if it is a public, nonviolent "mode of address" aimed at the community's sense of justice. Rawls here distinguishes two reasons favoring obedi- ence: the fair play obligation, which assumes knowing acceptance of the benefits of social cooperation, and what he calls a *natural duty* not to oppose just institutions, which does not. Although the distinction is not elaborated, Rawls was soon to deemphasize the former and highlight the latter.

By 1971, when his *A Theory of Justice* appeared, Rawls had con- cluded that although the principle of fair play (or of fairness) furnishes a foundation for the political obligations of officials, "[t]here is . . . no political obligation, strictly speaking, for citizens generally."[1] The prob- lem of political obligation for citizens generally is treated by the natural duty to support just institutions, and the principle of fairness is retained, in this context anyway, simply to underscore the especially grave duty of fidelity incumbent upon officials. The citizen's duty to obey just laws seems unproblematic to Rawls, and the duty to obey unjust laws is, in his view, the sticky point, which is overcome by combining the theory of justifiable civil disobedience—more or less as it appears in the essay included here—with a natural duty of civility, viz., "not to invoke the faults of social arrangements as a too ready excuse for not complying with them."[2] Rawls remains true to his 1963 view that the duty to obey the law is derived, not independent, in that he does not directly put it to the choosers in the "original position," unlike the more general principles—the duty of fair play, the duty to support just institutions, and (perhaps) the duty of civility—from which he believes it should be derivable if, in fact, it can be derived.

With the publication of *In Defense of Anarchism* (in 1971, coincidentally the year that Rawls's book appeared) Robert Paul Wolff challenged the assumption that there is a prima facie duty to obey, and he denied that the central project of political philosophy—which he defined to be the reconciliation of the authority of the state with the autonomy of the individual—was capable of solution. And, in 1973, M. B. E. Smith offered a point-by-point critique of the various grounds that had been proposed for the duty to obey: gratitude, fairness, consent, utility, and the natural duty to support just institutions. Smith clarified what was in dispute and what was not in the following way. No one seriously denies that there are prima facie moral duties with respect to a wide range of actions and act types; anarchists can agree with apologists for the state that there is, for example, a duty to not to commit murder—but the duty to obey a law forbidding murder is, for the anarchist, a derivative and even redundant one. Similarly, the anarchist can agree that there is an at least prima facie duty to obey the law where the consequences of disobedience would be sufficiently terrible. Here, though, the ground of the duty consists of the general duty not to bring about terrible consequences, rather than a general, prima facie duty to obey the law. It is the existence of a general, "gap-filling" duty to obey the law that is in dispute.

By means of an example that has become a landmark in this literature—the stop sign in the desert that can be ignored with complete safety—Smith subjects the claim that there is a prima facie duty to obey the law to general tests for assessing the weight of a putative prima facie duty. These tests show, Smith argues, that a general, prima facie duty to obey is of negligible weight, and therefore not morally significant. His conclusion is that there is no general duty to obey the law and that, in fact, the legality of an act is not even a good clue to its moral value. This conclusion, he suggests, should not be startling even though we might have difficulty affirming it. Our common linguistic and normative practices belie our willingness to assert that there is a general duty to obey the law. Nor will this conclusion license dire inferences about the legitimacy of the state, he suggests, unless some compelling reason can be

given why the concept of legitimate authority is linked—as is often assumed—with a general duty to obey the law.[3]

John Simmons's 1979 book, *Moral Principles and Political Obligations*,
remains in many ways the most thorough single discussion of many aspects of the duty to obey. His searching examination of consent theories
concludes that a general duty to obey the law cannot be founded on the
consent of the governed, and, in the excerpt included here, he turns to
the principle of fair play (or fairness) propounded by Hart and Rawls,
and criticized by Smith and by Robert Nozick in *Anarchy, State, and
Utopia* (1974). Simmons explores the significance of the fact that in
Rawls's rendering of the principle (unlike Hart's), the benefits of a fair,
cooperative scheme must be not merely be received but also *accepted* by
the person said to be bound. For Simmons, Rawls's requirement of
"positive acceptance" over and above "mere receipt" is intuitively appealing, but raises the troubling question whether the principle of fair
play, so understood, does not reintroduce the requirement of consent. If
in fact consent has been reintroduced, or has to be to yield an acceptable
principle of fair play, then the idea of fair play as an alternative to consent
theories will have failed. But without requiring some voluntary act
(other than or short of consent) as a basis for a fair play duty, Simmons
argues, the principle falls victim to Nozick's notorious "classical music"
counterexample: if everyone in town, including me, enjoys listening to
music broadcast by volunteers who sacrifice a day a year to operate the
community public address system, the antecedent conditions of the principle are satisfied, but it does not seem to follow, as the principle allows,
that I am bound to make a similar sacrifice. But what, short of consent,
can transform mere receipt of the benefit into the "positive acceptance"
needed?

Simmons defends the principle of fair play against the possible objection that requiring the acceptance of benefits collapses being benefited into consenting to the scheme that benefits. So long as all other of
the conditions of the principle are satisfied (and Simmons refines those
of Hart and Rawls), the possibility of accepting benefits while disclaim-
ing consent (which Simmons illustrates with a variation of Nozick's
"classical music" example) shows that the feared collapse of acceptance
into consent need not occur. A general account of political obligation is
a live possibility if an adequate account of acceptance can be worked
out. Can it? Simmons discusses the serious difficulty posed by the state's

provision of what he terms "open" benefits—what economists sometimes term "public goods," such as national defense, a stable economy, and so forth—that are practically impossible to avoid receiving. To the extent that the state provides open benefits, they seem incapable of being "accepted" rather than merely received. By examining further examples Simmons concludes that a defensible principle of fair play is not sufficiently general to solve the problem of political obligation. Rawls's shift in emphasis away from fairness to the natural duty to support just institutions may have been motivated by an anticipation of just such difficulties.

Taking issue with Wolff's claim that the central problem of political philosophy is reconciling the individual's moral autonomy with the legitimate authority of the state, Rolf Sartorius argues that the question of legitimate authority is independent of the question of political obligation. Sartorius elaborates an idea earlier suggested by Smith and by Robert Ladenson:[4] a right to rule does *not* entail a correlative duty to obey. Political authority necessarily involves claiming a right to occupy a field of activities best consigned to it—such as punishing wrongdoers—and having, in fact, a justification for doing so, but this claim of right and justification in monopolizing the use of coercion need not entail the existence of correlative duties of obedience, or even any *claim* that they exist.

Turning to the question of political obligation, Sartorius reviews the efforts to found a prima facie duty to obey on consent—actual, tacit, or hypothetical—and on fair play. Like Simmons, Sartorius despairs of consent theories and looks to the principle of fair play. Sartorius finds that, suitably modified, there is a valid principle of fair play that might serve as a basis for political obligation were it not for the essentially *coercive* nature of law. This inescapably coercive aspect of law undercuts the necessarily voluntaristic (though not necessarily consensual) setting that must exist before a valid principle of fair play can operate. Political association is, he concludes, necessarily a "one way street," on which the state owes a fiduciary duty toward its citizens, while citizens owe the state no duty other than, perhaps, a duty not to usurp its functions so long as it is faithfully discharging its trust.[5]

Joseph Raz's extensive writings on the subject of authority are represented here by his 1984 article, "The Obligation to Obey: Revision and Tradition." He notes Smith's distinction between the purported duty to *obey* the law and duties to *conform* to the law. Where what the law requires conforms to what justice or other moral reasons independently require, to speak of a duty to *obey* seems redundant (the duty having sufficient grounding without reference to what the law requires) or even perverse (as though the illegality of stealing, rather than its wrongness, would be a proper motive for not stealing). The existence of law sometimes *does* make a moral difference, and when it does, there is no paradox in speaking of a duty to obey the law.

The existence of law makes a moral difference where the lawmaker has superior knowledge of the subject or is in a position to solve a coordination problem, i.e., a problem that consists of the fact that each following her own inclinations would be worse for all (e.g., traffic and pollution problems). But these cases aren't generalizable, Raz argues: some individuals know more about, for example, automotive safety than the lawmaker, and laws addressed to coordination problems are typically overbroad (e.g., the nonexistent jam at the stop sign in the desert). The duty to obey, therefore, will vary from person to person and situation to situation. The only adequate foundation of a general duty to obey the law, Raz concludes, must be (as Thomas Hobbes and John Locke held) voluntary consent—what troubles us today is a diminished sense of loyal identification with the state as the formal expression of a community identity and the resulting lack of general consent.

Kent Greenawalt, in a chapter excerpted from his book, *Conflicts of Law and Morality*, examines the intuitively attractive claim that there is a logical link between the concept of a political authority and a duty of obedience on the part of those subject to authority. Extending a line of inquiry begun by Smith and Sartorius, Greenawalt analyzes the idea of legitimate political authority into a number of component elements, including a duty to obey. He then examines a series of examples of authority not associated with any duty to obey, and finds applicable in each a conception of legitimate authority. Having illustrated the possibility of legitimate authority without a duty to obey, Greenawalt turns to the question, What made the linkage seem so irresistible? He finds that a perceived practical *need* for a widespread disposition to acknowledge a duty to obey underlies the readiness to assume a *logical* correlation. This perception, however, rests on empirical assumptions that require support. Another explanation for our readiness to assume a necessary correlation of legitimate authority and obedience lies in the hope that it would assist in fixing the scope of the duty to obey—but in fact what fixing the scope of the duty to obey requires is a substantive moral inquiry rather than an appeal to the legitimacy of the government in a global sense.

The principle of fair play (or of fairness) continues to inspire the hope that it can be elaborated in a form that is unobjectionable, and serviceable as a nonconsensual basis for a general duty to obey the law. George Klosko pursues this line in his contribution, "Presumptive Benefit, Fairness, and Political Obligation." The principle's plausibility, however, varies according to the type of benefit a cooperative scheme conveys. Open or "nonexcludable" benefits—public goods such as public order and national defense—are ones whose receipt noncooperators have no real choice about, and as to these, Simmons and Rawls conclude, the principle of fair play is inapplicable.

This "limiting argument," as Klosko terms it, can be overcome by attending to a further distinction between "presumptively beneficial" and merely "discretionary" goods. Presumptively beneficial goods are, like Rawls's "primary" goods, ones that any reasonable person would value, while discretionary goods are ones that a person might reasonably refuse or disvalue. Robert Nozick's examples, Klosko argue, involve discretionary goods, like classical music, rather than presumptively beneficial ones, like security, safety, and satisfaction of basic needs. With respect to presumptively beneficial goods, "mere receipt" is sufficient to create a fair play duty to contribute one's fair share; *pace* Simmons and Rawls, voluntary acceptance and participation are not needed here. But what of discretionary goods, such as road repair? In the remainder of his chapter Klosko suggests how the argument from fairness might be extended to discretionary goods, where these are furnished by the state as part of a "package" including presumptively beneficial ones.

With the exception of Philip Soper, all of the authors included here at least tacitly accede to Wasserstrom's positivistic insistence that the law's requirements are recognizable independently of moral criteria. There have been other vigorous dissents. Ronald Dworkin, for example, has advanced an interpretive theory of law, according to which the law is identified with the morally best rendering of past political decisions. And John Finnis has defended a sophisticated version of natural law theory, which rejects as law those positive lawlike pronouncements that are too radically defective from the standpoint of morality. Soper himself has elsewhere written that the positivistic quest for a value-free test to answer the question *What is law?* should be abandoned in favor of a candidly normative engagement with the more pertinent question, *What is law, that I should obey it?*

Soper's contribution to this volume, "Legal Theory and the Claim of Authority," takes issue with the view suggested by Smith and embraced by Sartorius and Greenawalt that the concept of legitimate authority should simply be decoupled from the duty to obey the law. Such a decoupling is attractive as a way of saving the possibility of legitimate authority in case it turns out that there is no general duty to obey, but such a maneuver would not, in Soper's view, sufficiently respect the views and practices of "insiders," i.e., the lawyers and officials whose view of the law is from the inside rather than, like the philosopher's, from beyond. Insiders earnestly claim that law and morality are necessarily connected in the sense that citizens have a duty to obey that is not conditional upon the law's being correct by any external standard. Positivists deny the connection that insiders typically, if implicitly, assert even as positivists declare their project to be one of offering a descriptively adequate account of law as we find it. Something has to give, Soper argues, because the positivist's descriptive account is at odds with this well-entrenched feature of the phenomenon it seeks to describe. Just how entrenched this feature is, is shown by the insider's obliviousness to the philosophical critique of the duty to obey.

Taking aim at Raz's account, Soper endorses its conceptual analysis of the claims of authority (its "preemption," "content-independence," and "correlativity" aspects) while criticizing Raz's account of the *justification* of authority, on the ground that it mistakenly forsakes authority's "right to be wrong" by emphasizing its purported "greater likelihood of getting things right." In fact, as Raz admits, the likelihood of the law striking a better balance between competing considerations than, say, a civilian expert in the field is not sufficiently great morally to bind the expert. Soper points out that this result does not meet Raz's own criterion of explanatory adequacy, for insiders (and others!) are unlikely to accept the conclusion that, for example, the Grand Prix driver is morally free to drive as she thinks best, while the rest of us must accede to the legislature's superior wisdom. Soper concludes that philosophers should work harder at political theory before demanding that insiders curtail the law's claim to authority. Although, in later work,[6] Soper has questioned whether the normative claims conceptually linked to law are as strong as those defended here, his analysis has been influential.

Although the selections here largely repudiate the possibility of grounding political obligation generally on the consent of the governed, the classical consent theories of Hobbes and Locke are never far from the discussion, and their gravitational influence upon theorists hoping to discover a nonconsensual ground is easy to recognize. Nancy Hirschmann challenges the grip that this consent-centered understanding of obligation has exercised over political theory. Her chapter, "Freedom, Recognition, and Obligation: A Feminist Approach to Political Theory," argues that classical consent theory and its modern progeny reveal a pervasive, male-orientated bias. An unbiased account of political obligation will have to reflect women's experience of obligation, which does not square with the traditional view that obligations are binding only if freely consented to. Her critique seems to call for a second look at a "natural duty" account of political obligation.

Jeremy Waldron addresses some of the many difficulties that must be overcome by any account invoking natural duties. In particular, the duty to obey is thought to bind us only to the laws of our own government, or of the nation in which we are present, but it is usually supposed that the mark of natural duties is that they do not rest upon such contingencies as residence or voluntary assent—my natural duty not to murder applies in all times and places, but my duty to contribute to public works seems drastically more limited. How, then, can a natural duty theory explain the fact that the duty to obey ties persons not to laws generally but to the laws of one's own society? In answer, Waldron articulates a conception of a *range-limited* principle of justice that, combined with the fact that certain governments administer certain range-limited principles, can account for the fact that, for example, New Zealanders are bound to certain of the laws of New Zealand, while the French are not, without reintroducing the idea that in some sense New Zealanders have, as the French have not, *consented* to be bound by the laws of New Zealand.

Although consent has a role as a part of a criterion of justice and legitimacy, its bearing on the duty to obey is less direct, and more diffuse, on this account. Consent's proper role, in Waldron's view, is not in determining *whether* we are bound to do our part to support justice through necessary institutional means, but in determining whether claimant institutions have sufficient popular support to count as legitimate and effective. Thus, if the government of Montana by just means effectively addresses the needs of impoverished Montanans, and *if addressing these needs is a matter of justice*, then, Waldron suggests, the natural law theorist must face the fact that an outsider may have an obligation to respond to a financial appeal (demand?) from the state of Montana. This result will offend the intuitions of those who deny that obligations can simply be thrust upon us, but Waldron suggests that the discomfort arising here has more to do with our uneasiness about duties of beneficence than with the nonconsensual basis of political obligation. The natural duty theorist has to "bite the bullet" at some point and say, yes, like it or not, there is a duty to obey.

In his contribution, Leslie Green pointedly asks, "Who believes in political obligation?" The question is of interest because George Klosko, for one, has (elsewhere) argued that the existence of a duty to obey the law is a considered judgment of "most" people—including, but not limited to, Soper's "insiders." Green inquires whether this is so, and what it might mean if it were. The claim that "most" people believe that there is a general duty to obey the law may be taken in either an empirical or in an "armchair" sense. As a supposed deliverance of reflection, Green points out, the conviction that there is a duty to obey is a *theoretical* opinion rather than a judgment about a concrete, if hypothetical case. Therefore a coherentist moral epistemology, along the lines of Rawls's celebrated method of "reflective equilibrium," need no more account for such a conviction than any other pre-reflective opinion. If, as an empirical matter, it does turn out that "most" people do hold such an opinion, a skeptic about the duty to obey will have to explain why this error is commonly made, but "ideological shaping" of popular opinion by social influences seems equal to the task. But is there in fact any generally held belief in political obligation? Green examines purported empirical evidence and finds it ambiguous. The skeptic's case against the existence of a duty to obey cannot be put aside by these appeals to common sense, he concludes.

Mark Murphy's contribution to this volume is an effort to "refurbish" consent theory as an approach to grounding the duty to obey the law. To do so, he describes the way in which acting on abstract moral principles often involves *determinations*, or choices among acceptable means, no one of which is morally compelled. Moreover, many important "choiceworthy" moral ends, such as justice, can only be achieved by cooperative action. Consent "in the acceptance sense" to the rules of a cooperative scheme to achieve a choiceworthy end exists when the actor practically treats the group rule as her own determination of principle.

What is significant about consent in this sense is that it requires no "occurrent" or "attitudinal" event or disposition in order to bind morally. The "brute fact" that consent in these latter senses is often absent has been the Achilles' heel of consent theory. Consent in the acceptance sense, in contrast, requires no more than that the actor has made a determination of general principles that apply to her; and its moral bindingness flows from the fact that we are morally bound to act according to determinations of general moral principles that apply to us if failing to so act would frustrate the point of our having so determined. As a matter of empirical fact, it seems plausible to suppose that citizens employ their knowledge of the law in this way much more frequently than they declare their consent to its authority. As an illustration, Murphy points to drunk-driving laws that specify ("determine") blood alcohol levels. Citizens' surrender of judgment to the state's determinations on a range of such subjects is what constitutes the political authority of the state. And, to the extent that we are morally required to accept salient determinations of moral principle, we are not, Murphy argues, free to revoke our acceptance of law by the simple expedient of discontinuing our use of social rules in our practical decision making.

A FRAMEWORK FOR FURTHER INQUIRY

This anthology is intended to indicate the probable direction of further effort in this field, as well as to propel it along that way. Two main lines can be distinguished even though they must, ultimately, be rejoined. The first is the refinement of fair play and natural duty accounts of the duty to obey the law, and their reconciliation with the tenacious idea that the consent of the governed must, in some sense, be the foundation of legitimate government. The second line is to unpack the concept of authority, and specifically of political authority, and to exhibit what connection there is between political authority and a duty of obedience. The relationship between the two lines can perhaps best be exhibited by the following set of propositions:

1. X is an *authority* only if X at least implicitly makes claims distinctive of authority.

2. An authority X is a *legitimate* authority only if X's distinctive claims are true.

3. Political authority is a species of authority, whose distinctive claim is that persons subject to it have a general moral duty to obey its commands.

4. Political authority is legitimate only if it imposes a general moral duty of obedience on those subject to it (from 2 and 3).

5. There is no general duty to obey political authority X, even if X is (nearly) just.

6. Legitimate political authorities are possible and even actual.

The crunch comes in the subset {4,5,6}: not all of the members of this subset can be true; as a matter of logic, at least one of them has to be false. Much of the urgency of the question "Is there a duty to obey the law?" derives from the fact that a No answer calls into question the very possibility of a legitimate state. In other words, if there is no general duty to obey the law (as 5 states) then *either* legitimacy is not conditioned upon the existence of such a duty *or* there are no legitimate states, actual or possible.

Many of the authors included here have embraced 5, and at least two of them, Wolff and Simmons, have gone on to deny 6, embracing a view that has been termed *philosophical anarchism*. But others are hopeful that 6 can be saved by building a convincing case against 5 based on the principle of fair play (Klosko) or natural duty (Waldron, and perhaps Hirschmann) or consent (Murphy), or by yet other strategies, such as Ronald Dworkin's notion of "associative" obligations,[7] or Christopher Wellman's argument from the duty of beneficence.[8] This would allow one to maintain that there is a strong link between legitimate authority and a duty to obey, without having to give up on the possibility of a legitimate state.

Others, including Smith, Sartorius, and Greenawalt, accept 5 but save 6 by denying 4. For these three authors, the absence of a general duty to obey does not undermine the legitimacy of the state because there is no necessary correlation—at least, none as strong as 4 states—between legitimate authority and a general duty to obey. Waldron also doubts 4, but is not ready to accept 5.

The denial of 4 may seem appealing, as Soper points out, precisely because that move would reconcile 5 and 6. But 4 expresses a deeply held view of the nature of political authority, as Soper and others (most notably, Dworkin) have urged. Moreover, if 4 is denied, then either 2 or 3 must be denied also, because the conjunction of 2 and 3 entails 4. Raz affirms 1 and 3 but denies 4, and thus, by implication, denies 2. Raz argues that the legitimacy of state authority is not as closely tied to the imposition of a duty to obey as what 4 states, but he does not explain his implicit denial of 2, which is troubling in light of Soper's argument that 2 is true in the case of scientific authority and Raz's general claim that practical authority (of which political authority is a species) and scientific authority are structurally similar.

Soper affirms 3 (here, at least) and 4, and defends 2 in the case of scientific, though not political, authority. Thus, Soper's commitment to 4 is not compelled by adherence to 2 and 3, for he rejects 2 in its generality because it fails to apply to practical authority. Rather, Soper embraces 4 because it captures the views of "insiders," whose common convictions and practices must not be rejected lightly. Since insiders (and others) are at least as wedded to 6 as to 4, Soper's conclusion is that political philosophy has to work harder at refuting 5.

Green, finally, challenges the claim made by Klosko and Soper that the denial of 5 enjoys the presumption of correctness generally enjoyed by views endorsed by common sense or expert consensus. If confidence in 5 is to be undermined, that will have to be the result of theoretical work along the lines indicated above, rather than by appeal to "what we (or the experts) really think."

Although the tension within the set {4,5,6} could be resolved simply by denying the most dubious of its members, it may turn out on (yet) further examination that two or that all three require reformulation. In any case, it is clear that the nature of political authority, the legitimacy of that authority, and the duty to obey the law are implicated in a web of conceptual relationships that political and legal philosophers are still, two and a half millennia after the death of Socrates, only beginning to untangle.

NOTES

1. John Rawls, *A Theory of Justice* 113–14 (1971); and cf. John Rawls, "Legal Obligation and the Duty of Fair Play," in Sidney Hook, ed., *Law and Philosophy* 3–18 (New York: New York University Press, 1964).

2. *A Theory of Justice* at 355.

3. See M. B. E. Smith, "The Duty to Obey the Law," in Dennis Patterson, ed. *Companion to Philosophy of Law and Legal Theory* 465–74 (1996), for Smith's more recent view.

4. Robert Ladenson, "In Defense of a Hobbesian Conception of Law," 9 *Philosophy & Public Affairs* 134–59 (1980); "Legitimate Authority," 9 *American Philosophical Quarterly* 335–41 (1972).

5. See Rolf Sartorius, "Positivism and the Foundations of Legal Authority," in Ruth Gavison, ed., *Issues in Contemporary Legal Philosophy: The Influence of H. L. A. Hart* 43–61 (1987), for Sartorius's most recent statement of his view.

6. Philip Soper, "Law's Normative Claims," in Robert P. George, ed., *The Autonomy of Law: Essays on Legal Positivism* 215–47 (1996).

7. See Ronald Dworkin, *Law's Empire* 190–216 (1986); and cf. Leslie Green, "Associative Obligations and the State," in Allan C. Hutchinson and Leslie J. M. Green, eds., *Law and Community: The End of Individualism?* 93–118 (Toronto: Carswell, 1989); A. John Simmons, "Associative Political Obligations," 106 *Ethics* 247–73 (1996).

8. Christopher H. Wellman, "Liberalism, Samaritanism, and Political Legitimacy," 25 *Philosophy & Public Affairs* 211–37 (1996).

1

THE OBLIGATION TO OBEY THE LAW

Richard A. Wasserstrom

I

The question of what is the nature and extent of one's obligation to obey the law is one of those relatively rare philosophic questions which can never produce doubts about the importance of theory for practice. To ask under what circumstances, if any, one is justified in disobeying the law, is to direct attention to problems which all would acknowledge to be substantial. Concrete, truly problematic situations are as old as civil society.

The general question was posed—though surely not for the first time—well over two thousand years ago in Athens when Crito revealed to Socrates that Socrates' escape from prison could be easily and successfully accomplished. The issue was made a compelling one—though once again surely not for the first time—by Crito's insistence that escape was not only possible but also *desirable*, and that disobedience to law was in *this* case at least, surely justified. And the problem received at the hand of Socrates—here perhaps for the first time—a sustained theoretical analysis and resolution.

Just as the question of what is the nature and extent of one's obligation to obey the law demanded attention then—as it has throughout man's life in the body politic—it is no less with us today in equally vexing and perplexing forms. Freedom rides and sit-ins have raised the question of whether the immorality of segregation may justify disobeying the law. The all too awesome horrors of a nuclear war have seemed to some to require responsive action, including, if need be, deliberate but peaceful trespasses upon government-owned atomic testing grounds. And the rightness of disobedience to law in the face of court-ordered school integration has been insisted upon by the citizens of several states and acted upon by the governor of at least one.[1]

The problem is one of present concern and the questions it necessarily raises are real. But even if the exigencies of contemporary life were not such as to make this topic a compelling one, it is one which would still be peculiarly ripe for critical inquiry. In part this is so because despite their significance many of the central issues have been relatively neglected by legal or political philosophers and critics. Many of the important questions which bear upon the nature and extent of one's obligation to obey the law have been dealt with summarily and uncritically; distinguishable issues have been indiscriminately blurred and debatable conclusions gratuitously assumed.

More important is the fact that historically the topic has generally been examined from only one very special aspect of the problem. Those philosophers who have seriously considered questions relating to one's obligation to obey the law have considered them only in the context of revolution. They have identified the conditions under which one would, if ever, be justified in disobeying the law with the conditions under which revolution would, if ever, be justified; and they have, perhaps not surprisingly, tended thereby to conclude that one would be justified in disobeying the law if, and only if, revolution itself would in that case be justified.[2]

To view the problem in a setting of obedience or revolution is surely to misconstrue it. It is to neglect, among other things, something that is obviously true—that most people who disobey the law are not revolutionaries and that most acts of disobedience of the law are not acts of revolution. Many who disobey the law are, of course, ordinary criminals: burglars, kidnappers, embezzlers, and the like. But even of those who disobey the law under a claim of justification, most are neither advocates nor practitioners of revolution.[3]

If the traditional, philosophical treatment of this subject is unduly simplistic and restrictive, contemporary legal thought is seldom more instructive. It is distressing, for one thing, that those whose daily intellectual concern is the legal system have said so little on this subject. And it is disturbing that many of those who have said anything at all appear so readily to embrace the view that justified disobedience of the law is a rare, if not impossible, occurrence. What is so disturbing is not the fact that this view is held—although I think it a mistaken one—but rather that such a conclusion is so summarily reached or assumed.[4]

I must make it clear at the outset that it is not my purpose to devote the remainder of this article to a documentation of the claims just made concerning either historical or contemporary thought. I do not wish to demonstrate that people in fact do believe what they appear to believe about the possibility of justified disobedience to law. Nor do I wish to show why it is that people have come to believe what they appear to believe. Rather, in very general terms I am concerned here with *arguments*—with those arguments which have been or which might be given in support of the claim that because one does have an obligation to obey the law, one ought not ever disobey the law.

To describe the focus of the article in this manner is, however, to leave several crucial matters highly ambiguous. And thus, before the arguments can be considered properly, the following matters must be clarified.

A. There are several different views which could be held concerning the nature of the stringency of one's obligation to obey the law. One such view, and the one which I shall be most concerned to show to be false, can be characterized as holding that one has an *absolute* obligation to obey the law. I take this to mean that a person is never justified in disobeying the law; to know that a proposed action is illegal is to know all one needs to know in order to conclude that the action ought not to be done;[5] to cite the illegality of an action is to give a sufficient reason for not having done it. A view such as this is far from uncommon. President Kennedy expressed the thoughts of many quite reflective people when he said not too long ago:

> . . . [O]ur nation is founded on the principle that observance of the law is the eternal safeguard of liberty and defiance of the law is the surest road to tyranny.
>
> The law which we obey includes the final rulings of the courts as well as the enactments of our legislative bodies. Even among law-abiding men few laws are universally loved.
>
> But they are universally respected and not resisted.

Americans are free, in short, to disagree with the law, but not to disobey it. For in a government of laws and not of men, no man, however prominent or powerful, and no mob, however unruly or boisterous, is entitled to defy a court of law.

If this country should ever reach the point where any man or group of men, by force or threat of force, could long deny the commands of our court and our Constitution, then no law would stand free from doubt, no judge would be sure of his writ and no citizen would be safe from his neighbors.[6]

A more moderate or weaker view would be that which holds that, while one does have an obligation to obey the law, the obligation is a prima facie rather than absolute one. If one knows that a proposed course of conduct is illegal then one has a good—but not necessarily a sufficient—reason for refraining from engaging in that course of conduct. Under this view, a person may be justified in disobeying the law, but an act which is in disobedience of the law does have to be justified, whereas an act in obedience of the law does not have to be justified.

It is important to observe that there is an ambiguity in this notion of a prima facie obligation. For the claim that one has a prima facie obligation to obey the law can come to one of two different things. On the one hand, the claim can be this: the fact that an action is an act of disobedience is something which always does count against the performance of the action. If one has a prima facie obligation to obey the law, one always has that obligation—although, of course, it may be overridden by other obligations in any particular case. Thus the fact that an action is illegal is a relevant consideration in every case and it is a consideration which must be outweighed by other considerations before the performance of an illegal action can be justified.

On the other hand, the claim can be weaker still. The assertion of a prima facie obligation to obey the law can be nothing more than the claim that as a matter of fact it is *generally* right or obligatory to obey the law. As a rule the fact that an action is illegal is a relevant circumstance. But in any particular case, after deliberation, it might very well turn out that the illegality of the action was not truly relevant. For in any particular case the circumstances might be such that there simply was nothing in the fact of illegality which required overriding—*e.g.*, there were no bad consequences at all which would flow from disobeying the law in this case.

The distinction can be made more vivid in the following fashion. One person, *A*, might hold the view that any action in disobedience of the law is intrinsically bad. Some other person, *B*, might hold the view that no action is intrinsically bad unless it has the property, *P*, and that not all actions in disobedience of the law have that property. Now for *A*, the fact of disobedience is *always* a relevant consideration,[7] for *B*, the fact of disobedience may always be initially relevant because of the existence of some well-established hypothesis which asserts that the occurrence of any action of disobedience is correlated highly with the occurrence of *P*. But if in any particular case disobedience does not turn out to have the property, *P*, then, upon reflection, it can be concluded by *B* that the fact that disobedience is involved is not a reason which weighs against the performance of the act in question. To understand *B*'s position it is necessary to distinguish the relevance of *considering* the fact of disobedience from the relevance of the fact of disobedience. The former must always be relevant, the latter is not.

Thus there are at least three different positions which might be taken concerning the character of the obligation to obey the law or the rightness of disobedience to the law. They are: (1) One has an absolute obligation to obey the law; disobedience is never justified. (2) One has an obligation to obey the law but this obligation can be overridden by conflicting obligations; disobedience can be justified, but only by the presence of outweighing circumstances. (3) One does not have a special obligation to obey the law, but it is in fact usually obligatory, on other grounds, to do so; disobedience to law often does turn out to be unjustified.

B. It must also be made clear that when I talk about the obligation to obey the law or the possibility of actions which are both illegal and justified. I am concerned solely with *moral obligations* and *morally justified* actions. I shall be concerned solely with arguments which seek to demonstrate that there is some sort of a connection between the legality or illegality of an action and its morality or immorality. Concentration on this general topic necessarily renders a number of interesting problems irrelevant. Thus, I am not at all concerned with the question of why, in fact, so many people do obey the law. Nor, concomitantly, am I concerned with the nonmoral reasons which might and do justify obedience to law—of these, the most pertinent, is the fact that highly unpleasant consequences of one form or another are typically inflicted upon those who disobey the law. Finally there are many actions which are immoral irrespective of whether they also happen to be illegal. And I am not, except in one very special sense, concerned with this fact either. I am not concerned with the fact that the immorality of the action itself may be a sufficient reason for condemning it regardless of its possible illegality.

C. My last preliminary clarification relates to the fact that there is a variety of kinds of legal rules or laws and that there is a variety of ways in which actions can be related to these rules. This is an important point because many moral philosophers, in particular, have tended to assimilate all legal rules to the model of a typical law or legal order which is enforced through the direct threat of the infliction by the government of severe sanctions, and have thereby tended to assume that all laws and all legal obligations can be broken or disobeyed only in the manner in which penal laws can be broken or disobeyed. That this assimilation is a mistake can be demonstrated quite readily. There are many laws that, unlike the typical penal law, do not require or prohibit the performance of any acts at all. They cannot, therefore, be disobeyed. There are laws, for example, that make testamentary dispositions of property ineffective, unenforceable, or invalid, if the written instrument was not witnessed by the requisite number of disinterested witnesses. Yet a law of this kind obviously does not impose an obligation upon anyone to make a will. Nor, more significantly, could a person who executed a will without the requisite number of witnesses be said to have disobeyed the law. Such a person has simply failed to execute a valid will.[8]

The foregoing observations are relevant largely because it is important to realize that to talk about disobeying the law or about one's obligation to obey the law is usually to refer to a rather special kind of activity, namely, that which is exemplified by, among other things, actions in violation or disobedience of a penal law. It is this special type of activity which alone is the concern of this article.

II

One kind of argument in support of the proposition that one cannot be justified in disobeying the law is that which asserts the existence of some sort of *logical* or conceptual relationship between disobeying the law and acting immorally.[9] If the notion of illegality entails that of immorality then one is never justified in acting illegally just because part of the meaning of *illegal* is *immoral*; just because describing an action as illegal is—among other things—to describe it as unjustified.[10]

A claim such as this is extremely difficult to evaluate. For one has great difficulty in knowing what is to count as truly relevant—let alone decisive—evidence of its correctness. There is, nevertheless, a supporting argument of sorts which can be made. It might go something like this:

It is a fact which is surely worth noticing that people generally justify action that *seems to be* illegal by claiming that the action *is not really* illegal. Typically an actor who is accused of having done something illegal will not defend himself by pointing out that, while illegal, his conduct was nevertheless morally justified. Instead, he will endeavor to show in one way or another that it is really inaccurate to call his conduct illegal at all. Now it looks as though this phenomenon can be readily accounted for. People try to resist the accusation of illegality, it might be argued, for the simple reason that they wish to avoid being punished. But what is interesting and persuasive is the fact that people try just as hard to evade a charge of illegality even in those situations where the threat of punishment is simply not an important or even relevant consideration.

The cases of the recent sit-ins or freedom rides are apt. To be sure, the claim was that the preservation of segregated lunch counters, waiting rooms, and the like was morally indefensible. But an important justification for the rightness of the actions employed in integrating these facilities in the fashion selected rested upon the insistence that the perpetuation of segregation in these circumstances was itself illegal. One primary claim for the rightness of freedom rides was that these were not instances of disobeying the law. They were instead attempts to invoke judicial and executive protection of legal, indeed constitutional, rights. While there were some, no doubt, who might have insisted upon the rightness of sit-ins even if they were clearly illegal, most people were confident of the blamelessness of the participants just because it was plain that their actions were not, in the last analysis, illegal. Were it evident that sit-ins were truly illegal many might hold a different view about the rightness of sitting-in as a means to bring about integrated facilities.

Language commonly invoked in the course of disputes between

nations furnishes another equally graphic illustration of the same point. In the controversy over the status of Berlin, for instance, both the United States and Russia relied upon claims of legality and were sensitive to charges of illegality, to an appreciably greater extent than one would otherwise have supposed. And much the same can be said of the more recent dispute between India and China. Now if nations which have little to fear in the way of the imposition of sanctions for acting illegally are nevertheless extraordinarily sensitive to charges of illegal conduct, this also may be taken as evidence of the fact that *illegality* implies *immorality*.

Wholly apt, too, was the controversy over the Eichmann trial. To some, the fact that the seizure and trial of Eichmann by Israel was illegal was sufficient to cast grave doubts upon the justifiability of the proceedings. To others, the charge of illegality made it necessary to demonstrate that nothing really illegal had occurred. What is significant about all this is the fact that all of the disputants implicitly acknowledged that illegality was something which did have to be worried about.

Such in brief is the argument which might be advanced and the "evidence" which might be adduced to support it. I think that such an argument is not persuasive, and I can best show this to be so in the following fashion.

Consider the case of a law that makes it a felony to perform an abortion upon a woman unless the abortion is necessary to preserve *her* life. Suppose a teenager, the daughter of a local minister, has been raped on her way home from school by an escapee from a state institution for mental defectives. Suppose further that the girl has become pregnant and has been brought to a reputable doctor who is asked to perform an abortion. And suppose, finally, that the doctor concludes after examining the girl that her life will not be endangered by giving birth to the child.[11] An abortion under these circumstances is, it seems fair to say, illegal.[12] Yet, we would surely find both intelligible and appealing the doctor's claim that he was nonetheless justified in disobeying the law by performing an abortion on the girl. I at least can see nothing logically odd or inconsistent about recognizing both that there is a law prohibiting this conduct and that further questions concerning the rightness of obedience would be relevant and, perhaps, decisive. Thus I can see nothing logically odd about describing this as a case in which the performance of the abortion could be both illegal and morally justified.[13]

There is, no doubt, a heroic defense which can be made to the above. It would consist of the insistence that the activity just described simply cannot be both illegal and justified. Two alternatives are possible. First, one might argue that the commission of the abortion would indeed have been justified if it were not proscribed by the law. But since it is so prohibited, the abortion is wrong. Now if this is a point about the appropriateness of kinds of reasons, I can only note that referring the action to a valid law does not seem to preclude asking meaningful questions about the obligatoriness of the action. If this is a point about language or concepts it does seem to be perfectly intelligible to say that the conduct is both illegal and morally justified. And if this is, instead, an *argument* for the immorality of ever disobeying a valid law, then it surely requires appreciable substantiation and not mere assertion.

Second, one might take a different line and agree that other questions can be asked about the conduct, but that is because the commission of the abortion under these circumstances simply cannot be illegal. The difficulty here, however, is that it is hard to understand what is now meant by *illegal*. Of course, I am not claiming that in the case as I have described it, it is clear that the performance of the abortion must be illegal. It might not be. But it might be. Were we to satisfy all the usual tests that we do invoke when we determine that a given course of conduct is illegal, and were someone still to maintain that because the performance of the abortion is here morally justified it cannot be illegal, then the burden is on the proponent of this view to make clear how we are to decide when conduct is illegal. And it would further be incumbent upon him to demonstrate what seems to be highly dubious, namely, that greater clarity and insight could somehow be attained through a radical change in our present terminology. It appears to be a virtually conclusive refutation to observe that there has never been a legal system whose criteria of validity—no matter how sophisticated, how rational and how well defined—themselves guaranteed that morally justified action would never be illegal.

Thus an argument as strong as any of the above must fail. There is, of course, a weaker version which may be more appealing. If it is true that there is something disturbing about justifying actions that are conceded to be illegal, then one way to account for this is to insist that there is a logical connection between the concepts involved, but it is something less than the kind of implication already discussed. Perhaps it is correct that *illegal* does not entail *immoral*; *illegal* might nevertheless entail *prima facie immoral*. The evidence adduced tends to show that among one's moral obligations is the prima facie duty to obey the law.[14]

Once again, it is somewhat difficult to know precisely what to make of such a claim. It is hard to see how one would decide what was to count as evidence or whether the evidence was persuasive. At a minimum, it is not difficult to imagine several equally plausible alternative explanations of the disturbing character of accusations of illegal activity. In addition, to know only that one has a prima facie duty to obey the law is not to know a great deal. In particular, one does not know how or when that obligation can be overridden. And, of course, even if it is correct that acting illegally logically implies acting prima facie immorally, this in no way shows that people may not often be morally justified in acting illegally. At most, it demands that they have some good reason for acting illegally; at best, it requires what has already been hypothesized, namely, that the action in question, while illegal, be morally justified.

Thus, it is clear that if the case against ever acting illegally is to be made out, conceptual analysis alone cannot do it. Indeed, arguments of quite another sort must be forthcoming. And it is to these that I now turn.

III

One such argument, and the most common argument advanced, goes something like this: The reason why one ought never to disobey the law is simply that the consequences would be disastrous if everybody disobeyed the law. The reason why disobedience is never right becomes apparent once we ask the question "But what if everyone did that?"

Consider again the case of the doctor who has to decide whether he is justified in performing an illegal abortion. If he only has a prima facie duty to obey the law it looks as though he might justifiably decide that in this case his prima facie obligation is overridden by more stringent conflicting obligations. Or, if he is simply a utilitarian, it appears that he might rightly conclude that the consequences of disobeying the abortion law would be on the whole and in the long run less deleterious than those of obeying. But this is simply a mistake. The doctor would inevitably be neglecting the most crucial factor of all, namely, that in performing the abortion he was disobeying the law. And imagine what would happen if everyone went around disobeying the law. The alternatives are obeying the law and general disobedience. The choice is between any social order and chaos. As President Kennedy correctly observed, if any law is disobeyed, then no law can be free from doubt, no citizen safe from his neighbor.

Such an argument, while perhaps overdrawn, is by no means uncommon.[15] Yet, as it stands, it is an essentially confused one. Its respective claims, if they are to be fairly evaluated, must be delineated with some care.

At a minimum, the foregoing attack upon the possibility of justified disobedience might be either one or both of two radically different kinds of objection. The first, which relates to the consequences of an act of disobedience, is essentially a *causal* argument. The second questions the *principle* that any proponent of justified disobedience invokes. As to the causal argument, it is always relevant to point out that any act of disobedience may have certain consequences simply because it is an act of disobedience. Once the occurrence of the act is known, for example, expenditure of the state's resources may become necessary. The time and energy of the police will probably be turned to the task of discovering who it was who did the illegal act and of gathering evidence relevant to the offense. And other resources might be expended in the prosecution and adjudication of the case against the perpetrator of the illegal act. Illustrations of this sort could be multiplied, no doubt, but I do not think either that considerations of this sort are very persuasive or that they have been uppermost in the minds of those who make the argument now under examination. Indeed, if the argument is a causal one at all, it consists largely of the claim that any act of disobedience will itself cause, to some degree or other, general disobedience of all laws; it will cause or help to cause the overthrow or dissolution of the state. And while it is possible to assert that any act of disobedience will tend to further social disintegration or revolution, it is much more difficult to see why this must be so.

The most plausible argument would locate this causal efficacy in the kind of example set by any act of disobedience. But how plausible is this argument? It is undeniable, of course, that the kind of example that will be set is surely a relevant factor. Yet, there is nothing that precludes any proponent of justified disobedience from taking this into account. If, for example, others will somehow infer from the doctor's disobedience of the abortion law that they are justified in disobeying *any* law under *any* circumstances, then the doctor ought to consider this fact. This is a consequence—albeit a lamentable one—of his act of disobedience. Similarly, if others will extract the proper criterion from the act of disobedience, but will be apt to misapply it in practice, then this too ought to give the doctor pause. It, too, is a consequence of acting.[16] But if the argument is that disobedience would be wrong even if no bad example were set and no other deleterious consequences likely, then the argument must be directed against the principle the doctor appeals to in disobeying the law, and not against the consequences of his disobedience at all.

As to the attack upon a principle of justified disobedience, as a principle, the response "But what if everyone disobeyed the law?" does appear to be a good way to point up both the inherent inconsistency of almost any principle of justified disobedience and the manifest undesirability of adopting such a principle. Even if one need not worry about what others will be led to do by one's disobedience, there is surely something amiss if one cannot consistently defend his right to do what one is claiming he is right in doing.

In large measure, such an objection is unreal. The appeal to "But what if everyone did that?" loses much, if not all, of its persuasiveness once we become clearer about what precisely the "did that" refers to. If the question "But what if everyone did that?" is simply another way of asking "But what if everybody disobeyed the law?" or "But what if people generally disobeyed the laws?" then the question is surely quasi-rhetorical. To urge general or indiscriminate disobedience to laws is to invoke a principle that, if coherent, is manifestly indefensible. It is equally plain, however, that with few exceptions such a principle has never been seriously espoused. Anyone who claims that there are actions that are both illegal and justified surely need not be thereby asserting that it is right generally to disobey all laws or even any particular law. It is surely not inconsistent to assert both that indiscriminate disobedience is indefensible and that discriminate disobedience is morally right and proper conduct. Nor, analogously, is it at all evident that a person who claims to be justified in performing an illegal action is thereby committed to or giving endorsement to the principle that the entire legal system ought to be overthrown or renounced. At a minimum, therefore, the appeal to "But what if everyone did that?" cannot by itself support the claim that one has an absolute obligation to obey the law—that disobeying the law can never be truly justified.

There is, however, a distinguishable but related claim which merits very careful attention—if for no other reason than the fact that it is so widely invoked today by moral philosophers. The claim is simply this: While it may very well be true that there are situations in which a person will be justified in disobeying the law, it is surely not true that disobedience can ever be justified solely on the grounds that the consequences of disobeying the particular law were in that case on the whole less deleterious than those of obedience.[17]

This claim is particularly relevant at this juncture because one of the arguments most often given to substantiate it consists of the purported demonstration of the fact that any principle which contained a proviso permitting a general appeal to consequences must itself be incoherent. One of the most complete statements of the argument is found in Marcus Singer's provocative book, *Generalization in Ethics*:

> Suppose, . . . that I am contemplating evading the payment of income taxes. I might reason that I need the money more than the government does, that the amount I have to pay is so small in comparison with the total amount to be collected that the government will never miss it. Now I surely know perfectly well that if I evade the payment of taxes this will not cause others to do so as well. For one thing, I am certainly not so foolish as to publicize my action. But even if I were, and the fact became known, this would still not cause others to do the same, unless it also became known that I was being allowed to get away with it. In the latter case the practice might tend to become widespread, but this would be a consequence, not of my action, but of the failure of the government to take action against me. Thus there is no question of my act being wrong because it would set a bad example. It would set no such example, and to suppose that it must, because it would be wrong, is simply a confusion. . . . Given all this, then if the reasons mentioned would justify me in evading the payment of taxes, they would justify everyone whatsoever in doing the same thing. For everyone can argue in the same way—everyone can argue that if he breaks the law this will not cause others to do the same. The supposition that this is a justification, therefore, leads to a contradiction.

I conclude from this that, just as the reply "Not everyone will do it" is irrelevant to the generalization argument, so is the fact that one knows or believes that not everyone will do the same; and that, in particular, the characteristic of knowing or believing that one's act will remain exceptional cannot be used to define a class of exceptions to the rule. One's knowledge or belief that not everyone will act in the same way in similar circumstances cannot therefore be regarded as part of the circumstances of one's action. One's belief that not everyone will do the same does not make one's circumstances relevantly different from the circumstances of others, or relevantly different from those in which the act is wrong. Indeed, on the supposition that it does, one's circumstances could never be specified, for the specification would involve an infinite regress.[18]

Singer's argument is open to at least two different interpretations. One quite weak interpretation is this: A person cannot be morally justified in acting as he does unless he is prepared to acknowledge that everyone else in the identical circumstances would also be right in acting the same way. If the person insists that he is justified in performing a certain action because the consequences of acting in that way are more desirable than those of acting in any alternative fashion, then he must be prepared to acknowledge that anyone else would also be justified in doing that action whenever the consequences of doing that action were more desirable than those of acting in any alternative fashion. To take Singer's own example: A person, *A*, could not be morally justified in evading the payment of his taxes on the grounds that the consequences of nonpayment were *in his case* more beneficial, all things considered, than those of payment, unless *A* were prepared to acknowledge that any other person, *X*, would also be justified in evading his, *i.e.*, *X*'s taxes, if it is the case that the consequences of *X*'s nonpayment would in *X*'s case be more beneficial, all things considered, than those of payment. If this is Singer's point, it is, for reasons already elaborated, unobjectionable.[19]

But Singer seems to want to make a stronger point as well. He seems to believe that even a willingness to generalize in this fashion could not justify acting in this way. In part his argument appears to be that this somehow will permit everyone to justify nonpayment of taxes; and in part his argument appears to be that there is a logical absurdity involved in attempting to make the likelihood of other people's behavior part of the specification of the relevant consequences of a particular act. Both of these points are wrong. To begin with, on a common sense level it is surely true that the effect which one's action will have on other people's behavior is a relevant consideration. For as was pointed out earlier, if A determines that other people will be, or may be, led to evade *their* taxes even when the consequences of nonpayment will in their cases be less beneficial than those of payment, then this is a consequence of A's action which he must take into account and attempt to balance against the benefits which would accrue to society from his nonpayment. Conversely, if for one reason or another A can determine that his act of nonpayment will not have this consequence, this, too, must be relevant. In this sense, at least, other people's prospective behavior is a relevant consideration.

More importantly, perhaps, it is surely a mistake—although a very prevalent one in recent moral philosophy—to suppose that permitting a general appeal to consequences would enable everyone to argue convincingly that he is justified in evading his taxes. Even if I adopt the principle that everyone is justified in evading his taxes whenever the consequences of evasion are on the whole less deleterious than those of payment, this in no way entails that I or anyone else will always, or ever, be justified in evading my taxes. It surely need not turn out to be the case—even if no one else will evade his taxes—that the consequences will on the whole be beneficial if I succeed in evading mine. It might surely be the case that I will spend the money saved improvidently or foolishly; it might very well be true that the government will make much better use of the money. Indeed, the crucial condition which must not be ignored and which Singer does ignore is the condition which stipulates that the avoidance of one's taxes in fact be optimific, that is, more desirable than any other course of conduct.

The general point is simply that it is an empirical question—at least in theory—what the consequences of any action will be. And it would surely be a mistake for me or anyone else to suppose that that action whose consequences are most pleasing to me—in either the short or long run—will in fact be identical with that action whose consequences are on the whole most beneficial to society. Where the demands of self-interest are strong, as in the case of the performance of an unpleasant task like paying taxes, there are particular reasons for being skeptical of one's conclusion that the consequences of nonpayment would in one's own case truly be beneficial. But once again there is no reason why there might not be cases in which evasion of taxes would be truly justified, nor is there any reason why someone could not consistently and defensibly endorse nonpayment whenever these circumstances were in fact present.

There is one final point which Singer's discussion suggests and which does appear to create something of a puzzle. Suppose that I believe that I am justified in deliberately trespassing on an atomic test site, and thereby disobeying the law, because I conclude that this is the best way to call attention to the possible consequences of continued atmospheric testing or nuclear war. I conclude that the consequences of trespassing will on the whole be more beneficial than any alternative action I can take. But suppose I also concede—what very well may be the case—that if everyone were to trespass, even for this same reason and in the same way, the consequences would be extremely deleterious. Does it follow that there is something logically incoherent about my principle of action? It looks as though there is, for it appears that I am here denying others the right to do precisely what I claim I am right in doing. I seem to be claiming, in effect, that it is right for me to trespass on government property in order to protest atomic testing only if it is the case that others, even under identical circumstances, will not trespass. Thus, it might be argued, I appear to be unwilling or unable to generalize my principle of conduct.

This argument is unsound, for there is a perfectly good sense in which I am acting on a principle which is coherent and which is open to anyone to adopt. It is simply the principle that one is justified in trespassing on government property whenever—among other things—it happens to be the case that one can say accurately that others will not in fact act on that same principle. Whether anyone else will at any given time act on any particular principle is an empirical question. It is, to repeat what has already been said, one of the possible circumstances which can be part of the description of a class of situations. There is, in short, nothing logically self-contradictory or absurd about making the likelihood of even identical action one of the relevant justifying considerations. And there is, therefore, no reason why the justifiability of any particular act of disobedience cannot depend, among other things, upon the probable conduct of others.

IV

It would not be at all surprising if at this stage one were to feel considerable dissatisfaction with the entire cast of the discussion so far. In particular, one might well believe that the proverbial dead horse has received still another flaying for the simple reason that no one has ever seriously argued that people are never justified in disobeying the law. One might insist, for instance, that neither Socrates nor President Kennedy was talking about all law in all legal systems everywhere. And one might urge, instead, that their claims concerning the unjustifiability of any act of disobedience rest covertly, if not overtly, on the assumption that the disobedience in question was to take place in a society in which the lawmaking procedures and other political institutions were those which are characteristic of an essentially democratic, or free, society. This is, of course, an important and plausible restriction upon the original claim, and the arguments which might support it must now be considered.

While there are several things about a liberal, democratic or free society which might be thought to preclude the possibility of justified disobedience, it is evident that the presence of all the important constitutive institutions *cannot* guarantee that unjust or immoral laws will not be enacted. For the strictest adherence to principles of representative government, majority rule, frequent and open elections and, indeed, the realization of all of the other characteristics of such a society, in no way can insure that laws of manifest immorality will not be passed and enforced. And if even the ideal democratic society might enact unjust laws, no existing society can plausibly claim as much. Thus, if the case against the possibility of justified disobedience is to depend upon the democratic nature of the society in question, the case cannot rest simply on the claim that the only actions which will be made illegal are those which are already immoral.

What then are the arguments which might plausibly be advanced? One very common argument goes like this: It is, of course, true that even democratically selected and democratically constituted legislatures can and do make mistakes. Nevertheless, a person is never justified in disobeying the law as long as there exist alternative, "peaceful" procedures by which to bring about the amendment or repeal of undesirable or oppressive laws. The genuine possibility that rational persuasion and argument can bring a majority to favor any one of a variety of competing views, both requires that disapproval always be permitted and forbids that disobedience ever be allowed. This is so for several reasons.

First, it is clearly unfair and obviously inequitable to accept the results of any social decision-procedure only in those cases in which the decision reached was one of which one approves, and to refuse to accept those decisions which are not personally satisfying. If there is one thing which participation, and especially voluntary participation, in a decision-procedure entails, it is that all of the participants must abide by the decision regardless of what it happens to be. If the decision-procedure is that of majority rule, then this means that any person must abide by those decisions in which he was in a minority just as much as it means that he can insist that members of the minority abide when he is a member of the majority.

As familiar as the argument is, its plausibility is far from assured. On one reading, at least, it appears to be one version of the universalization argument. As such, it goes like this. Imagine any person, *A*, who has voted with the majority to pass a law making a particular kind of conduct illegal. *A* surely would not and could not acknowledge the right of any person voting with the minority justifiably to disobey that law. But, if *A* will not and cannot recognize a right of justified disobedience here, then *A* certainly cannot consistently or fairly claim any right of justified disobedience on his part in those cases in which he, *A*, happened to end up being in a minority. Thus, justified disobedience can never be defensible.

This argument is fallacious. For a person who would insist that justified disobedience was possible even after majoritarian decision-making could very plausibly and consistently acknowledge the right of any person to disobey the law under appropriate circumstances regardless of how that person had voted on any particular law. Consider, once again, the case already put of the doctor and the pregnant girl. The doctor can surely be consistent in claiming both that circumstances make the performance of the illegal abortion justified and that any comparable action would also be right irrespective of how the actor, or the doctor, or anyone else, happened to have voted on the abortion law, or any other law. The point is simply that there is no reason why any person cannot consistently: (1) hold the view that majority decision-making is the best of all forms of decision-making; (2) participate voluntarily in the decision-making process; and (3) believe that it is right for *anyone* to disobey majority decisions whenever the relevant moral circumstances obtain, *e.g.*, whenever the consequences of disobedience to that law at that time would on the whole be more deleterious than those of obedience.

But this may be deemed too facile an answer; it also may be thought to miss the point. For it might be argued that there is a serious logical inconsistency of a different sort which must arise whenever a voluntary participant in a social decision-procedure claims that not all the decisions reached in accordance with that procedure need be obeyed. Take the case of majority rule. It is inconsistent for anyone voluntarily to participate in the decision-process and yet at the same time to reserve the right to refuse to abide by the decision reached in any particular case. The problem is not an inability to universalize a principle of action. The problem is rather that of making any sense at all out of the notion of having a majority decide anything—of having a procedure by which to make group decisions. The problem is, in addition, that of making any sense at all out of the fact of voluntary participation in the decision-procedure—in knowing what this participation can come to if it does not mean that every participant is bound by all of the decisions which are reached. What can their participation mean if it is not an implicit promise to abide by all decisions reached? And even if the point is not a logical one, it is surely a practical one. What good could there possibly be to a scheme, an institutional means for making social decisions, which did not bind even the participants to anything?

The answer to this argument—or set of arguments—is wholly analogous to that which has been given earlier. But because of the importance and prevalence of the argument some repetition is in order.

One can simply assert that the notion of any social decision-making procedure is intelligible only if it entails that all participants always abide by all of the decisions which are made, no matter what those decisions are. Concomitantly, one can simply insist that any voluntary participant in the decision-process must be consenting or promising to abide by all decisions which are reached. But one cannot give as a plausible reason for this assertion the fact that the notion of group decision-making becomes incoherent if anything less in the way of adherence is required of all participants. And one cannot cite as a plausible reason for this assertion the fact that the notion of voluntary participation loses all meaning if anything less than a promise of absolute obedience is inferred.

It is true that the notion of a group decision-making procedure would be a meaningless notion if there were no respects in which a group decision was in any way binding upon each of the participants. Decisions which in no way bind anyone to do anything are simply not decisions. And it is also true that voluntary participation is an idle, if not a vicious, act if it does not commit each participant to something. If any voluntary participant properly can wholly ignore the decisions which are reached, then something is surely amiss.

But to say all this is not to say very much. Group decision-making can have a point just because it does preclude any participant from taking some actions which, in the absence of the decision, he might have been justified in performing. And voluntary participation can still constitute a promise of sorts that one will not perform actions which, in the absence of voluntary participation, might have been justifiable. If the fact of participation in a set of liberal political institutions does constitute a promise of sorts, it can surely be a promise that the participant will not disobey a law just because obedience would be inconvenient or deleterious to him. And if this is the scope of the promise, then the fact of voluntary participation does make a difference. For in the absence of the participation in the decision to make this conduct illegal, inconvenience to the actor might well have been a good reason for acting in a certain way. Thus, participation can create new obligations to behave in certain ways without constituting a promise not to disobey the law under any circumstances. And if this is the case, adherence to a principle of justified disobedience is not inconsistent with voluntary participation in the decision-making process.

Indeed, a strong point can be made. The notion of making laws through voluntary participation in democratic institutions is not even inconsistent with the insistence that disobedience is justified whenever the consequences of disobedience are on the whole more beneficial than those of obedience. This is so because a promise can be a meaningful promise even if an appeal to the consequences of performing the promise can count as a sufficient reason for not performing the promise.[20] And if this is the case for promises generally, it can be no less the case for the supposed promise to obey the law.

Finally, even if it were correct that voluntary participation implied a promise to obey, and even if it were the case that the promise must be a promise not to disobey on consequential grounds, all of this would still not justify the conclusion that one ought never to disobey the law. It would, instead, only demonstrate that disobeying the law must be prima facie wrong, that everyone has a prima facie obligation to obey the law. This is so just because it is sometimes right even to break one's own promises. And if this, too, is a characteristic of promises generally, it is, again, no less a characteristic of the promise to obey the law.

The notions of promise, consent, or voluntary participation do not, however, exhaust the possible sources of the obligation to obey the laws of a democracy. In particular, there is another set of arguments which remains to be considered. It is that which locates the rightness of obedience in the way in which any act of disobedience improperly distributes certain burdens and benefits among the citizenry. Professor Wechsler, for example, sees any act of disobedience to the laws of the United States as "the ultimate negation of all neutral principles, to take the benefits accorded by the constitutional system, including the national market and common defense, while denying it allegiance when a special burden is imposed. That certainly is the antithesis of law."[21]

On the surface, at least, Professor Wechsler's claim seems overly simple: it appears to be the blanket assertion that the receipt by any citizen, through continued, voluntary presence of benefits of this character necessarily implies that no act of disobedience could be justified. To disobey any law after having voluntarily received these benefits would be, he seems to suggest, so unjust that there could never be overriding considerations. This surely is both to claim too much for the benefits of personal and commercial security and to say too little for the character of all types of disobedience. For even if the receipt of benefits such as these did simply impose an obligation to obey the law, it is implausible to suppose that the obligation thereby imposed would be one that stringent.

But there is a more involved aspect of Professor Wechsler's thesis— particularly in his insistence that disobedience of the law, where benefits of this kind have been received, is the negation of all neutral principles. I am not at all certain that I understand precisely what this means, but there are at least two possible interpretations: (1) Unless everyone always obeyed the law no one would receive these obviously valuable benefits. (2) Since the benefits one receives depend upon the prevalence of conditions of uniform obedience, it follows that no one who willingly receives these benefits can justly claim them without himself obeying. The first has already been sufficiently considered.[22] The second, while not unfamiliar, merits some further attention.

In somewhat expanded form, the argument is simply this. What makes it possible for any particular person to receive and enjoy the benefits of general, personal and economic security is the fact that everyone else obeys the law. Now, if injustice is to be avoided, it is surely the case that any other person is equally entitled to these same benefits. But he will have this security only if everyone else obeys the law. Hence the receipt of benefits at others' expense requires repayment in kind. And this means universal obedience to the law.[23]

There are two features of this argument which are puzzling. First, it is far from clear that the benefits of security received by anyone necessarily depend upon absolute obedience on the part of everyone else. It just might be the case that an even greater quantum of security would have accrued from something less than total obedience. But even if I am wrong here, there is a more important point at issue. For reasons already discussed, it is undeniable that even in a democracy a price would be paid for universal obedience—the price that might have to be paid, for instance, were the doctor to refuse to perform the abortion because it was illegal. If this is so, then the fact that a person received benefits from everyone else's obedience does not necessarily entail that it is unjust for him to fail to reciprocate in kind. The benefit of general security might not have been worth the cost. A greater degree of flexibility on the part of others, a general course of obedience except where disobedience was justified, might have yielded a greater benefit. People may, in short, have done more or less than they should have. And if they did, the fact that anyone or everyone benefitted to some degree in no way requires that injustice can only be avoided through like and reciprocal conduct. If it is better, in at least some circumstances, to disobey a law than to obey it, there is surely nothing unjust about increasing the beneficial consequences to all through acts of *discriminate* disobedience.

If the argument based upon the effect of receipt of certain benefits is therefore not very persuasive, neither in most cases is the argument which is derived from the way in which any act of disobedience is thought to distribute burdens unfairly among the citizenry. The argument can be put very briefly: If there is one thing which any act of disobedience inevitably does, it is to increase the burdens which fall on all the law-abiding citizens. If someone disobeys the law even for what seems to be the best of reasons, he inevitably makes it harder—in some quite concrete sense—on everyone else. Hence, at a minimum this is a good reason not to disobey the law, and perhaps a sufficient reason as well.

This argument is appealing because there is at least one kind of case it fits very well. It is the case of taxation. For suppose the following, only somewhat unreal, conditions: that the government is determined to raise a specified sum of money through taxation, and that, in the long, if not the short, run it will do so by adjusting the tax rate to whatever percentage is necessary to produce the desired governmental income. Under such circumstances it could plausibly be argued that one of the truly inevitable results of a successfully executed decision to evade the payment of one's taxes—a decision made, moreover, on ostensibly justifiable grounds—is that every other member of society will thereby be required to pay a greater tax than would otherwise have been the case. Thus in some reasonably direct and obvious fashion any act of disobedience—particularly if undetected—does add to the burdens of everyone else. And surely this is to make out at least a strong case of prima facie injustice.

Now, for reasons already elaborated, it would be improper to conclude that evasion of one's taxes could never be justified. But the argument is persuasive in its insistence that it does provide a very good reason why evasion always must be justified and why it will seldom be justifiable. But even this feature of disobedience is not present in many cases. Tax evasion, as opposed to other kinds of potentially justified disobedience, is a special, far from typical case. And what is peculiar to it is precisely the fact that any act of disobedience to the tax laws arguably shifts or increases the burden upon others. Such is simply not true of most types of acts of disobedience because most laws do not prohibit or require actions which affect the distribution of resources in any very direct fashion.

Thus, if we take once again the case of the doctor who has decided that he is justified in performing an illegal abortion on the pregnant girl, it is extremely difficult, if not impossible, to locate the analogue of the shifting of burdens involved in tax evasion. How does the performance of the abortion thereby increase the "costs" to anyone else? The only suggestion which seems at all plausible is that which was noted earlier in a somewhat different context. Someone might argue that it is the occurrence of illegal actions which increases the cost of maintaining a police force, a judiciary and suitable correctional institutions. This cost is a burden which is borne by the citizenry as a whole. And hence, the doctor's illegal acts increase their burdens—albeit very slightly. The difficulty here is threefold. First, if the doctor's act is performed in secret and if it remains undetected, then it is hard to see how there is any shift of economic burden at all. Second, given the fact that police forces, courts and prisons will always be necessary as long as unjustified acts of disobedience are a feature of social existence, it is by no means apparent that the additional cost is anything but truly de minimis.[24] And third, the added costs, if any, are in the doctor's case assumed by the doctor *qua* member of the citizenry. He is not avoiding a burden; at most he adds something to everyone's—including his own—existing financial obligations. Thus, in cases such as these, it is not at all evident that disobedience need even be prima facie unjust and hence unjustified.

V

There is one final argument which requires brief elucidation and analysis. It is in certain respects a peculiarly instructive one both in its own right and in respect to the thesis of this article.

It may be true that on some particular occasions the consequences of disobeying a law will in fact be less deleterious on the whole than those of obeying it—even in a democracy. It may even be true that on some particular occasions disobeying a law will be just whereas obeying it would be unjust. Nevertheless, the reason why a person is never justified in disobeying a law—in a democracy—is simply this: The chances are so slight that he will disobey only those laws in only those cases in which he is in fact justified in doing so, that the consequences will on the whole be less deleterious than if he never disobeys any law. Furthermore, since anyone must concede the right to everyone to disobey the law when the circumstances so demand it, the situation is made still worse. For once we entrust this right to everyone we can be sure that many laws will be disobeyed in a multitude of cases in which there was no real justification for disobedience. Thus, given what we know of the possibilities of human error and the actualities of human frailty, and given the tendency of democratic societies to make illegal only those actions which would, even in the absence of a law, be unjustified, we can confidently conclude that the consequences will on the whole and in the long run be best if no one ever takes it upon himself to "second-guess" the laws and to conclude that in his case his disobedience is justified.[25]

The argument is, in part, not very different from those previously considered. And thus, what is to be said about it is not very different either. Nonetheless, upon pain of being overly repetitive, I would insist that there is a weak sense in which the argument is quite persuasive and a strong sense in which it is not. For the argument makes, on one reading, too strong an empirical claim—the claim that the consequences will in the long run always in fact be better if no one in a democracy ever tries to decide when he is justified in disobeying the law. As it stands, there is no reason to believe that the claim is or must be true, that the consequences will always be better. Indeed, it is very hard to see why, despite the hypothesis, someone might still not be justified in some particular case in disobeying a law. Yet, viewed as a weaker claim, as a summary rule, it does embody a good deal that is worth remembering. It can, on this level, be understood to be a persuasive reminder of much that is relevant to disobedience: that in a democracy the chances of having to live under bad laws are reduced; that in a democracy there are typically less costly means available by which to bring about changes in the law; that in a democracy—as in life in general—a justified action may always be both inaptly and ineptly emulated; and that in a democracy—as in life in general—people often do make mistakes as to which of their own actions are truly justified. These are some of the lessons of human experience which are easy to forget and painful to relearn.

But there are other lessons, and they are worth remembering too. What is especially troubling about the claim that disobedience of the law is never justified, what is even disturbing about the claim that disobedience of the law is never justified in a democratic or liberal society, is the facility with which its acceptance can lead to the neglect of important moral issues. If no one is justified in disobeying the Supreme Court's decision in *Brown v. Board of Educ.*[26] this is so because, among other things, there is much that is wrong with segregation. If there was much that was peculiarly wrong in Mississippi in 1963, this was due to the fact, among other facts, that a mob howled and a governor raged when a court held that a person whose skin was black could go to a white university. Disobeying the law is often—even usually—wrong; but this is so largely because the illegal is usually restricted to the immoral and because morally right conduct is still less often illegal. But we must always be sensitive to the fact that this has not always been the case, is not now always the case and need not always be the case in the future. And under concentration upon what is wrong with disobeying the law rather than upon the wrong which the law seeks to prevent can seriously weaken and misdirect that awareness.

NOTES

This is an expanded and substantially revised version of a paper, "Disobeying the Law," which was presented at the December 1961 meeting of the Eastern Division of the American Philosophical Society and which was published in 58 J. PHILOSOPHY 641 (1961).

This revision has been benefited by the helpful comments and suggestions of my colleagues, Professors Herbert Packer and Gerald Gunther; and especially of Professor Arnold Kaufman of the Department of Philosophy of the University of Michigan, presently a Fellow at the Center for Advanced Study in the Behavioral Sciences.

1. This is to say nothing of the stronger claim, involved in many of the war crimes prosecutions, that one does have a duty to disobey the law and, therefore, that one can be properly punished for having obeyed the law.

2. See, *e.g.*, AUSTIN, THE PROVINCE OF JURISPRUDENCE DETERMINED 53–55 (1954); HUME, A TREATISE OF HUMAN NATURE, bk. III, §§ 9, 10; LOCKE, THE SECOND TREATISE OF GOVERNMENT, chs. 18, 19.

3. A subject which has surely not received the philosophical attention it deserves is that of the nature of revolution. What, for instance, are the characteristics of a revolution? Must the procedures by which laws are made or the criteria of validity be altered? Or is it sufficient that the people who occupy certain crucial offices be removed in a manner inconsistent with existing rules? Must force or resistance accompany whatever changes or alterations are made? Whatever the answers may be to questions such as these, it is, I think, plain that particular laws may be disobeyed under a claim of justification without any of these features being present. One can *argue* that for one reason or another, any act of disobedience must necessarily lead to revolution or the overthrow of the government. But then this is an argument which must be demonstrated.

4. Professor Henry Hart, for example, in his extremely stimulating analysis of the aims of the criminal law seems to hold such a view. Professor Hart believes that the criminal law ought only be concerned with that conduct which is morally blameworthy. From this he infers that no real problem can ever be presented by laws which make knowledge of the illegality of an action one of the elements of the offense. And this is so because the "knowing or reckless disregard of legal obligation affords an independent basis of blameworthiness *justifying the actor's condemnation as a criminal*, even when his conduct was not intrinsically antisocial." Hart, *The Aims of the Criminal Law,* 23 LAW & CONTEMP. PROB. 401, 418

(1958). (Emphasis added.) Some such view can also be plausibly attributed to, among others, Professor Lon Fuller, see text at section II, and Professor Herbert Wechsler, see text at section IV. Of course, all of these scholars, or any other person holding such a view, might well insist that the position is tenable only if an important qualification is made, namely, that the legal system in question be that of an essentially democratic society. For a discussion of this more restricted claim, see text at section IV.

5. Because I am concerned with the question of whether one is ever *morally justified* in acting illegally, I purposely make the actor's knowledge of the illegality of the action part of the description of the act. I am not concerned with the question of whether ignorance of the illegality of the action ought to excuse one from moral blame.

6. *New York Times*, Oct. 1, 1962, p. 22, col. 6. The same qualification must be made here as was made in note 4 *supra*—President Kennedy may well have meant his remarks to be applicable only to the legal system which is a part of the set of political institutions of the United States.

7. To repeat, though, it surely is not necessarily conclusive, or sufficient, since an action in obedience to the law may under some other description be worse, or less justifiable, than disobedience.

8. See HART, THE CONCEPT OF LAW 27–48 (1961), particularly for the clearest and fullest extant philosophical analysis of the important distinguishing characteristics of different kinds of legal rules.

In this connection a stronger point than the one made above can be made. It is that there are many laws which, if they can be disobeyed at all, cannot be disobeyed in the way in which the typical criminal law can be disobeyed. For there are many laws that either impose or permit one to impose upon oneself any number of different legal obligations. And with many of these legal obligations, regardless of how created, it seems correct to say that one can breach or fail to perform them without thereby acting illegally or in disobedience of the law. One's obligation to obey the law may not, therefore, be coextensive with one's legal obligations. In the typical case of a breach of contract, for example, the failure to perform one's contractual obligations is clearly a breach of a legal obligation. Yet one can breach a contract and, hence, a legal obligation without necessarily acting illegally. This last assertion is open to question. And arguments for its correctness would not here be germane. It is sufficient to recognize only that failing to honor or perform some types of legal obligations may be a quite different kind of activity from violating or disobeying a law or order which is backed up, in some very direct fashion, by a governmentally threatened severe sanction.

9. It is worth emphasizing that I am not at all interested in the claim—which in many ways is an odd one to belabor—that there is a logical relationship be-

tween disobeying the law and acting illegally. See, *e.g.*, Carnes, *Why Should I Obey the Law?*, 71 ETHICS 14 (1960).

10. Professor Fuller may hold to some version of this view in his article, *Positivism and Fidelity to Law—A Reply to Professor Hart*, 71 HARV. L. REV. 630, 656 (1958), where, after characterizing the position of legal positivism as one which says that "On the one hand, we have an amoral datum called law, which has the peculiar quality of creating a moral duty to obey it. On the other hand, we have a moral duty to do what we think is right and decent." Professor Fuller goes on to criticize this bifurcation of law and morality on the grounds that "The 'dilemma' it states has the verbal formulation of a problem, but the problem it states makes no sense. It is like saying I have to choose between giving food to a starving man and being mimsey with the borogroves. I do not think it unfair to the positivistic philosophy to say that it never gives any coherent meaning to the moral obligation of fidelity to law."

Others who at least suggest adherence to such a position are: BAIER, THE MORAL POINT OF VIEW 134 (1958); NOWELL-SMITH, ETHICS 236–37 (1959); and WELDON, THE VOCABULARY OF POLITICS 57, 62, 66–67 (1953). And there are surely passages in Hobbes that could also be read in this way. See, *e.g.*, HOBBES, LEVIATHAN, chs. XIII, XVIII. The claim that *illegal* entails *immoral* is closely related to, but surely distinguishable from, the position that Professor Fuller, among many others, may also hold, namely, that there are certain minimum "moral" requirements that must be met before any rule can be a law.

11. These facts are taken from Packer & Gampell, *Therapeutic Abortion: A Problem in Law and Medicine*, 11 STAN. L. REV. 417 (1959), where they are introduced in a different context.

12. Such would seem to be the case in California, for example, where CAL. PEN. CODE § 274 makes the performance of an abortion a felony unless the abortion is necessary to preserve the life of the pregnant woman.

13. I am supposing, of course, that one would regard the performance of the abortion—in the absence of the relevant penal law—as clearly morally justified. If one disagrees with this assessment of the morality of the case, then some other example ought to be substituted. One likely candidate, drawn from our own history, is that of the inherent rightness in refusing to return an escaped Negro slave to his "owner." If one believes that refusing to do so would be clearly justifiable, then consider whether the existence of the fugitive slave laws necessarily rendered a continued refusal unjustified.

14. Sir W. David Ross, for example, suggests that the obligation to obey the law is a prima facie obligation which is a compound of three more simple prima facie duties. Ross, THE RIGHT AND THE GOOD 27–28 (1930).

15. Socrates, for instance, supposes that were he to escape he might properly be asked: "[W]hat are you about? Are you going by an act of yours to overturn

us—the laws and the whole state, as far as in you lies? Do you imagine that a state can subsist and not be overthrown, in which the decisions of law have no power, but are set aside and overthrown by individuals?" Plato, Crito. Analogous arguments can be found in, for example: Austin, The Province of Jurisprudence Determined 52–53 (1954); Hobbes, Leviathan, ch. XV; Hume, A Treatise of Human Nature, bk. III, pt. II, 3, 6, 8, 9; Toulmin, An Examination of the Place of Reason in Ethics 151 (1950).

16. For a very special and related version of this argument, see text at section V.

17. This is a particular illustration of the more general claim that for one reason or another utilitarianism cannot be a defensible or intelligible moral theory when construed as permitting one's moral obligation to do any particular action to be overridden by a direct appeal to the consequences of performing that particular action. For recent statements of the claim see, *e.g.*, Nowell-Smith, *op. cit. supra* note 10; Rawls, *Two Concepts of Rules*, 64 Philosophical Rev. 3 (1955), in Olafson, Society, Law, and Morality 420 (1961); Singer, Generalization in Ethics 61–138, 178–216 (1961); Toulmin, *op. cit. supra* note 15, at 144–65; Harrison, *Utilitarianism, Universalisation, and Our Duty To Be Just*, 53 Aristotelian Soc'y Proceedings 105 (1952–53).

For some criticisms of this restriction on utilitarianism see, *e.g.*, Wasserstrom, The Judicial Decision 118–37 (1961). But see Hart, *Book Review*, 14 Stan. L. Rev. 919, 924–26 (1962).

18. Singer, *op. cit. supra* note 17, at 149–50.

19. Neither Singer nor I have adequately refuted the confirmed ethical egoist who insists that he is prepared to generalize but only in the sense that X's nonpayment is justified if, and only if, the consequences of X's nonpayment would in X's case be more beneficial *to A* than those of payment. This is a problem which surely requires more careful attention than it typically receives. It will not do simply to insist that the egoist does not understand ordinary moral discourse. Instead, what must be demonstrated are the respects in which the egoist's position is an inherently unjust one. But to make this showing is beyond the scope of this article.

20. The point here is analogous to that made in the discussion of Singer's argument. Moral philosophers have often argued that one cannot appeal simply to the consequences of performing or not performing a particular promise as a reason for not performing that promise. And the reason why this is so is that the notion of having promised to do something would be unintelligible if the promisor could always, when the time came for performance, be excused if it were the case that the consequences of nonperformance were more beneficial than those of performance. This would make promising unintelligible, so the argument goes, because promising entails or means obligating oneself to do some-

thing. But if the appeal to consequences is what is to be determinative of one's obligations, then the promise becomes a wholly superfluous, meaningless act. Rawls, for instance, puts the point this way: "Various defenses for not keeping one's promise are allowed, but among them there isn't the one that, on general utilitarian grounds, the promisor (truly) thought his action best on the whole, even though there may be the defense that the consequences of keeping one's promise would have been *extremely* severe. While there are too many complexities here to consider all the necessary details, one can see that the general defense isn't allowed if one asks the following question: what would one say of someone who, when asked why he broke his promise, replied simply that breaking it was best on the whole? Assuming that his reply is sincere, and that his belief was reasonable (i.e., one need not consider the possibility that he was mistaken), I think that one would question whether or not he knows what it means to say 'I promise' (in the appropriate circumstances). It would be said of someone who used this excuse without further explanation that he didn't understand what defenses the practice, which defines a promise, allows to him. If a child were to use this excuse one would correct him; for it is part of the way one is taught the concept of a promise to be corrected if one uses this excuse. The point of having the practice would be lost if the practice did allow this excuse." Rawls, *supra* note 17, at 17, in OLAFSON, *op. cit. supra* note 17, at 429–30.

Now I am not concerned to dispute Rawls's remark if taken as descriptive of our institution of promising. For what I am here concerned with is the claim, implicit throughout, that promising would be a meaningless or pointless activity if the excuse were permitted. I should say though that the passage quoted from Rawls is not, I think, central to his main argument. I think I can show this to be a mistake through the following two examples.

(1) *A* has promised *B* that he will mow *B*'s lawn for *B* on Sunday. On Sunday, *A* is feeling lazy and so he refuses to mow the lawn.

(2) *A* is sitting home on Sunday, feeling lazy, when *B* calls him up and asks him to come over and mow *B*'s lawn. *A* refuses to mow the lawn.

Ceteris paribus, it would be the case that *A* is wrong in refusing to mow *B*'s lawn in example (1) but not blamable for refusing to mow *B*'s lawn in example (2). Why is this so? Because *A*'s promise to mow *B*'s lawn creates an obligation which in the absence of such a promise is nonexistent. If this is so, then permitting the general utilitarian defense does not make a promise a meaningless gesture. This is so because there are many situations in which, in the absence of having promised to do so, we are not, for example, obligated to inconvenience ourselves simply for another's convenience. Personal inconvenience then might be one excuse which must be inconsistent with the practice of promising, even if the general appeal to consequences is not. Thus, promising would and could have a real point even if the general appeal to consequences were a good defense.

21. Wechsler, *Toward Neutral Principles of Constitutional Law*, 73 HARV. L. REV. 1, 35 (1959).

22. See text at section III.

23. For a somewhat related characterization of the source of the obligation to obey the law, see Hart, *Are There Any Natural Rights?* 64 PHILOSOPHICAL REV. 175, 185 (1955), in OLAFSON, LAW, SOCIETY, AND MORALITY 173, 180–81 (1961): "A third very important source of special rights and obligations which we recognize in many spheres of life is what may be termed mutuality of restrictions. . . . In its bare schematic outline it is this: when a number of persons conduct any joint enterprise according to rules and thus restrict their liberty, those who have submitted to these restrictions when required have a right to a similar submission from those who have benefited by their submission. The rules may provide that officials should have authority to enforce obedience and make further rules, and this will create a structure of legal rights and duties, but the moral obligation to obey the rules in such circumstances is *due to* the co-operating members of the society, and they have the correlative moral right to obedience. In social situations of this sort (of which political society is the most complex example) the obligation to obey the rules is something distinct from whatever other moral obligations there may be for obedience in terms of good consequences (*e.g.*, the prevention of suffering); the obligation is due to the co-operating members of the society as such and not because they are human beings on whom it would be wrong to inflict suffering."

I would point out only two things. First, as Professor Hart himself asserts—in a passage not quoted—the existence of this right in no way implies that one is never justified in disobeying the law. The right which any participating member has in others' obedience can justifiably be infringed in appropriate circumstances. Second, and here perhaps Professor Hart disagrees for reasons already elaborated, there is no reason that I can see why an appeal to the consequences of disobeying a particular law cannot be a sufficient justification for infringing upon that right. It is surely conceivable, at least, that this is all the submission to rules which anyone ought to have given, and hence all the submission which anyone is entitled to expect from others.

24. Curiously, perhaps, given a legal system in which laws are in general good and hence in which the possibility of justified disobedience is rare, the special or added cost of an occasional act of justified disobedience is diminished still further.

25. For fuller analyses and assessments of this argument in different contexts see, *e.g.*, Rawls, *supra* note 17; WASSERSTROM, *op. cit. supra* note 17, at 118–71.

26. 347 U.S. 483 (1954).

2

THE JUSTIFICATION OF CIVIL DISOBEDIENCE

John Rawls

I. INTRODUCTION

I should like to discuss briefly, and in an informal way, the grounds of civil disobedience in a constitutional democracy. Thus, I shall limit my remarks to the conditions under which we may, by civil disobedience, properly oppose legally established democratic authority; I am not concerned with the situation under other kinds of government nor, except incidentally, with other forms of resistance. My thought is that in a reasonably just (though of course not perfectly just) democratic regime, civil disobedience, when it is justified, is normally to be understood as a political action which addresses the sense of justice of the majority in order to urge reconsideration of the measures protested and to warn that in the firm opinion of the dissenters the conditions of social cooperation are not being honored. This characterization of civil disobedience is intended to apply to dissent on fundamental questions of internal policy, a limitation which I shall follow to simplify our question.

II. THE SOCIAL CONTRACT DOCTRINE

It is obvious that the justification of civil disobedience depends upon the theory of political obligation in general, and so we may appropriately begin with a few comments on this question. The two chief virtues of social institutions are justice and efficiency, where by the efficiency of institutions I understand their effectiveness for certain social conditions and ends the fulfillment of which is to everyone's advantage. We should comply with and do our part in just and efficient social arrangements for at least two reasons: first of all, we have a natural duty not to oppose the establishment of just and efficient institutions (when they do not yet exist) and to uphold and comply with them (when they do exist); and second, assuming that we have knowingly accepted the benefits of these institutions and plan to continue to do so, and that we have encouraged and expect others to do their part, we also have an obligation to do our share when, as the arrangement requires, it comes our turn. Thus, we often have both a natural duty as well as an obligation to support just and efficient institutions, the obligation arising from our voluntary acts while the duty does not.

Now all this is perhaps obvious enough, but it does not take us very far. Any more particular conclusions depend upon the conception of justice which is the basis of a theory of political obligation. I believe that the appropriate conception, at least for an account of political obligation in a constitutional democracy, is that of the social contract theory from which so much of our political thought derives. If we are careful to interpret it in a suitably general way, I hold that this doctrine provides a satisfactory basis for political theory, indeed even for ethical theory itself, but this is beyond our present concern.[1] The interpretation I suggest is the following: that the principles to which social arrangements must conform, and in particular the principles of justice, are those which free and rational men would agree to in an original position of equal liberty; and similarly, the principles which govern men's relations to institutions and define their natural duties and obligations are the principles to which they would consent when so situated. It should be noted straightway that in this interpretation of the contract theory the principles of justice are understood as the outcome of a hypothetical agreement. They are principles which would be agreed to if the situation of the original position were to arise. There is no mention of an actual agreement nor need such an agreement ever be made. Social arrangements are just or unjust according to whether they accord with the principles for assigning and securing fundamental rights and liberties which would be chosen in the original position. This position is, to be sure, the analytic analogue of the traditional notion of the state of nature, but it must not be mistaken for a historical occasion. Rather it is a hypothetical situation which embodies the basic ideas of the contract doctrine; the description of this situation enables us to work out which principles would be adopted. I must now say something about these matters.

The contract doctrine has always supposed that the persons in the original position have equal powers and rights, that is, that they are symmetrically situated with respect to any arrangements for reaching agreement, and that coalitions and the like are excluded. But it is an essential element (which has not been sufficiently observed although it is implicit in Kant's version of the theory) that there are very strong restrictions on what the contracting parties are presumed to know. In particular, I interpret the theory to hold that the parties do not know their position in society, past, present, or future; nor do they know which institutions exist. Again, they do not know their own place in the distribution of natural talents and abilities, whether they are intelligent or strong, man or woman, and so on. Finally, they do not know their own particular interests and preferences or the system of ends which they wish to advance: they do not know their conception of the good. In all these respects the parties are confronted with a veil of ignorance which prevents any one from being able to take advantage of his good fortune or particular interests or from being disadvantaged by them. What the parties do know (or assume) is that Hume's circumstances of justice obtain: namely, that the bounty of nature is not so generous as to render cooperative schemes superfluous nor so harsh as to make them impossible. Moreover, they assume that the extent of their altruism is limited and that, in general, they do not take an interest in one another's interests. Thus, given the special features of the original position, each man tries to do the best he can for himself by insisting on principles calculated to protect and advance his system of ends whatever it turns out to be.

I believe that as a consequence of the peculiar nature of the original position there would be an agreement on the following two principles for assigning rights and duties and for regulating distributive shares as these are determined by the fundamental institutions of society: first, each person is to have an equal right to the most extensive liberty compatible with a like liberty for all; second, social and economic inequalities (as defined by the institutional structure or fostered by it) are to be arranged so that they are both to everyone's advantage and attached to positions and offices open to all. In view of the content of these two principles and their application to the main institutions of society, and therefore to the social system as a whole, we may regard them as the two principles of justice. Basic social arrangements are just insofar as they conform to these principles, and we can, if we like, discuss questions of justice directly by reference to them. But a deeper understanding of the justification of civil disobedience requires, I think, an account of the derivation of these principles provided by the doctrine of the social contract. Part of our task is to show why this is so.

III. THE GROUNDS OF COMPLIANCE WITH AN UNJUST LAW

If we assume that in the original position men would agree both to the principle of doing their part when they have accepted and plan to continue to accept the benefits of just institutions (the principle of fairness), and also to the principle of not preventing the establishment of just institutions and of upholding and complying with them when they do exist, then the contract doctrine easily accounts for our having to conform to just institutions. But how does it account for the fact that we are normally required to comply with unjust laws as well? The injustice of a law is not a sufficient ground for not complying with it any more than the legal validity of legislation is always sufficient to require obedience to it. Sometimes one hears these extremes asserted, but I think that we need not take them seriously.

An answer to our question can be given by elaborating the social contract theory in the following way. I interpret it to hold that one is to envisage a series of agreements as follows: first, men are to agree upon the principles of justice in the original position. Then they are to move to a constitutional convention in which they choose a constitution that satisfies the principles of justice already chosen. Finally they assume the role of a legislative body and guided by the principles of justice enact laws subject to the constraints and procedures of the just constitution. The decisions reached in any stage are binding in all subsequent stages. Now whereas in the original position the contracting parties have no knowledge of their society or of their own position in it, in both a constitutional convention and a legislature, they do know certain general facts about their institutions. For example, the statistics regarding employment and output required for fiscal and economic policy. But no one knows particular facts about his own social class or his place in the distribution of natural assets. On each occasion the contracting parties have the knowledge required to make their agreement rational from the appropriate point of view, but not so much as to make them prejudiced. They are unable to tailor principles and legislation to take advantage of their social or natural position; a veil of ignorance prevents their knowing what this position is. With this series of agreements in mind, we can characterize just laws and policies as those which would be enacted were this whole process correctly carried out.

In choosing a constitution the aim is to find among the just constitutions the one which is most likely, given the general facts about the society in question, to lead to just and effective legislation. The principles of justice provide a criterion for the laws desired; the problem is to find a set of political procedures that will give this outcome. I shall assume that, at least under the normal conditions of a modern state, the best constitution is some form of democratic regime affirming equal political liberty and using some sort of majority (or other plurality) rule. Thus it follows that on the contract theory a constitutional democracy of some sort is required by the principles of justice. At the same time it is essential to observe that the constitutional process is always a case of what we may call imperfect procedural justice: that is, there is no feasible political procedure which guarantees that the enacted legislation is just even though we have (let us suppose) a standard for just legislation. In simple cases, such as games of fair division, there are procedures which always lead to the right outcome (assume that equal shares is fair and let the man who cuts the cake take the last piece). These situations are those of perfect procedural justice. In other cases it does not matter what the outcome is as long as the fair procedure is followed: fairness of the process is transferred to the result (fair gambling is an instance of this). These situations are those of pure procedural justice. The constitutional process, like a criminal trial, resembles neither of these: the result matters and we have a standard for it. The difficulty is that we cannot frame a procedure which guarantees that only just and effective legislation is enacted. Thus even under a just constitution unjust laws may be passed and unjust policies enforced. Some form of the majority principle is necessary but the majority may be mistaken, more or less willfully, in what it legislates. In agreeing to a democratic constitution (as an instance of imperfect procedural justice) one accepts at the same time the principle of majority rule. Assuming that the constitution is just and that we have accepted and plan to continue to accept its benefits, we then have both an obligation and a natural duty (and in any case the duty) to comply with what the majority enacts even though it may be unjust. In this way we become bound to follow unjust laws, not always, of course, but provided the injustice does not exceed certain limits. We recognize that we must run the risk of suffering from the defects of one another's sense of justice; this burden we are prepared to carry as long as it is more or less evenly distributed or does not weigh too heavily. Justice binds us to a just constitution and to the unjust laws which may be enacted under it in precisely the same way that it binds us to any other social arrangement. Once we take the sequence of stages into account, there is nothing unusual in our being required to comply with unjust laws.

It should be observed that the majority principle has a secondary place as a rule of procedure which is perhaps the most efficient one under usual circumstances for working a democratic constitution. The basis for it rests essentially upon the principles of justice and therefore we may, when conditions allow, appeal to these principles against unjust legislation. The justice of the constitution does not insure the justice of laws enacted under it; and while we often have both an obligation and a duty to comply with what the majority legislates (as long as it does not exceed certain limits), there is, of course, no corresponding obligation or duty to regard what the majority enacts as itself just. The right to make law does not guarantee that the decision is rightly made; and while the citizen submits in his conduct to the judgment of democratic authority, he does not submit his judgment to it.[2] And if in his judgment the enactments of the majority exceed certain bounds of injustice, the citizen may consider civil disobedience. For we are not required to accept the majority's acts unconditionally and to acquiesce in the denial of our and others' liberties; rather we submit our conduct to democratic authority to the extent necessary to share the burden of working a constitutional regime, distorted as it must inevitably be by men's lack of wisdom and the defects of their sense of justice.

IV. THE PLACE OF CIVIL DISOBEDIENCE IN A CONSTITUTIONAL DEMOCRACY

We are now in a position to say a few things about civil disobedience. I shall understand it to be a public, nonviolent, and conscientious act contrary to law usually done with the intent to bring about a change in the policies or laws of the government.[3] Civil disobedience is a political act in the sense that it is an act justified by moral principles which define a conception of civil society and the public good. It rests, then, on political conviction as opposed to a search for self or group interest; and in the case of a constitutional democracy, we may assume that this conviction involves the conception of justice (say that expressed by the contract doctrine) which underlies the constitution itself. That is, in a viable democratic regime there is a common conception of justice by reference to which its citizens regulate their political affairs and interpret the constitution. Civil disobedience is a public act which the dissenter believes to be justified by this conception of justice and for this reason it may be understood as addressing the sense of justice of the majority in order to urge reconsideration of the measures protested and to warn that, in the sincere opinion of the dissenters, the conditions of social cooperation are not being honored. For the principles of justice express precisely such conditions, and their persistent and deliberate violation in regard to basic liberties over any extended period of time cuts the ties of community and invites either submission or forceful resistance. By engaging in civil disobedience a minority leads the majority to consider whether it wants to have its acts taken in this way, or whether, in view of the common sense of justice, it wishes to acknowledge the claims of the minority.

Civil disobedience is also civil in another sense. Not only is it the outcome of a sincere conviction based on principles which regulate civic life, but it is public and nonviolent, that is, it is done in a situation where arrest and punishment are expected and accepted without resistance. In this way it manifests a respect for legal procedures. Civil disobedience expresses disobedience to law within the limits of fidelity to law, and this feature of it helps to establish in the eyes of the majority that it is indeed conscientious and sincere, that it really is meant to address their sense of justice.[4] Being completely open about one's acts and being willing to accept the legal consequences of one's conduct is a bond given to make good one's sincerity, for that one's deeds are conscientious is not easy to demonstrate to another or even before oneself. No doubt it is possible to imagine a legal system in which conscientious belief that the law is unjust is accepted as a defense for noncompliance, and men of great honesty who are confident in one another might make such a system work. But as things are such a scheme would be unstable; we must pay a price in order to establish that we believe our actions have a moral basis in the convictions of the community.

The nonviolent nature of civil disobedience refers to the fact that it is intended to address the sense of justice of the majority and as such it is a form of speech, an expression of conviction. To engage in violent acts likely to injure and to hurt its incompatible with civil disobedience as a mode of address. Indeed, an interference with the basic rights of others tends to obscure the civilly disobedient quality of one's act. Civil disobedience is nonviolent in the further sense that the legal penalty for one's action is accepted and that resistance is not (at least for the moment) contemplated. Nonviolence in this sense is to be distinguished from nonviolence as a religious or pacifist principle. While those engaging in civil disobedience have often held some such principle, there is no necessary connection between it and civil disobedience. For on the interpretation suggested, civil disobedience in a democratic society is best understood as an appeal to the principles of justice, the fundamental conditions of willing social cooperation among free men, which in the view of the community as a whole are expressed in the constitution and guide its interpretation. Being an appeal to the moral basis of public life, civil disobedience is a political and not primarily a religious act. It addresses itself to the common principles of justice which men can require one another to follow and not to the aspirations of love which they cannot. Moreover by taking part in civilly disobedient acts one does not foreswear indefinitely the idea of forceful resistance; for if the appeal against injustice is repeatedly denied, then the majority has declared its intention to invite submission or resistance and the latter may conceivably be justified even in a democratic regime. We are not required to acquiesce in the crushing of fundamental liberties by democratic majorities which have shown themselves blind to the principles of justice upon which justification of the constitution depends.

V. THE JUSTIFICATION OF CIVIL DISOBEDIENCE

So far we have said nothing about the justification of civil disobedience, that is, the conditions under which civil disobedience may be engaged in consistent with the principles of justice that support a democratic regime. Our task is to see how the characterization of civil disobedience as addressed to the sense of justice of the majority (or to the citizens as a body) determines when such action is justified.

First of all, we may suppose that the normal political appeals to the majority have already been made in good faith and have been rejected, and that the standard means of redress have been tried. Thus, for example, existing political parties are indifferent to the claims of the minority and attempts to repeal the laws protested have been met with further repression since legal institutions are in the control of the majority. While civil disobedience should be recognized, I think, as a form of political action within the limits of fidelity to the rule of law, at the same time it is a rather desperate act just within these limits, and therefore it should, in general, be undertaken as a last resort when standard democratic processes have failed. In this sense it is not a normal political action. When it is justified there has been a serious breakdown; not only is there grave injustice in the law but a refusal more or less deliberate to correct it.

Second, since civil disobedience is a political act addressed to the sense of justice of the majority, it should usually be limited to substantial and clear violations of justice and preferably to those which, if rectified, will establish a basis for doing away with remaining injustices. For this reason there is a presumption in favor of restricting civil disobedience to violations of the first principle of justice, the principle of equal liberty, and to barriers which contravene the second principle, the principle of open offices which protects equality of opportunity. It is not, of course, always easy to tell whether these principles are satisfied. But if we think of them as guaranteeing the fundamental equal political and civil liberties (including freedom of conscience and liberty of thought) and equality of opportunity, then it is often relatively clear whether their principles are being honored. After all, the equal liberties are defined by the visible structure of social institutions; they are to be incorporated into the recognized practice, if not the letter, of social arrangements. When minorities are denied the right to vote or to hold certain political offices, when certain religious groups are repressed and others denied equality of opportunity in the economy, this is often obvious and there is no doubt that justice is not being given. However, the first part of the second principle which requires that inequalities be to everyone's advantage is a much more imprecise and controversial matter. Not only is there a problem of assigning it a determinate and precise sense, but even if we do so and agree on what it should be, there is often a wide variety of reasonable opinion as to whether the principle is satisfied. The reason for this is that the principle applies primarily to fundamental economic and social policies. The choice of these depends upon theoretical and speculative beliefs as well as upon a wealth of concrete information, and all of this mixed with judgment and plain hunch, not to mention in actual cases prejudice and self-interest. Thus unless the laws of taxation are clearly designed to attack a basic equal liberty, they should not be protested by civil disobedience; the appeal to justice is not sufficiently clear and its resolution is best left to the political process. But violations of the equal liberties that define the common status of citizenship are another matter. The deliberate denial of these more or less over any extended period of time in the face of normal political protest is, in general, an appropriate object of civil disobedience. We may think of the social system as divided roughly into two parts, one which incorporates the fundamental equal liberties (including equality of opportunity) and another which embodies social and economic policies properly aimed at promoting the advantage of everyone. As a rule civil disobedience is best limited to the former where the appeal to justice is not only more definite and precise, but where, if it is effective, it tends to correct the injustices in the latter.

Third, civil disobedience should be restricted to those cases where the dissenter is willing to affirm that everyone else similarly subjected to the same degree of injustice has the right to protest in a similar way. That is, we must be prepared to authorize others to dissent in similar situations and in the same way, and to accept the consequences of their doing so. Thus, we may hold, for example, that the widespread disposition to disobey civilly clear violations of fundamental liberties more or less deliberate over an extended period of time would raise the degree of justice throughout society and would ensure men's self-esteem as well as their respect for one another. Indeed, I believe this to be true, though certainly it is partly a matter of conjecture. As the contract doctrine emphasizes, since the principles of justice are principles which we would agree to in an original position of equality when we do not know our social position and the like, the refusal to grant justice is either the denial of the other as an equal (as one in regard to whom we are prepared to constrain our actions by principles which we would consent to) or the manifestation of a willingness to take advantage of natural contingencies and social fortune at his expense. In either case, injustice invites submission or resistance; but submission arouses the contempt of the oppressor and confirms him in his intention. If straightway, after a decent period of time to make reasonable political appeals in the normal way, men were in general to dissent by civil disobedience from infractions of the fundamental equal liberties, these liberties would, I believe, be more rather than less secure. Legitimate civil disobedience properly exercised is a stabilizing device in a constitutional regime, tending to make it more firmly just.

Sometimes, however, there may be a complication in connection with this third condition. It is possible, although perhaps unlikely, that there are so many persons or groups with a sound case for resorting to civil disobedience (as judged by the foregoing criteria) that disorder would follow if they all did so. There might be serious injury to the just constitution. Or again, a group might be so large that some extra precaution is necessary in the extent to which its members organize and engage in civil disobedience. Theoretically the case is one in which a number of persons or groups are equally entitled to and all want to resort to civil disobedience, yet if they all do this, grave consequences for everyone may result. The question, then, is who among them may exercise their right, and it falls under the general problem of fairness. I cannot discuss the complexities of the matter here. Often a lottery or a rationing system can be set up to handle the case; but unfortunately the circumstances of civil disobedience rule out this solution. It suffices to note that a problem of fairness may arise and that those who contemplate civil disobedience should take it into account. They may have to reach an understanding as to who can exercise their right in the immediate situation and to recognize the need for special constraint.

The final condition, of a different nature, is the following. We have been considering when one has a right to engage in civil disobedience, and our conclusion is that one has this right should three conditions hold: when one is subject to injustice more or less deliberate over an extended period of time in the face of normal political protests; where the injustice is a clear violation of the liberties of equal citizenship; and provided that the general disposition to protest similarly in similar cases would have acceptable consequences. These conditions are not, I think, exhaustive but they seem to cover the more obvious points; yet even when they are satisfied and one has the right to engage in civil disobedience, there is still the different question of whether one should exercise this right, that is, whether by doing so one is likely to further one's ends. Having established one's right to protest one is then free to consider these tactical questions. We may be acting within our rights but still foolishly if our action only serves to provoke the harsh retaliation of the majority; and it is likely to do so if the majority lacks a sense of justice, or if the action is poorly timed or not well designed to make the appeal to the sense of justice effective. It is easy to think of instances of this sort, and in each case these practical questions have to be faced. From the standpoint of the theory of political obligation we can only say that the exercise of the right should be rational and reasonably designed to advance the protester's aims, and that weighing tactical questions presupposes that one has already established one's right, since tactical advantages in themselves do not support it.

VI. CONCLUSION: SEVERAL OBJECTIONS CONSIDERED

In a reasonably affluent democratic society justice becomes the first virtue of institutions. Social arrangements irrespective of their efficiency must be reformed if they are significantly unjust. No increase in efficiency in the form of greater advantages for many justifies the loss of liberty of a few. That we believe this is shown by the fact that in a democracy the fundamental liberties of citizenship are not understood as the outcome of political bargaining nor are they subject to the calculus of social interests. Rather these liberties are fixed points which serve to limit political transactions and which determine the scope of calculations of social advantage. It is this fundamental place of the equal liberties which makes their systematic violation over any extended period of time a proper object of civil disobedience. For to deny men these rights is to infringe the conditions of social cooperation among free and rational persons, a fact which is evident to the citizens of a constitutional regime since it follows from the principles of justice which underlie their institutions. The justification of civil disobedience rests on the priority of justice and the equal liberties which it guarantees.

It is natural to object to this view of civil disobedience that it relies too heavily upon the existence of a sense of justice. Some may hold that the feeling for justice is not a vital political force, and that what moves men are various other interests, the desire for wealth, power, prestige, and so on. Now this is a large question the answer to which is highly conjectural and each tends to have his own opinion. But there are two remarks which may clarify what I have said: first, I have assumed that there is in a constitutional regime a common sense of justice the principles of which are recognized to support the constitution and to guide its interpretation. In any given situation particular men may be tempted to violate these principles, but the collective force in their behalf is usually effective since they are seen as the necessary terms of cooperation among free men; and presumably the citizens of a democracy (or sufficiently many of them) want to see justice done. Where these assumptions fail, the justifying conditions for civil disobedience (the first three) are not affected, but the rationality of engaging in it certainly is. In this case, unless the costs of repressing civil dissent injures the economic self-interest (or whatever) of the majority, protest may simply make the position of the minority worse. No doubt as a tactical matter civil disobedience is more effective when its appeal coincides with other interests, but a constitutional regime is not viable in the long run without an attachment to the principles of justice of the sort which we have assumed.

Then, further, there may be a misapprehension about the manner in which a sense of justice manifests itself. There is a tendency to think that it is shown by professions of the relevant principles together with actions of an altruistic nature requiring a considerable degree of self-sacrifice. But these conditions are obviously too strong, for the majority's sense of justice may show itself simply in its being unable to undertake the measures required to suppress the minority and to punish as the law requires the various acts of civil disobedience. The sense of justice undermines the will to uphold unjust institutions, and so a majority despite its superior power may give way. It is unprepared to force the minority to be subject to injustice. Thus, although the majority's action is reluctant and grudging, the role of the sense of justice is nevertheless essential, for without it the majority would have been willing to enforce the law and to defend its position. Once we see the sense of justice as working in this negative way to make established injustices indefensible, then it is recognized as a central element of democratic politics.

Finally, it may be objected against this account that it does not settle the question of who is to say when the situation is such as to justify civil disobedience. And because it does not answer this question, it invites anarchy by encouraging every man to decide the matter for himself. Now the reply to this is that each man must indeed settle this question for himself, although he may, of course, decide wrongly. This is true on any theory of political duty and obligation, at least on any theory compatible with the principles of a democratic constitution. The citizen is responsible for what he does. If we usually think that we should comply with the law, this is because our political principles normally lead to this conclusion. There is a presumption in favor of compliance in the absence of good reasons to the contrary. But because each man is responsible and must decide for himself as best he can whether the circumstances justify civil disobedience, it does not follow that he may decide as he pleases. It is not by looking to our personal interests or to political allegiances narrowly construed, that we should make up our mind. The citizen must decide on the basis of the principles of justice that underlie and guide the interpretation of the constitution and in the light of his sincere conviction as to how these principles should be applied in the circumstances. If he concludes that conditions obtain which justify civil disobedience and conducts himself accordingly, he has acted conscientiously and perhaps mistakenly, but not in any case at his convenience.

In a democratic society each man must act as he thinks the principles of political right require him to. We are to follow our understanding of these principles, and we cannot do otherwise. There can be no morally binding legal interpretation of these principles, not even by a supreme court or legislature. Nor is there any infallible procedure for determining what or who is right. In our system the Supreme Court, Congress, and the President often put forward rival interpretations of the Constitution. Although the Court has the final say in settling any particular case, it is not immune from powerful political influence that may change its reading of the law of the land. The Court presents its point of view by reason and argument; its conception of the Constitution must, if it is to endure, persuade men of its soundness. The final court of appeal is not the Court, or Congress, or the President, but the electorate as a whole.[5] The civilly disobedient appeal in effect to this body. There is no danger of anarchy as long as there is a sufficient working agreement in men's conceptions of political justice and what it requires. That men can achieve such an understanding when the essential political liberties are maintained is the assumption implicit in democratic institutions. There is no way to avoid entirely the risk of divisive strife. But if legitimate civil disobedience seems to threaten civil peace, the responsibility falls not so much on those who protest as upon those whose abuse of authority and power justifies such opposition.

NOTES

Originally presented at the meetings of the American Political Science Association, September 1966. Some revisions have been made and two paragraphs have been added to the last section. Copyright © 1968 by John Rawls.

1. By the social contract theory I have in mind the doctrine found in Locke, Rousseau, and Kant. I have attempted to give an interpretation of this view in: "Justice as Fairness," *Philosophical Review* (April 1958); "Justice and Constitutional Liberty," *Nomos*, VI (1963); "The Sense of Justice," *Philosophical Review* (July 1963). [Ed. note. See also "Distributive Justice," in Peter Laslett and W. G. Runciman, eds., *Philosophy, Politics and Society* (1967).]

2. On this point see A. E. Murphy's review of Yves Simon's *The Philosophy of Democratic Government* (1951) in the *Philosophical Review* (April 1952).

3. Here I follow H. A. Bedau's definition of civil disobedience. See his "On Civil Disobedience," *Journal of Philosophy* (October 1961).

4. For a fuller discussion of this point to which I am indebted, see Charles Fried, "Moral Causation," *Harvard Law Review* (1964).

5. For a presentation of this view to which I am indebted, see A. M. Bickel, *The Least Dangerous Branch* (Indianapolis, 1962), especially Chapters 5 and 6.

3

THE CONFLICT BETWEEN
AUTHORITY AND AUTONOMY

Robert Paul Wolff

1. THE CONCEPT OF AUTHORITY

Politics is the exercise of the power of the state, or the attempt to influence that exercise. Political philosophy is therefore, strictly speaking, the philosophy of the state. If we are to determine the content of political philosophy, and whether indeed it exists, we must begin with the concept of the state.

The state is a group of persons who have and exercise supreme authority within a given territory. Strictly, we should say that a state is a group of persons who have supreme authority within a given territory *or over a certain population.* A nomadic tribe may exhibit the authority structure of a state, so long as its subjects do not fall under the superior authority of a territorial state.[1] The state may include all the persons who fall under its authority, as does the democratic state according to its theorists; it may also consist of a single individual to whom all the rest are subject. We may doubt whether the one-person state has ever actually existed, although Louis XIV evidently thought so when he announced, "L'état, c'est moi." The distinctive characteristic of the state is supreme authority, or what political philosophers used to call "sovereignty." Thus one speaks of "popular sovereignty," which is the doctrine that the people are the state, and of course the use of "sovereign" to mean "king" reflects the supposed concentration of supreme authority in a monarchy.

63

Authority is the right to command, and correlatively, the right to be obeyed. It must be distinguished from power, which is the ability to compel compliance, either through the use or the threat of force. When I turn over my wallet to a thief who is holding me at gunpoint, I do so because the fate with which he threatens me is worse than the loss of money which I am made to suffer. I grant that he has power over me, but I would hardly suppose that he has *authority*, that is, that he has a right to demand my money and that I have an obligation to give it to him. When the government presents me with a bill for taxes, on the other hand, I pay it (normally) even though I do not wish to, and even if I think I can get away with not paying. It is, after all, the duly constituted government, and hence it has a *right* to tax me. It has *authority* over me. Sometimes, of course, I cheat the government, but even so, I acknowledge its authority, for who would speak of "cheating" a thief?

To *claim* authority is to claim the right to be obeyed. To *have* authority is then—what? It may mean to have that right, or it may mean to have one's claim acknowledged and accepted by those at whom it is directed. The term "authority" is ambiguous, having both a descriptive and a normative sense. Even the descriptive sense refers to norms or obligations, of course, but it does so by *describing* what men believe they ought to do rather than by *asserting* that they ought to do it.

Corresponding to the two senses of authority, there are two concepts of the state. Descriptively, the state may be defined as a group of persons who are *acknowledged* to have supreme authority within a territory—acknowledged, that is, by those over whom the authority is asserted. The study of the forms, characteristics, institutions, and functioning of *de facto* states, as we may call them, is the province of political science. If we take the term in its prescriptive signification, the state is a group of persons who have the *right* to exercise supreme authority within a territory. The discovery, analysis, and demonstration of the forms and principles of legitimate authority—of the right to rule—is called political philosophy.

What is meant by *supreme* authority? Some political philosophers, speaking of authority in the normative sense, have held that the true state has ultimate authority over all matters whatsoever that occur within its venue. Jean-Jacques Rousseau, for example, asserted that the social contract by which a just political community is formed "gives to the body politic absolute command over the members of which it is formed;

and it is this power, when directed by the general will, that bears . . . the name of 'sovereignty.' " John Locke, on the other hand, held that the supreme authority of the just state extends only to those matters which it is proper for a state to control. The state is, to be sure, the highest authority, but its right to command is less than absolute. One of the questions which political philosophy must answer is whether there is any limit to the range of affairs over which a just state has authority.

An authoritative command must also be distinguished from a persuasive argument. When I am commanded to do something, I may choose to comply even though I am not being threatened, because I am brought to believe that it is something which I ought to do. If that is the case, then I am not, strictly speaking, obeying a command, but rather acknowledging the force of an argument or the rightness of a prescription. The person who issues the "command" functions merely as the *occasion* for my becoming aware of my duty, and his role might in other instances be filled by an admonishing friend, or even by my own conscience. I might, by an extension of the term, say that the prescription has authority over me, meaning simply that I ought to act in accordance with it. But the person himself has no authority—or, to be more precise, my complying with his command does not constitute an acknowledgment on my part of any such authority. Thus authority resides in persons; they possess it—if indeed they do at all—by virtue of who they are and not by virtue of what they command. My duty to obey is a duty owed to them, not to the moral law or to the beneficiaries of the actions I may be commanded to perform.

There are, of course, many reasons why men actually acknowledge claims of authority. The most common, taking the whole of human history, is simply the prescriptive force of tradition. The fact that something has always been done in a certain way strikes most men as a perfectly adequate reason for doing it that way again. Why should we submit to a king? Because we have always submitted to kings. But why should the oldest son of the king become king in turn? Because oldest sons have always been heirs to the throne. The force of the traditional is engraved so deeply on men's minds that even a study of the violent and haphazard origins of a ruling family will not weaken its authority in the eyes of its subjects.

Some men acquire the aura of authority by virtue of their own extraordinary characteristics, either as great military leaders, as men of saintly character, or as forceful personalities. Such men gather followers and disciples around them who willingly obey without consideration of personal interest or even against its dictates. The followers believe that the leader has a *right to command*, which is to say, *authority*.

Most commonly today, in a world of bureaucratic armies and institutionalized religions, when kings are few in number and the line of prophets has run out, authority is granted to those who occupy official positions. As Weber has pointed out, these positions appear authoritative in the minds of most men because they are defined by certain sorts of bureaucratic regulations having the virtues of publicity, generality, predictability, and so forth. We become conditioned to respond to the visible signs of officiality, such as printed forms and badges. Sometimes we may have clearly in mind the justification for a legalistic claim to authority, as when we comply with a command because its author is an *elected* official. More often the mere sight of a uniform is enough to make us feel that the man inside it has a right to be obeyed.

That men accede to claims of supreme authority is plain. That men *ought* to accede to claims of supreme authority is not so obvious. Our first question must therefore be, Under what conditions and for what reasons does one man have supreme authority over another? The same question can be restated, Under what conditions can a state (understood normatively) exist?

Kant has given us a convenient title for this sort of investigation. He called it a "deduction," meaning by the term not a proof of one proposition from another, but a demonstration of the legitimacy of a concept. When a concept is empirical, its deduction is accomplished merely by pointing to instances of its objects. For example, the deduction of the concept of a horse consists in exhibiting a horse. Since there are horses, it must be legitimate to employ the concept. Similarly, a deduction of the descriptive concept of a state consists simply in pointing to the innumerable examples of human communities in which some men claim supreme authority over the rest and are obeyed. But when the concept in question is nonempirical, its deduction must proceed in a different manner. All normative concepts are nonempirical, for they refer to what ought to be rather than to what is. Hence, we cannot justify the use of the concept of (normative) supreme authority by presenting instances.[2] We must demonstrate by an *a priori* argument that there can be forms of human community in which some men have a moral right to rule. In short, the fundamental task of political philosophy is to provide a *deduction of the concept of the state*.

To complete this deduction, it is not enough to show that there are circumstances in which men have an obligation to do what the *de facto* authorities command. Even under the most unjust of governments there are frequently good reasons for obedience rather than defiance. It may be that the government has commanded its subjects to do what in fact they already have an independent obligation to do; or it may be that the evil consequences of defiance far outweigh the indignity of submission. A government's commands may promise beneficent effects, either intentionally or not. For these reasons, and for reasons of prudence as well, a man may be right to comply with the commands of the government under whose *de facto* authority he finds himself. But none of this settles the question of legitimate authority. That is a matter of the *right* to command, and of the correlative obligation *to obey the person who issues the command*.

The point of the last paragraph cannot be too strongly stressed. Obedience is not a matter of doing what someone tells you to do. It is a matter of doing what he tells you to do *because he tells you to do it*. Legitimate, or *de jure*, authority thus concerns the grounds and sources of moral obligation.

Since it is indisputable that there are men who believe that others have authority over them, it might be thought that we could use that fact to prove that somewhere, at some time or other, there must have been men who really did possess legitimate authority. We might think, that is to say, that although some claims to authority might be wrong, it could not be that *all* such claims were wrong, since then we never would have had the concept of legitimate authority at all. By a similar argument, some philosophers have tried to show that not all our experiences are dreams, or more generally that in experience not everything is mere appearance rather than reality. The point is that terms like "dream" and "appearance" are defined by contrast with "waking experience" or "reality." Hence we could only have developed a use for them by being presented with situations in which some experiences were dreams and others not, or some things mere appearance and others reality.

Whatever the force of that argument in general, it cannot be applied to the case of *de facto* versus *de jure* authority, for the key component of both concepts, namely "right," is imported into the discussion from the realm of moral philosophy generally. Insofar as we concern ourselves with the possibility of a just state, we *assume* that moral discourse is meaningful and that adequate deductions have been given of concepts like "right," "duty," and "obligation."[3]

What can be inferred from the existence of *de facto* states is that men *believe* in the existence of legitimate authority, for of course a *de facto* state is simply a state whose subjects believe it to be legitimate (i.e., really to have the authority which it claims for itself). They may be wrong. Indeed, *all* beliefs in authority may be wrong—there may be not a single state in the history of mankind which has now or ever has had a right to be obeyed. It might even be impossible for such a state to exist; that is the question we must try to settle. But so long as men believe in the authority of states, we can conclude that they possess the concept of *de jure* authority.[4]

The normative concept of the state as the human community which possesses rightful authority within a territory thus defines the subject matter of political philosophy proper. However, even if it should prove impossible to present a deduction of the concept—if, that is, there can be no *de jure* state—still a large number of moral questions can be raised concerning the individual's relationship with *de facto* states. We may ask, for example, whether there are any moral principles which ought to guide the state in its lawmaking, such as the principle of utilitarianism, and under what conditions it is right for the individual to obey the laws. We may explore the social ideals of equality and achievement, or the principles of punishment, or the justifications for war. All such investigations are essentially applications of general moral principles to the particular phenomena of (*de facto*) politics. Hence, it would be appropriate to reclaim a word which has fallen on bad days, and call that branch of the study of politics *casuistical politics*. Since there are men who acknowledge claims to authority, there are *de facto* states. Assuming that moral discourse in general is legitimate, there must be moral questions which arise in regard to such states. Hence, casuistical politics as a branch of ethics does exist. It remains to be decided whether political philosophy proper exists.

2. THE CONCEPT OF AUTONOMY

The fundamental assumption of moral philosophy is that men are responsible for their actions. From this assumption it follows necessarily, as Kant pointed out, that men are metaphysically free, which is to say that in some sense they are capable of choosing how they shall act. Being able to choose how he acts makes a man responsible, but merely choosing is not in itself enough to constitute *taking* responsibility for one's actions. Taking responsibility involves attempting to determine what one ought to do, and that, as philosophers since Aristotle have recognized, lays upon one the additional burdens of gaining knowledge, reflecting on motives, predicting outcomes, criticizing principles, and so forth.

The obligation to take responsibility for one's actions does not derive from man's freedom of will alone, for more is required in taking responsibility than freedom of choice. Only because man has the capacity to reason about his choices can he be said to stand under a continuing obligation to take responsibility for them. It is quite appropriate that moral philosophers should group together children and madmen as beings not fully responsible for their actions, for as madmen are thought to lack freedom of choice, so children do not yet possess the power of reason in a developed form. It is even just that we should assign a greater degree of responsibility to children, for madmen, by virtue of their lack of free will, are completely without responsibility, while children, insofar as they possess reason in a partially developed form, can be held responsible (i.e., can be required to take responsibility) to a corresponding degree.

Every man who possesses both free will and reason has an obligation to take responsibility for his actions, even though he may not be actively engaged in a continuing process of reflection, investigation, and deliberation about how he ought to act. A man will sometimes announce his willingness to take responsibility for the consequences of his actions, even though he has not deliberated about them, or does not intend to do so in the future. Such a declaration is, of course, an advance over the refusal to take responsibility; it at least acknowledges the existence of the obligation. But it does not relieve the man of the duty to engage in the reflective process which he has thus far shunned. It goes without saying that a man may take responsibility for his actions and yet act wrongly. When we describe someone as a responsible individual, we do not imply that he always does what is right, but only that he does not neglect the duty of attempting to ascertain what is right.

The responsible man is not capricious or anarchic, for he does acknowledge himself bound by moral constraints. But he insists that he alone is the judge of those constraints. He may listen to the advice of others, but he makes it his own by determining for himself whether it is good advice. He may learn from others about his moral obligations, but only in the sense that a mathematician learns from other mathematicians—namely by hearing from them arguments whose validity he recognizes even though he did not think of them himself. He does not learn in the sense that one learns from an explorer, by accepting as true his accounts of things one cannot see for oneself.

Since the responsible man arrives at moral decisions which he expresses to himself in the form of imperatives, we may say that he gives laws to himself, or is self-legislating. In short, he is *autonomous*. As Kant argued, moral autonomy is a combination of freedom and responsibility; it is a submission to laws which one has made for oneself. The autonomous man, insofar as he is autonomous, is not subject to the will of another. He may do what another tells him, but not *because* he has been told to do it. He is therefore, in the political sense of the word, *free*.

Since man's responsibility for his actions is a consequence of his capacity for choice, he cannot give it up or put it aside. He can refuse to acknowledge it, however, either deliberately or by simply failing to recognize his moral condition. All men refuse to take responsibility for their actions at some time or other during their lives, and some men so consistently shirk their duty that they present more the appearance of overgrown children than of adults. Inasmuch as moral autonomy is simply the condition of taking full responsibility for one's actions, it follows that men can forfeit their autonomy at will. That is to say, a man can decide to obey the commands of another without making any attempt to determine for himself whether what is commanded is good or wise.

This is an important point, and it should not be confused with the false assertion that a man can give up responsibility for his actions. Even after he has subjected himself to the will of another, an individual remains responsible for what he does. But by refusing to engage in moral deliberation, by accepting as final the commands of the others, he forfeits his autonomy. Rousseau is therefore right when he says that a man cannot become a slave even through his own choice, if he means that even slaves are morally responsible for their acts. But he is wrong if he means that men cannot place themselves voluntarily in a position of servitude and mindless obedience.

There are many forms and degrees of forfeiture of autonomy. A man can give up his independence of judgment with regard to a single question, or in respect of a single type of question. For example, when I place myself in the hands of my doctor, I commit myself to whatever course of treatment he prescribes, but only in regard to my health. I do not make him my legal counselor as well. A man may forfeit autonomy on some or all questions for a specific period of time, or during his entire life. He may submit himself to all commands, whatever they may be, save for some specified acts (such as killing) which he refuses to perform. From the example of the doctor, it is obvious that there are at least some situations in which it is reasonable to give up one's autonomy. Indeed, we may wonder whether, in a complex world of technical expertise, it is ever reasonable *not* to do so!

Since the concept of taking and forfeiting responsibility is central to the discussion which follows, it is worth devoting a bit more space to clarifying it. Taking responsibility for one's actions means making the final decisions about what one should do. For the autonomous man, there is no such thing, strictly speaking, as a *command*. If someone in my environment is issuing what are intended as commands, and if he or others expect those commands to be obeyed, that fact will be taken account of in my deliberations. I may decide that I ought to do what that person is commanding me to do, and it may even be that his issuing the command is the factor in the situation which makes it desirable for me to do so. For example, if I am on a sinking ship and the captain is giving orders for manning the lifeboats, and if everyone else is obeying the captain *because he is the captain*, I may decide that under the circumstances I had better do what he says, since the confusion caused by disobeying him would be generally harmful. But insofar as I make such a decision, I am not *obeying his command*; that is, I am not acknowledging him as having authority over me. I would make the same decision, for exactly the same reasons, if one of the passengers had started to issue "orders" and had, in the confusion, come to be obeyed.

In politics, as in life generally, men frequently forfeit their autonomy. There are a number of causes for this fact, and also a number of arguments which have been offered to justify it. Most men, as we have already noted, feel so strongly the force of tradition or bureaucracy that they accept unthinkingly the claims to authority which are made by their nominal rulers. It is the rare individual in the history of the race who rises even to the level of questioning the right of his masters to command and the duty of himself and his fellows to obey. Once the dangerous question has been started, however, a variety of arguments can be brought forward to demonstrate the authority of the rulers. Among the most ancient is Plato's assertion that men should submit to the authority of those with superior knowledge, wisdom, or insight. A sophisticated modern version has it that the educated portion of a democratic population is more likely to be politically active, and that it is just as well for the ill-informed segment of the electorate to remain passive, since its entrance into the political arena only supports the efforts of demagogues and extremists. A number of American political scientists have gone so far as to claim that the apathy of the American masses is a cause of stability and hence a good thing.

The moral condition demands that we acknowledge responsibility and achieve autonomy wherever and whenever possible. Sometimes this involves moral deliberation and reflection; at other times, the gathering of special, even technical, information. The contemporary American citizen, for example, has an obligation to master enough modern science to enable him to follow debates about nuclear policy and come to an independent conclusion.[5] There are great, perhaps insurmountable, obstacles to the achievement of a complete and rational autonomy in the modern world. Nevertheless, so long as we recognize our responsibility for our actions, and acknowledge the power of reason within us, we must acknowledge as well the continuing obligation to make ourselves the authors of such commands as we may obey. The paradox of man's condition in the modern world is that the more fully he recognizes his right and duty to be his own master, the more completely he becomes the passive object of a technology and bureaucracy whose complexities he cannot hope to understand. It is only several hundred years since a reasonably well-educated man could claim to understand the major issues of government as well as his king or parliament. Ironically, the high school graduate of today, who cannot master the issues of foreign and domestic policy on which he is asked to vote, could quite easily have grasped the problems of eighteenth-century statecraft.

3. THE CONFLICT BETWEEN AUTHORITY AND AUTONOMY

The defining mark of the state is authority, the right to rule. The primary obligation of man is autonomy, the refusal to be ruled. It would seem, then, that there can be no resolution of the conflict between the autonomy of the individual and the putative authority of the state. Insofar as a man fulfills his obligation to make himself the author of his decisions, he will resist the state's claim to have authority over him. That is to say, he will deny that he has a duty to obey the laws of the state *simply because they are the laws*. In that sense, it would seem that anarchism is the only political doctrine consistent with the virtue of autonomy.

Now, of course, an anarchist may grant the necessity of *complying* with the law under certain circumstances or for the time being. He may even doubt that there is any real prospect of eliminating the state as a human institution. But he will never view the commands of the state as *legitimate*, as having a binding moral force. In a sense, we might characterize the anarchist as a man without a country, for despite the ties which bind him to the land of his childhood he stands in precisely the same moral relationship to "his" government as he does to the government of any other country in which he might happen to be staying for a time. When I take a vacation in Great Britain, I obey its laws, both because of prudential self-interest and because of the obvious moral considerations concerning the value of order, the general good consequences of preserving a system of property, and so forth. On my return to the United States, I have a sense of reentering *my* country, and if I think about the matter at all, I imagine myself to stand in a different and more intimate relation to American laws. They have been promulgated by *my* government, and I therefore have a special obligation to obey them. But the anarchist tells me that my feeling is purely sentimental and has no objective moral basis. All authority is equally illegitimate, although of course not therefore equally worthy or unworthy of support, and my obedience to American laws, if I am to be morally autonomous, must proceed from the same considerations which determine me abroad.

The dilemma which we have posed can be succinctly expressed in terms of the concept of a *de jure* state. If all men have a continuing obligation to achieve the highest degree of autonomy possible, then there would appear to be no state whose subjects have a moral obligation to obey its commands. Hence, the concept of a *de jure* legitimate state would appear to be vacuous, and philosophical anarchism would seem to be the only reasonable political belief for an enlightened man.

NOTES

1. For a similar definition of "state," see Max Weber, *Politics as a Vocation*. Weber emphasizes the means—force—by which the will of the state is imposed, but a careful analysis of his definition shows that it also bases itself on the notion of authority ("imperative coordination").

2. For each time we offered an example of legitimate authority, we would have to attach to it a nonempirical argument proving the legitimacy.

3. Thus, political philosophy is a dependent or derivative discipline, just as the philosophy of science is dependent upon the general theory of knowledge and on the branches of metaphysics which concern themselves with the reality and nature of the physical world.

4. This point is so simple that it may seem unworthy of such emphasis. Nevertheless, a number of political philosophers, including Hobbes and John Austin, have supposed that *the concept* as well as the principles of authority could be derived from the concepts of power or utility. For example, Austin defines a command as a signification of desire, uttered by someone who will visit evil on those who do not comply with it (*The Province of Jurisprudence Determined*, Lecture I).

5. This is not quite so difficult as it sounds, since policy very rarely turns on disputes over technical or theoretical details. Still, the citizen who, for example, does not understand the nature of atomic radiation cannot even pretend to have an opinion on the feasibility of bomb shelters; and since the momentous choice between first-strike and second-strike nuclear strategies depends on the possibility of a successful shelter system, the uninformed citizen will be as completely at the mercy of his "representatives" as the lowliest slave.

4

IS THERE A PRIMA FACIE
OBLIGATION TO OBEY THE LAW?

M. B. E. Smith

It isn't a question of whether it was legal or illegal. That isn't enough. The question is, what is morally wrong.

—Richard Nixon, "Checkers Speech" 1952

M any political philosophers have thought it obvious that there is a prima facie obligation to obey the law; and so, in discussing this obligation, they have thought their task to be more that of explaining its basis than of arguing for its existence. John Rawls has, for example, written:

> I shall assume, as requiring no argument, that there is, at least in a society such as ours, a moral obligation to obey the law, although it may, of course, be overriden in certain cases by other more stringent obligations.[1]

As against this, I suggest that it is not at all obvious that there is such an obligation, that this is something that must be shown, rather than so blithely assumed. Indeed, were he uninfluenced by conventional wisdom, a reflective man might on first considering the question be inclined to deny any such obligation: As H. A. Prichard once remarked, "the mere receipt of an order backed by force seems, if anything, to give rise to the duty of resisting, rather than obeying."[2]

I shall argue that, although those subject to a government often have a prima facie obligation to obey particular laws (*e.g.*, when disobedience has seriously untoward consequences or involves an act that is *mala in se*), they have no prima facie obligation to obey all its laws. I do not hope to prove this contention beyond a reasonable doubt: My goal is rather the more modest one of showing that it is a reasonable position to maintain by first criticizing arguments that purport to establish the obligation and then presenting some positive argument against it.

First, however, I must explain how I use the phrase "prima facie obligation." I shall say that a person *S* has a prima facie obligation to do an act *X* if, and only if, there is a moral reason for *S* to do *X* which is such that, unless he has a moral reason not to do *X* at least as strong as his reason to do *X*, *S*'s failure to do *X* is wrong.[3] In this discussion it will also be convenient to distinguish two kinds of prima facie obligation via the difference between the two kinds of statement which ascribe them. A specific statement asserts that some particular person has a prima facie obligation to perform some particular act. In contrast, a generic statement (*e.g.*, "Parents have a prima facie obligation to care for their infant children") asserts that everyone who meets a certain description has a prima facie obligation to perform a certain kind of act whenever he has an opportunity to do so. I shall therefore say that a person *S* has a *specific* prima facie obligation to do *X* if, and only if, the specific statement "*S* has a prima facie obligation to do *X*" is true; and that he has a *generic* prima facie obligation to do *X* if, and only if, *S* meets some description D and the generic statement "Those who are D have a prima facie obligation to do *X*" is true.[4]

Now, the question of whether there is a prima facie obligation to obey the law is clearly about a generic obligation. Everyone, even the anarchist, would agree that in many circumstances individuals have specific prima facie obligations to obey specific laws. Since it is clear that there is in most circumstances a specific prima facie obligation to refrain from murder, rape, or breach of contract, it is plain that in these circumstances each of us has a specific prima facie obligation not to violate laws which prohibit these acts. Again, disobeying the law often has seriously untoward consequences; and, when this is so, virtually everyone would agree that there is a specific prima facie obligation to obey. Therefore, the interesting question about our obligation vis-à-vis the law is not "Do individual citizens ever have specific prima facie obligations to obey particular laws?," but rather "Is the moral relation of any government to its citizens such that they have a prima facie obligation to do certain things merely because they are legally required to do so?" This is, of course, equivalent to asking "Is there a generic prima facie obligation to obey the law?" Hereafter, when I use the phrase "the prima facie obligation to obey the law" I shall be referring to a generic obligation.

One final point in clarification: As used here, the phrase "prima facie" bears a different meaning than it does when used in legal writing. In legal materials, the phrase frequently refers to evidence sufficiently persuasive so as to require rebuttal. Hence, were a lawyer to ask "Is there a prima facie obligation to obey the law?," a reasonable interpretation of his question might be "May a reasonable man take mere illegality to be sufficient evidence that an act is morally wrong, so long as there is no specific evidence tending to show it is right?" Let us call this the "lawyer's question." Now, the question of primary concern in this inquiry is "Is there any society in which mere illegality is a moral reason for an act's being wrong?" The difference between these questions is that, were there a prima facie obligation to obey the law in the lawyer's sense, mere illegality would, in the absence of specific evidence to the contrary, be evidence of wrongdoing, but it would not necessarily be relevant to a determination of whether lawbreaking is wrong where there is reason to think such conduct justified or even absolutely obligatory. In contrast, if there is a prima facie obligation to obey the law in the sense in which I am using the phrase, the mere illegality of an act is always relevant to the determination of its moral character, despite whatever other reasons are present.[5] Hence, there may be a prima facie obligation to obey the law in the lawyer's sense and yet be no such obligation in the sense of the phrase used here. Near the end of this article I shall return briefly to the lawyer's question; for the present, I raise it only that it may not be confused with the question I wish to examine.

I

The arguments I shall examine fall into three groups: First, those which rest on the benefits each individual receives from government: second, those relying on implicit consent or promise; third, those which appeal to utility or the general good. I shall consider each group in turn.

Of those in the first group, I shall begin with the argument from gratitude. Although they differ greatly in the amount of benefits they provide, virtually all governments do confer substantial benefits on their subjects. Now, it is often claimed that, when a person accepts benefits from another, he thereby incurs a debt of gratitude towards his benefactor. Thus, if it be maintained that obedience to the law is the best way of showing gratitude towards one's government, it may with some plausibility be concluded that each person who has received benefits from his government has a prima facie obligation to obey the law.

On reflection, however, this argument is unconvincing. First, it may reasonably be doubted whether most citizens have an obligation to act gratefully towards their government. Ordinarily, if someone confers benefits on me without any consideration of whether I want them, and if he does this in order to advance some purpose other than promotion of my particular welfare, I have no obligation to be grateful towards him. Yet the most important benefits of government are not accepted by its citizens, but are rather enjoyed regardless of whether they are wanted. Moreover, a government typically confers these benefits, not to advance the interests of particular citizens, but rather as a consequence of advancing some purpose of its own. At times, its motives are wholly admirable, as when it seeks to promote the general welfare; at others, they are less so, as when it seeks to stay in power by catering to the demands of some powerful faction. But, such motives are irrelevant: Whenever government forces benefits on me for reasons other than my particular welfare, I clearly am under no obligation to be grateful to it.

Second, even assuming *arguendo* that each citizen has an obligation to be grateful to his government, the argument still falters. It is perhaps true that cheerful and willing obedience is the best way to show one's gratitude towards government, in that it makes his gratitude unmistakable. But, when a person owes a debt of gratitude towards another, he does not necessarily acquire a prima facie obligation to display his gratitude in the most convincing manner: A person with demanding, domineering parents might best display his gratitude towards them by catering to their every whim, but he surely has no prima facie obligation to do so. Without undertaking a lengthy case-by-case examination, one cannot delimit the prima facie obligation of acting gratefully, for its existence and extent depends on such factors as the nature of the benefits received, the manner in which they are conferred, the motives of the benefactor, and so forth. But, even without such an examination, it is clear that the mere fact that a person has conferred on me even the most momentous benefits does not establish his right to dictate all of my behavior; nor does it establish that I always have an obligation to consider his wishes when I am deciding what I shall do. If, then, we have a prima facie obligation to act gratefully towards government, we undoubtedly have an obligation to promote its interests when this does not involve great sacrifice on our part and to respect some of its wishes concerning that part of our behavior which does not directly affect its interests. But, our having this obligation to be grateful surely does not establish that we have a prima facie obligation to obey the law.

A more interesting argument from the benefits individuals receive from government is the argument from fair play. It differs from the argument from gratitude in contending that the prima facia obligation to obey the law is owed, not to one's government but rather to one's fellow citizens. Versions of this argument have been offered by H. L. A. Hart and John Rawls.

According to Hart, the mere existence of cooperative enterprise gives rise to a certain prima facie obligation. He argues that:

> when a number of persons conduct any joint enterprise according to rules and thus restrict their liberty, those who have submitted to these restrictions when required have a right to a similar submission from those who have benefitted by their submission. The rules may provide that officials should have authority to enforce obedience and make further rules, and this will create a structure of legal rights and duties, but the moral obligation to obey the rules in such circumstances is *due to* the cooperating members of the society, and they have the correlative moral right to obedience.[6]

Rawls' account of this obligation in his essay, *Legal Obligation and the Duty of Fair Play*,[7] is rather more complex. Unlike Hart, he sets certain requirements on the kinds of cooperative enterprises that give rise to the obligation: First, that success of the enterprise depends on near-universal obedience to its rules, but not on universal cooperation; second, that obedience to its rules involves some sacrifice, in that obeying the rules restricts one's liberty; and finally, that the enterprise conform to the principles of justice.[8] Rawls also offers an explanation of the obligation: He argues that, if a person benefits from participating in such an enterprise and if he intends to continue receiving its benefits, he acts unfairly when he refuses to obey its rules. With Hart, however, Rawls claims that this obligation is owed not to the enterprise itself, nor to its officials, but rather to those members whose obedience has made the benefits possible. Hart and Rawls also agree that this obligation of fair play—"fair play" is Rawls' term—is a fundamental obligation, not derived from utility or from mutual promise or consent.[9] Finally, both Hart and Rawls conceive of legal systems, at least those in democratic societies, as complex practices of the kind which give rise to the obligation of fair play; and they conclude that those who benefit from such legal systems have a prima facie obligation to obey their laws.

These arguments deserve great respect. Hart and Rawls appear to have isolated a kind of prima facie obligation overlooked by other philosophers and have thereby made a significant contribution to moral theory. However, the significance of their discovery to jurisprudence is less clear. Although Hart and Rawls have discovered the obligation of fair play, they do not properly appreciate its limits. Once these limits are understood, it is clear that the prima facie obligation to obey the law cannot be derived from the duty of fair play.

The obligation of fair play seems to arise most clearly within small, voluntary cooperative enterprises. Let us suppose that a number of persons have gone off into the wilderness to carve out a new society, and that they have adopted certain rules to govern their communal life. Their enterprise meets Rawls' requirements on success, sacrifice, and justice. We can now examine the moral situation of the members of that community in a number of circumstances, taking seriously Hart's insistence that cooperating members have a right to the obedience of others and Rawls' explanation of this right and its correlative obligation on grounds of fairness.

Let us take two members of the community, *A* and *B*. *B*, we may suppose, has never disobeyed the rules and *A* has benefitted from *B*'s previous submission. Has *B* a right to *A*'s obedience? It would seem necessary to know the consequences of *A*'s obedience. If, in obeying the rules, *A* will confer on *B* a benefit roughly equal to those he has received from *B*, it would be plainly unfair for *A* to withhold it from *B*; and so, in this instance, *B*'s right to *A*'s obedience is clear. Similarly, if, in disobeying the rule, *A* will harm the community, *B*'s right to *A*'s obedience is again clear. This is because in harming the community A will harm B indirectly, by threatening the existence or efficient functioning of an institution on which B's vital interests depend. Since A has benefitted from B's previous submission to the rules, it is unfair for A to do something which will lessen B's chances of receiving like benefits in the future. However, if A's compliance with some particular rule does not benefit B and if his disobedience will not harm the community, it is difficult to see how fairness to B could dictate that A must comply. Surely, the fact that A has benefitted from B's submission does not give B the right to insist that A obey when B's interests are unaffected. A may in this situation have an obligation to obey, perhaps because he has promised or because his disobedience would be unfair to some other member; but, if he does disobey, he has surely not been unfair to B.

We may generalize from these examples. Considerations of fairness apparently do show that, when cooperation is perfect and when each member has benefitted from the submission of every other, each member of an enterprise has a prima facie obligation to obey its rules when obedience benefits some other member or when disobedience harms the enterprise. For, if in either circumstance a member disobeys, he is unfair to at least one other member and is perhaps unfair to them all. However, if a member disobeys when his obedience would have benefitted no other member and when his disobedience does no harm, his moral situation is surely different. If his disobedience is then unfair, it must be unfair to the group but not to any particular member. But this, I take it, is impossible: Although the moral properties of a group are not always a simple function of the moral properties of its members, it is evident that one cannot be unfair to a group without being unfair to any of its members. It would seem, then, that even when cooperation is perfect, considerations of fairness do not establish that members of a cooperative enterprise have a simple obligation to obey all of its rules, but have rather the more complex obligation to obey when obedience benefits some other member or when disobedience harms the enterprise. This does not, it is worth noting, reduce the obligation of fair play to a kind of utilitarian obligation, for it may well be that fair play will dictate in certain circumstances that a man obey when disobedience would have better consequences. My point is merely that the obligation of fair play governs a man's actions only when some benefit or harm turns on whether he obeys. Surely, this is as should be, for questions of fairness typically arise from situations in which burdens or benefits are distributed or in which some harm is done.

The obligation of fair play is therefore much more complex than Hart or Rawls seem to have imagined. Indeed, the obligation is even more complex than the above discussion suggests, for the assumption of perfect cooperation is obviously unrealistic. When that assumption is abandoned, the effect of previous disobedience considered, an the inevitable disparity among the various members' sacrifice in obeying the rules taken into account, the scope of the obligation is still further limited; we shall then find that it requires different things of different members, depending on their previous pattern of compliance and the amount of sacrifice they have made.[10] These complications need not detain us, however, for they do not affect the fact that fairness requires obedience only in situations where noncompliance would withhold benefits from someone or harm the enterprise. Now it must be conceded that all of this makes little difference when we confine our attention to small, voluntary, cooperative enterprises. Virtually any disobedience may be expected to harm such enterprises to some extent, by diminishing the confidence of other members in its probable success and therefore reducing their incentive to work diligently towards it. Moreover, since they are typically governed by a relatively small number of rules, none of which ordinarily require behavior that is useless to other members, we may expect that when a member disobeys he will probably withhold a benefit from some other member and that he has in the past benefitted significantly from that member's obedience. We may therefore expect that virtually every time the rules of a small, voluntary enterprise call on a member to obey he will have a specific prima facie obligation to do so because of his obligation of fair play.

In the case of legal systems, however, the complexity of the obligation makes a great deal of difference. Although their success may depend on the "habit of obedience" of a majority of their subjects, all legal systems are designed to cope with a substantial amount of disobedience.[11] Hence, individual acts of disobedience to the law only rarely have an untoward effect on legal systems. What is more, because laws must necessarily be designed to cover large numbers of cases, obedience to the law often benefits no one. Perhaps the best illustration is obedience of the traffic code: Very often I benefit no one when I stop at a red light or observe the speed limit. Finally, virtually every legal system contains a number of pointless or even positively harmful laws, obedience to which either benefits no one or, worse still, causes harm. Laws prohibiting homosexual activity or the dissemination of birth control information are surely in this category. Hence, even if legal systems are the kind of cooperative enterprise that gives rise to the obligation of fair play, in a great many instances that obligation will not require that we obey specific laws. If, then, there is a generic prima facie obligation to obey the laws of any legal system, it cannot rest on the obligation of fair play. The plausibility of supposing that it does depends on an unwarranted extrapolation from what is largely true of our obligations within small, cooperative enterprises to what must always be true of our obligations within legal systems.

In his recent book, Rawls has abandoned the argument from fair play as proof that the entire citizenry of even just governments has a prima facie obligation to obey the law. He now distinguishes between obligations (*e.g.*, to be fair or to keep promises) and natural duties (*e.g.*, to avoid injury to others). Obligations, according to Rawls, are incurred only by one's voluntary acts, whereas this is not true of natural duties.[12] In his book, he retains the obligation of fair play (now "fairness"); but he now thinks that this obligation applies only to those citizens of just governments who hold office or who have advanced their interests through the government. He excludes the bulk of the citizenry from having a prima facie obligation to obey the law on the ground that, for most persons, receiving benefits from government is nothing they do voluntarily, but is rather something that merely happens to them.[13] He does not, however, take this to imply that most citizens of a reasonably just government are morally free to disobey the law: He maintains that everyone who is treated by such a government with reasonable justice has a natural duty to obey all laws that are not grossly unjust, on the ground that everyone has a natural duty to uphold and to comply with just institutions.[14]

It is tempting to criticize Rawls' present position in much the same way that I criticized his earlier one. One might argue that, while it is true that officeholders and those who have profited by invoking the rules of a just government must in fairness comply with its laws when disobedience will result in harm to that government or when it withholds a benefit from some person who has a right to it, it is simply false that fairness dictates obedience when disobedience does no harm or withholds no benefit. One might further argue that the utility of a just government is such that one has a prima facie duty to obey when disobedience is harmful to it, but that, so long as disobedience does no harm, the government's character is irrelevant to the question of whether one has a prima facie obligation to obey. These criticisms would, I think, show that if we are to base our normative ethics on an appeal to intuitively reasonable principles of duty and obligation, Rawls' present position is no more satisfying than is his earlier one. However, although certainly relevant to an assessment of Rawls' present position, these arguments cannot be regarded as decisive, for in his book Rawls does not rely on a bare appeal to moral intuition. He does not disregard the evidence of intuition, and he is glad to enlist its aid when he can; but, in putting forward particular principles of duty and obligation, he is more concerned with showing that they follow from his general theory of justice. Hence, to refute Rawls' present position, one would have to set out his elaborate theory and then show either that it is mistaken or that the particular claims he makes on its basis do not follow from it. Such a task is beyond the scope of this article; and I shall therefore be content to observe that Rawls' present position lacks intuitive support and, hence, that it rests solely on a controversial ethical theory and a complicated argument based upon it, neither of which have as yet emerged unscathed from the fire of critical scrutiny. His view deserves great respect and demands extended discussion, but it is not one which we must now accept, on pain of being unreasonable.

II

The second group of arguments are those from implicit consent or promise. Recognizing that among the clearest cases of prima facie obligation are those in which a person voluntarily assumes the obligation, some philosophers have attempted to found the citizen's obligation to obey the law upon his consent or promise to do so. There is, of course, a substantial difficulty in any such attempt, *viz.*, the brute fact that many persons have never so agreed. To accommodate this fact, some philosophers have invoked the concept of implicit promise or consent. In the *Second Treatise*, Locke argued that mere residence in a country, whether for an hour or a lifetime, constitutes implicit consent to its law.[15] Plato[16] and W. D. Ross[17] made the similar argument that residence in a country and appeal to the protection of its laws constitutes an implicit promise to obey.

Nevertheless, it is clear that residence and use of the protection of the law do not constitute any usual kind of consent to a government nor any usual kind of promise to obey its laws. The phrases "implicit consent" and "implicit promise" are somewhat difficult to understand, for they are not commonly used; nor does Locke, Plato, or Ross define them. Still, a natural way of understanding them is to assume that they refer to acts which differ from explicit consent or promise only in that, in the latter cases, the person has said "I consent . . ." or "I promise . . . ," whereas in the former, he has not uttered such words but has rather performed some act which counts as giving consent or making a promise. Now, as recent investigation in the philosophy of language has shown, certain speech acts are performed only when someone utters certain words (or performs some other conventional act) with the intention that others will take what he did as being an instance of the particular act in question.[18] And it is certain that, in their ordinary usage, "consenting" and "promising" refer to speech acts of this kind. If I say to someone, "I promise to give you fifty dollars," but it is clear from the context that I do not intend that others will take my utterance as a promise, no one would consider me as having promised. Bringing this observation to bear on the present argument, it is perhaps possible that some people reside in a country and appeal to the protection of its laws with the intention that others will take their residence and appeal as consent to the laws or as a promise to obey; but this is surely true only of a very small number, consisting entirely of those enamoured with social contract theory.[19]

It may be argued, however, that my criticism rests on an unduly narrow reading of the words "consent" and "promise." Hence, it may be supposed that, if I am to refute the implicit consent or promise arguments, I must show that there is no other sense of the words "consent" or "promise" in which it is true that citizens, merely by living in a state and going about their usual business, thereby consent or promise to obey the law. This objection is difficult to meet, for I know of no way to show that there is no sense of either word that is suitable for contractarian purposes. However, I can show that two recent attempts, by John Plamenatz and Alan Gewirth, to refurbish the implicit consent argument along this line have been unsuccessful.[20] I shall not quarrel with their analyses of "consent," though I am suspicious of them; rather, I shall argue that given their definitions of "consent" the fact that a man consents to government does not establish that he has a prima facie obligation to obey the law.

Plamenatz claims that there are two kinds of consent. The first, which is common garden-variety consent, he terms "direct." He concedes that few citizens directly consent to their government.[21] He suggests, however, that there is another kind of consent, which he calls "indirect," and that, in democratic societies, consent in this sense is widespread and establishes a prima facie obligation to obey the law. Indirect consent occurs whenever a person freely votes or abstains from voting.[22] Voting establishes a prima facie obligation of obedience because:

> Even if you dislike the system and wish to change it, you put yourself by your vote under a [prima facie] obligation to obey whatever government comes legally to power. . . . For the purpose of an election is to give authority to the people who win it and, if you vote knowing what you are doing and without being compelled to do it, you voluntarily take part in a process which gives authority to these people.[23]

Plamenatz does not explain why abstention results in a prima facie obligation, but perhaps his idea is that, if a person abstains, he in effect acknowledges the authority of whoever happens to win.

The key premise then in the argument is that "the purpose of an election is to give authority to the people who win it," and it is clear that Plamenatz believes that this implies that elections do give authority to their winners. In assessing the truth of these contentions, it is, of course, vital to know what Plamenatz means by "authority." Unfortunately, he does not enlighten us, and we must therefore speculate as to his meaning. To begin, the word "authority," when used without qualification, is often held to mean the same as "legitimate authority." Since prima facie obligation is the weakest kind of obligation, part of what we mean when we ascribe authority to some government is that those subject to it have at least a prima facie obligation to obey. However, if this is what Plamenatz means by "authority," his argument simply begs the question: For, in order to be justified in asserting that the purpose of an election is to confer authority and that elections succeed in doing this, he must first show that everyone subject to an elected government has a prima facie obligation to obey its law, both those eligible to vote and those ineligible.

It is possible, however, that Plamenatz is using "authority" in some weaker sense, one that does not entail that everyone subject to it has a prima facie obligation to obey. If this is so, his premises will perhaps pass, but he must then show that those who are eligible to take part in conferring authority have a prima facie obligation to obey it. However, it is difficult to see how this can be done. First, as Plamenatz recognizes, voting is not necessarily consenting in the "direct" or usual sense, and merely being eligible to vote is even more clearly not consenting. Hence, the alleged prima facie obligation of obedience incurred by those eligible to vote is not in consequence of their direct consent. Second, Plamenatz cannot appeal to "common moral sentiment" to bolster his argument: This is because if we really believed that those eligible to vote have a prima facie obligation to obey, an obligation not incurred by the ineligible, we should then believe that the eligible have a stronger obligation than those who are ineligible. But, as far as I can tell, we do not ordinarily think that this is true. Finally, Plamenatz cannot rely on a purely conceptual argument to make his point. It is by no means an analytic truth that those subject to elected governments have a prima facie obligation to obey the law.[24] The radical who says, "The present government of the United States was freely elected, but because it exploits people its citizens have no obligation to obey it," has perhaps said something false, but he has not contradicted himself. Plamenatz's argument is therefore either question-begging or inconclusive, depending on what he means by "authority."

Gewirth's argument is similar to Plamenatz's in that he also holds that a person's vote establishes his prima facie obligation of obedience. He argues that men consent to government when "certain institutional arrangements exist in the community as a whole," including "the maintenance of a method which leaves open to every sane, noncriminal adult the opportunity to discuss, criticize, and vote for or against the government."[25] He holds that the existence of such consent "justifies" government and establishes the subject's prima facie obligation to obey because:

> The method of consent combines and safeguards the joint values of freedom and order as no other method does. It provides a choice in

the power of government which protects the rights of the electorate more effectively than does any other method. It does more justice to man's potential rationality than does any other method, for it gives all men the opportunity to participate in a reasoned discussion of the problem of society and to make their discussion effective in terms of political control.[26]

As it stands, Gewirth's argument is incomplete. He makes certain claims about the benefits of government by consent which are open to reasonable doubt. Some communists, for example, would hold that Gewirth's method of consent has led to exploitation, and that human rights and freedom are better protected by the rule of the party. This aside, Gewirth's argument still needs strengthening. The fact that certain benefits are given only by government with a method of consent establishes only that such a government is better than one which lacks such a method. But, to show that one government is better than another, or even to show that it is the best possible government, does not prove that its subjects have a prima facie obligation to obey its laws: There is a prior question, which remains to be settled, as to whether there can be a prima facie obligation to obey any government. Gewirth does not carry the argument farther in his discussion of "consent," but earlier in his paper he hints as to how he would meet this objection. He argues that "government as such" is justified, or made legitimate, by its being necessary to avoid certain evils.[27] Indeed, although he does not explicitly so state, he seems to think that utilitarian considerations demonstrate that there is a prima facie obligation to obey any government that protects its subjects from these evils, but that there is an additional prima facie obligation to obey a government with a method of consent because of the more extensive benefits it offers. In the next section, I shall discuss whether a direct appeal to utility can establish a prima facie obligation to obey the law.

III

I shall consider three utilitarian arguments: the first appealing to a weak form of act-utilitarianism, the second and third to rule-utilitarian theories. To my knowledge, the first argument has never been explicitly advanced. It is nevertheless worth considering, both because it possesses a certain plausibility and because it has often been hinted at when philosophers, lawyers, and political theorists have attempted to derive an obligation to obey the law from the premise that government is necessary to protect society from great evil. The argument runs as follows:

> There is obviously a prima facie obligation to perform acts which have good consequences. Now, government is absolutely necessary for securing the general good: The alternative is the state of nature in which everyone is miserable, in which life is "solitary, poor, nasty, brutish and short." But, no government can long stand in the face of widespread disobedience, and government can therefore promote the general good only so long as its laws are obeyed. Therefore, obedience to the law supports the continued existence of government and, hence, always has good consequences. From this it follows that there is a prima facie obligation to obey the law.

On even brief scrutiny, however, this argument quickly disintegrates. The first thing to be noticed is that its principle of prima facie obligation is ambiguous. It may be interpreted as postulating either (a) an obligation to perform those acts which have any good consequences, or (b) an obligation to perform optimific acts (*i.e.*, those whose consequences are better than their alternatives). Now, (a) and (b) are in fact very different principles. The former is obviously absurd. It implies, for example, that I have a prima facie obligation to kill whomever I meet, since this would have the good consequence of helping to reduce overpopulation. Thus, the only weak act-utilitarian principle with any plausibility is (b). But, regardless of whether (b) is acceptable—and some philosophers would not accept it[28]—the conclusion that there is a prima facie obligation to obey the law cannot be derived from it, inasmuch as there are obvious and familiar cases in which breach of a particular law has better consequences than obedience. The only conclusion to be derived from (b) is that there is a specific prima facie obligation to obey the law whenever obedience is optimific. But no generic prima facie obligation to obey can be derived from weak act-utilitarianism.[29]

The second utilitarian argument appeals not to the untoward consequences of individual disobedience, but rather to those of general disobedience. Perhaps the most common challenge to those who defend certain instances of civil disobedience is "What would happen if every-one disobeyed the law?" One of the arguments implicit in this question is the generalization argument, which may be expanded as follows:

> No one can have a right to do something unless everyone has a right to do it. Similarly, an act cannot be morally indifferent unless it would be morally indifferent if everyone did it. But, everyone's breaking the law is not a matter of moral indifference; for no government can survive in such a circumstance and, as we have already agreed, government is necessary for securing and maintaining the general good. Hence, since the consequences of general disobedience would be disastrous, each person subject to law has a prima facie obligation to obey it.

In assessing this argument, we must first recognize that the generalization argument is a moral criterion to be applied with care, as virtually everyone who has discussed it has recognized.[30] If we simply note that if everyone committed a certain act there would be disastrous consequences and thereupon conclude that there is a prima facie obligation not to commit acts of that kind, we will be saddled with absurdities. We will have to maintain, for example, that there is a prima facie obligation not to eat dinner at five o'clock, for if everyone did so, certain essential services could not be maintained. And, for similar reasons, we will have to maintain that there is a prima facie obligation not to produce food. Now, those who believe that the generalization argument is valid argue that such absurdities arise when the criterion is applied to acts which are either too generally described or described in terms of morally irrelevant features. They would argue that the generalization argument appears to go awry when applied to these examples because the description "producing food" is too general to give the argument purchase and because the temporal specification in "eating dinner at five o'clock" is morally irrelevant.[31]

However, such a restriction on the generalization argument is fatal to its use in proving a prima facie obligation to obey the law. This is because a person who denies any such obligation is surely entitled to protest that the description "breaking the law" is overly general, on the ground that it refers to acts of radically different moral import.[32] Breaking the law perhaps always has some bad consequences; but sometimes the good done by it balances the bad or even outweighs it. And, once we take these differences in consequences into account, we find that utilitarian generalization, like weak act-utilitarianism, can only establish a specific prima facie obligation to obey the law when obedience is optimific. Were everyone to break the law when obedience is optimific, the consequences would undoubtedly be disastrous; but it is by no means clear that it would be disastrous if everyone broke the law when obedience is not optimific. Since no one knows, with respect to any society, how often obedience is not optimific, no one can be certain as to the consequences of everyone acting in this way. Indeed, for all we know, if everyone broke the law when obedience was not optimific the good done by separate acts of law-breaking might more than compensate for any public disorder which might result. In sum, even if the generalization argument is regarded as an acceptable principle of prima facie obligation, the most it demonstrates is that there is a specific prima facie obligation to obey the law whenever the consequences of obedience are optimific.

Some readers—especially those unfamiliar with the recent literature on utilitarianism[33]—may suspect that this last argument involves sleight of hand. They may object:

> In your discussion of the generalization argument, you argued that we have no way of knowing the consequences if everyone disobeyed when obedience was not optimific. But, your argument rests on the premise that the act-utilitarian formula can be perfectly applied, whereas this is in fact impossible; The consequences of many acts are difficult or impossible to foretell: and so, were we all to attempt to be act-utilitarians, we would either make horrendous mistakes or be paralyzed into inaction. In constructing a rule-utilitarian theory of prima facie obligations, we should therefore concentrate not on the consequences of everyone following certain rules, but rather on the consequences of everyone trying to follow them. And, it seems reasonable to believe that, on such a theory, the rule "Obey the law" would receive utilitarian blessing.

As it stands, this objection is overdrawn. My argument does not presuppose that persons can generally succeed in applying the act-utilitarian formula: I merely speculated on the consequences of everyone behaving in a certain way; and I made no assumption as to what made them act that way. Moreover, the objection severely overestimates the difficulty in being a confirmed act-utilitarian. Still, the objection makes one substantial point that deserves further attention. Rule–utilitarian theories which focus on the consequences of everyone accepting (although not always following) a certain set of rules do differ markedly from the generalization argument; and so the question remains as to whether such a theory could establish a prima facie obligation to obey the law. I shall therefore discuss whether the most carefully developed such theory, that given by R. B. Brandt,[34] does just this.

In Brandt's theory, one's obligations are (within certain limits) relative to his society and are determined by the set of rules whose acceptance in that society would have better consequences than would acceptance of any other set.[35] According to this theory, then, there can be a generic prima facie obligation to obey the law within a given society if, and only if, general acceptance of the rule "Obey the law," as a rule of prima facie obligation, would have better consequences than were no rule accepted with respect to obeying the law, as well as better consequences than were some alternative rule accepted (*e.g.*, "Obey the law when obedience to the law is optimific," or "Obey the law so long as it is just"). Now, to many it may seem obvious that the ideal set of rules for any society will contain the rule "Obey the law," on the ground that, were its members not generally convinced of at least a prima facie obligation to obey, disobedience would be widespread, resulting in a great many crimes against person and property. But, there are two reasons to doubt such a gloomy forecast. First, we must surely suppose that in this hypothetical society the laws are still backed by sanctions, thereby giving its members a strong incentive to obey its laws. Second, we must also assume that the members of that society accept other moral rules (*e.g.*, "Do not harm others," "Keep promises," "Tell the truth") which will give them a moral incentive to obey the law in most circumstances. It is, in short, a mistake to believe that unless people are convinced that they have a generic prima facie obligation to obey the law, they cannot be convinced that in most circumstances they have a specific prima facie obligation to obey particular laws. We may therefore expect that, even though members of our hypothetical society do not accept a moral rule about obedience to the law per se, they will still feel a prima facie obligation to act in accordance with the law, save when disobedience does no harm. There is, then, no reason to think that an orgy of lawbreaking would ensue were no rule about obedience to the law generally recognized; nor, I think, is there any good reason to believe that acceptance of the rule "Obey the law" would in any society have better consequences than were no such rule recognized. And, if this is so, there is surely no reason to think that recognition of this rule would have better consequences than recognition of some alternative rule. In sum, Brandt's theory requires that we be able to determine the truth-value of a large number of counter-factual propositions about what would happen were entire societies persuaded of the truth of certain moral rules. But, even if we assume—and it is hardly clear that we should[36]—that we can reliably determine the truth-value of such counter-factuals through "common sense" and our knowledge of human nature, Brandt's form of rule utilitarianism gives no support for the proof of a prima facie obligation to obey the law.

IV

In the foregoing discussion, I have played the skeptic, contending that no argument has as yet succeeded in establishing a prima facie obligation to obey the law. I want now to examine this supposed obligation directly. I shall assume *arguendo* that such an obligation exists in order to inquire as to how it compares in moral weight with other prima facie obligations. As we shall see, this question is relevant to whether we should hold that such an obligation exists.

To discuss this question, I must, of course, first specify some test for determining the weight of a prima facie obligation. It will be recalled that I defined "prima facie obligation" in terms of wrongdoing: To say that a person S has a prima facie obligation to do an act X is to say that S has a moral reason to do X which is such that, unless he has a reason not to do X that is at least as strong, S's failure to do X is wrong. Now, we are accustomed, in our reflective moral practice, to distinguish degrees of wrongdoing. And so, by appealing to this notion, we can formulate two principles that may reasonably be held to govern the weight of prima facie obligations: First, that a prima facie obligation is a serious one if, and only if, an act which violates that obligation and fulfills no other is seriously wrong; and, second, that a prima facie obligation is a serious one if, and only if, violation of it will make considerably worse an act which on other grounds is already wrong.[37] These principles, which constitute tests for determining an obligation's weight, are closely related, and application of either to a given prima facie obligation is a sufficient measure; but I shall apply both to the presumed prima facie obligation to obey the law in order to make my argument more persuasive.

First, however, we should convince ourselves of the reliability of these tests by applying them to some clear cases. I suppose it will be granted that we all have a prima facie obligation not to kill (except perhaps in self-defense), and that this obligation is most weighty. Our first test corroborates this, for, if a person kills another when he is not defending himself and if he has no specific prima facie obligation to kill that person, his act is seriously wrong. By contrast, our prima facie obligation to observe rules of etiquette—if indeed there is any such obligation—is clearly trifling. This is borne out by our test, for if I belch audibly in the company of those who think such behavior rude, my wrongdoing is at most trivial. The same results are obtained under our second test. If I attempt to extort money from someone my act is much worse if I kill one of his children and threaten the rest than if I merely threatened them all; and so the obligation not to kill again counts as substantial. Similarly, the prima facie obligation to observe the rules of etiquette is again trivial, for if I am rude during the extortion my act is hardly worse than it would have been had I been polite.

By neither of these tests, however, does the prima facie obligation to obey the law count as substantial. As for the first test, let us assume that while driving home at two o'clock in the morning I run a stop sign. There is no danger, for I can see clearly that there was no one approaching the intersection, nor is there any impressionable youth nearby to be inspired to a life of crime by my flouting of the traffic code. Finally, we may assume that I nevertheless had no specific prima facie obligation to run the stop sign. If, then, my prima facie obligation to obey the law is of substantial moral weight, my action must have been a fairly serious instance of wrongdoing. But clearly it was not. If it was wrong at all— and to me this seems dubious—it was at most a mere peccadillo. As for the second test, we may observe that acts which are otherwise wrong are not made more so—if they are made worse at all—by being illegal.[38] If I defraud someone my act is hardly worse morally by being illegal than it would have been were it protected by some legal loophole. Thus, if there is a prima facie obligation to obey the law, it is at most of trifling weight.

This being so, I suggest that considerations of simplicity indicate that we should ignore the supposed prima facie obligation to obey the law and refuse to count an act wrong merely because it violates some law. There is certainly nothing to be lost by doing this, for we shall not thereby recommend or tolerate any conduct that is seriously wrong, nor shall we fail to recommend any course of action that is seriously obligatory. Yet, there is much to be gained, for in refusing to let trivialities occupy our attention, we shall not be diverted from the important questions to be asked about illegal conduct, *viz.*, "What kind of act was it?," "What were its consequences?," "Did the agent intend its consequences?," and so forth. Morality is, after all, a serious business; and we are surely right not to squander our moral attention and concern on matters of little moral significance.

To illustrate what can be gained, let us consider briefly the issue of civil disobedience. Most philosophers who have written on the subject have argued that, at least in democratic societies, there is always a strong moral reason to obey the law. They have therefore held that civil disobedience is a tactic to be employed only when all legal means of changing an unjust law have failed, and that the person who engages in it must willingly accept punishment as a mark of respect for the law and recognition of the seriousness of lawbreaking. However, once we abandon the notion that civil disobedience is morally significant per se, we shall judge it in the same way we judge most other kinds of acts, that is, on the basis of their character and consequences. Indeed, we can then treat civil disobedience just as we regard many other species of illegal conduct. If breaking the law involves an act which is *mala in se* or if it has untoward consequences, we are ordinarily prepared to condemn it and to think that the malefactor ought to accept punishment. But if lawbreaking does not involve an act that is *mala in se* and if it has no harmful consequences, we do not ordinarily condemn it, nor do we think that its perpetrator must accept punishment, unless evading punishment itself has untoward consequences. If we adopt this view of civil disobedience, we shall have done much to escape the air of mystery that hovers about most discussions of it.

Of course, this is not to say it will be easy to determine when civil disobedience is justified. Some have maintained that the civil disobedience of the last decade has led to increasing violation of laws which safeguard people and property.[39] If this is true, each instance of disobedience which has contributed to this condition has a share in the evil of the result. Others maintain that such disobedience has had wholly good consequences, that it has helped to remedy existing injustice and to restrain government from fresh injustice.[40] Still others think its consequences are mixed. Which position is correct is difficult to determine. I myself am inclined to believe that, although the consequences have been mixed, the good far outweigh the bad; but I would be hard pressed to prove it. What is clear, however, is that either abandoning or retaining the supposed prima facie obligation to obey the law will not help settle these questions about consequences. But, if we do abandon it, we shall then at least be able to focus on these questions without having to worry about a prima facie obligation of trivial weight that must nevertheless somehow be taken into account. Finally, if we abandon the prima facie obligation to obey the law, we shall perhaps look more closely at the character of acts performed in the course of civil disobedience, and this may, in turn, lead to fruitful moral speculation. For example, we shall be able to distinguish between acts which cannot conceivably violate the obligation of fair play (*e.g.*, burning one's draft card) and acts which may do so (*e.g.*, tax refusal or evasion of military service). This in turn may provide an incentive to reflect further on the obligation of fair play, to ask, for example, whether Rawls is right in his present contention that a person can incur the obligation of fair play only so long as his acceptance of the benefits of a cooperative enterprise is wholly voluntary.

V

It is now time to take stock. I initially suggested that it is by no means obvious that there is any prima facie obligation to obey the law. In the foregoing, I have rejected a number of arguments that purport to establish its existence. The only plausible argument I have not rejected is the one of Rawls that purports to prove that there is a natural duty to obey the laws of reasonably just governments. However, I did note that his position lacks intuitive support and rests on a controversial ethical theory which has not yet withstood the test of critical scrutiny. Finally, I have shown that even if such an obligation is assumed, it is of trivial weight and that there are substantial advantages in ignoring it. I suggest that all of this makes it reasonable to maintain that there is in no society a prima facie obligation to obey the law.

Before I conclude my discussion, however, I want to tie up one loose thread. Near the beginning of my argument I distinguished the question to be discussed from that which I called the lawyer's question, "May a reasonable man take mere illegality to be sufficient evidence that an act is morally wrong, so long as he lacks specific evidence that tends to show that it is right?" Since I have raised the question, I believe that, for the sake of completeness, I should consider it, if only briefly. To begin, it seems very doubtful that there is, in the lawyer's sense, a prima facie obligation to obey the law. It is undoubtedly true that most instances of lawbreaking are wrong, but it is also true that many are not: This is because there are, as Lord Devlin once remarked, "many fussy regulations whose breach it would be pedantic to call immoral,"[41] and because some breaches of even non-fussy regulations are justified. Now, unless—as in a court of law—there is some pressing need to reach a finding, the mere fact that most *A*s are also *B* does not, in the absence of evidence that a particular *A* is not *B*, warrant an inference that the *A* in question is also a *B*: In order for this inference to be reasonable, one must know that virtually all *A*s are *B*s. Since, then, it rarely happens that there is a pressing need to reach a moral finding, and since to know merely that an act is illegal is not to know very much of moral significance about it, it seems clear that, if his only information about an act was that it was illegal, a reasonable man would withhold judgment until he learned more about it. Indeed, this is not only what the fictitious reasonable man would do, it is what we should expect the ordinary person to do. Suppose we were to ask a large number of people: "Jones has broken a law; but I won't tell you whether what he did is a serious crime or merely violation of a parking regulation, nor whether he had good reason for his actions. Would you, merely on the strength of what I have just told you, be willing to say that what he did was morally wrong?" I have conducted only an informal poll; but, on its basis, I would wager that the great majority would answer "I can't yet say—you must tell me more about what Jones did."

More importantly, it appears to make little difference what answer we give to the lawyer's question. While an affirmative answer establishes a rule of inference that an illegal act is wrong in the absence of specific information tending to show it to be right, it is a rule that would in fact virtually never be applied in any reasonable determination of whether an illegal act is wrong. If, on the one hand, we have specific information about an illegal act which tends to show it to be right, then the rule is irrelevant to our determination of the act's moral character. Should we be inclined, in this instance, to hold the act wrong we must have specific information which tends to show this: and it is clear that our conclusions about its moral character must be based on this specific information, and not on the supposed reasonableness of holding illegal conduct wrong in the absence of specific information tending to show it is right. On the other hand, if we have specific information tending to show that an illegal act is wrong and no information tending to show it is right, the rule is applicable but otiose: Since we have ample specific reason to condemn the act, the rule is superfluous to our judgment. It would seem, then, that the rule is relevant only when we have no specific information about the illegal conduct's rightness or wrongness: and this, I suggest, is something that virtually never occurs. When we are prompted to make a moral judgment about an illegal act, we virtually always know something of its character or at least its consequences; and it is these that we consider important in determining the rightness or wrongness of lawbreaking. In short, it seems to make little difference what answer we give to the lawyer's question; I raise it here only that it may hereafter be ignored.

In conclusion, it is, I think, important to recognize that there is nothing startling in what I am recommending, nothing that in any way outrages common sense. Even the most conscientious men at times violate trivial and pointless laws for some slight gain in convenience and, when they do so, they do not feel shame or remorse. Similarly, when they observe other men behaving in a like fashion, they do not think of passing moral censure. For most people, violation of the law becomes a matter for moral concern only when it involves an act which is believed to be wrong on grounds apart from its illegality. Hence, anyone who believes that the purpose of normative ethics is to organize and clarify our reflective moral practice should be skeptical of any argument purporting to show that there is a prima facie obligation to obey the law. It is necessary to state this point with care: I am not contending that reflective and conscientious citizens would, if asked, deny that there is a prima facie obligation to obey the law. Indeed, I am willing to concede that many more would affirm its existence than deny it. But, this is in no way inconsistent with my present point. We often find that reflective people will accept general statements which are belied by their actual linguistic practice. That they also accept moral generalizations that are belied by their actual reflective moral practice should occasion no surprise.

This last point may, however, be challenged on the ground that it implies that there is in our reflective moral practice no distinction between raw power and legitimate authority. As I noted above, the concept of legitimate authority is often analyzed in terms of the right to command, where "right" is used in the strict sense as implying some correlative obligation of obedience. Given this definition, if it is true that the principle "There is a prima facie obligation to obey the law" is not observed in our reflective moral practice, it follows that we do not really distinguish between governments which possess legitimate authority (*e.g.*, that of the United States) and those which do not (*e.g.*, the Nazi occupation government of France). And this, it may justly be held, is absurd. What I take this argument to show, however, is not that the principle is enshrined in our reflective morality, but rather that what we ordinarily mean when we ascribe legitimate authority to some government is not captured by the usual analysis of "legitimate authority." It is a mistake to believe that, unless we employ the concept of authority as it is usually analyzed, we cannot satisfactorily distinguish between the moral relation of the government of the United States vis-à-vis Americans and the moral relation of the Nazi occupation government vis-à-vis Frenchmen. One way of doing this, for example, is to define "legitimate authority" in terms of "the right to command and to enforce obedience," where "right" is used in the sense of "what is morally permissible." Thus, according to this analysis of the notion, the government of the United States counts as having legitimate authority over its subjects because within certain limits there is nothing wrong in its issuing commands to them and enforcing their obedience, whereas the Nazi occupation government lacked such authority because its issuing commands to Frenchmen was morally impermissible. It is not my intention to proffer this as an adequate analysis of the notion of legitimate authority or to suggest that it captures what we ordinarily mean when we ascribe such authority to some government. These are difficult matters, and I do not wish to address myself to them here. My point is rather that the questions

"What governments enjoy legitimate authority?" and "Have the citizens of any government a prima facie obligation to obey the law?" both can be, and should be, kept separate.

NOTES

I wish to thank Judith Jarvis Thomson, Hugo A. Bedau, Gerald Barnes, Murray Kiteley, Robert Ackermann, and Stanley Rothman, for their criticism of earlier drafts of this article.

1. Rawls, *Legal Obligation and the Duty of Fair Play*, in LAW AND PHILOSOPHY 3 (S. Hook ed. 1964).

2. H. A. PRICHARD, *Green's Principles of Political Obligation*, in MORAL OBLIGATION 54 (1949).

3. The distinction between prima facie and absolute obligation was first made by W. D. Ross in THE RIGHT AND THE GOOD ch. 2 (1930). My account of prima facie obligation differs somewhat from Ross'; but I believe it adequately captures current philosophical usage. As for absolute obligation, I shall not often speak of it; but when I do, what I shall mean by "*S* has an absolute obligation to do *X*" is that "*S*'s failure to do *X* is wrong."

4. My motive for distinguishing generic and specific prima facie obligations is simply convenience, and not because I think it provides a perspicuous way of classifying prima facie obligations. As a classification it is obviously defective: The two kinds of obligation overlap, since in a trivial sense every specific obligation can be construed as a generic one; and there are some prima facie obligations (*e.g.*, the obligation to keep one's promise), that fit neither definition.

5. An example may help to make the point clear. If I promise that I will meet someone at a certain time, I have a prima facie obligation to keep my promise. Now, were this merely a prima facie obligation in the lawyer's sense, without evidence to the contrary the fact that I had promised would be sufficient to hold that a breach of my promise was wrong, yet it would not be evidence of wrongdoing were there reason to believe the breach was justified or even obligatory. But, in fact, this is not what we think of promising. We think that if someone promises to do a thing there is a strong moral reason for him to do it and that, although this reason may sometimes be opposed by stronger reasons to the contrary, its weight does not disappear. In such cases, my promise is yet relevant to what I am absolutely obligated to do, although it is not always determinative. But, even when this reason is outweighed, it still discloses its existence by imposing fresh prima facie obligations (*e.g.*, to tell the person I promised why I broke it). Hence, there is a prima facie obligation to keep one's promise in the sense in which I here use the phrase.

6. Hart, *Are There Any Natural Rights?* 64 PHIL. REV. 185 (1955). I must note that Hart does not use the phrase "prima facie obligation," maintaining that his argument establishes an obligation *sans phrase* to comply with the rules of cooperative enterprises. However, since his use of "obligation" seems much the same as my use of "prima facie obligation," I shall ignore his terminological scruples.

7. Rawls, *supra* note 1. The same argument appears, although in less detail, in Rawls, *Justice as Fairness*, 67 PHIL. REV. 164 (1958), and Rawls, *The Justification of Civil Disboedience*, in CIVIL DISOBEDIENCE: THEORY AND PRACTICE (H. A. Bedau, ed. 1969).

8. Rawls, *Legal Obligation and the Duty of Fair Play*, in LAW AND PHILOSOPHY 10 (S. Hook, ed. 1964). According to Rawls, the principles of justice are
that everyone have an equal right to the most extensive liberty compatible with a like liberty for all; . . . [and] that inequalities are arbitrary unless it is reasonable to expect that they will work out for everyone's advantage and provided that the positions and offices to which they attached or from which they may be gained are open to all.
Id. at 11.

9. *Id.* at 13; Hart, *supra* note 6, at 185.

10. Those intrigued by the mention of these additional factors may be interested to know that, when imperfect cooperation is taken into account, it can be shown that considerations of fairness establish no more than: (1) that a member A of a cooperative enterprise has a prima facie obligation to obey when his obedience will benefit some other member B from whose submission A has previously benefitted and it is not the case that B has withheld from A more significant benefits than A withholds from B; and (2) that A has a prima facie obligation to obey when his disobedience harms the enterprise and there is some other member B from whose submission A has previously benefitted and B has by his disobedience harmed the enterprise less than the harm which would be done by A's disobedience.

As for the effect of disparity in sacrifice, it was only recently suggested to me that this factor must be taken into account, and I have not yet attempted to determine its effects precisely. A moment's reflection discloses, however, that this additional factor would make the obligation still more complex. Were anyone to attempt a precise specification of the citizen's obligations vis-à-vis the laws of his government, he would have to master these complexities; but my task is not so ambitious.

11. Indeed, it seems strange that Rawls should have attempted to base the prima facie obligation to obey the law on fair play, since he maintains that this latter obligation is incurred within cooperative enterprises that depend on near-universal cooperation. Rawls, *Legal Obligation and the Duty of Fair Play*, in LAW AND PHILOSOPHY 10 (S. Hook, ed. 1964).

12. J. Rawls, A THEORY OF JUSTICE 108 (1971).

13. *Id.* at 336, 344.

14. *Id.* at 334–37, 350–62.

15. J. Locke, TWO TREATISES OF GOVERNMENT Bk. 11, ¶ 119 (1690).

16. I Plato, DIALOGUES 435 (B. Jowett, transl. 1892).

17. Ross, *supra* note 3, at 27.

18. *Cf.* Strawson, *Intention and Convention in Speech Acts*, 73 PHIL. REV. 439, 448–49, 457–59 (1964).

19. A similar argument could also be made utilizing the analysis of promising in J. Searle, SPEECH ACTS: AN ESSAY IN THE PHILOSOPHY OF LANGUAGE 60 (1969).

20. Another recent tacit consent theory is found in J. Tussman, Obligation and the Body Politic (1960). I shall not discuss this theory, however, because it has already received adequate criticism in Pitkin, *Obligation and Consent I*, 59 AM. POL. SCI. REV. 990 (1965). Nor shall I discuss Pitkin's own "hypothetical consent" theory that obedience is owed to those governments to which one ought to consent, because in her discussion of how political obligation is justified she does not appeal to the concept of hypothetical consent. She takes the problem of justifying political obligation to be the question "Why am I ever obligated to obey even legitimate authority?" She gives the question short shrift, however, replying that it is simply part of the meaning of the phrase "legitimate authority" that those subject to legitimate authority have a prima facie obligation to obey it. *See* Pitkin, *Obligation and Consent II*, 60 AM. POT. SCI. REV. 39, 45–49 (1966).

21. J. Plamenatz, MAN AND SOCIETY 228, 238–39 (1963).

22. *Id.* at 239–40.

23. *Id.*

24. A defender of Plamenatz, John Jenkins, appears to hold that something like this is an analytic truth, maintaining that:

> if a person supposes that he has no obligation to a successful candidate because that candidate happens not to be the person for whom he cast his vote, then there is an excellent case for saying that the man has failed to understand the nature of the electoral process.

Jenkins, *Political Consent*, 20 PHIL. Q. 61 (1970).

This seems a silly claim. Many who voted for George McGovern believe themselves to be under no obligation to Richard Nixon. Some are highly educated and close observers of the political scene. Were such a person to explain his belief that he is not obligated to Nixon solely on the ground that he did not vote for him, we might think him mistaken or wish that he had chosen a better reason, but we should have no reason at all to think that he fails to understand "the nature of the electoral process."

25. Earlier in his discussion Gewirth distinguishes three senses of "consent": an "occurrence" sense, a "dispositional" sense, and an "opportunity" sense. *Id.* at 131. It is only the last that will concern us here, since he admits that the prima facie obligation to obey the law cannot be shown by relying on the occurrence or the dispositional senses. Gewirth, *Political Justice*, in SOCIAL JUSTICE 138 (R. Brandt, ed. 1962).

26. *Id.* at 139.

27. *Id.* at 135.

28. For example, some philosophers would hold that there is a prima facie obligation to refrain from acts which have undesirable consequences, but not that there is an obligation to perform the one act which has the best consequences. *See, e.g.*, M. G. Singer, GENERALIZATION IN ETHICS, ch. 7 (1961).

29. For purposes of clarification, I should emphasize that I am here concerned with act-utilitarianism as a theory of prima facie, not absolute, obligation. There is no incongruity here. The consequences of acts count as having great moral significance on virtually every moral theory; and so, one need not be a strict act-utilitarian in order to maintain the principle that there is a prima facie obligation to act optimifically. Indeed, for a strict act-utilitarian such as Bentham, it is pointless to worry about whether there is a prima facie obligation to obey the law: He would hold that there is an absolute obligation to obey the law when, and only when, obedience is optimific, and would there end the discussion. At most, an act-utilitarian would hold that the rule "Obey the law" is a useful rule of thumb, to be followed only when the consequences of obedience or disobedience are difficult to discern.

30. Singer, *supra* note 28, at ch. 4.

31. I have borrowed these cases and this strategy for handling them from Singer. *Id.* at 71–83.

32. According to Singer, a mark of a description's being overly general is that the generalization argument is "invertible" with respect to it, *i.e.*, the consequences of everyone's doing the act (given that description) is disastrous and the consequences of everyone's failing to do it is also disastrous. *Id.* at 76–77. It is relevant to note that the generalization argument is plainly invertible with respect to the description "breaking the law." Sometimes breaking the law is the only way to avoid a great evil; and so, if everyone were always to obey the law, such evils could never be avoided.

33. That the generalization argument and weak act-utilitarianism offer the same advice on the topic of obedience to the law should surprise no one familiar with D. Lyons, FORMS AND LIMITS OF UTILITARIANISM (1965). Lyons there shows that act-utilitarianism and the generalization argument are extensionally equivalent. There is, it should be noted, a substantial difference between Lyons' argument for equivalence and the argument I have here offered. Lyons argues

for equivalence on a priori grounds, whereas I have relied on the empirical impossibility of determining the consequences of everyone disobeying the law when obedience is not optimific.

34. Brandt, *Toward a Credible Utilitarianism*, in MORALITY AND THE LANGUAGE OF CONDUCT 107 (H. N. Casteñeda & G. Nakhnikian, eds. 1963). In the following I shall not be attacking a position Brandt holds, but only an argument that might be offered on the basis of his theory. In fact, in *Utility and the Obligation to Obey the Law*, in LAW AND PHILOSOPHY 43, 47–49 (S. Hook ed. 1964) Brandt expresses doubt as to whether there is such an obligation.

35. According to Brandt's theory, there is an absolute obligation to perform an act if it

conforms with that learnable set of rules the recognition of which as morally binding—roughly at the time of the act—by everyone in the society of the agent, except for the retention by individuals of already formed and decided moral convictions, would maximize intrinsic value.

Brandt, *Toward a Credible Utilitarianism*, in MORALITY AND THE LANGUAGE OF CONDUCT 107 (H. N. Casteñeda & G. Nakhnikian, eds. 1963). He distinguishes three levels of rules, the first stating prima facie obligations and the latter two dealing with cases in which lower-level rules conflict. At every level, however, those in the favored set of rules are those whose recognition would have the best consequences, *i.e.*, consequences better than were any alternative rule accepted, as well as better than were no such rule accepted. *Id.* at 118–19.

36. As an illustration of the difficulty, Brandt suggests that the first-level rule "Keep your promises" is neither the one that we accept nor the rule about promising that would maximize utility. *Id.* at 131–32. I think he is right to say that it is not the rule we accept, but how does he know that some more complex rule maximizes utility?

37. The second principle may be thought objectionable on the ground that it trivializes obviously weighty prima facie obligations. It may perhaps be held that, were a man to kill a thousand persons, his act would not have been much worse had he killed but one more. The principle therefore seems to imply that the prima facie obligation not to kill that one person is trivial. The objection is plausible, but misguided. Surely there is a substantial moral difference between killing a thousand persons and killing a thousand-and-one—exactly the difference between killing one person and killing none. To deny this is to imply that the thousand-and-first person's life has little moral significance. At first glance, however, we may be inclined to take the difference to be trivial, because both acts are so monstrous that we should rarely see any point in distinguishing between them. That this objection might be raised against the principle was pointed out to me by Anne Bowen.

38. I have taken this point from I. W. Blackstone, COMMENTARIES 54:

Neither do divine or natural *duties* (such as, for instance, the worship of God, the maintenance of children, and the like) receive any stronger sanction from being also declared to be duties by the law of the land. The case is the same as to crimes and misdemeanors, that are forbidden by the superior laws, and therefore styled *mala in se,* such as murder, theft, and perjury; which contract no additional turpitude from being declared unlawful by the inferior legislature.

39. C. Whittaker, *First Lecture,* in LAW, ORDER AND CIVIL DISOBEDIENCE (1967).

40. *See* H. Zinn, DISOBEDIENCE AND DEMOCRACY (1968).

41. P. Devlin, THE ENFORCEMENT OF MORALS 27 (1965).

5

THE PRINCIPLE OF FAIR PLAY

A. John Simmons

I. HART AND RAWLS ON FAIR PLAY

Many consent theorists have recognized as grounds of political obligation acts which are not consensual acts, promises, or contracts. Primarily through utilizing what I call "consent-implying" acts, Locke and other consent theorists confusedly, and unintentionally, acknowledged the existence of grounds of political obligation which were not deliberate undertakings. These grounds were acts which seemed to bind the individual to the state, and seemed to be related to consent in some way: they were recognized as morally significant acts, but were mistakenly subsumed under the title of consent. Specifically, the "consent-implying" acts in question were the "enjoyments" of the benefits of government within the state.

The problem, then, has become one of understanding the significance of these sorts of acts in new (i.e., not consent-related) terms. If we allow that these acts, which are not consensual in character, may nonetheless generate political obligations, how are we to explain this possibility? One sort of explanation which has enjoyed some popularity during the last two decades relies on what has been called "the Principle of Fair Play"[1] (or "the Principle of Fairness"). I suggest that this principle might be regarded in some ways as an extension of certain consent theory intuitions; but more often, it is regarded as simply a replacement for consent theory. H. L. A. Hart, for instance, in the first concise formulation of the principle of fair play, writes:

　　A third important source of special rights and obligations which we recognize in many spheres of life is what may be termed mutuality of restrictions, and I think political obligation is intelligible only if we see what precisely this is and how it differs from the other right–creating transactions (consent, promising) to which philosophers have assimilated it.[2]

Hart's comments on the principle (and on its application to political cases) are fairly sparse, but I want to examine them briefly by way of introduction. Hart's explanation of the "special transaction" he has in mind runs as follows:

　　When a number of persons conduct any joint enterprise according to rules and thus restrict their liberty, those who have submitted to these restrictions when required have a right to a similar submission from those who have benefited by their submission. The rules may provide that officials should have authority to enforce obedience . . . but the moral obligation to obey the rules in such circumstances is due to the cooperating members of the society, and they have the correlative moral right to obedience.[3]

While Hart does not refer to this source of special rights and obligations in terms of fairness or fair play, he does note later that "in the case of mutual restrictions we are in fact saying that this claim to interfere with another's freedom is justified because it is fair."[4] We can understand him, then, to be claiming that in the situation described, a beneficiary has an obligation to "do his fair share" by submitting to the rules when they require it; others who have cooperated before have a right to this fair distribution of the burdens of submission.

　　Clearly, Hart intends to restrict the generation of rights and obligations under the principle of fair play to certain special contexts. Not just any situation in which we would be inclined to talk of fair play will suffice. The salient features of these special contexts seem to be: (1) a number of individuals participate in an "enterprise"; (2) a set of rules (according to which individuals are uniformly restricted in their actions) governs the enterprise; (3) when some (or all) of the participants follow the rules, certain benefits accrue to some (or all) of the participants—but these benefits may be gotten in at least some cases without following the rules when one's turn comes. Under these conditions, when a person (who must presumably be a participant, although Hart does not specify this) benefits from others having followed the rules, he has an "obligation of fair play" also to follow the rules, and those who have followed the rules have a right to his cooperation.

A large number of questions concerning this account come immediately to the fore. What is to be counted as "an enterprise"? (Will any "project" be "an enterprise"? Must participants be "members," or have joined in some way?) Why is a set of rules necessary? (Mightn't a principle of fair play apply as well to nonrule-governed enterprises?) How do we specify the class of beneficiaries to whom obligations are ascribed? (Who counts as a participant, and who as an "outsider"?) Must a "fair share" of benefits be received to obligate the recipient to do his "fair share" in following the rules? The list can go on. Obviously, Hart's account leaves out far more than it fills in (but in fairness, it was not intended as a complete account—Hart's essay does not profess to give this principle any more than a superficial treatment). What is needed for our present purposes is a fuller discussion of both the principle itself and its application to political cases.

Both needs are best met by John Rawls's 1964 essay, "Legal Obligation and the Duty of Fair Play." In it Rawls builds on Hart's account to give both a more complete account of the principle of fair play and an extensive discussion of its application to constitutional democracies. (Rawls's later account of the principle in *A Theory of Justice* is substantially the same; in many respects, however, the account presently under discussion is more detailed and hence more suitable for present purposes.)[5] The ways in which Rawls elaborates on and adds to Hart's principle are, I think, interesting. Rawls's central presentation of the principle of fair play runs:

> The principle of fair play may be defined as follows. Suppose there is a mutually beneficial and just scheme of social cooperation, and that the advantages it yields can only be obtained if everyone, or nearly everyone, cooperates. Suppose further that cooperation requires a certain sacrifice from each person, or at least involves a certain restriction of his liberty. Suppose finally that the benefits produced by cooperation are, up to a certain point, free; that is, the scheme of cooperation is unstable in the sense that if any one person knows that all (or nearly all) of the others will continue to do their part, he will

still be able to share a gain from the scheme even if he does not do his part. Under these conditions a person who has accepted the benefits of the scheme is bound by a duty of fair play to do his part and not to take advantage of the free benefits by not cooperating.[6]

The context within which obligations (or duties—Rawls is not particularly concerned here with the distinction between them) of fair play can arise, as described by Rawls, can be seen to exhibit three important features parallel to those we discerned in Hart's account:

1. There must be an active scheme of social cooperation. This does not really advance us much beyond Hart's "enterprise," but I think that both writers clearly intended that the principle cover a broad range of schemes, programs, enterprises, etc., differing in size and in significance. Thus, a tenant organization's program to improve conditions in their apartment building, and an entire political community's cooperative efforts to preserve social order, both seem to qualify as "enterprises" or "schemes of social cooperation" of the appropriate sort. Rawls does set two explicit conditions, however, which help us limit the class of "schemes" he has in mind. First, they must be "mutually beneficial." This condition is, I think, implicit in Hart's account as well; indeed, the principle would be obviously objectionable in its absence. Second, the schemes must be just. This condition is nowhere alluded to by Hart, and I will consider it carefully in part II. In his later discussions of the principle (see note 5), Rawls introduces the term "institution" to replace "scheme of social cooperation." I find this term not only equally nebulous, but unnecessarily restrictive. Surely fair play considerations apply to many schemes which do not involve anything we would want to call an "institution." When nine friends decide to collect newspapers from neighbors to sell as scrap, in order to raise money for their softball team, their scheme hardly seems to constitute an "institution" (at the very least, we would say that this seems too "formal" a title). Yet when one of the nine plays on the team while failing to help in the collections, surely our criticism would be made in terms of "fair play."

2. Cooperation under the scheme involves at least a restriction of one's liberty. Rawls does not mention here, as Hart does, that this restriction be in accord with a system of rules which govern the scheme by determining the requirements of cooperation (although his later "institutional" language does follow Hart's requirement). Frankly, I can see

no good reason to insist on the rule-governedness of the enterprise. Might not an enterprise be of the right sort which, say, assigned burdens fairly but not in accord with any preestablished rules? Cannot doing one's part be obligatory under considerations of fair play even if "one's part" is not rule-specified? Consider again the example of the paper collection. Must there be a set of rules which specifies the part which each participant must play in the collection? It seems that it would be obligatory for each to do "his part" in the scheme, even if that "part" is not clearly defined by rules. But perhaps my objection simply involves a stricter reading of "system of rules" than either Hart or Rawls has in mind.

3. The benefits yielded by the scheme may be gotten in at least some cases by someone who does not cooperate when his turn comes; here Rawls again makes explicit a condition which Hart clearly has in mind (since "free riding" is a problem only when this condition obtains). But Rawls adds to this the condition that the benefits in question can be obtained only if nearly all of the participants cooperate. I confess that I again do not see the necessity of this condition. Would it be any less unfair to take the benefits of the cooperative sacrifices of others if those benefits could be obtained even if one-third or one-half of the participants neglected their responsibilities toward the scheme? Would this make that neglect justifiable? Surely not. A scheme which requires uniform cooperation when only 50 percent cooperation is needed may perhaps be an inefficient scheme; but it is not clear that this would make considerations of fair play inapplicable. Consider a community scheme to preserve water pressure which prohibits watering lawns in the evening, when in fact if half of the members watered their lawns there would be no lowering of water pressure. Surely this is an inefficient plan, compared to alternatives. But once the plan was instituted, would a member be any more justified in watering his lawn in the evening than if only a few people's so doing would lower the water pressure? I think it is clear that he would not be. Certainly free riding is more dangerous to the scheme's successful provision of benefits when Rawls's requirement obtains; it may then be even more objectionable in those cases. But this additional objectionable element seems to have nothing to do with considerations of *fair play*.[7]

Rawls's account, then, seems to conform to either the letter or the spirit of Hart's account fairly consistently. One significant addition

Rawls makes, however, is to move beyond Hart's simple requirement that an individual have benefited from the scheme in order to become bound. Rawls specifies that the obligation depends on "our having accepted and our intention to continue accepting the benefits of a just scheme of cooperation. . . ."[8] We have, then, a move from mere benefaction in Hart's case, to a positive *acceptance* of benefits in Rawls's account. (The "intention to continue accepting benefits" seems quite beside the point here, and Rawls drops that clause in later versions; I will ignore it.) While the distinction between benefiting and accepting benefits is usually not easy to draw in actual cases, that there is such a distinction, and that it is of great significance to moral questions, is undeniable. Suppose that I am kidnapped by a mad doctor and dragged to his laboratory, where he forces on me an injection of an experimental drug. When I discover that the result of the injection is a great increase in my intelligence and strength, it is undeniable that I have benefited from the injection; but it would be a simple abuse of language to say that I had "accepted" the benefits which I received. Or consider the difference between the cases in which a stranger (a) sneaks into my yard while I am out of town and mows my lawn, and (b) asks me if I'd like to have my lawn mowed, and proceeds to mow it after receiving an affirmative response. In both cases I have clearly received a benefit (in fact, the same benefit), but only in the latter would we say that I had "accepted" that benefit. It seems clear from these examples that we can distinguish, at least in some cases, between mere receipt and positive acceptance of benefits. And it seems equally clear that this distinction may play a crucial role in determining whether or what obligations arise from my having benefited from another's actions.

To have accepted a benefit in the right sense, I must have wanted that benefit when I received it, or have made some effort to get the benefit, or at least not have actively attempted to avoid getting it. I will try to be more precise about this distinction later; here I want only to suggest that Rawls apparently does not see mere benefaction as sufficient to generate an obligation of fair play. He stresses instead the necessity that the benefits be voluntarily accepted by the beneficiary.

This restriction of the principle, of course, seems quite intuitive, for it seems to place us less at the mercy of the whims of cooperative schemes (see my criticism of Nozick's arguments in part IV). And while I have suggested that Rawls has added to Hart's account in imposing this restriction, once again it is possible that such a restriction was intended by Hart. For he does note that "not all obligations to other persons are deliberately incurred, though I think it is true of all special rights that they arise from previous voluntary actions."[9] In other words, while obligations of fair play need not be deliberately incurred, a voluntary action is required. And what is this voluntary action? It is possible that Hart refers simply to the voluntary act of joining the cooperative scheme. But it is also possible that the voluntary act Hart has in mind as a necessary condition for the generation of obligations of fair play is the voluntary acceptance of benefits from the scheme. Since mere receipt of benefits need not involve any voluntary act, Hart may then have in mind the same sort of restriction on the principle as Rawls. At any rate, the problems associated with this distinction will receive fuller consideration in parts IV and V.

II. FAIR PLAY AND JUSTICE

Before continuing, however, I want to return to consider briefly one of Rawls's conditions for the generation of obligations of fair play: the condition states that only when the scheme or institution in question is just can any obligations of fair play (relative to that scheme) arise. This claim is part of a more general thesis that we can never be bound to support or comply with unjust arrangements; although Rawls never advances this general thesis in so many words, it follows from his (unacceptable) claim that *all* obligations are accounted for by the principle of fair play,[10] conjoined with the absence of any natural duties which could account for such a bond. I argue elsewhere that Rawls was mistaken in his claim that consent to an unjust institution could not bind. It remains now to be asked if the principle of fair play can be limited in application to contexts of just cooperative schemes.[11] An answer to this question is, of course, of some importance, since Rawls's condition would limit significantly the principle's application in both political and nonpolitical settings.

Rawls's requirement that the scheme of cooperation be just is put forward quite casually in the paper we have been considering; although he calls it an "essential condition," as far as I can see, he offers no defense of this claim. Even in the more recent statement of this requirement in

A Theory of Justice, we are given little in the way of a justification of it. While he suggests that the condition is necessary to guarantee the requisite "background conditions" for obligation,[12] he elaborates on this point only by using the bad argument which concerns the fact that "extorted promises are void ab initio." As I have argued in the case of consent, the injustice of an institution (or cooperative scheme) need not have any effect on the voluntariness of my membership in or acceptance of benefits from that scheme. And since it is a failure in terms of voluntariness that renders extorted promises nonbinding, Rawls's argument appears to be a non sequitur in the case of fair play, as well as consent.

As Rawls supplies us with no real arguments for this "justice condition," let us try to construct some for him. Two sorts of arguments suggest themselves as defenses of this condition: the first concerns the purpose of the scheme or the ends it promotes, while the second concerns more directly distribution within the scheme. Our first argument would run as follows: we cannot have obligations to do the morally impermissible, or to support schemes whose purposes are immoral or which promote immoral ends. Since unjust schemes fall within this category, we cannot have an obligation to cooperate within unjust schemes. Now, there are a number of obvious problems with this defense of Rawls's "justice condition." Some of these are discussed elsewhere where I defend the possibility of binding consent being given to unjust institutions. But another problem is this: why does Rawls only disqualify *unjust* schemes, rather than all schemes which promote or aim at *immoral* ends? Why does Rawls not include the more general prohibition?

The reason is, I think, that while these immoral ends of the scheme provide us with a reason for working against it, the justice condition is meant to be tied to the principle in a more intimate fashion. But what is this fashion? Thus far, nothing we have said about fair play seems to have anything to do with the moral status of the scheme's purposes. The intuitive force of the principle of fair play seems to be preserved even for, e.g., criminal conspiracies. The special rights and obligations which arise under the principle are thought to do so because of the special relationships which exist between the cooperating participants; a fair share of the burdens is thought to be owed by a benefiting participant simply because others have sacrificed to allow him to benefit within a cooperative scheme. No reference is made here to the morally acceptable status of the scheme. Simple intuitions about fair play, then, do not seem to provide a reason for disqualifying unjust cooperative schemes. Rather, they suggest that obligations of fair play can, at least sometimes, arise within such schemes.

But perhaps another sort of support can be given to Rawls's condition. This second argument concerns distribution within the scheme, and it certainly has the Rawlsian flavor. We suggest, first, that what the justice condition does is, in effect, amend the principle to read that a person is bound to do his fair share in supporting a cooperative scheme only if he has been allocated a fair share of the benefits of the scheme. Previously, the principle of fair play required only that the individual have accepted benefits from the scheme in order to be bound, where now it requires that he have accepted benefits and have been allocated at least a fair share of benefits. The role of the justice condition now appears to be important and an intimate feature of our intuitions about fair play. For if a scheme is just, each participant will be allocated a fair share of the benefits of cooperation; thus, anyone who benefits from the scheme at all has the opportunity to benefit to the extent of a fair share (although he may *accept* less than this). We are guaranteed that the principle of fair play will apply only to individuals who have been fairly treated. Our feeling that a person ought not to have to share equally in supporting a scheme that treats him unfairly is given voice in this condition. The justice condition, then, on this argument, serves the purpose of assuring that a man is bound to do his fair share only if he is allocated a fair share of benefits (and *accepts* some of them).

I think that this is an important feature of our intuitions about fair play, and it also seems a natural way of reading Rawls. In fact, this may be the argument that Rawls is suggesting when, in elaborating on the principle, he notes that if the scheme is just, "each person receives a fair share when all (himself included) do their part."[13] (Rawls's observation is, strictly speaking, false; the justice of a scheme does not guarantee that each person either receives or accepts a fair share.) But if this *is* the argument Rawls intends for his justice condition, there are serious difficulties for it to overcome. The motivation for including the requirement is (on this reading) to guarantee that an individual not become bound to carry a fair share of the burdens of a cooperative scheme if he has been allocated less than a fair share of its benefits; it is unfair to demand full cooperation from one to whom full benefits are denied. But if *this* is our reason for including the justice condition, we have surely included too much. Why should we think that the whole scheme must be just for this sort of intuition to be given play? Rawls's justice condition requires that *everyone* be allocated a fair share of benefits if *anyone* is to be bound by an obligation of fair play. But the reasons we have given for including this condition seem only to require that for a particular individual to be bound, *he* must be allocated a fair share. This says nothing about the allocation of benefits in general, or about what benefits *others* are allocated. If some individuals within an unjust scheme are allocated less than a fair share of benefits, then our reasons would support the view that *they* are not bound to carry a fair share of the burdens. But nothing said yet about feelings of fair play seems to exempt from obligation those individuals to whom a fair share of benefits is in fact allocated within an *unjust* scheme. So again the point of Rawls's justice condition comes into doubt.

These arguments may prompt us to think more about the notion of a "fair share" of the burdens of cooperation. For if we understand by this phrase a share of the total burden proportionate to the share of the total benefits allocated to the individual, then we may have no problem in accepting that anyone who accepts *any* benefits from a cooperative scheme is bound to do his "fair share." Our belief that only an individual who is allocated a fair share of the benefits is bound to cooperate may be false. For it seems eminently fair to hold that each is bound to cooperate to the extent that he is allowed to benefit from a cooperative scheme; thus, those who are allocated the largest shares of benefits owe the largest share of burdens. But even one who is allocated a very small share of the benefits is bound to carry a small share of the burdens (provided he accepts the benefits).

Now, it is clear that these intuitions cannot be given full play in the case of schemes whose burdens cannot be unequally distributed. But there may seem to be other difficulties involved in the interpretation of the fair play principle sketched above. First, it seems to entail that the better off are bound to support unjust schemes which favor them, and the more discriminatory the scheme, the more strongly they must support it. And second, it seems to entail that those who are allocated tiny, unfair shares of the benefits are still bound to cooperate with the unjust scheme which mistreats them. These may again seem to be good reasons to limit the principle's application to just schemes. I think this appearance is misleading. First, the principle under discussion does not entail that the better off must support unjust schemes which favor them. While it does specify that they are obligated to repay by cooperation the sacrifices made in their behalf by the other members, the injustice of the scheme is a strong reason for opposing it, and a reason which gains in strength with the degree of injustice. Thus, there are moral considerations which may override the obligations of fair play (depending, of course, on the degree of the injustice of the scheme, among other things). And if we think of the burdens as sacrifices to be made, it seems only fair that the unjustly favored should be heavily burdened. As for the apparent result that the unjustly treated are still bound to support the scheme (even if to a lesser degree) which discriminates against them, this result can also be seen to be mistaken. For if we remember that benefits must be *accepted* in order for an individual to be bound under the principle, the unfairly treated have the option of refusing to accept benefits, hence sparing themselves the obligation to support a scheme which treats them unfairly (and they have, as well, the duty to oppose such unjust schemes, regardless of what obligations they are under). The idea, then, is that only if they willingly accept the benefits of the scheme are participants bound to bear the burdens of cooperation, and only then in proportion to the benefits allocated to them.

I am not sure just how much of the Hart-Rawls conception of the principle of fair play this analysis captures. But the considerations raised above seem to me to be good reasons for rejecting Rawls's "justice condition." While we can, of course, agree with Rawls that intolerably unjust schemes ought not to be furthered (and ought, in fact, to be opposed), there is no logical difficulty, at least, in holding that we may sometimes have obligations of fair play to cooperate within unjust schemes. And the arguments suggest that there may be no nonlogical difficulties either.

III. FAIR PLAY AND POLITICAL OBLIGATION

To this point we have given a sketchy analysis of various aspects of the principle of fair play and the contexts within which it is supposed to apply. In part IV I will consider in more detail how defensible the principle will be when applied to actual cases, and in part V, when applied specifically to political cases. Here I want to pause to consider the way in which the principle of fair play is supposed to yield an account of political obligation, and the changes which this new account introduces into our conception of that obligation.

We may observe that each of the different accounts of the ground of political obligation would involve its own special conception of the content of the obligation, as well as the obligee to whom the obligation is owed. The move from consent theory's account to an account utilizing the principle of fair play illustrates this point. On the consent theory account, remember, the ground of the obligation is some deliberate consensual act, promise, or contract; this account entails that both the content of the obligation and the identity of the obligee are dependent on the specific nature of the act performed (and on the context within which it is performed). Thus, the content is determined by determining what is consented to, promised, etc., and the obligee is identified as simply the other party involved in the transaction. On the other hand, an account of political obligation using the principle of fair play (like Hart's) departs from this analysis in significant ways. The specific features of the act which is the ground of the obligation are far less central to a determination of the content of the obligation. For here the ground in question is simply any acceptance of benefits provided through the sacrifices of other participants in a cooperative scheme; the content is, for any such case, doing one's part within the scheme. And the obligee, on the fair play account, is the class of participants in the scheme in question (with the exception of the obligor).

This is not to say, of course, that there are not important continuities between the consent theory account of political obligation and the account using the principle of fair play. Both are "obligation-centered" accounts,[14] and as such both stress the essential voluntariness of the generation of the obligation. On both accounts, a voluntary act is the ground of our political bonds, although the consent theorist insists on the need for a deliberate undertaking where the "fair play theorist" does not. And of course, the fact that the acceptance of benefits may often be what I have called a "consent-implying act" further illustrates this continuity. But this continuity is not to be mistaken for a sign of identity between the two accounts: both Hart and Rawls are quite clear that the principle of fair play is not just a special principle of consent. Nonetheless, John Ladd, for instance, has interpreted the principle in this way. In commenting on Rawls's "Legal Obligation and the Duty of Fair Play,"

Ladd notes that "it provides us with a model of consent through participation rather than through contract."[15] I have already argued sufficiently against this sort of error elsewhere; it is just one more example of the more than frequent confusion in contemporary literature between what I have called acts which are "signs of consent" and acts which merely "imply consent."

I have already suggested several ways in which the "fair play account" (as I shall hereafter call it) of political obligation alters the way we see the ground, the content, and the obligee for the obligation in question. But I have not yet mentioned the advantages which this account is supposed by its advocates to have over the more traditional account offered by consent theory. Neither, unfortunately, have its advocates. It is, however, fairly easy to guess what advantages one might believe the fair play account to have. First, this account involves viewing political communities in a different way from consent theory; specifically, they are viewed as "communities" in a fairly strict sense. We are to understand political communities as being fundamentally, or at least in part, cooperative enterprises on a very large scale. Citizens thus are thought to stand in a cooperative relationship to their fellows, rather than in an adversary relationship with the government. And this former view may seem to some more realistic than the latter.

But clearly the major advantage which the fair play account of political obligation is thought by its advocates to have is that it provides a general account of our political bonds. No deliberate undertaking is necessary to become obligated under the principle of fair play. One can become bound without trying to and without knowing that one is performing an act which generates an obligation.[16] Since mere acceptance of benefits within the right context generates the obligation, one who accepts benefits within the right context can become bound unknowingly. This is an important difference from consent theory's account, which stressed the necessity of a deliberate undertaking. Thus, while one can neither consent nor accept benefits (in the right sense) unintentionally, one can accept benefits without being aware of the moral consequences of so doing (while being unaware of the moral consequences of consenting defeats the claim that consent was given). The significance of this difference, of course, lies in the possibility of giving a *general* account of political obligation in the two cases. Consent theory's failure to give a general account stemmed from the lack of citizens in modern states who had voluntarily undertaken political obligations in the sense required. At least initially, however, it seems much more plausible to suggest that most or all of us have accepted benefits, as is required to be bound under the principle of fair play. Thus, the possibility of giving a general account using this principle seems to be vastly increased over one which uses a principle of consent. This would *not* be the case, however, if accepting benefits in the right sense required having an understanding of the moral consequences of such acceptance, for certainly most citizens who receive the benefits of government do not have such an understanding.

Exactly what "accepting the benefits of government" amounts to, of course, is not yet entirely clear. Neither is the identity of the "cooperative scheme" embodied in political communities. These points will be discussed as we continue. My aim here has been simply to mention what might seem to be advantages of the fair play account: whether these "advantages" are genuine remains to be seen. But regardless of the advantages this account may have over the consent theory account, it surely falls short of this latter account on one score. Consent is a *clear* ground of obligation. If we are agreed on anything concerning moral requirements, it is that promising and consenting generate them. In specifying a different ground of obligation, the account using the principle of fair play draws away from the paradigm of obligation-generating acts. And to those who are strongly wedded to this paradigm of consent, like Robert Nozick, the principle of fair play may seem a sham.

IV. NOZICK'S ARGUMENTS

In chapter 5 of *Anarchy, State, and Utopia*,[17] Nozick argues against accepting the principle of fair play as a valid moral principle, not just in political settings, but in any settings whatsoever. While he seems to rely more on the snowball effect of deviously arranged examples than on argument, Nozick nonetheless makes a persuasive case against the principle. I will consider Nozick's presentation centrally in the remainder of my examination of the principle, in that it seems to touch at least briefly on most of the problems we will want to discuss.

Nozick begins by describing a cooperative scheme of the sort he thinks Hart and Rawls have in mind, and then suggests that benefaction within that scheme may *not* bind one to do one's part:

> Suppose some of the people in your neighborhood (there are 364 other adults) have found a public address system and decide to institute a system of public entertainment. They post a list of names, one for each day, yours among them. On his assigned day (one can easily switch days) a person is to run the public address system, play records over it, give news bulletins, tell amusing stories he has heard, and so on. After 138 days on which each person has done his part, your day arrives. Are you obligated to take your turn? You *have* benefited from it, occasionally opening your window to listen, enjoying some music or chuckling at someone's funny story. The other people *have* put themselves out. But must you answer the call when it is your turn to do so? As it stands, surely not. Though you benefit from the arrangement, you may know all along that 364 days of entertainment supplied by others will not be worth your giving up *one* day. You would rather not have any of it and not give up a day than have it all and spend one of your days at it. Given these preferences, how can it be that you are required to participate when your scheduled time comes?[18]

On the basis of this example and others, Nozick concludes that we are never bound to cooperate in such contexts (unless we have given our consent to be constrained by the rules of the cooperative scheme).

Now Nozick does not, to be fair, simply pick the weakest form of the principle of fair play and then reject it for its inadequacy in hard cases; he has, in fact, a suggestion for improving the principle in response to the cases he describes. Having noticed, I suppose, that the case described above favors his conclusions largely because of the negligible value of the benefits received (can we even imagine the day-long efforts of our painfully dull neighbors to entertain us as a benefit?), Nozick suggests that "at the very least one wants to build into the principle of fairness the condition that the benefits to a person from the actions of others are greater than the cost to him of doing his share."[19] There is certainly something right about this; something like this must be built into the idea of a *useful* cooperative scheme. On the other hand, we can imagine a defender of the principle saying, "if you weren't prepared to do your part you oughtn't to have taken *any* benefits from the scheme, no matter how insignificant." Nozick, of course, has more to say on this point, and so do I.

Even if we do modify the principle with this condition, however, Nozick has other arguments against it: "The benefits might only barely be worth the costs to you of doing your share, yet others might benefit from *this* institution much more than you do; they all treasure listening to the public broadcasts. As the person least benefited by the practice, are you obligated to do an equal amount for it?"[20] The understood answer is "No," but we might agree with this answer without agreeing that it tells against the principle. For if we understand by "doing one's part" or "doing one's fair share" not necessarily "doing an equal part," but rather "doing a part proportionate to the part of the benefits received," then the one who benefits least from a cooperative scheme will *not* be bound to share equally in the burdens of cooperation. I argued for this interpretation in part II, and if we accept it, Nozick's PA system example may no longer seem so troublesome. For mightn't we be willing to admit that the individual in question, because he benefited so little, was bound to cooperate, but not to the same extent as others who benefit more from the scheme? Would being obligated to do one's part in the PA scheme seem quite so objectionable if one's part was only, say, an hour's worth of broadcasting, as opposed to the PA enthusiasts', whose parts were one and a half days of broadcasting? There are, perhaps, not clear answers to these questions, and certainly the "too-available" character of the benefits causes some difficulties here (these problems will surface again later).

But surely the defender of the principle of fair play will have more fundamental objections to Nozick's case than these. In the first place, the individual in Nozick's PA example does not seem to be a *participant* in the scheme in the sense that Hart and Rawls may have in mind. While he does live in the neighborhood within which the scheme operates, and he does benefit from it, he is still very much of an "innocent bystander." The PA system scheme has been built up around him in such a way that he could not escape its influence. And, of course, the whole force of Nozick's example lies in our feeling that others should not be able to *force* any scheme they like upon us, with the attendant obligations. The PA case would be precisely such a case of "forced" obligation. So naturally we may find Nozick's criticism of the principle of fair play convincing, if we believe the principle to entail that we *do* have obligations under the PA scheme.

But it seems clear that Hart at least, and probably Rawls as well, did not mean for the principle to apply to such cases of "innocent bystanders." Hart, remember, begins his specification of the principle with: "When a number of persons conduct any joint enterprise. . . ." He then goes on to suggest that those who benefit from others following the rules are bound to cooperate as well. This way of stating the principle does seem to leave open the possible reading that anyone at all who benefits, whether he be a participant or not, is obligated to cooperate. And Nozick must be relying on such a reading if he believes his PA system case to be one to which Hart's principle applies. But this reading does not seem to capture the *spirit* of Hart's remarks; the beneficiaries who are bound under Hart's principle must, I think, be among those persons who are "conducting" the enterprise. This seems to me to be implicit in Hart's remarks. It is certainly a shame that he did not make it explicit, for that would have guarded the principle against the implausible sort of reading that Nozick utilizes, in which the principle binds *everyone* who benefits from the enterprise, regardless of his relation to it.

And a principle which had those results *would* be an outrageous one. People who have no significant relationship at all with some cooperative scheme may receive incidental benefits from its operation. Thus, imagine yourself a member of some scheme which benefits you immensely by increasing your income. Your friends and relatives may benefit incidentally from the scheme as well if, say, you now become prone to send them expensive presents. But the suggestion that their benefiting in this way obligates them to do their part in the scheme is absurd.

That Hart did not have in mind such an outrageous principle can be seen as follows, if any doubt remains. He wants the principle to serve in giving an account of political obligation. The benefits which citizens receive within the cooperative scheme of a political community may be thought of primarily as the benefits of the rule of law. It is the receipt of these benefits that binds each citizen to his fellow citizens. But, of course, other people besides citizens receive benefits from those citizens' maintaining the rule of law. People residing in neighboring nations, for instance, benefit from this. But Hart surely does not want to maintain that, e.g., Canadian citizens are bound to the political community in the

United States simply because Canadians *also* benefit from the U.S. citizens' cooperative efforts to maintain the rule of law!

My suggestion is that Hart and Rawls should be read as holding that only beneficiaries who are also participants (in some significant sense) are bound under the principle of fair play. And on this reading, of course, Nozick's PA system example does not seem to be a case to which the principle applies; the individual in question is not a participant in the scheme, having had nothing to do with its institution, and having done nothing to lead anyone to believe that he wished to become involved in the scheme. The example, then, cannot serve as a counterexample to Hart's principle. In fact, all of Nozick's examples in his criticisms of Hart are examples in which an "outsider" has some benefit thrust on him by some cooperative scheme to which he is in no way tied (see Nozick's "street-sweeping," "lawn-mowing," and "book-thrusting" examples).[21] But if I am right, these examples do not tell against the principle of fair play, since the benefits accruing to "outsiders" are not thought by Hart and Rawls to bind under that principle.

The problem of specifying who are "outsiders," and consequently, whose benefits will count, is a serious one, especially in the political applications of the principle; I will have more to say about that in part V. And it seems that the problem may provide ammunition for a serious counterattack by someone like Nozick against the principle of fair play. We have maintained, remember, that only "participants" or "insiders" in the cooperative scheme are candidates for being obligated under the principle to do their share in cooperating. Those "outsiders" who benefit from the scheme's operation are not bound under the principle of fair play. But how exactly do we differentiate between these outsiders and the insiders? What relationship must hold between an individual and a cooperative scheme for him to be said to be a participant in some significant sense?

This is a hard question to answer, but we have already considered some cases where an individual is *not* a participant in the right sense. Thus, merely being a member of some group, other members of which institute a scheme, is not enough to make one a participant or an "insider." Although Nozick's man is a "member" of an identifiable group, namely his neighborhood, this "membership" does not suffice to make him a participant in any scheme his neighbors dream up. Normally, we would want to say that for an individual to be a real participant in a cooperative scheme, he must have either (1) pledged his support, or tacitly agreed to be governed by the scheme's rules, or (2) played some active role in the scheme after its institution. It is not enough to be associated with the "schemers" in some vague way; one must go out and do things to become a participant or an "insider" and to potentially be bound under the principle of fair play.

Now, we can imagine an opponent of the principle accepting these remarks concerning whose benefiting will count, and accepting our criticism of Nozick's PA system counterexample, and still responding to our discussion by posing the following dilemma: We are agreed, the Nozickian begins, that "outsiders" fall outside the scope of Hart's principle; not just anyone who benefits from a cooperative scheme will be bound to do his share in it. And we are agreed that mere membership in some group, other members of which conduct some cooperative scheme, is insufficient to make one an "insider." And we are agreed that one becomes an "insider" by the means described above, perhaps among others. But the problem is this. In becoming an "insider," one must do something which involves either an express or a tacit undertaking to do one's part in the scheme. So if the principle of fair play can bind only "insiders" in a cooperative scheme, it will bind only those individuals who have *already* become bound to do their part in the scheme in becoming "insiders." The principle is superfluous; it collapses into a principle of consent. All and only those individuals who have actually undertaken to do their part in the scheme are bound by the principle of fair play to do their part in the scheme. Benefiting under the scheme is quite irrelevant, for benefiting only counts under the principle for "insiders." But "insiders" are already bound to the scheme, whether they benefit from it or not.

This argument, if it is acceptable, counts heavily against the principle of fair play, for that principle was supposed to show us how individuals could become bound to some cooperative enterprise *without* actually giving their consent to it. But if the principle can only plausibly be thought to bind those who have already consented to going along with the enterprise, the principle's usefulness becomes highly doubtful. We can explain whatever obligations participants in the enterprise are thought to have simply in terms of the principles of consent and fidelity, quite independent of considerations of fair play. We cannot become participants in the right sense without having given at least tacit consent to do our part in the scheme.

But is this sort of argument acceptable? Is it true that I cannot become a participant in the right sense without giving at least tacit consent to the scheme? Surely many participants in cooperative schemes have given their consent, either express or tacit, and are bound to their schemes regardless of what else they do to bind themselves. But these are not the individuals with whom Hart and Rawls are primarily concerned. With all our discussion of "participation," we are overlooking a feature of the principle of fair play which Rawls (and Hart, I've suggested) saw as essential to the generation of the obligation. The principle of fair play does not specify that all participants in cooperative schemes are bound to do their part, or even that all participants who benefit from the schemes are so bound. It states rather that those who *accept* the benefits of a cooperative scheme are bound to cooperate. This distinction between accepting benefits and merely receiving benefits has been lost somewhere in the shuffle. It is a distinction which is completely overlooked in Nozick's discussion of the principle of fair play. But it seems to me that this distinction is crucial in settling the problem of how to distinguish participants (or "insiders") from "outsiders."

For Rawls and Hart, the principle of fair play accounts for the obligations of those whose active role in the scheme consists of accepting the benefits of its workings. One becomes a participant in the scheme precisely by accepting the benefits it offers; the other ways in which one can become a participant are not important to considerations of fair play. And individuals who have merely *received* benefits from the scheme have the same status relative to it as those who have been unaffected by the scheme; they are not in any way bound to do their part in the scheme unless they have independently undertaken to do so. If, as I suggested, the acceptance of benefits constitutes the sort of "participation" in a scheme with which Rawls and Hart are concerned, we can understand why neither Rawls nor Hart specifically limits the application of the principle to *participants* in the scheme. This limitation has already been accomplished by making obligation conditional on the acceptance of benefits. This means, of course, that the principle cannot be read as the outrageous one which requires anyone at all who benefits from the scheme to do his part in it (this is the reading I earlier attributed to

Nozick); it is limited in application to those who are participants in the scheme, in the name of having accepted benefits.

But understanding the principle in this way also helps us see why the Nozickian line of argument we have considered cannot succeed. The Nozickian tried to persuade us that an individual could not become a participant, or an "insider," without doing something which amounted to giving his consent to do his part in the scheme. The obligations generated relative to the scheme could be explained in terms of consent. But it seems clear that a man can accept benefits from a scheme, and be a participant in that sense, without giving his consent to the scheme. And further, such acceptance of benefits does seem to obligate him to do his part. Let me support and clarify this claim with an example.

Imagine that in Nozick's neighborhood the need for public entertainment is not the only matter of concern. There is also a problem with the neighborhood's water supply; the water pumped through the pipes is sufficiently polluted to make nearly everyone desire corrective action of some sort. But the government is sufficiently unresponsive to make them sure that they will have to handle the problem themselves. So a neighborhood meeting is called, at which a majority votes to dig a public well near the center of the neighborhood, to be paid for and maintained by the members of the neighborhood.

Some of the members clearly give their consent to the proposed scheme. Others, who vote against the proposal, do not. Jones, in particular, announces angrily that he wants to have nothing to do with the scheme and that he will certainly not pledge his support. Nothing, he claims, could make him consent to such a ridiculous enterprise. But in spite of his opposition, the well is dug, paid for, and maintained by the other members of the neighborhood. Jones, as expected, contributes nothing to this effort.

Now the benefits of clear, fresh water are available to the neighborhood, and Jones begins to be envious of his neighbors, who go the well daily. So he goes to the well every night and, knowing that the water will never be missed, takes some home with him for the next day. It seems clear to me that Jones is a perfect example of a "free rider." And it also seems clear that, having accepted benefits from the scheme (indeed, he has gone out of his way to obtain them), he has an obligation to do his part within it. But he certainly does not seem to have *consented* to the scheme. We have, then, a case in which an individual has an obligation to do his part within a cooperative scheme which is *not* accounted for by a principle of consent. We would, I think, account for that obligation precisely in terms of fair play. Jones has made himself a participant in the scheme by accepting its benefits, although he has refused to give his consent.

So the Nozickian argument does not succeed. One might, rather feebly I think, try to maintain that Jones's taking the water was a way of giving tacit consent to the scheme. Hopefully, the reader will already be convinced of the unpersuasiveness of such a position. But if not, we can suppose instead that Jones goes to the well during the day, taking the water while shouting, "Don't think this means I'm coming into your stupid scheme! I'll never consent to share the burdens of this enterprise!" Certainly under those conditions, to call the taking of the water a consensual act would be ludicrous.

I have tried to show, then, that the principle of fair play does not collapse into a principle of consent. While many participants in cooperative schemes will be bound to do their parts because they have consented to do so, many others will be bound because they have accepted benefits from the scheme. The obligations of the latter will fall under the principle of fair play. We should not think, because of the peculiarity of Jones's position in our example, that only the obligations of free riders like Jones will be accounted for by the principle. It is possible to *go along* with a cooperative scheme (as Jones does not) without consenting to it, becoming bound through one's acceptance of benefits. In fact, I think that *most* participants in cooperative schemes do nothing which can be thought to constitute consent. It is not necessary to refuse to give one's consent, as Jones does, in order not to give it. Consent is not given to a scheme by any behavior short of express dissent. Most participants in cooperative schemes simply "go along with" the schemes, taking their benefits and carrying their burdens. But if they do not expressly undertake to support the schemes, and if their behavior does not constitute a response to a clear choice situation, I do not think that we can ascribe consent to them. Certainly by going along with a scheme, we lead others to *expect* certain future performances from us; but this does not show that we have *undertaken* to perform according to expectations. Thus, the obligations which participants in cooperative schemes have (relative to those schemes) will not normally be grounded in consent. It remains to be seen, however, under what conditions any participants in a scheme can be obligated to do their parts in it, for we have not yet discussed carefully the important notion of the acceptance of benefits.

The reading of the principle which I have given obviously places a very heavy load on the notion of "acceptance," a notion to which we have as yet given no clear meaning. Rawls and Hart certainly give us no help on this count; in spite of the fact that Rawls stresses the need for "voluntary acceptance" in all of his accounts of the principle, he never gives us any clues as to what this "voluntary acceptance" is supposed to be. It is not, as I suggested in part I, at all easy to distinguish in practice between benefits that have been accepted and those that have only been received, although some cases clearly seem to fall on the "merely received" side. Thus, benefits we have actively resisted getting, and those which we have gotten unknowingly or in ways over which we had no control at all, seem *not* to be benefits we have accepted. To have accepted a benefit, I think, we would want to say that an individual must either (1) have tried to get (and succeeded in getting) the benefit, or (2) have taken the benefit willingly and knowingly.

I suggested a moment ago that Nozick seems to have completely overlooked the distinction now under consideration. This can be seen in the fact that all of his supposed counterexamples to the principle seem to be cases of merely receiving, rather than accepting, benefits from some scheme (and this fact was, of course, responsible for my earlier charge that the individuals in Nozick's examples did not seem to be participants). But if the principle of fair play requires acceptance of benefits, then Nozick's examples may fail to be counterexamples.

Consider Nozick's examples of the programs that involve "thrusting books" into unsuspecting people's houses,[22] and the people on your street taking turns sweeping the street.[23] Clearly, the benefits in question are merely received, not accepted. "One cannot," Nozick writes, "whatever one's purposes, just act so as to give people benefits and then demand (or seize) payment. Nor can a group of persons do this."[24] I am suggesting, contra Nozick, that the principle of fair play does *not* involve justifying this sort of behavior; people are bound under the principle only when they have accepted benefits.

Nozick's first-line example, the PA scheme, however, is slightly more difficult. For here the benefits received are not forced upon you, as in the "book-thrusting" case, or gotten in some other way which is outside your control (as in the case of the person who mows your lawn while you're out of town, which I mentioned in part I). Rather, the benefits are what I will call "open"; while they can be avoided, they cannot be avoided without considerable inconvenience. Thus, while I can avoid the (questionable) benefits the PA system provides by remaining indoors with the windows closed, this is a considerable inconvenience (and eventually, at least, more than this). The benefits are "open" in the sense that I cannot avoid receiving them, even if I want to, without altering my life-style (economists often have such benefits in mind in speaking of "public goods"). Many benefits yielded by cooperative schemes (in fact most benefits, I should think) are "open" in this way. A neighborhood organization's program to improve the neighborhood's appearance yields benefits which are "open." They cannot be avoided without avoiding the neighborhood altogether. And the benefits of government, which we have spoken of frequently, are mostly of this sort. The benefits of the rule of law, protection by the armed forces, pollution control, etc., can be avoided only by emigration.

We can contrast these cases of "open" benefits with benefits which are only "readily available." If instead of a PA system, Nozick's group had decided to rent a building in the middle of town in which live entertainment was continuously available to neighborhood members, the benefits of the scheme would only be "readily available." A good example of the distinction under consideration would be the distinction between two sorts of police protection, one sort being an "open" benefit, the other being only "readily available." Thus, the benefits which I receive from the continuous efforts of police officers who patrol the streets, capture criminals, and eliminate potential threats to my safety are benefits which are "open." They can be avoided only by leaving the area which the police force protects. But I may also request *special* protection by the police, if I fear for my life, say, or if I want my house to be watched while I'm away. These benefits are "readily available." Benefits which are "readily available" can be easily avoided without inconvenience.

Now, I think that clear cases of the acceptance of benefits, as opposed to receipt, will be easy to find where benefits which are only "readily available" are concerned. Getting these benefits will involve going out of one's way, making some sort of effort to get the benefit, and hence there will generally be no question that the benefit was accepted in the sense we have described. It will be in cases like these that the principle of fair play seems most clearly to apply. These will be cases where our actions may clearly fall short of constituting *consent* to do our part in the scheme in question, but where our acceptance of benefits binds us to do our part because of considerations of fair play. When we accept benefits in such cases, it may be necessary that we be aware that the benefits in question *are* the fruits of a cooperative scheme, in order for us to be willing to ascribe any obligations of fair play; but it will *not* be necessary that some express or tacit act of consent have been performed.

The examples of "open" benefits are, of course, harder to handle. Nozick's comments seem quite reasonable with respect to them. Surely, it is very implausible to suggest that if we are unwilling to do our part, we must alter our life-styles in order to avoid enjoying these benefits. As Nozick suggests, there is certainly no reason why, when the street-sweeping scheme comes to your town, you must "imagine dirt as you traverse the street, so as not to benefit as a free rider."[25] Nozick's comments here do not, however, strike against the principle of fair play in any obvious way, for as I have interpreted it, the principle does not apply to cases of mere receipt of benefits from cooperative schemes; and the cases where the benefits are "open" in this way seem to be cases of mere receipt of benefits. Certainly, it would be peculiar if a man, who by simply going about his business in a normal fashion benefited unavoidably from some cooperative scheme, were told that he had voluntarily accepted benefits which generated for him a special obligation to do his part.

This problem of "acceptance" and "open benefits" is a serious one, and there are real difficulties involved in solving it. It may look, for instance, as if I am saying that a genuine acceptance of open benefits is impossible. But I would not want to be pushed so far. It seems to me that it is possible to accept a benefit which is (in one sense) unavoidable; but it is not at all the *normal* case that those who receive open benefits from a scheme have also accepted those benefits. In the case of benefits which are only "readily available," receipt of the benefits is generally *also* acceptance. But this is not so in the case of open benefits. I suggested earlier that accepting a benefit involved either (1) trying to get (and succeeding in getting) the benefit, or (2) taking the benefit willingly and knowingly. Getting benefits which are "readily available" normally involves (1), trying to get the benefit. It is not clear, however, how one would go about *trying* to get an open benefit which is not distributed by request but is rather received by everyone involved, whether they want it or not. If open benefits can be accepted, it would seem that method (2) of accepting benefits is the way in which this is normally accomplished. We can take the open benefits which we receive willingly and knowingly. But doing so involves a number of restrictions on our attitudes toward and beliefs about the open benefits we receive. We cannot, for instance, regard the benefits as having been forced upon us against our will, or think that the benefits are not worth the price we must pay for them. And taking the benefits "knowingly" seems to involve an understanding of the status of those benefits relative to the party providing them. Thus, in the case of open benefits provided by a cooperative scheme, we must understand that the benefits *are* provided by the cooperative scheme in order to accept them.

The necessity of satisfying such conditions, however, seems to significantly reduce the number of individuals who receive open benefits, who can be taken to have *accepted* those benefits. And it will by no means be a standard case in which all beneficiaries of a cooperative scheme's workings have accepted the benefits they receive.

I recognize, of course, that problems concerning "acceptance" remain. But even if they did not, my reading of the principle of fair play, as binding only those who have accepted benefits, would still face difficulties. The fact remains that we *do* criticize persons as "free riders" (i.e., in terms of fair play) for not doing their part, even when they have *not* accepted benefits from a cooperative scheme. We often criticize them merely because they *receive* benefits without doing their part in the cooperative scheme. Let us go back to Nozick's neighborhood and imagine another, more realistic, cooperative scheme in operation, this one designed to beautify the neighborhood by assigning to each resident a specific task involving landscaping or yard work. Homeowners are required to care for their yards and to do some work on community property on weekends. There are also a number of apartments in the neighborhood, but because the apartment grounds are cared for by the landlords, apartment dwellers are expected to help only on community property (they are expected to help because even tenants are granted full community membership and privileges; and it is reasoned that all residents have an equal interest in the neighborhood's appearance, at least during the time they remain there). Two of these apartment dwellers, Oscar and Willie, refuse to do their part in the scheme. Oscar refuses because he hates neatly trimmed yards, preferring crabgrass, long weeds, and scraggly bushes. The residents do not feel too badly about Oscar (although they try to force him out of the neighborhood), since he does not seem to be benefiting from their efforts without putting out. He hates what they are doing to the neighborhood. Willie, however, is another case altogether. He values a neat neighborhood as much as the others; but he values his spare time more than the others. While he enjoys a beautiful neighborhood, the part he is expected to play in the cooperative scheme involves too much of his time. He makes it clear that he would prefer to have an ugly neighborhood to joining such a scheme.

So while the others labor to produce an almost spotless neighborhood, Willie enjoys the benefits resulting from their efforts while doing nothing to help. And it seems to me that Willie is *just* the sort of person who would be accused by the neighborhood council of "free riding," of unfairly benefiting from the cooperative efforts of others; for he receives exactly the same benefits as the others while contributing nothing. Yet Willie has not accepted the benefits in question, for he thinks that the price being demanded is too high. He would prefer doing without the benefits to having the benefits and the burdens.

So it looks as if the way in which we have filled out the principle of fair play is not entirely in accord with some common feelings about matters of fair play; for these common feelings do not seem to require acceptance of benefits within the scheme, as our version of the principle does. It is against these "ordinary feelings about fair play" (and not against the "filled-out" principle we have been describing), I think, that Nozick's arguments, and the "Nozickian" arguments we've suggested, strike most sharply.

But Willie's position is *not* substantially different from that of the salesman, Sam, whose sole territory is the neighborhood in question. Sam works eight hours every day in the neighborhood, enjoying its beauty, while Willie (away at work all day) may eke out his forty weekly hours of enjoyment if he stays home on weekends. Thus, Sam and Willie receive substantially the same benefits (if there is a "prestige" benefit which Willie receives from living in a beautiful neighborhood, we can imagine that Sam has a corresponding prestige in the fellowship of salesmen for having risen to being awarded such a beautiful territory). Neither Sam nor Willie has done anything at all to ally himself with the cooperative scheme, and neither has "accepted" the fruits of that scheme, although both "receive" them. Willie is a "member" of the community only because the council voted to award "membership" to tenants, and he has made no commitments; to make the parallel complete, we can even suppose that Sam, beloved by all the residents, is named by the council an "honorary member." But if the neighborhood council accused Sam, the salesman, of "free riding," and demanded that *he* work on community property, their position would be laughable. Why, though, should Willie, who is like Sam in all important respects, be any *more* vulnerable to such accusations and demands?

The answer is that he is *not* any more vulnerable; if ordinary feelings about obligations of fair play insist that he *is* more vulnerable, those feelings are mistaken. But in fairness to Nozick, the way that Hart and Rawls phrase their account of the principle of fair play *does* sometimes look as if it expresses those (mistaken) feelings about fair play. As Rawls states it,

> The main idea is that when a number of persons engage in a mutually advantageous cooperative venture according to rules, and thus restrict their liberty in ways necessary to yield advantages for all, those who have submitted to these restrictions have a right to a similar acquiescence on the part of those who have benefited from their submission. We are not to gain from the cooperative labors of others without doing our fair share.[26]

This certainly looks like a condemnation of Willie's actions. Of course, the way in which Rawls fills out this idea, in terms of accepting benefits and taking advantage of the scheme, points in quite a different direction; for on the "filled-out" principle, Willie is not bound to cooperate, and neither is the salesman.

It looks, then, as if we have a choice to make between a very general principle (which binds all beneficiaries of a scheme) which is *very* implausible, and a more limited principle which is more plausible. I say that we have a choice to make simply because it seems clear that the limited principle is *much* more limited than either Hart or Rawls realized. For if my previous suggestions were correct, participants in cooperative schemes which produce "open" benefits will not always have a right to cooperation on the part of those who benefit from their labors. And this does not look like a result that either Hart or Rawls would be prepared to accept.

There is a great deal more that needs to be said about the principle of fair play, but this is not the place to say it. The results that we have produced to this point are adequate, I think, to evaluate the principle's usefulness in developing an account of political obligation. My arguments have suggested that the principle neither collapses altogether, as the "Nozickian" line of argument tried to persuade us, nor applies in as general a fashion as the Hart-Rawls account seems to want. What we must say about the political applications of the principle is, I assume, fairly obvious by now.

V. THE PRINCIPLE IN POLITICAL COMMUNITIES

When we move to political communities, the "schemes of social cooperation" with which we will be concerned will naturally be schemes on a rather grand scale. We may, with Rawls, think that the maintenance of the legal order should be "construed as a system of social cooperation,"[27] or perhaps we will want to identify all the workings of that set of political institutions governing "political society" generally as the operation of "the most complex example" of a cooperative scheme (as Hart seems to).[28] The details of the interpretation which we accept are not particularly important here. We must simply imagine a cooperative scheme large enough that "doing our part" will involve all of the things normally thought of as the requirements of political obligation; and regardless of how we characterize this scheme in its particulars, the difficulties which an account of political obligation utilizing the principle of fair play will involve will be common to all particular versions. One limitation on this account, of course, is obvious from the start. Only political communities which at least appear to be reasonably democratic will be candidates for a "fair play account" to begin with. For only where we can see the political workings of the society as a voluntary, cooperative venture will the principle apply. Thus, a theorist who holds that the acceptance of benefits from a cooperative scheme is the *only* ground of political obligation will be forced to admit that in at least a large number of nations, *no* citizens have political obligations. Rawls recognizes this limitation, claiming only that the principle accounts for political obligations in "constitutional democracies" (he, of course, withdraws even this limited claim in *A Theory of Justice*). Hart does not seem aware of the problem, but one assumes that he would not disagree with Rawls's early position.

To return, whatever specific cooperative scheme we identify as the one to be considered in giving an account of political obligation using the principle of fair play, the account will face problems that we have already discussed at length in the preceding portions of this chapter. To begin, we face an immediate problem of "membership," of distinguishing the "insiders" from the "outsiders." Ideally, of course, the account wants all and only the citizens of the state in question to be the "insiders" relative to the cooperative scheme in operation in the state. The "all" in "all and only" can be sacrificed here, since an account which only applies to some members of a political community is not obviously objectionable; but the "only" in "all and only" must not be compromised. We cannot accept an account of political obligation which binds noncitizens to do their part in a foreign country's cooperative political enterprises.

But, as I suggested, the immediate problem lies in the need to establish that at least a large number of citizens of the states to which the principle is supposed to apply are related to the scheme in the right way to be bound under the principle. We are, after all, born into political communities; and being "dropped into" a cooperative scheme does not seem significantly different from having a scheme "built up around you," as in the cases mentioned earlier in part IV. Most citizens, even in constitutional democracies, seem to be very much in the same sort of position as Nozick's man. They are not obviously tied to the grand cooperative scheme of political life any more than Nozick's man is tied to his PA scheme.

I tried to suggest earlier, of course, that the right way to distinguish the "insiders" relative to some scheme was through the notion of the "acceptance" of benefits from that scheme. While it is clear that at least most citizens in most states *receive* benefits from the workings of their legal and political institutions, how plausible is it to say that they have voluntarily *accepted* those benefits, in even the cases of the most democratic political societies now in existence? Not, I think, very plausible. The benefits in question have been mentioned before: the rule of law, protection by armed forces, pollution control, maintenance of highway systems, avenues of political participation, etc. But these benefits are what we have called "open" benefits. It is precisely in cases of such "open" benefits that it is least plausible to suggest that benefits are being *accepted* by most beneficiaries. It will, of course, be difficult to be certain about the acceptance of benefits in actual cases; but on any natural understanding of the notion of "acceptance" which seems relevant here, our having accepted open benefits involves our having had certain attitudes toward and beliefs about the benefits we have received (as noted in part IV). Among other things, we must understand that the benefits flow from a cooperative scheme, rather than regarding them as "free" for the taking. And we must, for instance, think that the benefits we receive are worth the price we must pay for them, so that we would take the benefits if we had a choice between taking them (with the burdens involved) or leaving them. These kinds of beliefs and attitudes are necessary if the benefaction is to be plausibly regarded as constituting voluntary participation in the cooperative scheme.

But surely most of us do not have these requisite attitudes toward or beliefs about the benefits of government. At least many citizens barely notice (and seem disinclined to think about) the benefits they receive. And many more, faced with high taxes, with military service which may involve fighting in foreign "police actions," or with unreasonably restrictive laws governing private pleasures, believe that the benefits received from governments are not worth the price they are forced to pay. While such beliefs may be false, they seem nonetheless incompatible with the "acceptance" of the open benefits of government. Further, it must be admitted that, even in democratic political communities, these benefits are commonly regarded as purchased (with taxes) from a central authority, rather than as accepted from the cooperative efforts of our fellow citizens. We may feel, for instance, that if debts are owed at all, they are owed not to those around us, but to our government. Again, these attitudes seem inconsistent with the suggestion that the open benefits are accepted, in the strict sense of "acceptance." Most citizens will, I think, fall into one of these two classes: those who have not "accepted" because they have not taken the benefits (with accompanying burdens) willingly, and those who have not "accepted" because they do not regard the benefits of government as the products of a cooperative scheme. But if most citizens cannot be thought to have voluntarily accepted the benefits of government from the political cooperative scheme, then the fair play account of political obligation will not be suitably general in its application, even within democratic states. And if we try to make the account more general by removing the limitations set by our strict notion of "acceptance," we open the floodgates and turn the principle of fair play into the "outrageous" principle discussed earlier. We seem forced by such observations to conclude that citizens generally in no actual states will be bound under the principle of fair play.

These suggestions raise serious doubts about the Hart-Rawls contention that at least some organized political societies can be thought of as ongoing cooperative schemes on a very large scale. While such a claim may be initially attractive, does it really seem reasonable to think of any actual political communities on the model of the kinds of neighborhood cooperative schemes we have discussed in this chapter? This seems to me quite unrealistic. We must remember that where there is no consciousness of cooperation, no common plan or purpose, no cooperative scheme exists. I do not think that many of us can honestly say that we regard our political lives as a process of working together and making necessary sacrifices for the purpose of improving the common lot. The centrality and apparent independence of governments does not make it natural to think of political life in this way. No doubt we all have our own reasons for obeying the law and going along with the other demands made by our political systems. Prominent among these reasons, I suspect, are blind habit, fear of sanctions, and the conviction that some prohibited acts are "mala in se." Even among the thoughtful and "morally aware," it must be a rare individual who regards himself as engaged in an ongoing cooperative venture, obeying the law because fair play demands it, and with all of the citizens of his state as fellow participants.

Perhaps, then, we ought not to think of modern political communities as essentially or in part large-scale cooperative ventures. No doubt there is a sense in which society in general (and political society in particular) can be understood as a "cooperative venture," even though no consciousness of cooperation or common purpose is to be found. Social man is thought of as governed by public systems of rules designed to regulate his activities in ways which increase the benefits accruing to all. Perhaps it is this rather loose sense of "cooperative scheme" which Hart and Rawls have in mind when they imagine political communities as cooperative schemes.[29] But we should remember that whatever intuitive plausibility the principle of fair play has derives from our regarding it as an acceptable moral principle for cooperative schemes in the *strict* sense. Clearly, the considerations which lead us to accept the principle of fair play as determining our obligations in the context of a neighborhood organization's cooperative programs may in no way be mirrored in the context of "cooperative schemes" understood in the loose sense mentioned above. So that while talk of cooperative schemes on the level of political communities may not be obviously objectionable, such cooperative schemes will not be among those to which we should be inclined to apply the principle of fair play.[30] All of this is not to say that we cannot *imagine* a political community being the sort of cooperative venture to the operations of which the principle of fair play might apply. In fact, we needn't imagine at all, since we have such a community painted in vivid detail in Rousseau's *Social Contact*. But Rousseau's society is not one with which we are familiar in actual political life.

These brief remarks all point toward the conclusion that at very best the principle of fair play can hope to account for the political obligations of only a very few citizens in a very few actual states; it is more likely, however, that it accounts for no such obligations at all. While we have seen that the principle does not "collapse" into a principle of consent, we have also seen that in an account of political obligation, the principle has very little to recommend it, either as a supplement to or a replacement for principles of fidelity and consent. In particular, the main advantage which the fair play account was thought to have over consent theory's account, namely, an advantage in *generality,* turns out to be no advantage at all. We will not, then, advance very far with the suggestions of Hart and Rawls concerning the usefulness of the principle of fair play. And it seems that the principle will also not be able to help us solve the original problem with which this chapter began. It will not provide a satisfactory explanation of our intuitions concerning the binding character of Locke's "consent-implying enjoyments."

NOTES

1. The principle was given this name in John Rawls's essay "Legal Obligation and the Duty of Fair Play," in Hook (ed.), *Law and Philosophy*. Similar, but unnamed, principles had been previously discussed in C. D. Broad, "On the

Function of False Hypotheses in Ethics," *International Journal of Ethics* 26 (April 1916), and in Hart, "Are There Any Natural Rights?" *Philosophical Review* 64 (1955). On the utilitarian's difficulties with fair play, see David Lyons, *Forms and Limits of Utilitarianism,* Oxford University Press, 1965, chap. V.

2. "Are There Any Natural Rights?" p. 185.

3. Ibid.

4. Ibid., pp. 190–191.

5. Actually, Rawls gives at least four different accounts of the principle of fair play. His first, in "Justice as Fairness" (*Philosophical Review* 68 [April 1958]), follows Hart's account exactly, with the exception of an added requirement that participants in the practice "accept its rules as fair" (p. 179). I will discuss Rawls's 1964 account. Later versions, in "The Justification of Civil Disobedience" (in H. Bedau [ed.], *Civil Disobedience: Theory and Practice,* Pegasus, 1969) and *A Theory of Justice,* do not differ substantially from the 1964 account.

6. "Legal Obligation and the Duty of Fair Play," pp. 9–10.

7. This argument also seems to me to provide an effective response to a recent attack on the principle of fair play made by M. B. E. Smith (in "Is There a Prima Facie Obligation to Obey the Law?"). Smith argues that failing to cooperate in a scheme after receiving benefits is only unfair if by this failure we deny someone else benefits within the scheme. But my example is precisely a case in which the failure to cooperate may not deny anyone else benefits within the scheme. And still it looks as if failure to cooperate is unfair, for by failing to do his part, the individual takes *advantage* of the others, who act in good faith. Whether or not my cooperation is necessary for benefiting other members, it is not fair for me, as a participant in the scheme, to decide not to do my part when the others do theirs. For these reasons, Smith's argument is unpersuasive, as is J. R. Pennock's similar position in "The Obligation to Obey the Law and the Ends of the State," in S. Hook (ed.), *Law and Philosophy,* New York University Press, 1964.

8. "Legal Obligation and the Duty of Fair Play," p. 10.

9. Hart, "Are There Any Natural Rights?" p. 185.

10. Rawls, *A Theory of Justice,* p. 112.

11. Here considering the principle of fair play only as one of several principles of obligation (i.e., one which does not account for obligations of fidelity and consent, as it does on Rawls's view).

12. Rawls, *A Theory of Justice,* p. 343.

13. Ibid., p. 112.

14. By an "obligation-centered" account I mean simply an account according to which most or all of the people bound by political bonds are bound by obligations (in the strict sense of "obligation" [which presupposes a voluntary, transactional basis—*Ed.]*). *"Obligation-centered" accounts are to be opposed, of course,*

to *"duty-centered"* accounts, according to which most or all of those bound are bound by duties.

15. John Ladd, *"Legal and Moral Obligation,"* in Pennock and Chapman (eds.), *Nomos XII: Political and Legal Obligation,* p. 21.

16. This point is made clearly in Hart's account of the principle.

17. Nozick, *Anarchy, State, and Utopia,* pp. 90–95. Nozick calls the principle "the principle of fairness," using Rawls's more recent name for it.

18. Ibid., p. 93.

19. Ibid., p. 94.

20. Ibid.

21. Ibid., pp. 94–95.

22. Ibid., p. 95.

23. Ibid., p. 94.

24. Ibid., p. 95.

25. Ibid., p. 94.

26. Rawls, *A Theory of Justice,* p. 112.

27. Rawls, *"Legal Obligation and the Duty of Fair Play,"* p. 17.

28. Hart, *"Are There Any Natural Rights?"* pp. 185–186.

29. See Rawls, *A Theory of Justice,* e.g., pp. 4, 84. Rawls seems to be saying that a system of rules defines a cooperative scheme even where no individuals regard themselves as engaged in a cooperative scheme.

30. Perhaps Rawls would not accept the need to give "microlevel" support for a principle to be applied on a "macrolevel." See Nozick's discussion of these points in *Anarchy, State, and Utopia,* pp. 204–206. But it is doubtful that the principle of fair play can even be understood as a principle for the macrostructure of society.

6

POLITICAL AUTHORITY AND
POLITICAL OBLIGATION

Rolf Sartorius

The two most fundamental questions of political theory are:

(1) Under what conditions, if any, may those in power claim to rule as a matter of moral right? This I shall call the question of *political authority;* and
(2) Under what conditions, if any, may the citizen lie under a prima facie moral obligation to obey those who claim political authority? This I shall call the question of *political obligation.*

Many have seemed to assume that the sets of conditions in question must be identical.[1] Given this equation, the answers that one gives to this pair of questions are likely to be influenced by the question with which one begins. Our intuitions, I believe, tug in opposite directions.

If one is skeptical of the claim that the bare fact that the law requires something may be in and of itself a good reason for doing it, and one finds wanting traditional philosophical arguments designed to establish the contrary, one will deny the existence of political obligation and conclude forthwith that the notion of political authority is spurious as well. Such is the position of philosophical anarchist Robert Paul Wolff.[2] On the other hand, if one believes that government at least sometimes is properly viewed as more than a well-organized group of successful thugs, one will affirm the possibility of political authority and conclude forthwith that the conditions under which it is realized also constitute

143

the foundations of political obligation. Such is the position of Elizabeth Anscombe in a paper the central theme of which I shall turn to shortly.[3]

My strategy in this essay will be to separate completely the questions of political authority and political obligation. My conclusion is that those in political power may often correctly claim a moral right to rule but that those under their power may not, under any philosophically interesting conditions, be said to have a correlative moral obligation to obey the law. My argument will be that the conditions that constitute the grounds of political authority undercut the possibility of the only reasonable grounds of political obligation being satisfied. The basic idea is simply this: Within human associations in general, the grounds of obligations to those in authority are voluntaristic in nature; this is the central insight contained in theories that would ground special associational obligations in tacit *consent* or considerations having to do with what fairness requires against the background of one's *voluntary* acceptance of the benefits of others' cooperation. The striking feature of modern life under government, however, is that opting out is no real option; any benefits that one receives are the result of government exercising its monopoly over the use of coercion, including the all-important power of compulsory taxation. These nonvoluntaristic aspects of life under government are necessary and desirable because rational individuals would not voluntarily undertake obligations to act cooperatively in enforcing people's rights in a state-of-nature situation. Government, on this view, holds a *trust;* it has both the right and the responsibility to act in certain ways for the benefit of its citizens, but these beneficiaries have no correlative obligation to do what it requires in the course of its exercising its putative beneficence. The analogies to questions concerning the nature and grounds of parental authority and filial obligation are, I believe, quite close, and I shall attempt to exploit them along the way.

I. POLITICAL AUTHORITY

To have political authority, as opposed to mere political power, is to have a right to engage in certain forms of behavior unavailable to the private citizen in each of the following ways:

   (1) It is to have a moral and legal capacity to perform certain actions of which only duly constituted authorities acting in their official

role are capable. As a private citizen, I am simply incapable of voting for a bill in my state legislature, adjudicating a legal dispute, or arresting a law breaker. Such capacities are what I shall call the performative aspects of legislative, judicial, and executive authority;

(2) To the extent that the exercise of political authority involves the use of coercion, such ordinarily impermissible behavior must be justified *qua* use of coercion. This justification gives rise to what Robert Ladenson describes as a justification-right;[4] and

(3) Political authority is also the basis of a claim-right against would-be, unauthorized usurpers of official activities. The kangaroo court has no right to conduct a trial; the lynch mob has no right to carry out even an officially valid sentence of death.

On this account, then, political authority is a morally justified form of authorship constituted by certain moral capacities, justification-rights, and claim-rights. As Ladenson notes, such authority is not correlated with any duties of obedience on the part of those over whom authority is exercised.[5] Although the question of whether or not there is a prima facie moral obligation to obey the law under certain conditions is at this stage left open, it is clear that it is not to be derived from the existence of political authority as it has been described above. Further, within limits,[6] one cannot infer from the existence of political authority as it has been described that the institutional framework within which such authority is exercised is just. *"Indeed, conceding someone the right to rule . . . is logically compatible with believing that the particular governmental institutions under which he or she acts ought not to exist at all."*[7]

I believe that a similar analysis is required of the nature of parental authority. Only a parent has the capacity to issue binding directives to his or her children; no matter how wise or well intentioned, my neighbor issuing an order to my children that they brush their teeth after each meal simply cannot amount to an act of "laying down the law." My neighbor may threaten my children with harm and, indeed, may carry out the threat for a breach of some command, either his or my own, but only I may punish. I have the requisite capacities and the justification-right for exercising those capacities. Further, as parent, I have a claim-right against my neighbor should he attempt to usurp my authority; he simply has no right to seek to control the activities of my children in the way in which I do. As is the case with political authority, on this account there is no implication of a correlative (filial) obligation. A parental statement "Because I told you to!" does not, on this account of parental authority, provide a morally relevant reason for action. Also, again within limits, one cannot infer from the existence of legitimate parental authority that the particular framework within which it is exercised can withstand moral scrutiny. Perhaps I am a rotten parent and my children ought to be put in a foster home—maybe even the one operated by that neighbor of mine. Until a competent court so decides, however, I have rights over my children that my neighbor does not.

If the foregoing general account of the *nature* of associational authority is accepted, at least some direction is given to the search for its genesis. The source of authority on such an account must be found in the foundations of the capacities, justification-rights, and claim-rights in question. Although I reject the conclusion that she draws from her analysis on the question of political obligation, I find Anscombe's *On the Source of the Authority of the State* a most fruitful place to begin.

According to Anscombe, governmental authority, like parental authority, "arises from the necessity of a task whose performance requires . . . obedience on the part of those for whom the task is supposed to be done."[8] One finds oneself subject to either form of authority "willy-nilly," as Anscombe puts it;[9] the authority arises from the necessity of the task rather than the approval, let alone the consent, of those in whose name it is carried out. Although Anscombe recognizes the aspects of authority that I have already identified, she describes the claim-right aspect (as against, for instance, an "interfering outsider") as "secondary" and presumably would say the same of the justification-right and capacity aspects.[10] On her view, "obedience/disobedience are the [logically] primary correlates of authority."[11] It is also clear that by obedience Anscombe understands the existence of an obligation to obey rather than merely customary compliance. She is, therefore, adopting the very view of the relationship between authority and obligation that I reject. Yet I believe that her account of the foundations of authority as she understands it takes us a long way toward an account of the foundations of authority as I understand it. That is, the foundation of political (and parental) authority arises from the necessity of a task whose successful performance requires customary compliance on the part of those for whom the task is supposed to be done.

Anscombe realizes that the mere existence of a task that needs to be done does not suffice to establish that one who undertakes to perform the task has a right to do so. Those who kidnap babies and rear them with love and kindness do not thereby acquire parental rights; those who usurp legitimate government authority and exercise it benevolently do not thereby acquire the right to rule. Something more is needed, and, according to Anscombe, "[i]t must either be necessary that he should perform the task or be his right to do it, before he can derive a right to certain things from the fact that they are necessary for the performance of the task."[12]

Consider first the relatively unproblematic case of parental authority. Children require certain forms of physical, emotional, and intellectual support if they are to survive and mature into healthy adults. They require direction which, if it is to be successful, must by and large be generally accepted. Biological parents are typically capable of and willing to provide such support and direction, but this is not enough to establish traditional parental rights.[13] In our society, biological parents do have such rights because there are customary principles of positive morality which give them the right to perform the required tasks when they are willing and able to do so. Having the right to perform the tasks, they have the right to what is necessary to their successful performance. This embraces the bundle of capacities, justification-rights, and claim-rights discussed earlier. The rights in question are not of a kind which are correlated with an obligation to obey because they need not be so correlated.

The task of government, as I conceive it, is to protect moral rights that exist outside of government.[14] Whether or not these rights receive recognition through customary morality is not important. What is important is that what H. L. A. Hart has called the rules of recognition, change, and adjudication[15] receive customary acceptance.[16] These rules provide remedies for what Locke described as the "inconveniences"[17] of a state-of-nature situation in which rights may only be enforced through resort to self-help. Following Hart, I understand the notion of the acceptance of the fundamental rules constitutive of a modern legal system in terms of a complex practice in which both officials and private citizens are involved in their own quite different ways. Although I believe there are a number of shortcomings in Hart's account,[18] for the present purposes it is more important to note a central point of agreement: Like

Hart, I do not assume that the acceptance of such rules involves their moral approval by those who accept them. Although the acceptance of such rules may, of course, be motivated or accompanied by certain moral attitudes, the point is that on such a positivistic account they need not be.[19] It is thus that the existence of social rules does not *normally* give rise to valid claims of moral right on the part of those who act under them. On the account that I have presented, positive rights become moral rights only when they involve what is necessary for the successful carrying out of a task that must be performed for the benefit of those on whose behalf authority is exercised.

I have followed Ladenson in claiming that acknowledging the existence of legitimate authority is compatible with denying the morality of the particular framework within which it is exercised; I have also noted, however, that I believed that this was true only within limits. On my view, the perpetration of gross injustice destroys the foundations of authority even though the customary acceptance of the rules that confer it persists. To speak of the authority of those who had the power to send Jews to Nazi death camps or of parents who engage in gross forms of child abuse is on my account to make a claim that has no moral content whatsoever. What constitutes gross injustice will depend on one's view of just what rights it is the task of government to protect as well as one's view of what powers it is necessary for those in authority to have in order to protect those rights. To the extent to which the answers to such questions are inherently controversial, so must be the answer to the question of what constitutes the sphere of legitimate political authority. Where welfare statists find legitimacy, libertarians will see only theft on a grand scale being carried out under the color of authority.

I believe that the substantive moral rights that exist outside of government both set the task for and constrain the legitimate range of political authority. But contrary to state-of-nature theorists like Locke and Nozick,[20] I do not believe that the only rights that government may exercise are ones which in principle could have been transferred to it by individuals seeking to transform a state-of-nature situation into civil society. Although primitive forms of a right to punish and seek reparation surely could exist simply as forms of self-protection outside of government, clearly the complex procedures that are associated with modern legislation, adjudication, and law enforcement could not. To think of an individual in a state of nature as having a *right* to subject another to a jury trial, for instance, is simply absurd. This is not to deny that government is morally bound to observe the moral constraints associated with the notion of the rule of law; it is merely to claim that *only* governments can be so bound. As Anscombe puts it, the institution of government "creates the character of an act as one of *doing justice on* the wronger of others."[21]

Skeletal as it may be, I believe that the foregoing is a correct account of the nature and foundations of political authority. Although there is no implication on this account that the citizen has a prima facie moral obligation to obey the law, there is no implication that he does not. The question of political obligation thus remains open, and it is to it that I shall now turn.

II. POLITICAL OBLIGATION

Might the mere fact that the law requires one to do something be a morally relevant consideration in favor of doing it?[22] I find that an affirmative answer to this question has little more appeal than the philosophical claim that material objects do not exist or that the existence of God may be established a priori. I do not believe that murder is any more wrongful where the law prohibits it than where it does not. Nor do I believe that making a prohibited U-turn where it is obviously completely safe to do so is a prima facie wrong that stands in need of justification.[23] I do believe, however, that it is possible to explain the sources of appeal of at least some of the arguments that have been thought to establish the existence of a prima facie obligation to obey the law. By explaining them, I hope not only to explain them away but to deepen our understanding of the need for and the nature of political authority. All of the arguments that I shall be concerned with contain an important *voluntaristic* element and in each case, I shall contend, it is that element that provides the clue to identifying whatever insights they conceal beneath the mask of the mistaken answer which they provide to the question of political obligation.

There are a number of familiar arguments that rely on the notion of hypothetical consent. These arguments assume that in a state-of-nature situation one's rights would at best be insecure and at worst one's life itself would be "solitary, poore, nasty, brutish, and short."[24] If one were to find oneself in such circumstances, one would agree to the institution of political authority and acknowledge an obligation to obey the laws enacted under it. Even if this counterfactual claim were correct, it is difficult to see how it could establish the existence of an obligation of obedience. Assume that you know of my sweet tooth and poor teeth and you force your way into my home and install a time lock on my candy cabinet. Suppose I would have asked you to do this if you had proposed the idea to me. Surely this establishes neither that you in fact had the authority to do what you did nor that I lie under any obligation to you not to remove the time lock if I can. To the extent to which your interference with my liberty is successful, the fact is that I had no choice in the matter and the moral import normally contained in the notion of consent is therefore absent. Hypothetical consent is just what the name implies—unreal and thus without binding force.

It is, indeed, questionable that one would even consent to the institution of political authority *and* to the obligation to obey the laws enacted under it if one found oneself in a state-of-nature situation. With respect to the institution of authority, each individual would surely stand to benefit by the existence of (a just) government, and each individual would also benefit by others undertaking an obligation to obey the law; however, any given individual would have the best of reasons not to enter into any such general agreement. It is only general compliance with the law that is necessary in order for government to succeed in carrying out its task; any given individual can rightly reason that his obedience is unnecessary and that it is in his interest not to incur an avoidable obligation to obey the law.[25] To assume that there is some moral principle which requires one not to attempt to be a free rider in such a situation is surely just as problematic as assuming that there is an obligation to obey the law.[26]

The move from the claim that one would agree to the institution of government and obedience to its laws to the claim that one has in fact, *tacitly,* so consented has seemed to writers like Locke but a small one. Continued residence and the enjoyment of the benefits that government bestows, which included for Locke the protection of private property rights, are familiar candidates for signs of such agreement that are implicit rather than explicit. The problem is that consent, whether express or tacit, must be fully voluntary in order to bind. Hume was surely correct when he remarked that it was simply not a live option for the average citizen to leave the country of his birth and native language, and to abandon his friends, family, employment, and cultural ties.[27] As an account of the putative foundation of political obligation it thus seems to me that any theory of an implied social contract must fail. In accordance with the analysis of the foundations of political authority presented earlier, however, it might be said that such theories contain an important grain of truth. The satisfaction of the acceptance conditions for the social rules of recognition, change, and adjudication of which Hart speaks might be taken as representing a kind of tacit consent on the global level on the part of the citizenry to recognize the authority of those who act under such rules.

Philosophers might have been less sanguine about the prospects of developing a plausible theory of tacit consent had they taken a closer look at what can be said for express consent as a ground of political obligation. Many naturalized citizens of the United States have taken oaths of allegiance in which they have solemnly sworn to uphold the Constitution and the laws made under it. What, if anything, is to be said about the obligations that they have thereby incurred? With respect to those who as a last resort have fled to this country in order to escape severe repression, I believe that there is nothing to be said for the claim that they have incurred a moral obligation of obedience to law by going through the naturalization process. Such a notion has no more merit than the idea that I might require you to acknowledge all kinds of burdensome obligations to me as a condition for my saving your life when there is no real risk or cost to myself in doing so. As for those who had a real choice in the matter and who came here perhaps merely because they believed that their material prospects would be better than in their homelands, I suggest that we must once again distinguish questions of political authority from questions of political obligation. A sincere and freely given oath to uphold the Constitution is plausibly taken to represent an acknowledgement of the character of political authority; it may be taken as evidence that one both understands and endorses the claims of those in power (and of those who will legitimately succeed them) to the right to rule. Beyond that, it may also be the case that one who has taken such an oath has also undertaken a moral obligation not to act in ways which would subvert the political structure by engaging in revolutionary violence and other such illegal activities at least as long as that

structure remains more or less as just as it was when he chose to participate as a citizen within it.

Nevertheless, the claim that the naturalized citizen has in virtue of
his oath of allegiance incurred a prima facie moral obligation to obey
any valid law enacted under the Constitution seems to be false. My
misgivings here, I think, have the same root as my uneasiness with the
notion that traditional marriage vows "to love, honor, and obey till
death do us part" could really bind in anything like the manner that the
words literally suggest. The difficulty, I suspect, is that one simply cannot
make such global promises. One can, of course, say the right words, but
they cannot bind. It is as if there were a legal provision that voided the
intended effect of issuing blank checks with one's signature written on
them. On this view, the notion of a fully general moral obligation to
obey the law, whatever its content and without regard to the consequences of obeying it, represents a moral blank check that government
is free to fill in at will or at least within very broad limits. It is for this
reason that this view seems to me to be oblivious to the facts of the
moral practices that surround the making and keeping of voluntary
agreements, whether by express or tacit consent. If understanding political obligation in terms of express consent must fail for these reasons,
contractarian theories of political obligation built upon the notion of
tacit consent must fail as well.

A voluntaristic account of political obligation which does not rely
on any form of the notion of consent to obey the law looks rather to
the implications of the voluntary acceptance of the benefits of others'
obedience. What has come to be known as the principle of fair play is
defined by Rawls as follows:

> Suppose there is a mutually beneficial and just scheme of social coop-
> eration, and that the advantages it yields can only be obtained if every-
> one, or nearly everyone, cooperates. Suppose further that cooperation
> requires a certain sacrifice from each person, or at least involves a
> certain restriction of his liberty. Suppose finally that the benefits pro-
> duced by cooperation are, up to a certain point, free: that is, the
> scheme of cooperation is unstable in the sense that if any one person
> knows that all (or nearly all) of the others will continue to do their
> part, he will still be able to share a gain from the scheme even if he
> does not do his part. Under these conditions a person who has ac-

cepted the benefits of the scheme is bound by a duty of fair play to do his part and not to take advantage of the free benefit by not cooperating.[28]

H. L. A. Hart's account is similar and, like Rawls, he believes that it provides a foundation for political obligation:

> [W]hen a number of persons conduct any joint enterprise according to rules and thus restrict their liberty, those who have submitted to these restrictions when required have a right to a similar submission from those who have benefited by their submission. The rules may provide that officials should have authority to enforce obedience . . . but the moral obligation to obey the rules in such circumstances is due to the co-operating members of the society, and they have the correlative moral right to obedience.[29]

Let us first consider the principle of fairness as a general moral principle and then turn to the question of what bearing it has on the question of political obligation.[30]

Unlike Rawls, I do not believe that a cooperative scheme need be fully just in order for obligations of fairness to arise under it. Burdens and benefits might be distributed in an unfair manner, for instance, but one still might rightly be claimed to have an obligation to contribute one's fair share to the extent to which one has in fact benefited.[31] As to Nozick's objection that the principle is totally unacceptable because it would permit some to foist obligations on others by foisting benefits on them,[32] I believe the proper response is to interpret Hart and Rawls as requiring genuinely voluntary acceptance of the benefits in question. Obligations do not arise in the counterexamples that Nozick raises because, as A. John Simmons puts it, "benefits we have actively resisted getting, and those we have gotten unknowingly or in ways over which we have no control at all, seem clearly *not* to be benefits we have accepted."[33]

As so interpreted, it may appear that the principle of fair play is no independent moral principle at all because it collapses into a principle of consent. Voluntary acceptance of the benefits arising under a cooperative practice in which one participates willingly and with understanding of the rules which underlie it might seem tantamount to the giving of one's tacit consent to do one's fair share as required by the rules. Indeed, this may often be the case; Simmons has convinced me, however, that it need not always be.[34] For example, I might explicitly refuse to give my consent to participate in the initiation of a cooperative practice because I quite sincerely believe that it will not work. If it does, however, and I choose to enjoy the benefits of it, I may incur an obligation to bear a fair share of the burdens involved in its organization and maintenance.

There is one major modification that I wish to make in the Hart-Rawls-Simmons account of the principle of fair play. The principle is presented by them as a universal moral principle that attaches obligations to the voluntary acceptance of benefits that arise within continuing conventional cooperative practices irrespective of the understanding of those involved in the practices. Suppose a group of individuals unwittingly acted in a coordinated manner that produced valuable benefits for some group of passive but grateful bystanders, or a group of people deliberately engaged in what they took to be a cooperative practice of providing charitable benefits to others, or a group of people again knowingly cooperated but the members lacked totally the notion of fairness. In such cases there is nothing morally objectionable in free riding by those beneficiaries who can. Therefore, I would put the principle of fair play in a hypothetical rather than a categorical form: If there is a mutually beneficial cooperative social practice, and if associated with that practice is the conventional acceptance of a norm requiring those who voluntarily accept the benefits of it to do their fair share of assuming its burdens, then those who have so benefited have an obligation to do what the rules of the practice require. In this form, and with the proviso that "the benefits to a person from the actions of the others are greater than the cost to him of doing his share,"[35] I believe that the principle of fairness is a general moral principle to which we often rightly appeal.

There are surely acts that the law prohibits which it would be unfair to perform even if the law did not prohibit them. There are other acts performance of which would be unfair because of the fact that general compliance with what the law requires establishes certain conventional practices that would not otherwise exist, *e.g.,* parking regulations.[36] What is at issue, however, is whether or not there is a prima facie moral obligation, based on considerations of fairness, to obey any valid law (or judicial or executive order) enacted within the bounds of legitimate legal authority. Those who have claimed that there is seem to have believed that it derives from the acceptance of the benefits of general compliance with the law. It is the general practice of compliance with law, and the quite general benefits of peace and security to which this practice gives rise, that are seen as providing the foundation for a fully general obligation to obey the law.

Within a just society, the general pattern of compliance with what the law requires would be *voluntary* in the sense that the *normal motive* for obedience would not be the fear of legal sanctions but rather the belief that what the law required was right independent of the fact that the law required it.[37] Likewise, the acceptance of the benefits of general compliance would be voluntary in the sense that these benefits would be perceived as genuinely desirable and worth what was involved in each citizen doing his fair share in paying for the costs of their production. If this were all there were to it, there would be considerable plausibility in grounding a general obligation to obey the law in the principle of fair play; however, this is not all there is to it. Lurking in the background is the omnipresent threat of legal authority exercising the coercive powers upon which it claims a monopoly. All of the benefits in question are ultimately financed through compulsory taxation; disobedience to law is at the risk of incurring legal sanctions; and one really has no choice in accepting the benefits in question. The voluntaristic features present in cooperative social practices to which the principle of fair play applies are simply missing. The grounds for the application of the principle are thus undercut.[38]

III. CONCLUSION

There is something of a paradox here, an understanding of which both explains why there is a strong temptation to appeal to the principle of fair play as a foundation for political obligation and why any such attempt must ultimately fail. Within a fully just society, the law would provide only genuine benefits and require of each citizen that he do no more than shoulder his fair share of the burdens of providing those benefits. The requirements would be identical to those that would be generated by the principle of fair play with respect to the very same schedule of benefits as they might arise in a voluntary association. Because the distinctive character of government lies in its exercise of a monopoly on the use of coercive force, however, political associations are not volun-

tary associations. Given the nature of the need for them and the existence of customary rules definitive of legal authority, those exercising
political power may, under the right conditions, claim a moral right to
rule. Such political authority, however, is not associated with the existence of a general prima facie obligation on the part of citizens to obey
the law. Owing to its essentially coercive character, a political association
is inherently a one-way street. Those who legitimately wield the powers
of government have the right to rule and the responsibility to do so for
the benefit of, and with an eye to the protection of, the rights of those
they govern. Those they govern lie under no general obligation to obey
them and may, indeed, seek to remove from authority those who abuse
the awesome powers of government. It is thus that I conclude: Government holds a *trust*.

NOTES

The author wishes to thank the Reason Foundation and Liberty Fund, Inc., for
their support in the writing of this article.

1. *See, e.g.,* Anscombe, *On the Source of the Authority of the State,* 20 RATIO 1
(1978).

2. *See generally* R. Wolff, IN DEFENSE OF ANARCHISM (1970).

3. *See generally* Anscombe, *supra* note 1.

4. *See* Ladenson, *In Defense of a Hobbesian Conception of Law,* 9 PHILOSOPHY &
PUB. AFF. 134, 137–40 (1980).

5. *See id.* at 141.

6. *See* text *infra* at notes 19–21.

7. Ladenson, *supra* note 4, at 143 (emphasis in original).

8. Anscombe, *supra* note 1, at 6.

9. *See id.* (emphasis omitted).

10. *See id.*

11. *Id.*

12. *Id.* at 18.

13. In Plato's *Republic,* for instance, biological parents would not have such
rights. *See generally* Plato, THE REPUBLIC (F. Cornford, trans. 1957).

14. The story is a bit more complicated than this simple slogan suggests. *See*
Sartorius, *Government Regulation and Intergenerational Justice,* to be published in
ESSAYS ON DEREGULATION (B. Johnson & T. Machan, eds. 1981).

15. *See* H. L. A. Hart, THE CONCEPT OF LAW 89–96 (1961).

16. For Hart's understanding of the phenomenon of the acceptance of rules, see H. L. A. Hart, *supra* note 15, at 54–60.

17. J. Locke, *Second Treatise Of Civil Government* § 127, in Two Treatises of Government 119, 185 (T. Cook ed. 1947).

18. *See* Sartorius, *Hart's Concept of Law,* in More Essays in Legal Philosophy 131 (R. Summers, ed. 1971)(originally published in 52 Archiv fur Rechts und Sozialphilosophie 161 [1966]); Woozley, *The Existence of Rules,* 1 Nous 63 (1967).

19. *See* Sartorius, *supra* note 18, at 176–77.

20. *See generally* J. Locke, *supra note* 17; R. Nozick, Anarchy, State, and Utopia (1974).

21. Anscombe, *supra* note 1, at 21 (emphasis in original).

22. This question does not assume any distinction between constitutional provision, statute, judicial or executive order, or ruling of an administrative agency.

23. The line of argument suggested here is developed in Smith, *Is There a Prima Facie Obligation to Obey the Law?,* 82 Yale L.J. 950 (1973).

24. T. Hobbes, Leviathan 186 (C. Macpherson, ed. 1968).

25. For a general discussion of the problems surrounding the voluntary provision of public goods, see Sartorius, *The Limit of Libertarianism,* in Liberty and the Rule of Law 87 (R. Cunningham, ed. 1979).

26. For a tentative discussion of just such a principle, see *id.* at 127.

27. D. Hume, *Of the Original Contract,* in Hume's Moral and Political Philosophy 356, 363–64 (H. Aiken, ed. 1948).

28. Rawls, *Legal Obligation and the Duty of Fair Play,* in Law and Philosophy 1, 9–10 (S. Hook, ed. 1964).

29. Hart, *Are There Any Natural Rights?,* 64 Philosophical Rev. 175, 185 (1955) (emphasis deleted).

30. I follow very closely here the extremely valuable account found in Simmons, *The Principle of Fair Play,* 8 Philosophy & Pub. Aff. 307 (1979).

31. *See id.* at 312–17.

32. *See* R. Nozick, *supra* note 20, at 95.

33. Simmons, *supra* note 30, at 327 (emphasis in original).

34. *See id.* at 323–26.

35. R. Nozick, *supra* note 20, at 94.

36. In this connection, see A. Woozley, Law and Obedience 139 (1979).

37. *See also* H. L. A. Hart, *supra* note 15, at 193.

38. Simmons also argues in this way. *See* Simmons, *supra* note 30, at 333–37.

7

THE OBLIGATION TO OBEY: REVISION AND TRADITION

Joseph Raz

The turbulent sixties, years of the civil rights movement and of the Vietnam War, brought, as a by-product of civil strife and widespread discontent, renewed interest in the question of the duties an individual owes his society. It was soon to give way to a preoccupation with what society owes to its members, that is to the swelling of interest in theories of justice and individual rights. But before it did so a good deal of common ground seemed to have been established among many of the political and moral theorists who did and still do attend to the issue. It is summed up by the view that every citizen has a prima facie moral obligation to obey the law of a reasonably just state. Its core intuition is the belief that denying an obligation to obey its laws is a denial of the justice of the state. This is believed to be so either on instrumentalist grounds or on grounds of fairness. The instrumentalist contends that the state will not be able to function if its citizens are not obligated to obey its laws and respect that obligation for the most part. The fairness argument has it that anyone who denies an obligation to obey in a just state takes unfair advantage of others who submit to such an obligation.

I have joined several theorists who challenge this consensus.[1] There have, of course, always been those who deny the existence of an obligation to obey the law on the ground that no state can be just. Their most powerful philosophical spokesman in recent years has been Robert Paul Wolff.[2] The challenge posed by the arguments referred to is that they claim that even in a just state, if there can be such, there is no general obligation to obey the law. Not even all those who deny the existence of a general obligation to obey the law have realized its full implications. If there is no general obligation to obey, then the law does not have general authority, for to have authority is to have a right to rule those who are subject to it. And a right to rule entails a duty to obey. I shall contend below that in a very real sense this conclusion returns to the main line of thought of the founders of modern political theory. However, it appears to be a novel position and not surprisingly has led to a number of misunderstandings that this article aims to help dispel.

I. GOVERNMENT WITHOUT AUTHORITY

Let us start by considering the (apparent) paradox of the just government. Most political theorists acknowledge that there is no general obligation to obey the law of an unjust state. But, it is contended, there is an obligation to obey the law of a reasonably just state, and the greater its justice the stricter, or at any rate the clearer, the obligation. But is this so? Isn't the reverse the case? The morality of a government's laws measures, in part, its justice. Its laws are moral only if there is a moral obligation to perform the actions which they impose a legal obligation to perform. That moral obligation cannot be due to the existence of an obligation to obey the law. To establish an obligation to obey the law one has to establish that it is relatively just. It is relatively just only if there is a moral obligation to do that which it imposes legal obligations to do. So the moral obligations on which the claim that the law is just is founded are prior to and independent of the moral obligation to obey the law. The alleged moral obligation to obey arises from these independent obligations to act as the law requires.

Since the obligation to obey the law derives from these other moral obligations, its weight or strictness reflects their weight. The stricter they are the stricter is the obligation to obey. But if so, then the obligation to obey the law is at best redundant. It may make a moral difference if it exists in an unjust state, for there it imposes a moral obligation where none exists. But in a just state, it is at best a mere shadow of other moral duties. It adds nothing to them. Since the obligation to obey exists only in a just state, it is at best redundant.

Consider the question whether there is a legal obligation to obey the law. The obligation exists, but it is hardly ever mentioned, for it is the shadow of all the specific legal obligations. The law requires one to pay tax, refrain from murder, assault, theft, libel, breach of contract, etc. Hence, tautologically, one has a legal obligation to pay tax, refrain from murder, assault, theft, libel, breach of contract, etc. A short, though empty and uninformative, way of describing one's legal duties is to say that one has a legal duty to obey the law. One has a legal duty to obey the law because one has a legal duty to obey this law and that, and so on, until one exhausts the list. It is likewise, the paradox can be interpreted as alleging, with the moral duty to obey the law. It exists only to the extent that there are other, independent moral duties to obey each of the laws of the system. It is merely their shadow.

In fact the paradox is even worse. The obligation to obey the law is no mere shadow. It would be, were it to exist, a moral perversion. Consider legal duties such as the duty not to commit murder and not to rape. Clearly there are moral duties to refrain from murder and from rape. Equally clearly we approve, if we do, of the laws prohibiting such acts, because the acts they forbid are morally forbidden.[3] Moreover, we expect morally conscientious people to comply with these laws because the acts they forbid are immoral. I would feel insulted if it were suggested that I refrain from murder and rape because I recognize a moral obligation to obey the law. We expect people to avoid such actions whether or not they are legally forbidden, and for reasons which have nothing to do with the law. If it turns out that those reasons fail, that it is only respect for the law which restrains them from such acts, then those people lose much of our respect.

But if the obligation to obey the law is not a morally correct reason by which the morally conscientious person should guide his action, at least not in such elementary and fundamental areas of the law as those mentioned, then can there be such an obligation? Can there be a moral obligation to perform an action if to take the existence of the obligation as one's reason for the action it enjoins would be wrong, or ill-fitting?

So much for the apparent paradox of the just law. The more just and valuable the law is, it says, the more reason one has *to conform to it,* and the less *to obey it.* Since it is just, those considerations which establish its justice should be one's reasons for conforming with it, i.e., for acting as it requires. But in acting for these reasons one would not be obeying the law, one would not be conforming because that is what the law requires. Rather one would be acting on the doctrine of justice to which the law itself conforms.

I called the paradox merely 'apparent' because it is overstated. For reasons we will examine in the next section, sometimes the law makes a moral difference. In particular sometimes the law is just, although no independent obligation attaches to what it requires. In these cases it is morally obligatory to act as the law requires because it so requires. But even though overstated the alleged paradox is instructive. It challenges the existence of a general obligation to obey the law. To succeed it need only establish that in some fairly central cases there is no such obligation. From this point of view it matters not that some laws are not like the laws against murder and rape. If a legal prohibition of murder neither imposes an independent moral obligation nor makes the duty not to murder stricter or weightier than it was without the law, then the case is made. The prohibitions of murder, rape, enslavement, imprisonment and similar legal prohibitions are central to the laws of all just legal systems. Their existence cannot be dismissed as marginal or controversial. If these laws do not make a difference to our moral obligations, then there is no *general* obligation to obey the law. There may be a moral obligation to obey some laws, but this was never in contention.

The argument so far depends on two assumptions both of which are open to challenge. First, the argument assumes that to refrain from murder or any other moral perversion solely because the law proscribes it is morally distorted and undesirable. It may be objected that while this is not the best motive for refraining from murder it is not the worst either. It is better for example than sparing a person's life because he will then suffer a more painful death. Second, it assumes that the reasons for obeying the law, when such can be found, must derive from the reasons for having laws with that particular content. It may be objected that the reasons for obedience normally thought of as constituting the obligation to obey have nothing to do with the desirability of any particular law but with the desirability of the existence of a legal system and a structure of government by laws as a whole.

The argument of the following pages will help rebut these objections and will bolster the assumptions, especially the second one.[4] My present purpose is more modest. Even if the alleged paradox fails to disprove the existence of an obligation to obey, it succeeds in making us reexamine some of our assumptions about the functions of law in society. It reveals that much of the good that the law can do does not presuppose any obligation to obey.

Once more a simplified picture will help bring out the point more clearly. Let us assume that in its sole proper function, the law prohibits murder, neglect of children by their parents, and other similar immoralities. On this assumption it is plausible to claim that the law's direct function is to motivate those who fail to be sufficiently moved by sound moral considerations. The conscientious, knowledgeable person will do what the law requires of him regardless of whether the law exists or not. The law is not for him. It is for those who deny their moral duties. It forces them to act as they should by threatening sanctions if they fail to do so. By addressing the self-interest of those who fail to be properly moved by moral considerations, the law reassures the morally conscientious. It assures him that he will not be taken advantage of, will not be exploited by the unscrupulous.

This oversimplified picture demonstrates the good a government without authority can do.[5] One can threaten and penalize people without having authority over them. One can also have an organization to issue and carry out threats without authority over them either. We can imagine the law enforcement functions we have in mind being carried out by people who are paid salaries, or given other incentives to enforce and to administer the laws. The personnel in charge of the implementation of the law need not necessarily be subject to the authority of the government or its law; they may be doing a job under a contract. Their actions are morally permissible for reasons independent of the law. Even when they encroach on the personal liberty of the offender, they need not invoke the law in justification. They treat offenders in ways morally appropriate for those who renege on their moral duties.

The picture is oversimplified. But it is so in what it leaves out, not in what it says. Governments fulfill the functions we described, but they do much else besides. Some of their other functions do not presuppose the recognition of authority either. It is an important fact about the modern state that to an ever greater extent it affects our fortunes by means other than exercising, or claiming to exercise, authority over us. In many states the government, or public authorities generally, are the largest employer in the country, control much of the infrastructure through a state monopoly on the provision of mail, telephone, airport and seaport services and the like. The armed forces are the largest clients for many high technology industries, and so on. The details vary from state to state, but the overall picture is rather similar.

The effects of this concentration of economic power are evident in the state's growing use of its economic muscle to achieve aims which in previous times would have required legislation or administrative actions. Governments attempt to affect the direction of industrial development, the level of economic activity, the rate of inflation, the level of unemployment, the regional distribution of wealth in the country, and other objectives through their economic power alone. Even non-economic objectives such as racial equality in employment are sometimes pursued by the use of economic power, rather than by the exercise of authority. It is often argued that the awarding of governmental contracts only to equal opportunity employers is the best way of pursuing such objectives.

Many of these developments are relatively recent and raise difficult questions about the adequacy of the existing machinery for controlling governmental powers. The machinery evolved primarily as a check on the government's exercise of legislative and administrative power. It is ill suited today to supervise the economic activities of public authorities. Nevertheless, it is clear that only the degree to which governments affect their populations by non-governmental means is new, for governments have always affected individuals by changing their physical or economic environment by means which do not invoke its authority. Governments have built roads, dug canals, constructed state buildings and monuments, employed people and the like for as long as political society has existed.

II. ON THE FOUNDATION OF POLITICAL AUTHORITY

Governments affect us through their intervention in the market by changing the physical environment, and by providing the morally unscrupulous or misguided with self-interested reasons to do that which they ought to do, but which moral reasons fail to make them do. Focusing on these aspects of governmental activity helps dispel the myth that denying the existence of an obligation to obey the law amounts to denying the possibility of a just government. This myth is based on a misperception of the aims and means of governmental action. If in principle governments can discharge all the mentioned functions without authority, then they can do so justly as well as unjustly. From our perspective it does not matter if the same ends can be achieved by other means, ones which do not involve the existence of governments. I am not challenging the justice of alternative modes of social organization, nor comparing their precise merits. I only seek to establish that those who favor the continued exercise of many of the existing functions of governments cannot argue from that to the existence of a general obligation to obey the law. For those functions can be discharged by governments independently of such an obligation.

One objection may be that the argument overlooks that at least government officials must accept governmental authority for government to function as described. If the officials do not obey the law, then the morally unscrupulous, for example, will have no fear that legal sanctions may be applied to them. The contract model answered this objection, because officials would serve the government by consent, rather than because they recognize its authority. This may not be a very practical arrangement in some cases. A more important objection may be that, where governments do not exercise any authority, not even over their officials, one may well doubt whether they are governments at all rather than corporations who voluntarily undertake some good social services. Be that as it may, the functions described which are normally carried out by governments can in principle be carried out without authority. Furthermore, let us remind ourselves that the argument does not require that nobody is under the authority of government. It only claims there is no general obligation to obey the law, i.e., that not everyone is under an obligation to obey all the laws, not even in a relatively just society.

My basic position is not that no one has any moral reason ever to take account of the existence of the law. I argue that the extent of the obligation to obey varies from person to person. In no case is the moral obligation as extensive as the legal obligation. Consider three typical situations in which ordinary citizens do find themselves under an obligation to obey.

First, imagine that I use in the course of my employment tools which may create a safety hazard to passersby. The government has issued safety regulations detailing the equipment which may be used and the safety measures that I must take to make their use safe. The government experts who laid down these safety regulations are experts in their field. Their judgment is much more reliable than mine. I am therefore duty bound to obey the regulations which they have adopted.

Second, we all have reason to preserve the countryside. In areas visited by many people, this goal would be enhanced if no one had barbecues. In fact everyone has barbecues in those areas. The damage is done and my refraining from a barbecue will not help. The situation is so bad that my having a barbecue will not make even a small difference. At long last the government steps in and forbids having barbecues except in a few designated locations. Because the regulation might reverse the trend, I have an obligation to obey this law.

Third, I disagree with the government's policy of allowing the construction of nuclear power plants. I can try to block the roads leading to the construction sites to stop building material and machinery from reaching the workers. Doing so will be against the law. It will also, if successful to any degree, encourage other people to take the law into their own hands when they think they can force the government to change its policies. This will undermine the ability of the government to discharge its functions. Despite this lapse on the government's part, I still regard it as a relatively just and moral government. I have an obligation to obey the law and avoid breaking it in the way described.

In one respect the last case differs from the first two. Though I am obligated to obey the law, the obligation does not show that the law or government has authority over me regarding the issue in question. In the first two cases my obligation to obey results from the law's authority. It knows best, or it can best arrange matters. Hence, I had better accept its instructions and obey. In the last case there are no such assumptions. It is merely that I will undermine the government's ability to do good. That reason can, and often does, apply to people not subject to the authority of the government. A foreign state may restrain its action in order not to undermine the ability of my government to fulfill its useful functions. But a foreign state is not subject to the authority of the government.[6]

More important are the features the three cases have in common. (1) They are typical cases. Much of planning law, laws concerning safety at work, regulations regarding standards of manufactured goods such as cars, pharmaceuticals and the like, rules concerning the safe maintenance of cars, or concerning standards of safe driving, qualifications required for engaging in certain occupations, and many more, all belong to the first category. Standards for the preservation of the environment, for the protection of scarce resources, for the raising of revenue through taxation to finance public projects, welfare services or other valuable projects, and many more belong in most cases to the second category. Any act aimed at forcing public authorities to change their policies or actions by unlawful means belongs to the third category. Some laws are more likely to be broken for these reasons than others, but the violation of any law can, on occasion, be used for such a purpose.

(2) In all the examples, the law makes a difference to one's moral obligations. The moral obligation is a prima facie one; it may be overridden by contrary considerations. But for the law, I might well have adopted different safety precautions. I accept the superior reliability of the law on such issues, and defer to its judgment. I would not have had any reason to avoid having barbecues in the beauty spots of the second example, but for the introduction of the law which gives rise to the expectation that the widespread but damaging practice will come to an end, or at least that it will be sufficiently reduced so that my self-restraint will make a difference, however little. Finally, had the blockade of the nuclear power plant site not been against the law, it would not have been an act tending to undermine the ability of the government to carry out its proper functions. That is why it is proper to talk in all these cases of my obligation to obey some laws.

(3) None of the cases separately, nor all of them together offer an argument capable of being generalized to point to a general obligation to obey. The contrary is the case. They highlight the degree to which the obligation is limited and varies in accordance with circumstances. The first case depends on the law's superior knowledge. But if I am the greatest living expert on pharmaceuticals, then the law has no authority over me regarding the safety of pharmaceuticals. Sometimes I have the option of investing time, money and mental effort in a problem to solve it myself, or to go to a knowledgeable friend and follow his advice. The law, in cases of the first type, is like a knowledgeable friend and the same range of options are available. (So that in such matters the range of the law's authority over individuals varies from one person to another.)

The second example concerns not the law's superior knowledge, but its ability to achieve goals which individuals have reason to pursue, but cannot do so effectively on their own, because their realization requires coordinating the actions of large numbers of people. Although central to the normal functioning of the law, such cases cannot be generalized to generate an obligation to obey the law of a relatively just state.

First, not all laws purport to fulfill such a function. Laws of the kind involved in the first class of cases, as well as laws like the prohibition of rape and murder differ from laws which coordinate the efforts of large groups. In the former cases, the reasons for acting in accord with the law apply with the same stringency in each case regardless of the degree of general conformity with the law. Every time someone murders or recklessly engages in a risky activity he acts wrongly, harming or risking others. Not so in our second example. Here the existence of reasons for the action, and their weight, depend on general conformity, or the likelihood of it. Some laws are of this character, others are not. The reasons which lead one to acknowledge the law's authority in cases of coordination do not apply elsewhere. Second, laws striving to achieve coordination address masses of people, and are designed to be enforced and regulated through the activities of judicial and administrative institutions. They are drafted not merely to state most accurately the actions required if coordination is to be achieved, but also to be easily comprehended, and to avoid giving rise to administrative corruption, the harassment of individuals, and other undesirable by-products of the operation of the legal machine. A person who understands the situation will often have reason to go beyond the law, and to do more than the law requires in pursuit of the same coordinating goal. Alternatively, he may find that on occasion he has no reason to follow certain aspects of the law. They may be the inevitable simplifications the law has to embrace to be reasonably understood and efficiently enforced. There is no reason for an individual not faced with the same considerations to conform to the law on such occasions.

The third type of example is often invoked to supplement the previous two and plug the remaining holes. It is argued that if the law is reasonably just, then cases like those of the first two types exist in large numbers. In other cases one ought to obey the law, for otherwise one would undermine its ability to function effectively. The argument is based on a false premise. Law breaking is liable to undermine the effectiveness of the government in many cases. In others, violations of law have no such effect. Offenses never known to anyone or violating the interests of one private individual only, as with many torts and breaches of contract, generally do not diminish the government's effectiveness. There may be other reasons for conforming with the law in some of these cases, but the threat to the effectiveness of government and the law is not among them.

These three types of arguments illustrated by our examples are not the only ones which lead to obligations to obey some laws or others. I have discussed them, because, other than consent and voluntary commitments, they most commonly give rise to an obligation to obey. They usefully illustrate the main points which need emphasizing. First, that the extent of the duty to obey the law in a relatively just country varies from person to person and from one range of cases to another. There is probably a common core of cases regarding which the obligation exists and applies equally to all. Some duties based on the coordinative argument (e.g., duty to pay tax) and on the bad example argument (e.g., avoiding political terrorism) are likely to apply equally to all citizens. Beyond this core, the extent of the obligation to obey will vary greatly. Second, the extent of the obligation depends on factors other than whether the law is just and sensible. It may depend on the expertise of the individual citizen, as in cases of the first kind, or on the circumstances of the occasion for the violation, as often in cases of the third kind.

III. REVISIONISM IS TRADITIONALISM

John Finnis's article "The Authority of Law in the Predicament of Contemporary Social Theory"[7] exemplifies some of the confusions which pervade our reflections on the obligation to obey. His central claim is that the law presents itself as a seamless web: its subjects are not allowed to pick and choose.[8] This is certainly the case. But Finnis does not even pause to indicate that he draws from this the conclusion that we are not allowed to pick and choose, let alone present any reason in support of it. For him, if this is how the law presents itself, then this is how we ought to take it. To be sure, if we have an obligation to obey the law, then the conclusion does indeed follow. But one cannot presuppose that we have such an obligation in order to provide the reason ("the law is a seamless web") for claiming that we have an obligation to obey. This would be a most vicious circle indeed. Does he perchance imply that we cannot pick and choose, for if we do the whole system of law and order will be undermined and will eventually collapse? He certainly does not argue to that effect, nor does he consider the case to the contrary which I have presented above and previously.[9] Under these circumstances one hesitates to foist any particular interpretation on Finnis's statement.

Dr. Finnis's intriguing article contains similar throwaway points which leave the reader wondering how they are meant to be taken. Does he really believe that "apart from the law" a person "could reasonably be relatively indifferent to the concerns and interests of persons whose activities . . . do not affect him or at least do not benefit him"?[10] There are no doubt people who do hold that we have no moral obligations to people who do not benefit us. But such a broad statement has no hope of carrying conviction without any word in its defense. Moreover, most of those people will take the point as militating against there being an obligation to obey the law, at least to the extent that it requires us to benefit strangers. Finnis regards it as a further reason to believe in an obligation to obey.

Finnis tells us that, even if farmers have a duty not to pollute the river they may misguidedly dispute this, and therefore the way to get them to do their moral duty is to have a moral obligation to obey the law. They will then refrain from pollution because the law requires them to do so. But that will be the case only if they will not make a mistake about their obligation to obey the law, and only if the lawmakers will not make a mistake about the obligation not to pollute the rivers. Even if these conditions are met, they constitute an argument for the existence of an obligation to obey the law only if the lawmakers are not likely to make fewer mistakes than the farmers on other issues as well. For the obligation to obey is general and what is won in the absence of pollution can easily be lost in the maltreatment of old age pensioners or of the mentally ill.

Those who emphasize the danger of every person deciding for himself, whether case for the law's authority over any range of questions is good or not, often overlook this last point. Human judgment errs. It falls prey to temptations and bias distorts it. This fact must affect one's considerations. But which way should it incline one? The only general answer which I find persuasive is that it depends on the circumstances. In some areas and regarding some people, caution requires submission to authority. In others it leads to denial of authority. There are risks, moral and other, in uncritical acceptance of authority. Too often in the past, the fallibility of human judgment has led to submission to authority from a misguided sense of duty where this was a morally reprehensible attitude.

Finnis's elegant discussion of the river pollution case illustrates one way in which the law can do good, and when it does it should certainly be obeyed.[11] It is a good illustration of an occasion on which the existence of the law makes a difference. While some laws make a difference, I doubt that all do. Some of the examples used above show how greatly many legal rules, all equally central to the law, differ from the river pollution example. One should not be so captivated by one paradigm that others go unnoticed. Consider the river pollution case itself. Finnis quite reasonably directs our attention to a time when coordination, though desirable, does not obtain and the law steps in to secure it. But travel ten years on. By now, let us simplify, either the scheme introduced by the law has taken root and is the general practice, or it has long since been forgotten and is honored only in the breach. In the second case, my conforming with the law will serve no useful purpose unless it happens to protect me from penalties, or to stop my behavior being misunderstood by others. There is then no point in obeying the law. There is reason to conform with it if the scheme is in general effective. But, as is evident by comparing this case with the previous one where the law is the same but the practice of conformity is missing, that reason is not the law but the actual practice.

All the questions I raise can be answered. I have stated my answers in previous publications and supplemented them above. Finnis seems to disagree, but he fails to tell us why. He properly explains why the law is a way of achieving coordination,[12] but he never even attempts to show that coordination requires general obedience to law.[13]

I should make clear my agreement with Finnis in his doubts about the value of social choice and game theory as guides to moral decisions. This is not the occasion to go into such issues. But we should remember that all the arguments concerning an obligation to obey which were canvassed so far were essentially instrumental arguments. They assumed that we have reason to promote or protect certain states of affairs, and examined whether recognition of an obligation to obey the law, or obedience to law, is a way of doing so. But are there not non-instrumental reasons for obeying the law?

Non-instrumental reasoning is central to a distinguished tradition in political philosophy. Today one of the most common arguments, often repeated in different forms, is based on alleged considerations of fairness. It is unfair, it claims, to enjoy benefits derived from the law without contributing one's share to the production of those benefits. As has been pointed out many times before, this argument is of dubious validity when one has no choice but to accept the benefits, or even more generally, when the benefits are given to one who doesn't request them, and in circumstances which do not imply an understanding concerning the conditions attached to their donation and receipt. Besides, even where it is unfair not to reciprocate for services received, or not to contribute one's share to the production of a good of general public value, it cannot be unfair to perform innocuous acts which neither harm any one, nor impede the provision of any public good. Many violations of law are such innocuous acts. Therefore, appeals to fairness can raise no general obligation to obey the law.

The more traditional non-instrumental justification of the obligation to obey the law relies on contract and consent. Not all consent theorists base either the validity of the consent or the reasons for giving it on non-instrumental reasons. Hobbes wished to derive it all from enlightened self interest. Locke allowed moral reasons to enter the argument, but they are instrumental reasons. Consent to obey is designed to bring greater conformity with the natural law and greater respect for the natural rights of men than is likely to be achieved in a state of nature. Rousseau was the most important eighteenth-century thinker to highlight the intrinsic value of the social contract as the act which constitutes civil society, as well as the personality of those who belong to it.

Consent to obey the law of a relatively just government indeed establishes an obligation to obey the law.[14] The well-known difficulty with consent as the foundation of political authority is that too few have given their consent. This argument in its customary form can be right and wrong at the same time. Consent or agreement requires a deliberate, performative action, and to be binding it has to be voluntarily undertaken. Many people, however, have never performed anything remotely like such an action. The only time I did was during my national military service, in circumstances where failure to take the oath would have led to being court-martialled. I would not have made the oath but for these circumstances, and I do not think I was ever bound to observe this coerced undertaking.

Nevertheless, this objection is also misguided. There are other ways of incurring voluntary or semi-voluntary obligations. Consider a family or a friendship. There are obligations which friends owe each other, and which are in a sense voluntary obligations, as it is obligatory neither to form friendships nor to continue with them once formed. Yet we do not undertake these obligations by an act of promise or consent. As does friendship, these obligations arise from the developing relations between people. Loyalty is an essential duty arising from any personal relationship. The content of this duty helps us to identify the character of the relationship. If the duty precludes your having sex with another person, then your relations are of one character; and if it precludes publicizing disagreements between you, then you have relations of another kind, and so on. In other words, duties of loyalty are semi-voluntary, because the relationship itself is not obligatory. Moreover, they are non-instrumentally justified because they are part of what makes the relationship into the kind of relationship it is. (I am assuming that having the particular relationship, friendship, is itself of intrinsic value.)

What has this excursion into the normative aspect of personal relations to do with the obligation to obey the law? It demonstrates the possibility of one kind of obligation to obey which arises out of a sense of identifying with or belonging to the community. Such an attitude, if directed to a community which deserves it, is intrinsically valuable. It is not however obligatory. One does not have a moral duty to feel a sense of belonging in a community; certainly there is no obligation to feel that one belongs to a country (rather than one's village, or some other community). I talk of a feeling that one belongs, but this feeling is nothing other than a complex attitude comprising emotional, cognitive and normative elements. Feeling a sense of loyalty and a duty of loyalty constitutes, here too, an element of such an attitude.

The government and the law are official or formal organs of the community. If they represent the community or express its will justly and accurately, then an entirely natural indication of a member's sense of belonging is one's attitude toward the community's organization and laws. I call such an attitude respect for law. It is a belief that one is under an obligation to obey because the law is one's law, and the law of one's country. Obeying it is a way of expressing confidence and trust in its justice. As such, it expresses one's identification with the community. Respect for law does not derive from consent. It grows, as friendships do; it develops as does one's sense of membership in a community. Nevertheless, respect for law grounds a quasi-voluntary obligation. An obligation to obey the law is in such cases part and parcel of one's attitude toward the community. One feels that one betrays the community if one breaks the law to gain advantage, or out of convenience, or thoughtlessness, and this regardless of whether the violation actually harms anyone, just as one can be disloyal to a friend without harming him or any of his interests, without even offending him.

An obligation to obey which is part of a duty of loyalty to the community is a semi-voluntary obligation, because one has no moral duty to identify with this community. It is founded on non-instrumental considerations, for it constitutes an attitude of belonging which has intrinsic value, if addressed to an appropriate object. Vindicating its existence does not therefore establish the existence of a general obligation to obey the law. For good or ill there are many who do not feel this way about their country, and many more who do not feel like this about its formal legal organization. It is sometimes said that the denial of a general obligation to obey is of recent vintage. It is in many ways the opposite. At the birth of modern political theory in the seventeenth and eighteenth centuries, there was one clear orthodoxy: if there is a general obligation to obey the law, it exists because it was voluntarily undertaken. That is the view defended in this article. The fathers of modern political theory also believed that such obligations were indeed voluntarily undertaken. If this view is no longer true today it is because the societies we live in are less homogeneous, more troubled about their own identity, and about the role of government and the law in the social fabric. Society has changed, not political theory.

NOTES

1. *See* Smith, *Is There a Prima Facie Obligation to Obey the Law?*, 82 YALE L. J. 950 (1973); A. Woozley, LAW AND OBEDIENCE (1979); A. Simmons, MORAL PRINCIPLES AND POLITICAL OBLIGATION (1979); J. RAZ, THE AUTHORITY OF LAW (1979); Sartorius, *Political Authority and Political Obligation,* 67 VA. L. REV. 3 (1981).

2. R. Wolff, IN DEFENSE OF ANARCHISM (1970).

3. Here as elsewhere in this article I am assuming that the immorality of an

action, even if a necessary condition for the justice of a law prohibiting it, is never a sufficient condition.

4. The first objection is indecisive. The fact that some motives for action according to law are worse than the desire to obey may be nothing more than the ranking of evils. It may show merely that we normally regard intellectual confusion (the belief in an obligation to obey and action for it) as a lesser evil than cruelty, hatred, etc.

5. My analysis here is loose and informal. It runs parallel to the ingenious discussion of the pre-state existence of voluntary protection associations in R. Nozick's ANARCHY, STATE AND UTOPIA (1974). I do not share his picture of the working of the invisible hand, nor his understanding of people's moral rights and duties. But my argument parallels his in the emphasis on the extent to which governments do or can carry out functions which do not presuppose possession of authority.

6. In other words, I agree with R.P. Wolff's contention that sometimes one has reason to obey someone who claims authority for reasons which do not amount to submission to his authority. *See,* R. Wolff, *supra* note 2, at 15–16.

7. Finnis, *The Authority of Law in the Predicament of Contemporary Social The-ory,* 1 NOTRE DAME J. L. ETHICS & PUB. POL'Y 115 (1984).

8. *Id.* at 120.

9. J. Raz, THE AUTHORITY OF LAW, ch. 12 (1979).

10. *Id.*

11. *Id.* at 134–37.

12. *Id.* at 134–35.

13. Throughout I am using "coordination" in its ordinary signification, rather than in the narrow and artificial sense it has been given in some recent writings in game theory.

14. I discuss the issue at some length in my *Authority and Consent,* 67 VA. L. REV. 103 (1981).

8

LEGITIMATE AUTHORITY AND THE DUTY TO OBEY

Kent Greenawalt

I move from an introductory exploration of the claims of law and the nature of moral judgment to the moral reasons for obeying the law because it is the law. Do we have a good moral reason for complying with a rule because it is a valid law of the state in which we reside or are citizens? Although an overall decision whether or not to obey the law on a particular occasion will also depend on independent reasons for doing what the law prescribes and on moral reasons for noncompliance, appraising reasons for obeying the law as such is an important component of the decision.

This chapter concentrates not on substantive moral arguments but on a conceptual claim—that the concept of political authority includes the notion that those subject to such authority have a duty to obey. The chapter indicates that the conceptual claim is either wrong or not right in a way that is helpful, that it represents an unsatisfactory approach to determining the scope of a duty to obey.

After first analyzing the significance of the claim that political authority and a duty to obey are indissolubly linked, I suggest various aspects of authority and different ways in which authority may be understood. By breaking down distinguishable aspects of authority, I show that one can make sense of a concept of political authority that does not include a duty to obey. Whatever factual premises and moral arguments might be advanced in favor of including a duty to obey within the concept of political authority bear more straightforwardly on substantive reasons in favor of that duty. I conclude that concern about the concept of political authority tends to obscure rather than clarify the relevance of those arguments.

THE CLAIMED LINKAGE OF POLITICAL AUTHORITY AND THE DUTY TO OBEY AND ITS SIGNIFICANCE

Many writers on political obligation have assumed that an aspect of the concept of legitimate political authority[1] is a moral duty to obey laws issued by the authority. The idea is that one cannot acknowledge a government is legitimate and at the same time deny one has a duty to obey. Hannah Pitkin, for example, has said, "Part of what 'authority' means is that those subject to it are obligated to obey."[2] According to Joseph Raz, "legitimate authority implies an obligation to obey on the part of those subject to it."[3] Elizabeth Anscombe has written, "authority is a regular right to be obeyed in a domain of decision."[4] And Richard Flathman has suggested that if one does not understand this linkage, he does not understand the semantic rules governing the concepts of authority and law.[5]

How is this thesis to be taken? It might mean only that the definition of terms like *political authority*[6] and *legitimate government* simply includes a duty to obey. This exercise in definition is dubious but in any event, a thesis of linkage based on it would not be very interesting. What is interesting is a claim that some independent features of authority and legitimate government imply a duty to obey—that, for example, any government that is morally justified in coercing its citizens has a right to be obeyed. An example of such a claim is traditional social contract theory, which treats the right to govern and the duty to obey as arising from the same acts of consent.

Elsewhere, we inquired whether or not an aspect of law is to make a claim to obedience. Even when such claims are made, they are not necessarily morally compelling, and when they are not morally compelling, a citizen may justifiably reject them. Here the question is whether or not a citizen who acknowledges his government is generally justified in coercing its subjects must also accept a duty of obedience. Justified coercion is a minimal condition of what one means by legitimate government; the duty to obey is what follows if that duty invariably attaches to legitimate government. Doubts about the comprehensiveness of the law's claim to obedience circumscribe the likely scope of such a duty. If a good government adopts valid laws whose scope is much broader than any expected compliance, a conclusion that the government is legitimate presumably would not acknowledge a duty to obey that reaches further than official hopes about obedience.

Why would a joinder of authority and a duty to obey matter? A showing that legitimate authority and an obligation to obey are always linked would not establish that anyone actually has a duty to obey.[7] Perhaps on examination we shall find, as Robert Wolff claims,[8] that no legitimate governments exist. Nor would a linkage necessarily affect the arguments for whether people have a duty to obey; legitimate government might rest on precisely those bases commonly suggested for a duty to obey.[9] Nonetheless, the joinder could be significant in at least three different respects.

It might yield a kind of presumption about the duty to obey. Some people may implicitly acknowledge the legitimacy of their government but doubt that they have a duty to obey. Whether their coming to understand that the justification for government coercion implies a duty to obey will move them toward acceptance of the duty or toward doubt about the justifiability of the coercion may depend on the strength of their initial convictions; but if most people are quite firm in believing their governments are morally warranted in coercing, the linkage between legitimate government and the duty to obey, when recognized, will support belief in a duty to obey. In a somewhat more complex way, the linkage might have a similar effect for scholars and others who take widespread convictions on ethical questions as evidence of what is ethically correct.[10] If a duty to obey necessarily follows from legitimate government, then the belief of the great majority of people that government is justified in coercing subjects would serve to confirm the existence of the duty.[11]

A second matter of importance concerns the apparent weight of arguments for legitimate government and a duty to obey. Some claims might have much more obvious relevance for legitimate government than for a duty to obey. For example, the assertion that life would be horrible in the absence of government bears plainly on whether or not, at a minimum, the best possible form of government is legitimate. Were the linkage to duty to obey acknowledged, we could see that the reason favoring the best government's legitimacy would also be a reason for the subjects of that government having a duty to obey—a point that might not have been clear initially.

A third way in which the linkage could be important is in construing the import of voluntary undertakings by which people establish or accept institutions of authority. One source of legitimate authority, for example, is consent. We might find instances in which people rather clearly consent to a government's legitimacy without saying anything about a duty to obey. If a duty to obey is logically linked to legitimate authority, the consent to legitimacy would carry with it an implied promise to obey, much as traditional social contract theory has assumed.

Standing alone, the claim that authority and a duty to obey are linked cannot establish either that government is legitimate or that people should obey; for all the preceding reasons, however, the claim could affect our outlook on political obligation.

AUTHORITY WITHOUT A DUTY TO OBEY

In this section, I try to identify common major elements of the concept of political authority, including a duty to obey. I then inquire which of these elements are essential for any idea of legitimate government and suggest that the duty to obey is not among them.

Aspects of Political Authority

The idea of legitimate political authority is associated with at least seven elements:

1. Persons with political authority are justified in issuing certain kinds of directives to those they govern.
2. They are justified in using force to induce compliance with these directives.
3. Other persons in the society are not warranted in issuing the kinds of directives appropriate for political authority,[12] and they also lack the right to employ coercive force on behalf of their wishes.[13]

4. The governed should pay attention to the directives of the persons with authority.
5. The governed should not interfere with the exercise of force by those with authority.
6. The governed should cooperate with enforcement efforts.
7. The governed should obey the directives of those with authority.

If the question of what distinguishes a legitimate government from a well-organized band of criminals were posed, these features of legitimate authority might be mentioned.

One can sensibly distinguish a proper government from a band of robbers without conceding a duty to obey the government. Not every kind of legitimate practical authority[14] carries such a duty. In nonpolitical and imaginary political settings we can easily conceive of authority existing without such a duty. Although these settings differ from actual political societies in important respects, the general possibility of authority without a duty to obey has crucial implications for political authority as we know it.

Authority Without a Duty to Obey

Illustration 1:
Five business partners decide that spending a summer vacation together would be fun. To simplify planning and forestall undue diversion from business efforts, they assign one partner, Ann, responsibility to look into possibilities and make suggestions while the other partners concentrate on firm affairs. If a suggestion of hers appeals to the other four, that will be fine; but all understand that no one need take the vacation if he or she does not prefer it to a vacation alone.

Among the partners, Ann has authority to develop common vacation plans. Similar efforts by other partners will be inappropriate. Each partner should consider carefully any plans Ann puts forward; none need look at plans proposed by another partner in violation of their agreement. No partner need accept any of Ann's plans, and none is expected to submerge his or her own interests in a desirable vacation.[15] Although Ann's authority, unlike that of a government, involves no right to coerce, the example shows that we can speak meaningfully of practical authority when others are not under a duty to do what the person in authority suggests.

One instance of legitimate and coercive practical authority that is not accompanied by an obligation to obey arises in the relationship between parents and very young children. Parents may compel their children to do things that others may not compel them to do. Although parental authority over young children concerns the relationships of parents to outsiders, it also helps justify actions of the parent when those are challenged by the child after he or she matures.[16] If an older child expresses dismay over something his parents did when the child was young, the parents might respond, "Well, we thought that would be best and we were the ones who were supposed to decide."[17]

A still sharper illustration of a similar kind of authority occurs if Beth, with full mental capacity, authorizes Carol to do something to her later, while Beth is asleep, unconscious, or wildly irrational. Carol's authority, conferred by Beth's consent, will be exercised under circumstances in which Beth has no duty to obey because she is physically or psychologically incapable of obeying. If these illustrations involving subjects incapable of obeying or perceiving a duty to obey[18] seem too remote, I turn to practical authority over persons who can perceive duties.

Parental authority over older children is one variety of such authority. Most family upbringing links legitimate parental authority with a child's duty to obey, and children typically feel some such duty, although it usually weakens as children mature and relationships with parents become more reciprocal. Before concluding too quickly that parental relationships with older children support the linkage of authority with a duty to obey, we should consider a conceivable attitude of an older child.

Illustration 2:
Doris, a sixteen-year-old, thinks the following: My parents can tell me to do things that no one else can tell me to do. The way our society is organized, parents need to be given powers over children, and in my rational moments I don't resent the power my own parents have to influence my behavior. Since I want their love and the things they give me, and I believe lying is wrong, I usually do what they tell

me. Often I think what they say is right. Still, I have seen enough other parents and children to think that my own parents have a lot of rotten ideas about what is good for me and for others. So I really do not suppose I have some general duty to do what they tell me.

Doris recognizes the moral legitimacy of her parents' authority in a significant sense, but without conceding a moral duty to follow their directions. Although such disrespect of parental views may rarely be combined with such easy acceptance of parental authority, Doris's attitude is certainly not absurd;[19] and, although most parents aspire to greater confidence in their judgment, many families might survive tolerably well if teenage children held Doris's point of view, particularly if the children conceded the appropriateness of parent inquiry about their activities and placed a high value on telling the truth.

Is such a limited sense of authority possible in the political realm?

Illustration 3:
In a small society technology produces an amazing device that permits a user to know what changes in legal norms are warranted, to ascertain the legality of all individual behavior, and to impose appropriate civil or penal consequences. The device is subject to extreme abuse in the hands of someone untrustworthy. Members of the society agree that only one device will exist, and that all legislative, executive, and judicial functions will be concentrated in a single director, to be elected by the assembled society for a one-year term. Former directors are ineligible for the office and a new director's first job is to discover if the outgoing director has acted properly.

In these highly fanciful circumstances, an honest director would be exercising legitimate political authority. Because of the device's effectiveness, society would be viable even if citizens did not recognize any moral duty to comply with the director's rules. The people in such a society would have a clear sense of legitimate political authority without necessarily accepting a corresponding moral duty to obey the authority. In that context at least, a coherent moral view could include acknowledgment of legitimate government without acceptance of a moral duty to obey.

THE ELEMENTS OF POLITICAL AUTHORITY
AND ACTUAL SOCIETIES

Central and Peripheral Aspects of Authority

I now return, with these examples in mind, to the seven aspects of legitimate political authority that I suggested earlier. The warrant to issue certain kinds of directives is undoubtedly part of the essential core of political authority. This warrant is what has been called a "justification right"; the government asserts the justification in the face of a possible claim that it is doing something morally wrong.[20] The justified use of force to induce compliance with directives is similar, though its status is different in one respect. We could imagine a society in which human beings were so altruistic, or in which informal restraints of social opinion were so effective, that physical coercion was unnecessary. In such a society, persons with authority to issue directives for the entire society might lack justified enforcement power. This, indeed, is perhaps the most comprehensible notion of what society would be like if the state were to "wither away," as Marx supposed. Given human beings as they now are or will be in the foreseeable future, however, the authority to coerce is an essential aspect of legitimate government in a large complex society.

The notion of political authority implies some exclusivity. More than one person or organization may have authority to do something—parents, for example, share authority over their children—but to say that one person has authority to do something means that some others lack the right to do that thing.[21] To acknowledge that a government is legitimate is to concede that it may issue directives and engage in exercises of enforcement that would be inappropriate for other persons and organizations. Such an acknowledgment therefore involves acceptance of a duty not to do those things that are appropriately reserved to government officers. To this extent, the minimal notion of political authority includes a claim by the government and those who support it against usurpation of its functions by others.[22]

The first three elements of political authority, just discussed, are sufficient to differentiate a legitimate government from an invader's army of occupation[23] or an extremely powerful criminal syndicate. Because the foreign army is committing a moral wrong in trying to control people's lives, subjects have no duty to accept its use of force and are morally justified in trying to supplant it. Prudence and concern for the welfare of others may often dictate observance of the army's directives, but the subjects will not concede that their issuance is justified.

Consideration of a government's rules and noninterference with its enforcement efforts, the fourth and fifth elements of political authority, are not quite at the core of that concept as are the government's justification rights and the duty not to usurp, but imagining a concession of legitimacy that does not include them is difficult. If the enforcement efforts of political authorities were as foolproof as those of the director and his device in illustration 3, subjects would not need to regard themselves as under a *moral* duty to consider the state's rules or to refrain from interfering with enforcement. Prudence alone would dictate those actions, because disregard of the rules would lead to one's punishment; and attempted interference would be futile. Given actual circumstances, however, a person could not reasonably say that the government acts appropriately in making and enforcing rules but that he is morally free to disregard the rules and interfere with enforcement.[24] Interference, say in preventing a police arrest, is not identical to usurpation, since the interferor need not attempt to take on functions of the government; but a general privilege to interfere would not be consonant with the moral appropriateness of the enforcement efforts. Similarly, claiming that one is free not to pay any attention to the government's morally appropriate directives would be odd.

This conclusion about the duties to consider directives and not interfere with enforcement does not settle the scope of the two duties. Has one a duty to consider *all* government directives that are applicable to one's behavior, to refrain from interference in *all* situations,[25] or may these duties be more limited? My comments below with respect to a duty to obey suggest why I think only the more limited scope of these duties follows from the government's legitimacy.

Possible moral duties to cooperate in enforcement and to obey occupy a more questionable status than the duties of consideration and noninterference. If government enforcement were quite effective, the government might do without a claimed right to the help of citizens; and help may sometimes misfire or have destructive effects on relations between citizens. In a family situation, for example, a mother may discourage one son from informing on another, telling him to mind his own business, although the mother certainly would not brook one son's interference with her efforts to punish the other. Further, if enforcement were reasonably effective and citizens felt themselves to be under fairly powerful independent moral restraints from doing serious harm to their fellows, a sense of a duty to obey rules just because they issue from legitimate political authority might not be needed.[26] Thus, duties of obedience and cooperation are less central to the concept of political authority than other elements, and we can imagine acknowledgments of legitimacy that would not include them.

Factual Premises That Underlie the Claimed Linkage of Authority and the Duty to Obey

If the concept of legitimate authority does not include as a core element a duty to obey, and an acknowledgment that political authority is legitimate need not carry the assumption of such a duty, why has the linkage of political legitimacy and a duty to obey seemed so plausible? The answer lies in premises about the importance of government and the requirements of effective government and in the implications of those premises for individual duties.

The first underlying premise is that humans need government. If government were unnecessary, an idea of legitimate government might still exist, but we would be undisturbed if an account of individual duties rendered such governments highly vulnerable.

The second premise is that a sense of duty to obey is necessary to ensure the survival or effective working of legitimate government. The bare necessity of obedience itself is not sufficient to establish this premise. Even in our fanciful society governed by the director with a magical device, a fair degree of obedience would be required for society to be viable. Here, the absence of a need for a sense of moral duty to obey derives from the ability of sanctions to guarantee obedience. Some actual governments, including foreign occupation forces, may be able to terrorize the governed sufficiently to get effective obedience without a sense of duty to obey, but these governments will not be conceded legitimacy by most who attend to these matters. That some actual governments can succeed without a sense of duty to obey does not establish that legitimate governments can do so. Perhaps some of the very features that may render a government legitimate, such as a substantial degree of personal liberty, will tie the government's success to its subjects' sense of duty. And even if some legitimate governments can survive without a sense of duty, they might support a tolerable life for citizens less effectively than if a sense of duty were present.

If government is necessary for social life, if a sense of a duty to obey is necessary for legitimate government to work effectively, and if morality embodies standards that allow human beings to live tolerably well together, the conclusion follows that individuals have some duty to obey. So viewed, the linkage of legitimate political authority and a duty to obey is seen to rest on empirical premises about what is needed for effective legitimate government. The point is implicit in the discussion of Elizabeth Anscombe, who writes, "Authority arises from the necessity of a task whose performance requires a certain sort and extent of obedience on the part of those for whom the task is supposed to be done."[27]

If the crucial empirical premise behind the linkage of legitimate authority and a duty to obey concerns the need for the duty, the question immediately presents itself whether the premise is well founded and, if so, how far it reaches. Ascertaining what sorts of attitudes subjects of governments deemed legitimate actually have would be a start. If legitimate governments in stable societies survive without a wide sense of duty to obey, that would show that the obedient attitude is not always essential to the continued existence of such governments, though this attitude might still be viewed as something that will *improve* life under any legitimate government. If the obedient attitude is present in societies with legitimate governments, we could conjecture about the effects of its dissipation.

Why the Linkage of Authority and a Duty to Obey Does Not Assist in Determining the Scope of the Duty

The nature of this empirical inquiry leads us to take care about the precise nature of the attitudes necessary to effective government. Let us suppose that some sense of duty is needed for effective government. Must citizens have a sense of duty to obey all laws in every situation, or is some less inclusive sense adequate?

Someone who begins with the assumption that the duty to obey simply follows conceptually from legitimate government will suppose that any act of the legitimate government generates the duty. He may concede that the duty to obey does not attach to directives of legitimate authority insofar as neither officers nor citizens expect or hope for obedience.[28] More significantly, he may also grant that because of faulty procedures or substantive injustice, some acts of an *otherwise* legitimate government are not acts of legitimate political authority, and carry no duty to obey based on their being acts of legitimate authority. What this person will not say is that an act intended to affect behavior that derives from legitimate political authority can fail to carry a duty to obey.

Yet the empirical perspective reveals the possibility of just such a category. Some government directives, for example, certain parking regulations, that are within the realm of legitimate authority and are enforced may have their purposes adequately served without a sense of duty to obey. Once we understand the empirical underpinnings of the assertion that legitimate political authority implies a duty to obey, we see that it becomes an open question how widely that duty need be conceived.

Our examination of the claimed conceptual linkage of political authority and a duty to obey has produced some important conclusions. The conceptual linkage is not of the powerful logical sort that has been supposed. Rather, it rests on empirical premises and on a normative approach that derives duties from the necessities of social existence. Even if the linkage is accurate in the sense that any acknowledgment that a government is legitimate implies acceptance of some moral duty to obey some of its directives, the linkage does not aid us in fixing the scope of the duty.

Any assertion that an acknowledgment that a government is legitimate automatically implies a duty to obey all its directives would be patently false. Within the traditions of natural law and social contract, ample room exists for claiming that some acts of otherwise legitimate political authority are outside the scope of authority, are illegitimate, and carry no right to be obeyed. Anyone wishing to deny this conclusion must employ substantive arguments, not rely on implications of the concept of legitimate authority.[29]

Once this point is granted, we can see that asking whether a government is legitimate in general or in particular actions is hardly the most helpful way to decide the nature or scope of a duty to obey. We need rather to examine the claimed substantive reasons for obedience. Within that more fruitful inquiry, the moral status of the government may make an important difference; but it is not always determinative.

NOTES

1. Perhaps "legitimate authority" may be redundant, but I employ the phrase to make clear that I am talking about political power that is not only accepted but is normatively justified in some sense. Compare William McBride's suggestion in The "Fetishism of Illegality and the Mystifications of 'Authority' and 'Legitimacy,' " 18 *Ga. L. Rev.* 863, 874 (1984), that " 'authority' denotes nothing further than the idea of possessing the ability ('power') to coerce and of exercising that power when such possession and exercise are considered acceptable by some other person." A critic could, of course, recognize that a government had "authority" in this sense without conceding that its exercise of power was at all morally legitimate.

2. Pitkin, "Obligation and Consent—II," 60 *Am. Pol. Sci. Rev.* 39, 40 (1966).

3. Raz, "Authority and Consent," 67 *Va. L. Rev.* 103, 117 (1981).

4. Anscombe, "On the Source of the Authority of the State," 20 *Ratio* 1, 3 (1978).

5. Flathman, *Political Obligation* 89–90 (1972). See also Beran, "In Defense of the Consent Theory of Political Obligation and Authority," 87 *Ethics* 260 (1977).

6. Plainly the term *authority* must be qualified or limited in some way if a duty to obey is to be plausible, since the kind of "authority" an expert has—what has been called authority as a personal characteristic (see Anscombe, note 4 supra, at 2)—clearly involves no duty to comply with the expert's recommendations. Richard DeGeorge distinguishes executive authority from nonexecutive authority, including in the latter category epistemic authority, authority based on competence, and authority based on personal authenticity or excellence. *The Nature and Limits of Authority* 22, 42–43 (1985).

7. See Flathman, note 5 supra at 99, 104–105.

8. Wolff, *In Defense of Anarchism* (1976).

9. See A. John Simmons, *Moral Principles and Political Obligations,* 42–43 (1979).

10. Such a position is consistent with belief that the great majority of people may be mistaken concerning some moral questions.

11. One needs to say a little more about the content of the beliefs. If everyone thinks some legitimate government exists but half think only liberal democracy is legitimate and half think only communism is legitimate, the universal belief that some government is legitimate might not provide strong evidence that either liberal democracy or communism is legitimate.

12. Some kinds of directives, such as a specification of one's tax liabilities, appropriate emanate only from government sources. Other kinds of directives, such as prohibitions of willful killing, may also appropriately issue from other

sources, such as church authorities; what distinguishes political authority in these areas are directives about the methods of enforcement, including the use of coercive physical force.

13. Some forms of physical coercion are permitted to parents and others with supervisory responsibilities over children.

14. As I have already indicated (note 6 supra), to acknowledge someone as an authority in the sense of being an expert would not, of course, imply any duty to obey. What I wish to show is that even what may be called "practical authority" need not carry with it a duty to obey. Various senses of authority are perceptively explored in Raz, "Authority and Consent," 67 *Va. L. Rev.* 103, 106–118 (1981). See also R. DeGeorge, note 6 supra.

15. Someone who wants to vacation with the other partners may end up settling for a less than optimal location, but that will be because he or she prefers a joint vacation at that place to a single vacation at the most desired place.

16. These comments are meant to deflect the possible criticism that a special sense of authority is involved here, one that essentially concerns parents and outsiders, rather than the relation *between* parents and child. Clear examples of this special sense of authority are authority over zoo animals or parks. The text tries to show that parental authority over young children cannot be so reduced.

17. Of course, the existence of authority would not fully justify the parents' action if it were based on seriously faulty judgment, but part of an adequate justification would include the claim of authority, and one possible ground of complaint on the child's part would be met.

18. I draw this distinction because young children have a capacity to obey before they can perceive a duty to obey.

19. G. J. Warnock, *The Object of Morality* 44 (1971), has suggested more generally that "one may accept a rule—that is, admit that it *is* a rule and even that it is wholly proper that there should be that rule—and yet think, consistently and reasonably, that one need not comply with it."

20. See Ladenson, "In Defense of a Hobbesian Conception of Law," 9 *Phil. & Pub. Affs.* 134, 139–41 (Winter 1980); Sartorius, "Political Authority and Political Obligation," 67 *Va. L. Rev.* 3, 5 (1981); Smith, "Is There a Prima Facie Obligation to Obey the Law?" 82 *Yale L. J.* 950, 976–76 (1973). John Simmons correctly suggests that the term *right* is not required here to convey the central idea of justification. Simmons, "Voluntarism and Political Association," 67 *Va. L. Rev.* 19, 23 (1981). Compare Richard DeGeorge's distinction between performatory executive authority and imperative executive authority, note 6 supra at 63.

21. A broader sense of authority includes any legal or moral right to do something. In this sense, everyone may have authority to help the poor. But only the government may help the poor by spending money that comes from payments coerced from subjects.

22. See Sartorius, note 20 supra at 5. The generalization in the text does not establish what amounts to usurpation or whether or not what would otherwise be usurpation can be warranted if the government is ineffective. Private vigilantes might argue that private punishment is either an appropriate supplement to state activity or at least justifiable when the legitimate government performs inadequately.

23. In some circumstances, a foreign army of occupation may temporarily exercise legitimate authority, as when it has fought a just war, the government of its enemy has collapsed, and conditions are not yet propitious for creation of a new government; the legitimacy of the army's power might be recognized by some subjects of the enemy state. That is not the sort of example I have in mind in the text.

I pass over the questions raised when remnants of legitimate authority combine with an occupying power to enforce basic criminal provisions that remain unchanged.

24. See Simmons, note 20 supra at 24.

25. I mean here only whether or not there is a prima facie moral duty not to interfere in all situations. Even if such a duty existed, it might on occasion be outweighed by other considerations.

26. One can imagine, as in the family situation, a duty to obey without a duty to cooperate, but the reverse is implausible. The main purpose of most compulsory norms of criminal law is to prevent the behavior in question; enforcement against an offender is a second best alternative. If a subject has a moral duty to cooperate fully that includes turning himself in and confessing, must he not also have a duty to refrain from the behavior in the first place? And if the subject has a moral duty to *help* the government enforce the law against others, the duty's basis must be a moral responsibility to help reduce unpunished criminal behavior, which would also encompass a duty not to commit unsanctioned violations himself.

27. Anscombe, note 4 supra at 6. See also id. at 9. Anscombe apparently does not recognize the distinction I have drawn between needing obedience and needing a sense of duty to obey.

28. He might, of course, collapse this category of norms one does not have a duty to obey into a category of illegitimate norms, discussed in text, claiming that governments never legitimately adopt norms broader than the behavior they seek to control. That view is overly simplistic.

29. I do not deny the possibility that one might carefully formulate a notion of legitimate political authority such that every directive of legitimate authority would carry a duty to be obeyed. But, in that event, the concept of legitimate authority would itself have to be framed with reference to the relevant substantive arguments concerning a duty to obey.

9

PRESUMPTIVE BENEFIT, FAIRNESS, AND POLITICAL OBLIGATION

George Klosko

In this article I explore the possibility of grounding general political obligations upon the principle of fairness. Recent scholars have forcefully criticized the traditional arguments in favor of political obligation, calling into question the possibility of a general theory of obligation founded upon the assumptions of liberal political theory.[1] These scholars criticize the principle of fairness, and I will attempt to respond to their objections.[2] I am especially concerned with countering one specific argument which I call the "limiting argument," variations of which are advanced by numerous scholars, including Rawls and Nozick. Section I briefly examines the principle of fairness and presents the limiting argument. Section II counters objections to the principle, including the limiting argument, and discusses the circumstances under which the principle is able to create prima facie political obligations. Section III applies the principle to wider questions of political obligation.

I

The principle of fairness was originally formulated by H. L. A. Hart in 1955:

> [W]hen a number of persons conduct any joint enterprise according to rules and thus restrict their liberty, those who have submitted to

these restrictions when required have a right to a similar submission from those who have benefited by their submission.[3]

The main thrust of the principle is that those who benefit from the cooperative efforts of others have an obligation to cooperate as well. As analyzed by recent scholars, the principle of fairness rests upon a more general moral principle, referred to by Lyons as "the just distribution of benefits and burdens."[4] According to Rawls, "We are not to gain from the cooperative labors of others without doing our fair share."[5] As we shall see, the principle applies rather differently to cooperative schemes providing different kinds of goods, and so we must sort out different goods and consequent differences in the principle's application.

To begin with, goods provided by cooperation can be termed "excludable" or "nonexcludable." Excludable goods can be provided to some members of a given community while being denied to specified others. Familiar instances of such goods abound. For instance, A, B, C, and D can combine forces in order to dig a well for their own consumption, and deny access to the well to E. Or they can combine their resources to build an auditorium and not let others enter. Nonexcludable goods, in contrast, cannot be denied to specified others. Frequently, if provided at all, they must be provided to all members of some community. Familiar examples of nonexcludable goods are the rule of law, relief from various forms of pollution and other environmental hazards, and national defense.[6] These goods and others like them that also depend upon the cooperation of large numbers of people are often referred to as public goods. The two main features of public goods are (a) that they are nonexcludable and (b) that they depend upon the cooperation of large numbers of people.[7]

The principle of fairness applies rather clearly to cooperative schemes that provide excludable goods ("excludable schemes"). If A, B, C, and D cooperate to dig a well, for instance, others who partake of the benefits have an obligation to share the burdens. Thus the cooperators would be justified in refusing to provide benefits to E, who did not share in the labor. This would be especially clear if E had been asked to cooperate but had declined. Similarly, E would possess a clear entitlement to the labors of his fellows only if he had shared in that labor. The nature of E's expected contribution would of course depend upon the nature of the scheme in question and would vary with different sorts of schemes; it might consist, for example, in physical labor, restraints on his pattern of consumption, or financial contributions. But in general, such contributions are necessary to justify receipt of excludable goods, and it is apparent that individuals attain obligations to excludable schemes only when they actively pursue the benefits such schemes provide. There is a strong presumption that individuals should decide for themselves whether they will be forced to make sacrifices or have their liberty curtailed. Thus the decision whether E will join in digging the well should be made by E rather than by the members of the well-digging scheme. Because E can be excluded from the benefits, he incurs obligations only if he chooses not to be excluded. Excludable schemes are readily viewed as voluntary associations, membership in which has strong contractarian overtones.[8] These aspects of excludable schemes render the application of the principle of fairness relatively trouble-free.

Greater complexity is encountered when we turn to schemes providing nonexcludable goods ("nonexcludable schemes"). Because the benefits provided by such schemes are nonexcludable, individuals are no longer able to decide whether or not to receive them. Accordingly, the contractarian implications of the receipt of such benefits are blurred. Several commentators argue that because the benefits in question will be provided to E more or less regardless of what he does, receipt of the benefits does not obligate him to participate in the scheme's labors. We can refer to this as the "limiting argument," because it severely limits the principle's applicability in important ways. Rawls, for one, argues in this way. According to him, the principle of fairness entails that one is not obligated to contribute to a cooperative venture unless one "has voluntarily accepted the benefits of the arrangement or taken advantage of the opportunities it offers to further one's interests."[9] Because he is unable to identify the requisite binding actions that create general political obligations, Rawls believes that the principle of fairness does not give rise to such obligations."[10]

The principle of fairness can be used most plausibly to establish political obligations by appealing to society's provision of important public goods. But because the recipients of public goods are not free to accept or reject them, according to the limiting argument, receipt of such goods does not create obligations to help provide them. If the principle is to have important political implications, the limiting argument must be defused.

II

It seems that the force of the limiting argument can itself be limited if we look more closely at its application to public goods. But before examining this subject directly, we must establish an important preliminary point. Whether or not the principle of fairness is able to ground obligations to contribute to nonexcludable schemes, it is evident that the principle (or some functional equivalent) is necessary for the proper maintenance of such schemes. As we have noted, public goods (a) are nonexcludable and (b) require the cooperation of large numbers of people. If we assume that the cooperation in question is viewed as burdensome by those asked to cooperate and that the number of people required to provide the goods in question is sufficiently large, because the goods are nonexcludable and will be provided to individuals whether or not they cooperate, it is in their interest to enjoy them without cooperating. In other words, it is in their interest to be "free riders."

The problem of free riders—otherwise referred to as the problem of the commons, or the prisoner's dilemma—has of course been widely discussed in recent years.[11] The dilemma is clear. In a large group, if n people must cooperate for some benefit to be provided, there are two possibilities. If n others will cooperate, the benefit will be provided whether or not A cooperates. In this case it is in his interest to enjoy the benefit without sharing the burden. If n others will not cooperate, the benefit will not be provided; by cooperating A would simply bear useless burdens. Even if A were not selfish and wished to contribute his share, it would not be rational for him to do so, unless he were assured that n others would also contribute. Of course if everyone acted on the basis of this reasoning, the benefits in question would not be provided. Thus to ensure that the benefits are provided, a sufficient number of individuals must somehow be induced to cooperate. The obvious solution, as stated by Hardin, is "mutual coercion, mutually agreed upon."[12] But coercion will ensure that goods are provided only if nonagreers can be forced to cooperate, and it is not just to coerce them unless they have obligations—rooted in the principle of fairness—to cooperate.[13]

Now, according to the limiting argument, the principle of fairness does not create obligations for nonagreers to contribute to nonexcludable schemes. This conclusion is supported by a series of ingenious examples presented by Nozick. For instance, Nozick describes the case of a group of neighbors who band together and institute a public address system designed to provide the neighborhood with entertainment and other broadcasting. If there are 364 other neighbors, each of whom runs the system for one day, is A obligated to take over the broadcasts when his day comes? Nozick assumes that A has benefited from the scheme by listening to the broadcasts but would prefer not to give up a day.[14] Another example concerns a neighborhood street-sweeping association. Must A sweep the street when his turn comes, even if he does not care a great deal about clean streets? If he refuses to do so, must he "imagine dirt" as he crosses the street so as not to benefit as a free rider?[15] Nozick clearly believes that A is not obligated in cases of this sort: "One cannot, whatever one's purposes, just act so as to give people benefits and then demand (or seize) payment. Nor can a group of persons do this."[16] According to Nozick, the principle of fairness does not "serve to obviate the need for other persons' *consenting* to cooperate and limit their activities."[17] Nozick presents additional examples, but they are similar to the ones we have noted.[18]

What is striking about Nozick's examples is that they concern the provision of goods that are of relatively little value. To some extent Nozick's choice of such examples is probably rhetorical. But I think it is more than that. If we were to substitute examples of schemes providing more significant benefits, the force of Nozick's arguments would be blunted.

The principle of fairness is able to generate obligations to contribute to nonexcludable schemes if certain conditions are met. The main conditions are that the goods in question must be (i) worth the recipients' effort in providing them and (ii) "presumptively beneficial."[19] The implications of (i) will be discussed below. As for (ii), by "presumptively beneficial" goods (or presumptive goods) I mean something similar to Rawls's primary goods, "things that every man is presumed to want."[20] Since we are concerned with public goods, we can confine our attention to presumptively beneficial public goods (presumptive public goods). These are public analogues of Rawls's primary goods. Basically, such goods must be necessary for an acceptable life for all members of the community. To apply Rawls's description of primary goods, presumptive public goods are things it is supposed that all members of the community want, whatever else they want, regardless of what their rational plans are in detail.[21]

The notion of presumptive public goods is still undoubtedly unclear in various respects. But we need not attempt to explicate the precise contents of this class. Certain goods can be named that can be presumed to be necessary for an acceptable life for all members of the community. Though the number of these goods is perhaps small, such things as physical security, protection from a hostile environment, and the satisfaction of basic bodily needs appear obviously to fit the bill. For our purposes, it is not necessary to extend the list into more controversial areas. Providing presumptive public goods such as these is widely recognized as a central purpose of government.[22]

The principle of fairness applies more readily to the provision of presumptive public goods than to the provision of public goods in general. As we have noted, there is a strong presumption that individuals should decide for themselves whether they are going to be required to make sacrifices. The cooperative schemes on which we will concentrate provide public goods that are indispensable to the welfare of the community. In these cases the indispensability of the goods overrides the outsider's usual right to choose whether he wishes to cooperate.[23]

The examples discussed by Nozick concern the provision of goods that are clearly not presumptively beneficial. We can refer to goods that are of less value—goods that may be desirable but should not be viewed as essential to people's well-being—as "discretionary" goods. Nozick's presentation of the limiting argument appears to work because there is something inherently questionable about restricting an individual's liberty in order to give him something that he could easily do without, even if the benefits of receiving such goods outweigh the burdens of helping to provide them. Accordingly, if we look at similar examples, but substitute presumptive public goods, we will come to different conclusions.

In criticizing Nozick, Simmons focuses on the fact that the non-agreers in Nozick's examples do not appear to participate in the schemes in question in the proper sense.[24] Simmons writes: "Certainly, it would be peculiar if a man, who by simply going about his business in a normal fashion benefited unavoidably from some cooperative scheme, were told that he had voluntarily accepted benefits which generated for him a special obligation to do his part."[25] In his own account of the principle of fairness, Simmons attempts to overcome this difficulty by explicating the concept of "accepting" a public good in such a way that, by "accepting," the individual comes to participate in a given cooperative scheme in some meaningful sense.[26] On the whole, "accepting" excludable benefits is a less troublesome notion. In most cases this can be explicated as voluntary pursuit of given benefits. The connection between acceptance of some benefit and participation in a cooperative scheme is also generally clear here, as, by pursuing the benefit, A would seem meaningfully to participate in the scheme. Simmons's attempt to elucidate a concept of "accepting" a nonexcludable benefit that also entails meaningful participation can be read as an attempt to circumvent the limiting argument. Because of his emphasis upon participation, Simmons proposes that public goods are not "accepted" unless the acceptor has certain attitudes and beliefs, and especially unless he is aware of the status of the benefits as products of a cooperative scheme.[27] These aspects of Simmons's position need not be discussed here. I believe that they are questionable, and they have been criticized before.[28] For our purposes it is sufficient to note that Simmons's focus on the bystander's degree of participation appears to be misplaced. A more important aspect of the principle is the magnitude (or lack thereof) of the benefits provided. As the following examples will show, as long as the benefits in question are sufficiently large, someone "who by simply going about his business in a normal fashion" benefits unavoidably from a cooperative scheme does indeed incur an obligation to contribute to the scheme.

Example 1. Let us assume that A lives in a small territory, X, that is surrounded by hostile territories, the rulers of which declare their intention of massacring the X-ites. Accordingly, the X-ites band together for their joint protection. Since the circumstances in which they find themselves are similar to those the Israelis believe themselves to confront, let us assume that they institute measures similar to those in practice in Israel: compulsory military service for men and women; mandatory service in the reserves, including a substantial period of yearly active duty until a relatively advanced age; provisions for rapid mobilization of reservists; and so forth. Because these provisions are obviously burdensome to all affected, A, who would prefer to go about his business as usual, decides not to comply. Under these circumstances, assuming that a number of X-ites sufficient to ensure the safety of X and its inhabitants do comply, A would obviously be a free rider. Though the mutual-protection scheme has simply sprung up around him, there can be little doubt that he has an obligation to do his part. Now, the circumstances sketched here do not rule out the possibility of other factors in A's situation that would justify his failure to comply. For instance, A might be a conscientious objector, or his health might not be equal to the rigors of military service. However, these circumstances do not rule out an obligation to serve. Obligations are not necessarily binding; they can be overridden by conflicting moral claims. The circumstances sketched in this example present A with a prima facie obligation to do his part, which, in the light of the gravity of the situation indicated, would seem likely to be overridden by only the most stringent extenuating circumstances.

Example 2. Here we can consider less extreme circumstances. Let us assume that the territory of Y is beset by severe air pollution, generated primarily by automobiles. People with certain lung conditions already find it difficult to breathe, and if things keep up, the more general population will soon be affected similarly. The Y-ites therefore band together to impose various restrictions on driving privileges and decree that all automobiles must be modified to cut down on pollution. Again, because these restrictions are burdensome, B would prefer not to comply. But again, assuming that a sufficient number of his fellows do comply, if he does not, he will be a free rider. Under these circumstances, B incurs an obligation to comply. Though, again, this obligation could be overridden by a variety of mitigating circumstances, the obligation is no less real for that.

Example 3. Let us assume that the territory of Z is in an arid region and so heavily dependent upon irrigation for its agriculture. Let us also assume that all inhabitants of the territory depend upon agriculture for their livelihood, either directly or indirectly: some are farmers; others work in food-processing facilities; others sell things to the farmers or food processors; and so forth. Finally, let us assume that Z is beset by drought and that the irrigation system will not be able to supply enough water to save the year's crop unless the community's water consumption is drastically curtailed. Accordingly, the Z-ites band together to draw up a set of guidelines restricting the use of water: no lawn watering, no car washing, showers instead of baths, dishwashing once a day, and so forth. C would of course prefer not to comply, but again, assuming that a sufficient number of Z-ites do comply, if he does not, he will be a free rider. Again, I think it is clear that C has an obligation to comply, though this obligation too can be overridden by other factors.

In all three examples, the goods in question satisfy both conditions (i) and (ii) above. They are (i) worth their costs to their recipients as well as (ii) presumptively beneficial. In regard to condition (i), the benefits and burdens under consideration are those of the relevant community as a whole, rather than of each particular member.[29] Many important cooperative schemes involve complex forms of cooperation, in which the burdens borne by different individuals may differ appreciably. The principle of fairness requires not that the burdens people bear be identical, but, in Lyons's words, only that they be "associated as integrated elements in a co-operative scheme."[30] In an army, to take an obvious example, those individuals who are killed or severely wounded in action bear heavier burdens than other soldiers, some of whom may have relatively pleasant duties. But this in itself would not free the former from their obligation to serve, as long as there were good grounds for assigning both groups their tasks and the assignments were fair.[31]

These points can be illustrated by examples. A situation in which condition (i) would appear not to be satisfied is the account of the city of Melos described in Book V of Thucydides, from which I extrapolate certain details. Let us say that the Melians are willing to fight for their freedom, which is a supreme good in their eyes (Thucydides V. 112). They are confronted, however, by an irresistible Athenian force, and if they resist and are defeated, they are all likely to be killed (V. 101–3). Under circumstances such as these, the Melians could organize measures for their defense. But because these measures are highly unlikely to succeed, I do not believe that the individual citizen has an obligation to cooperate. Along similar lines, in 1836 the defenders of the Alamo were surrounded by a powerful Mexican army and asked to surrender. The defenders of course decided to resist and were killed. Under these circumstances, I do not believe that the group can obligate a dissenting individual to cooperate in resistance. Here too the benefits to be gained by successful resistance are (we will assume) presumptive, but the chances of success are so slight that the burdens of cooperating outweigh them. It is interesting to note that Colonel Travis, the defenders' commanding officer, did not require that his men stay and resist. He offered anyone who wished to escape the opportunity to do so. Hopeless causes require volunteers.

Cases such as Melos and the Alamo should be distinguished from more complex cases in which benefits outweigh burdens for the relevant community, but not for particular individuals. Thus in a military campaign it may be necessary to sacrifice some soldiers for the good of the larger unit. As long as the military enterprise as a whole satisfies conditions (i) and (ii), the immediate benefit of this unfortunate group's mission is sufficiently large, and the members of the group are chosen fairly, the circumstances would not affect their obligation to serve.

A nonmilitary example concerns the enormous benefits that would result if scientists were allowed to experiment upon human beings, especially unwilling ones. Let us assume that the resulting benefits would be nonexcludable and that all members of society would benefit equally. Though the benefits in question here are presumptive, the costs involved are so severe as to make one question the desirability of instituting the necessary measures. However, if we were to alter the circumstances of this example so that the members of the community were faced with some terrible plague, which threatened to kill a high percentage of them and which also could probably be averted if scientists were able to experiment upon unwilling human subjects, then perhaps the necessary measures should be undertaken and individuals would be obligated to comply. (This case suggests institutions not unlike those described by Shirley Jackson in "The Lottery.")

As these examples suggest, there are serious practical difficulties to be overcome in deciding whether condition (i) is satisfied in any given case. These difficulties can be lessened to some extent by the requirement that for condition (i) to be satisfied, the benefits must obviously outweigh the burdens (for the community as a whole, and so for the typical individual). Since individuals bear significant burdens simply by being required to comply with cooperative schemes, the obligation to comply should cease when the burdens themselves merely approach the benefits. The question of assessing the relative magnitudes of benefits and burdens is pursued in Section III, though numerous aspects of this complex subject cannot be discussed in this article. We will set such problems aside, under the assumption that the overall position is clear.

I conclude, then, that if conditions (i) and (ii)—and the condition mentioned in the next paragraph—are met, then individuals have obligations to contribute to cooperative schemes that provide nonexcludable goods. Examples 1–3 show that an individual's degree of participation in a scheme does not necessarily affect his obligations towards it. Nor does it seem that Nozick and other proponents of the limiting argument are correct in asserting that the individual incurs obligations only by consenting to schemes.

Before moving on to the next section, we should note an additional condition that schemes must satisfy. Because obligations to support co-operative schemes are grounded upon a broad principle of the fair distribution of burdens and benefits, they hold only as long as the costs and benefits of the schemes in question are fairly distributed.[32] We can say that a scheme in which this condition is met passes the "fair distribution" test and so is "fair." Because of the complexity of the distribution of benefits and burdens in actual schemes, however, it may be difficult to say whether any given scheme passes this test. Similarly, it may be difficult to say at exactly what point the pattern of distribution in a given scheme moves from being fair to being unfair. But it is clear that at the point at which a given scheme begins to fail the test, individuals' obligations to it are dissolved.[33]

III

Considered as a basis for political obligation the principle as discussed so far has an obvious weakness. Though it obligates individuals to contribute to the provision of presumptive public goods, it does not create obligations to help provide discretionary public goods. Though repairing roads, to take an obvious example, has been a function of governments for thousands of years, the principle of fairness, as formulated so far, does not obligate individuals to do (or to pay) their fair shares in this regard.[34] So we must consider whether the principle can be extended to cover discretionary public goods as well.[35]

One conclusion that might be drawn from our discussion is that the principle of fairness justifies obligations to support only governments providing only presumptive public goods, that is, minimalist governments. This is similar to the conclusion reached by Nozick in *Anarchy, State, and Utopia*, though his means of getting there are quite different. I believe, however, that the principle can establish wider obligations. There are many difficult problems connected with these extended obligations that cannot be discussed in detail here. The remainder of this article will present what I believe is a defensible approach.

One possible solution to our problem is as follows. Though the members of scheme X, which provides a single discretionary public good, cannot demand that A contribute, perhaps if the functions of X were multiplied so that it provided numerous discretionary goods, at some point A would become obligated. The intuition here is that, though by definition no single discretionary good is presumptively beneficial, when a large number of such goods are provided together, the package as a whole becomes presumptively beneficial. Though clean streets or public parks or public transportation are not each by themselves presumptive public goods, through some transformation of differences of quantity into differences of quality the collection of such goods becomes presumptively beneficial. I do not believe that this approach is promising. First, it is unlikely that we would be able to elucidate the requisite mechanism of transformation. More important, if A cannot justly have his liberties infringed upon by being obligated to contribute to the provision of one good he could do without, it seems tyrannical to infringe upon his liberties still more by demanding that he contribute to other similar goods in addition to that one. Though the package of discretionary public goods provided by a modern government might make A's life much easier or more pleasant, the fact that he could do without them seems crucial here.

A more promising solution lies in extending the functions of cooperative schemes that have been set up to provide presumptive goods. Nozick's examples show that a group of individuals cannot band together to provide some discretionary public good and then declare that A is also obligated to contribute. Even if the principle cannot obligate individuals to support schemes that furnish *only* discretionary goods, however, Nozick has not shown that it cannot generate obligations to help provide discretionary goods if a given scheme also provides presumptive goods. There are significant differences between the initial infringement upon A's liberty when he is obligated to help provide presumptive goods and the added infringement when he is obligated to help with discretionary goods as well.

In regard to the provision of discretionary public goods, we can divide recipients into two classes: those for whom it is and those for whom it is not the case that the added benefits received outweigh the added burdens of cooperating. Obviously, if members of the second group can be shown to have obligations to contribute, then the same is true of members of the first. So in the following discussion I concentrate on members of the second group.

Now it is at first sight unclear that these individuals have such obligations. As we have noted above, if a given scheme fails to pass the fair distribution test, the individual's obligations to it no longer hold. Let us assume that B, C, and D, who have banded together to provide presumptive public goods, decide also to provide a discretionary public good. In such a case we can presume that they benefit from their added cooperation. Thus if the added cooperation required of A is not beneficial to him, the cooperative scheme cannot be fair, and he should not be obligated to cooperate.[36]

It seems, however, that additional factors should be considered. The case discussed in the previous paragraph concerns *added* infringement, rather than initial infringement. In cases of added infringement, the problem is not to explain why A should contribute to a scheme that does not (yet) command his support, but rather why he should make additional contributions to a scheme to which he is already obligated.[37] For the obligations already imposed on A to be justified, it must have been shown that the scheme in question has a legitimate claim to his support. For A not to be obligated to cooperate in this additional task, then, it must be possible to demonstrate that because the scheme has taken on this added task, participation in it will no longer be beneficial to A, or that the scheme has become sufficiently unfair to suspend his obligations.

In the kind of case under consideration, the additional benefits A receives are part of a package of benefits that scheme X provides, some components of which he cannot do without. We saw above that if X provides presumptive public goods, the indispensability of the goods overrides A's usual right to decide for himself whether he wishes to accept the benefits and burdens of cooperating with X. I see no reason why this set of circumstances is overturned by the fact that X has also undertaken to supply discretionary public goods, unless it can be shown that because of the assumption of these added functions, cooperation with X will no longer benefit A, or that because of these added functions the scheme is no longer fair.

Showing the unfairness of the scheme in such cases does not promise to be easy. The task is not to show that if A is asked to contribute to a given discretionary good his added burdens would outweigh his added benefits or that in regard to this particular good the scheme is unfair. The benefits and burdens associated with X are packages, and ordinarily it will be difficult clearly to distinguish the added burdens required by a given discretionary good from the existing burdens required by the presumptive goods.[38] Thus it must be shown that if X takes on this added function, the scheme as a whole will no longer satisfy the requisite conditions.

It seems, then, that if it can be shown that X is justified in infringing upon A's liberty by providing him with presumptive public goods, it will be difficult to demonstrate that A is not obligated to undertake the added burdens associated with the provision of discretionary goods. Obviously, it will be easier for proponents of X to justify commanding the support of individuals like A if the discretionary goods X provides are limited to those (a) that are clearly in the interest of everyone and (b) the benefits and burdens of which tend to fall out fairly.[39]

We are left with the following position: If A is obligated to contribute to the provision of some presumptive public good(s) supplied by scheme X, then he is also obligated to support X's provision of discretionary public goods *a, b, c,* and so forth, unless it can be shown that his costs in cooperating with X outweigh his benefits, or that X is unfair.

The position sketched here can be further supported if we turn briefly to the question of placing the burden of proof in the cases under consideration. Because of our general belief that individuals should not have obligations imposed upon them against their wills, there is a strong presumption that in all cases in which a nonagreer is confronted with obligations, the scheme's members must show that the goods produced are presumptive, the (typical) nonagreer's gains would outweigh his losses, and the scheme is fair. The nonagreer did not ask to join the scheme; he can be presumed not to be obligated to it, unless its members can justify their demands. The presumption here is consistent with our discussion so far. In regard to excludable schemes, the placement of the burden of proof is not ordinarily a pressing issue. In general, A's obligation to such a scheme depends upon his voluntary pursuit of the benefit it provides. We can assume that he will pursue a given benefit only when he believes that it outweighs the accompanying burden and he also believes that the scheme is fair. We have seen the conditions that nonexcludable schemes must satisfy. It seems that in general proponents of such schemes would be able to meet their burden of proof. As we have noted, A will be obligated to support scheme X only when it provides goods that are presumptively beneficial. The importance of such goods should be recognized by agreers and nonagreers alike. The provision of even presumptive public goods does not create obligations unless the (average) individual's benefits outweigh his burdens in cooperating and the scheme is fair. Here too, the importance of presumptive goods should lessen the difficulty of demonstrating that they justify their costs, while the nature of such goods, especially their being characterized by nonrival consumption, should lessen the difficulty of showing that they are distributed fairly. Still, in any given case, the burden of proof rests upon the scheme's members.

Nozick appears to agree with this placement of the burden of proof, though he does not mention presumptive goods or the need to show that schemes are fair. He writes: "At the very least one wants to build into the principle of fairness the condition that the benefits to a person from the actions of the others are greater than the costs of doing his share."[40] Nozick's language suggests that a scheme's members must show that the benefits outweigh the costs—not that an individual A whose support the members demand must show that they do not.

The cases examined in the two previous paragraphs concern *initial* infringements upon A's liberty. In each of these cases A is asked to support a scheme to which he is not already obligated, and the burden of proving that the scheme is presumptive, beneficial, and fair falls upon its supporters. However, when we turn to cases of *added* infringement the burden of proof shifts. Whereas, in our previous cases, A can be presumed not to be obligated unless the scheme's members can show that he is, in cases of added infringement A can be presumed to be obligated unless he can show that he is not. Though X has undertaken to perform additional functions, it still supplies a package of goods some components of which are presumptively beneficial. Thus we can presume that A is still obligated to X. Moreover, for A to have incurred his original obligations to X, its proponents must have been able to demonstrate that X satisfies the necessary conditions. Their arguments can be presumed to stand, unless it can be shown that the relevant circumstances have changed. Because the proponents can be presumed to have met their burden of proof and A is still presumed to be obligated, it is incumbent upon him to show that the nature of the scheme has changed in important respects and that because of this, the presumption of obligation no longer holds. Unless A can satisfy both of these conditions, his obligation to X remains.

Therefore, in order for A, who is obligated to scheme X, which provides presumptive goods, not to be obligated to do his share in helping X to provide additional, discretionary goods, it must be possible to demonstrate that if X assumes these added functions, it will no longer satisfy the requisite conditions. Moreover, not only must it be possible to show this, but the burden of showing it rests upon A.

Modern societies are of course enormously complex, with governments that undertake wide ranges of discretionary functions, not all of which meet the criteria discussed above. But there can be little doubt that many discretionary functions do meet them. Among such functions are tasks we have come to expect that governments perform—for example, support of transportation and communication, regulation of health and safety, provision of parks and recreation facilities, and public education. Thus if the principle of fairness does not create obligations to support everything that modern governments do, it does appear to create obligations for most citizens to support an important range of functions that we have come to associate with good government.

NOTES

I wish to thank Michael J. Smith and the editors of *Philosophy & Public Affairs* for valuable criticisms and suggestions.

1. A. J. Simmons, *Moral Principles and Political Obligations* (Princeton: Princeton University Press, 1979); C. Pateman, *The Problem of Political Obligation* (New York: Wiley, 1979); also J. Rawls, *A Theory of Justice* (Cambridge: Harvard University Press, 1971), pp. 113–14.

2. Simmons, *Moral Principles and Political Obligations*, chap. 5; Pateman, *Problem of Political Obligation*, pp. 121–29. (Pateman refers to the argument based on the principle of fairness as the "benefits argument.") For Rawls's criticism, see below. Important discussions of the principle of fairness are found in Rawls, *Theory of Justice*, secs. 18 and 52; Rawls, "Legal Obligation and the Duty of Fair Play," in *Law and Philosophy*, ed. S. Hook (New York: New York University Press, 1964); R. Arneson, "The Principle of Fairness and Free-Rider Problems," *Ethics* 92 (1982); R. Nozick, *Anarchy, State, and Utopia* (New York: Basic Books, 1974), pp. 90–95; D. Lyons, *Forms and Limits of Utilitarianism* (Oxford: Oxford

University Press, 1965), pp. 161–77. For further references, see G. Klosko, "The Principle of Fairness and Political Obligation," *Ethics* 97 (1987).

3. H. L. A. Hart, "Are There Any Natural Rights?" *Philosophical Review* 64 (1955): 185.

4. Lyons, *Forms and Limits of Utilitarianism*, p. 164.

5. Rawls, *Theory of Justice*, p. 112; the underlying moral principle is analyzed by Arneson, "Principle of Fairness."

6. The dividing line between excludable and nonexcludable goods is of course rough. Many familiar goods that are generally regarded as nonexcludable (e.g., access to public roads and sidewalks) could conceivably be denied to specified people. However, in cases in which denying access would be prohibitively expensive or inconvenient, the goods in question should be viewed as nonexcludable.

7. Other features of public goods, especially "nonrival consumption," are of less immediate concern; on public goods, see E. and J. Browning, *Public Finance and the Price System* (New York: Macmillan, 1979), pp. 21–24; M. Olson, *The Logic of Collective Action* (Cambridge: Harvard University Press, 1971), pp. 14–15, with numerous references. Throughout I assume that public goods are produced by "large" groups; in Olson's terminology, in such groups the contribution of any given member does not perceptibly affect the burdens or benefits of the other members (*Logic of Collective Action*, chap. 1). See also J. Buchanan, "Ethical Rules, Expected Values, and Large Numbers," *Ethics* 76 (1965).

8. But as Simmons shows, the principle of fairness does not collapse into a principle of contract (*Moral Principles and Political Obligations*, pp. 126–27).

9. Rawls, *Theory of Justice*, pp. 111–12.

10. Rawls, *Theory of Justice*, pp. 113–16: similarly Nozick, *Anarchy, State, and Utopia*, p. 95; F. Miller and R. Sartorius, "Population Policy and Public Goods," *Philosophy & Public Affairs* 8 (1979): 166; N. Bell, "Nozick and the Principle of Fairness," *Social Theory and Practice* 5 (1978).

11. It is discussed in regard to the principle of fairness by Arneson, "Principle of Fairness."

12. G. Hardin, "The Tragedy of the Commons," *Science*, n.s. 162 (1968); Buchanan, "Ethical Rules."

13. I do not of course wish to rule out the possibility that some other moral principles could create such obligations. Questions of coercion will not be discussed here. I assume that if nonagreers have obligations to cooperate, at least some of which correspond to commonly recognized political obligations, some coercion is justified.

14. Nozick, *Anarchy, State, and Utopia*, pp. 93–94.

15. Nozick, *Anarchy, State, and Utopia*, p. 94

16. Nozick, *Anarchy, State, and Utopia*, p. 95.

17. Nozick, *Anarchy, State, and Utopia*, p. 95; Nozick's emphasis.

18. Cf. Simmons's similar examples in *Moral Principles and Political Obligations*, pp. 133–35.

19. The approach developed here is first suggested in Klosko, "Principle of Fairness." An additional condition is that the overall distribution of benefits and burdens in any given scheme must be fair; this is discussed briefly below. The complexities here will be set aside except where they are unavoidable.

20. Rawls, *Theory of Justice*, p. 62.

21. Rawls, *Theory of Justice*, p. 92.

22. The identification of certain goods as presumptively beneficial depends upon at least a minimal background of suitable values and beliefs. The question of deciding whether all members of a given community *actually* benefit from a given good raises severe problems that cannot be discussed here. In general, the criterion to be employed is a rough standard of "reasonable" beliefs. To say that good G is essential to community C is tantamount to saying that there are strong, reasonable grounds for believing that the members of C regard (or should regard) G as necessary for acceptable lives. One cannot rule out the possibility that because of unusual beliefs (and other extenuating factors), certain members of C might find G of considerably less value. In cases in which it could not be shown that a given good benefits a particular individual to the requisite extent, he would be freed from obligations he would otherwise have. The specific factors involved in such cases, however, will generally be so peculiar as to confirm the presumption of benefit in more usual cases. For some suggestions bearing on these problems, see the remarks below in Section III concerning burden of proof.

23. Strong evidence that the obligations discussed below arise from the principle of fairness and not from some other moral principle is the connection between the obligations A incurs and the behavior of *others*. Fairness obligations are distinctive in that they stem from the behavior of others, as opposed to the performances of the individual himself that are generally necessary to ground other obligations. (The need for such performances provides the basis for the limiting argument.) Because the questions discussed in this article concern "political obligation" as traditionally regarded, I see no need to confine the term "obligation" to self-imposed moral requirements; see R. B. Brandt, "The Concepts of Obligation and Duty," *Mind* 73 (1964): 384–93. Cf. Pateman, *Problem of Political Obligation*, pp. 28–30 and passim; also H. Beran, "Ought, Obligation and Duty," *Australasian Journal of Philosophy* 50 (1972). Excellent general discussions of obligation may be found in Brandt, "Concepts of Obligation and Duty," and Simmons, *Moral Principles and Political Obligations*, chap. 1. Cf. the discussion of people's attitudes towards various obligations to Klosko, "Principle of Fairness."

24. Simmons, *Moral Principles and Political Obligations*, p. 122.

25. Simmons, *Moral Principles and Political Obligations*, p. 131.

26. Simmons, *Moral Principles and Political Obligations*, pp. 129–36.

27. Simmons, *Moral Principles and Political Obligations*, pp. 131–32.

28. Arneson, "Principle of Fairness," p. 228; G. Kavka, review of *Moral Principles and Political Obligations* by A. J. Simmons, *Topoi* 2 (1983): 228.

29. Many problems can arise in defining the community relevant to the provision of particular benefits. These must be set aside. In general, we can assume that a given community can be identified as the collection of individuals who benefit directly from the cooperative scheme in question. By "directly" here, I mean in contrast to various "spillover" benefits that often unavoidably affect other parties. For instance, the existence of law and order in community P could well be construed as beneficial to the inhabitants of neighboring community Q, in that Q is freed from certain problems associated with bordering upon an anarchical society. (I borrow this example from the Ph.D. dissertation of Scott Lowe [University of Virginia, 1986].) Interesting questions could be raised about whether the communities discussed in this article must be antecedently identifiable as such, without reference to the provision of public goods. These issues cannot be explored here.

30. Lyons, *Forms and Limits of Utilitarianism*, p. 164.

31. Lyons, *Forms and Limits of Utilitarianism*, pp. 164–77.

32. This is emphasized by Rawls (*Theory of Justice*, pp. 111–12, 342–43); see Simmons, *Moral Principles and Political Obligations*, pp. 109–14.

33. Pateman's criticisms of the principle center upon the unfairness of the distribution of important goods in existing societies (*Problem of Political Obligation*, pp. 121–29). Her arguments require the establishment of controversial factual claims, whereas I do not believe that the factual issues bear directly upon the theoretical validity of the principle—unless one were to argue that, in principle, no society could satisfy the fair distribution test. Thus though Pateman's arguments suggest that the overall distribution of presumptive public goods is unjust to certain groups, especially minorities and the poor, I do not believe that she has shown that the overall distribution in most societies is so unfair as to dissolve all obligations. Similarly, even if she were able to show that certain individuals are treated so unfairly in existing societies as to dissolve their obligations, this would not necessarily entail that the overall distribution of presumptive public goods is so unfair that obligations sufficiently widespread to satisfy Simmons's criterion of "generality" (*Moral Principles and Political Obligations*, pp. 55–56) would not remain.

34. This important objection was first brought to my attention by Brian Barry.

35. On reasons for regarding the repair of roads as nonexcludable, see note 6

above. Because the other examples discussed in this section are similar, the relevant qualifications need not be added in regard to each.

36. A cooperative scheme can be unjust for reasons other than lack of fairness in the distribution of benefits and burdens, e.g., if it requires the commission of injustice, as for example in a gang of thieves. Or a scheme can be unfair even if each member's participation benefits him. This would hold if some members benefited much more than others. In the interest of clarity, I avoid such complexities in the subsequent discussion.

37. The temporal language used throughout the discussion here should be taken to indicate logical rather than temporal relationships.

38. There are exceptions here, especially cases in which A is asked to undertake particular tasks, generally manual labor, associated with the provision of particular goods. Not only are burdens of this sort easily distinguished from other components of one's package of burdens, but they are particularly onerous in that they are generally comprised of labor that many people find unpleasant (e.g., sweeping streets, mowing lawns)—i.e., that verges on forced labor—and also disrupt people's normal routines. Thus it is not surprising that the examples presented by Nozick and other opponents of the principle often entail burdens of this sort (see also note 18 above).

39. Enormous gray areas are encountered in the provision of discretionary public goods. Because such goods are not presumptively beneficial, they are likely to be viewed quite differently by different members of society, and many familiar discretionary goods benefit some members of society more than others. The formidable difficulties associated with determining (1) exactly what goods should be supplied and (2) exactly how they should be supplied in those common cases in which there are possible alternatives, cannot be discussed here. It should be noted, however, that the procedures through which such decisions are made must be fair to all participants.

40. Nozick, *Anarchy, State, and Utopia*, p. 94.

10

LEGAL THEORY AND THE CLAIM OF AUTHORITY

Philip Soper

I. INTRODUCTION

The Thesis

In the first part of this article I provide a conceptual account of the claim of authority: what do we typically mean when we make such claims? In the second part, I consider the implications of this account for certain standard models of law, in particular those forms of legal positivism that insist that a theory of law must include a description of the normative claims made by those who accept or enforce the legal system.[1]

The general thesis I shall defend is that the standard claim of authority within legal systems is inconsistent with the basic tenet of positivism. Legal officials claim what positivism denies—namely, that there is a necessary connection between law and morality. Thus, even if positivism is true, insiders in their capacity as legal officials will act as if positivism were false. Put another way, if positivism correctly completes its project of depicting the normative claims that officials make for law, then the model that emerges will be one in which the "essence" of positivism (the denial of a necessary connection between law and morality) is incompatible with the "essence" of law (a belief in just such a connection).

Preliminaries

I am not sure that the concept of authority I defend will seem controversial. Indeed, the interesting aspects of the thesis, in my view, are its consequences rather than its inherent contestability. But if I am wrong in this assessment, I do not know how I could shore up the argument to convince someone who finds it implausible. The argument is basically an empirical one about what a careful observer of the phenomenon of legal life will see. As in all such cases, it is hard to know what to say to someone who just doesn't see it that way. Continued disagreement, it seems, could only be resolved by further examples from legal life and further attempts to see why different perceptions of the same phenomenon persist.

I said that my claim is primarily an empirical one. That characterization seems to commit me to the view that one can separate the conceptual or descriptive part of an inquiry (what do we mean when we claim authority?) from the normative part (how are such claims justified?). This separation, common to much of the literature, is thought by many today to be suspect.[2] As will become clear, I too think that the separation is useful at best only as an aid in understanding a concept whose conceptual and normative dimensions are essentially connected.

Keeping the connections in mind can help resolve disagreements over both the descriptive and the normative issues. Thus a descriptive thesis about what it means to assert authority that has the consequence of making it very difficult ever to justify such assertions is for that very reason suspect. But the converse is also true. A thesis about how to justify claims of authority may be uncontroversial precisely because it is based on a watered-down and inaccurate view of what we mean when we make such claims. In fact, the account I shall defend differs from recent discussions of authority and its justification in just this respect: recent discussions concentrate primarily on the problem of justification and suggest solutions that easily solve that problem, but at the cost of distorting the typical claims we make when we assert authority. I shall defend what seems to me a more accurate conceptual account, even though I do so at the admitted cost of thereby exacerbating the problem of justification.

Consequences

It may be helpful to begin with a preview of the second half of the paper—with the implications of the general thesis, rather than its defense. One consequence is this: if the thesis is true, it is no longer possible to pursue the question of the connection between law and morality as simply a conceptual matter. Conceptual or descriptive analysis has been and, with a few exceptions, remains the dominant approach in legal theory. Most positivists assume that we can tell simply as a matter of linguistic analysis or sociological observation that law and morality are not necessarily connected. If the thesis is correct, this approach fails because it produces a concept of law that is inconsistent with the concept used by insiders. Conceptual analysis cannot resolve this dispute, but can only confirm *that the dispute exists*. The corollary of this conclusion is that further disagreement between positivists and insiders about the connection between law and morality makes sense only as a dispute within political theory: we must confront directly the claim that insiders make about the moral value of law and show either that it is or that it is not a valid claim—as a matter of substantive moral philosophy.

There is a second consequence of the thesis. Suppose that I am right about the typical posture of the law when it claims authority and that one result, as suggested, is that we must evaluate this claim on its merits as a matter of political theory. Philosophers, of course, have been doing that for a long time, even if legal positivists have not. The currently fashionable conclusion seems to be that there is no general obligation to obey the law, no general connection between the existence of law and its moral relevance to decisions about what to do.[3] The problem is that this conclusion of political philosophy is also at odds with the typical claim of insiders. The claim of authority that I shall describe and defend is remarkably resistant to, one might even say blissfully oblivious of, the debates within political theory about whether law obligates just in virtue of its existence. Insiders continue to claim that law always morally obligates, whatever political theorists say.

This resistance of the practice of insiders to the critique of the philosopher points to the major unresolved problem in the current literature—that of explaining how theory is related to the data it attempts to explain. In ethics, this problem appears in the question of how intuitions are related to the moral theory that is used to evaluate or justify them: where these do not coincide, does one change the intuition or the moral theory? In metaethics the question is what to do if the claim about the meaning of a moral term is inconsistent with the moral language that people actually use: Does one change one's language? Or does one continue to make the moral claims and tell the philosopher that he is wrong—the meaning he assigns to the term is so far from coinciding with the practice that it simply is not the same term? Coherence seems to require that one give some account of this relation between data and theory and try to harmonize them. Either theory controls, or the data control, or, as I think is now increasingly recognized, both interact in some mutually dependent way that represents at least a temporary coherence or unity of thought.

Apply these remarks to the present thesis. If theory controls, and the conclusion fashionable among philosophers is correct, then insiders should modify their claims: the claim that law creates obligations just in virtue of its existence should be qualified to allow for exceptions where sound political theory shows no obligation results—for example, laws that are very unjust or otherwise misguided or pointless in particular circumstances. On the other hand, if the data control, and it is true, as the thesis asserts, that insiders persist in their claims about the obligatory force of law despite all the (recent) advice of moral philosophers to the contrary, then it is the fashionable conclusion of the moral philosopher that is wrong, and we need to think again about how to justify the view that law always obligates—a view that has, after all, been endorsed by such diverse, if old-fashioned, thinkers as Plato, Kant, and Hobbes. A third possibility is to deny that either data or theory has a veto power over the other, and to look instead for some way of reconciling the more extreme positions of both: philosophers should try harder to justify the pervasive claims that are made for the moral force of law; and law, in turn, should relax the claims it makes by, for example, voiding convictions where the laws that are broken fail to satisfy the conditions for imposing moral obligation.

Of course there are other possible explanations for the continued discrepancy between what legal officials claim and what philosophers suggest they are entitled to claim. The cynic will observe that persons interested in maintaining power are likely to claim justifications even if there is no basis for such claims. But this explanation requires an assumption of cynicism that neither I nor the legal theorists I have in mind make. The question is not the psychological one of what might motivate people to claim more than they can justify, for that begs the question: the issue is whether the claim *is* justified. The discrepancy arises because the typical attitude of the insider is that law obligates just in virtue of its existence. That belief, not well thought out, not very self-conscious about its moral assumptions, is the datum that conflicts with and is resistant to the moral philosopher's fashionable conclusion.[4]

Reactions

So much for the thesis and its general consequences for both legal and political theory. Consider now two possible reactions to the thesis that will help locate it in relation to other strands of thought in contemporary legal theory. One reaction to the claim about what people mean when they assert legal authority is that it is obvious and does not require argument. That conclusion, for example, seems to be Ronald Dworkin's. In *Law's Empire* Dworkin takes it for granted that the concept of law as used by insiders purports to justify state coercion on the basis of past political decisions;[5] he then tries to show what theory of adjudication is necessary in order to make plausible this claimed connection between past facts and the justified use of force. The thesis I shall defend differs in two ways from the one assumed by Dworkin. First, I shall offer some evidence for the thesis, rather than simply assume it to be true. Second, the claim I think insiders make about the justification of state coercion is not contingent on getting the theory of adjudication correct. Dworkin's theory of adjudication, after all, is controversial. If his theory of adjudication—or any other—were an essential link in the connection between state decisions and justified coercion, the link would often not exist and the claim of justification would be false. In contrast, the claim of authority I think insiders make does not depend on getting the theory of adjudication correct, any more than it depends on legislators getting the content of the law correct: insiders, to be sure, try to get both things right; but they claim that their decrees obligate even if they turn out to be wrong in either of these respects. Dworkin, in short, is right about the connection insiders assert between law and morality; he is wrong about (or ignores) what insiders claim is necessary to maintain that connection.[6]

A second possible reaction to the thesis I have described is illustrated in recent work of Neil MacCormick. MacCormick recognizes that positivism's claim about the separation of law and morality must be defended not on conceptual but on moral grounds. He accordingly defends positivism by arguing that individual sovereignty of conscience is a good thing and would be fostered by acceptance of the view that there is no necessary connection between law and morality.[7] MacCormick's mistake is a mistake in political theory, just as Dworkin's is a mistake in legal theory. Dworkin focuses on too narrow a view of what insiders claim when they assert a connection between law and morality; MacCormick has too narrow a view about how one contests the insider's claim. The question is not whether it would be a good thing if morality and law were connected; the question is whether they are connected.[8] The issue, in short, is not a matter for stipulation in either legal or political theory; it is a matter of deciding what is the case in terms of already existing concepts whose asserted connections we must test by ordinary, if controversial, political theory.

II. THE CLAIM OF AUTHORITY

Conceptual Features

I shall introduce my views about authority by considering three features of the concept that are widely accepted in the literature as characteristic of claims of authority: preemption, content-independence, and correlativity.

Preemption. That assertions of authority are intended to preempt individual decisions in some sense is generally conceded. Disagreement exists, however, over just what is preempted. H. L. A. Hart, for example, says that a speaker claiming authority "intends his hearer to take [the speaker's] will instead of [the hearer's] own as a guide to action and so to take it in place of any deliberation or reasoning of his own."[9] Joseph Raz (whose views I shall be using as the primary foil for my own discussion) disagrees: assertions of authority do not preempt *deliberation*; they only preempt *action* on the basis of such deliberation.[10]

This disagreement is a minor but revealing one. Raz, I think, is technically correct; if I direct my child to come in from his football game and practice the piano, it doesn't matter to me whether he makes his own calculation about the proper amounts of time to allocate to football and music. As long as he does as directed and does not *act* on the basis of his deliberations my intent in issuing the directive is satisfied. But why does it matter if one puts the point in the stronger terms that Hart uses? What error does one make if one says that assertions of authority intend to preempt, not just action inconsistent with what is ordered, but even deliberation about whether to take the action? In practical terms, after all, both ways of making the point seem to come to the same thing. I may not care whether my son deliberates about my directive as long as he obeys; but I also don't care whether he mutters under his breath, or whistles a tune, or thinks about his girlfriend or continues any other aspect of his mental life—just as long as it doesn't interfere with practicing the piano. Deliberations, in short, are for all practical purposes rendered irrelevant by my directive. What, then, hinges on whether one thinks authorities intend to preempt deliberations as well as action?

One possibility is that these alternative descriptions matter because a problem of justification results if authority is construed in one way rather than the other. If deliberation about the merits of command action is prohibited, assertions of authority might seem to require that "surrender of judgment" that many see as inconsistent with the demands of autonomy.[11] But this answer is unsatisfactory. Raz's own explanation of how authority is reconciled with autonomy, or example, requires only that there be good reasons for accepting authority—that is, "sufficient reasons to follow its directives regardless of the balance of reasons on the merits of such action."[12] Authority, in short, is consistent with autonomy whether or not deliberation about the merits of the action is permitted *so long as one is not prohibited from deliberating about the decision to accept authority—that is, so long as one can deliberate about the decision not to deliberate about the merits of the action.*

But is even this last qualification necessary? I have just suggested that the problem of justification is unaffected by either the deliberation-excluding or the deliberation-permitting view. Could the same be said of a view that describes authority as preempting deliberation about the very question of the authority's right to command? Can authority bootstrap itself, as it were, into legitimacy by claiming the same preemptive force for its claim to legitimacy that it claims with respect to the content of its directives?

An affirmative answer to this question might be thought to raise serious doubts about the compatibility of autonomy and authority. But I do not think we can reject out of hand even this stronger view about what we normally intend when we claim authority. Consider the ordinary military command. The suggestion that such commands are meant to preempt a soldier's deliberation, not only about the action to be taken, but also about the lawfulness of the command, is not farfetched, or else we would have had far less trouble dealing with Nuremberg-like defenses in the case of soldiers who blindly follow apparently legitimate authority. If this is so, if legal authorities typically or even frequently purport to foreclose individual deliberation about both the merits of action and the merits of the claim of legitimacy ("double preemption," as I shall call it), then the conflict between authority and autonomy might seem to require overhauling either the conceptual claim or the moral theory.

The conception of authority I shall defend in many ways supports precisely the view suggested here: law typically intends to preempt (in the sense of rendering practically irrelevant) deliberation about both the content of the law and the legitimacy of the legal system. Some might think that this view presents an insurmountable justification problem: if that is what people mean when they claim authority, the claim could never be justified. But there is a persistent strain in political theory, most obvious in Hobbes, that is best understood as endorsing just such a double preemption thesis: a de facto Sovereign's claim to legitimacy is as much exempted from second-guessing as are the specific commands of the Sovereign. The important point, as the reference to Hobbes suggests, is that this view of authority could still be consistent with the demand that the exercise of authority be justified in some final sense by appeal to reason and the demands of autonomy. All that is required is that one shift the point of justification back one level: the problem now will be to offer sufficient reasons (as Hobbes tries to) for accepting an assertion that the subject is to deliberate *neither* about the merits of action *nor* about the merits of the claim of legitimacy. Reason in the end would still justify (because subjects could still deliberate, as Hobbes does, about this claim of double preemption); but it would be justification of a far more potent claim—a claim that action must be taken even though the action is wrong on its merits *and* even though the directing authority is wrong in its assumption about its own legitimacy.

Content-independence. Closely connected with all three preemption theses—the deliberation-excluding, the deliberation-permitting, and the doubly preempting—is a second feature, alluded to in the last sentence. Hart calls it "content-independence."[13] Again, there are differences in the way this feature is described in the literature, but I do not think that critical issues depend on the particular formulation; nor do I think that the general idea is controversial, even though its precise formulation and range of application are elusive. "Content-independence" refers to the fact that the justification for complying with authority is to be sought outside the evaluation of the particular action commanded. More generally, "a reason is content-independent if there is no direct connection between the reason and the action for which it is a reason."[14]

Content-independent reasons help explain how speech acts, such as commands and requests can alter a normative situation. These speech acts are alike in purporting to give the hearer new reasons for action that are independent of the "ordinary" reasons revealed by a direct evaluation of the action. But commands and requests differ (in part) in the implicit claim that is made about whether the content-independent reasons are supposed to displace the ordinary reasons. A strong claim ("complete independence") arises where one intends the content-independent reasons to be sufficient to determine action without reference to the ordinary reasons, thus (for all practical purposes) displacing them. A weaker claim ("partial independence") arises where such displacement is not intended. Requests are examples of the weaker claim. My request to my son to practice the piano gives him a new, independent reason to do so (for example, filial respect), *to be considered along with* whatever reasons already bear on practicing. Thus it would not be inconsistent with my intent (as it would be if I had commanded or ordered him to practice) for my son to weigh the content-independent reason created by my request along with the ordinary reasons that bear on practicing— and act accordingly.[15] In contrast, assertions of legal authority, like commands, claim complete independence. The consequence is that an authoritative legal directive, if it is legitimate, requires action even if the authority is mistaken in its evaluation of the action.

It is easy to see why content-independence is closely connected with the preemption thesis. If authorities expect to be obeyed even if their estimates about what is to be done are mistaken, individual deliberation about the content of directives is necessarily irrelevant. In short, content independence (in the complete form claimed by law) entails preemption. But it is important to recognize that the converse is not true: preemption does not entail content-independence (either partial or complete); thus the concepts are not equivalent. An authority could preempt individual deliberation without at the same time claiming that it is to be followed whether or not it is correct. Indeed, this is a major difference between theoretical and practical authority.

Consider the expert who gives advice on a technical matter—say, the half-life of radioactive material in a nuclear plant. His advice is intended to preempt independent evaluations by nonexperts because his judgment is more likely than theirs to yield correct results. But it would be very odd indeed for the expert to suggest that even if it turned out that his calculations were wrong, his advice should still be followed. Theoretical authority derives its legitimacy from the assumption that the content of its judgments is correct: the reasons for recognizing the authority are reasons for accepting this assumption.

Practical authority, in contrast, is content-independent in precisely the way that theoretical authority is not. The typical claim of the legal authority is that directives are to be followed even if they are wrong— and that claim is a far stronger one than is entailed by the preemption thesis alone. Thus it is not quite accurate to say, as Raz does, that "there is no point in having authorities unless their determinations are binding even if mistaken."[16] What one *should* say is that there is no point in having authorities if the question whether they are mistaken is to be determined in each case by individual evaluation. But there could be a point in having authority which preempts direct evaluation of directives, but conditions its legitimacy on its being right about their content— even though it will have to be shown wrong in some other way than through direct individual evaluation of the content (for example, through the evidence of other experts).

Correlativity. In addition to preemption and content-independence, claims of authority exhibit a third, more controversial feature, which has been called the "correlativity" thesis.[17] The correlativity thesis asserts that legitimate commands result in correlative duties on the part of subjects to comply. Controversy over this thesis reflects once again the interdependence of the conceptual and normative enterprises. Increasing doubt about the existence of a general duty to obey the law, coupled with unwillingness to brand general assertions of authority within ordinary legal systems as illegitimate, leads to proposals to sever the correlation: states should be seen as legitimately ordering subjects to comply; but neither states nor subjects need therefore conclude that subjects have duties to obey.

On this issue I agree with Raz: a view that denies the correlation between the assertion of authority and the assertion of a duty to obey is simply not "faithful to the main features of the notion of political authority prevalent in our culture."[18] Imagine a situation in which

> the political authorities of a country do not claim that the inhabitants are bound to obey them. . . . [C]ourts [imprison] people without finding them guilty of any offense. Damages are ordered, but no one has a duty to pay them. The legislature never claims to impose duties of care or of contribution to common services. It merely pronounces that people who behave in certain ways will be made to suffer.[19]

Such a society, says Raz, never existed, and if it did, we would not regard it as exercising political authority.

Though I am in agreement with Raz on this issue, two points about the kind of argument that he advances here for the correlativity thesis are worth emphasizing. First, the argument is mainly an empirical one that replies to the suggestion that correlativity exacerbates the problem of justification with a shrug of the shoulders: that just happens to be the concept that is used by every political society we know; that is, the data must control. Second, the empirical claim is based on the viewpoint of legal *officials* (or the legal system). Indeed, if the question were whether *citizens* typically view law as resulting in moral duties, one could not avoid taking into account the so-called bad-man view of law. The society that Raz invites us to imagine, however farfetched as an example of the claim of authority implicitly endorsed by political officials, is not at all farfetched when considered, for example, from the viewpoint of some economic models that purport to show how much of the law, even the criminal law, can be seen as "taxes" on conduct, rather than as fines or impositions of duties. The important point is that questions of what authority means are to be taken from the viewpoint of the system itself, not from the possible viewpoint of those who, like Holmes or some economists, might prove brave enough to convert all sanctions into taxes.

Normative Features

The above features are conceptual features: they are descriptions of the scope of the claim that is made when legal authority is asserted. I come now to two normative theses about authority. They are normative theses because they concern substantive questions of political theory about how to justify claims of authority or about how authority ought to be exercised. One of these theses, which Raz calls the "dependence" thesis, purports to set conditions that any exercise of authority ought to observe. The other thesis, the "justification" thesis (or the "normal justification thesis." as Raz calls it), is more basic: it purports to describe the normal way that one justifies claims of authority, even when authorities are acting within the constraints of the dependence thesis.

It is these two normative theses that contrast most sharply with the claims of authority that I shall defend. These theses also graphically illustrate the discrepancy between the "theory" of the moral philosopher and the "data" provided by the claims that are actually made within legal systems. I shall argue that, *from the viewpoint of the legal system,* (1) the dependence thesis is true, if at all, only in a trivial sense that does not provide significant constraints on the exercise of authority; and (2) the justification thesis is wrong.

The dependence thesis asserts that, even though authorities may preempt deliberation on the merits of directives, their decisions should be based on the same reasons that would apply independently to the subjects of the directives. The justification thesis states that the typical way of justifying authority "involves showing that the alleged subject is likely better to comply with reasons which apply to him . . . if he accepts the directives of the alleged authority as authoritatively binding and tries to follow them, rather than trying to follow the reasons which apply to him directly."[20]

A simple example will help illustrate both theses as well as summarize the discussion thus far. The United States has recently raised the speed limit from fifty-five to sixty-five miles per hour on rural interstates. Prior to the fuel shortage that followed the formation of OPEC, the speed limit had been seventy miles per hour on interstates. The decision to lower the speed limit was based primarily on considerations of fuel economy and safety, but as the fuel crisis eased, growing numbers of people—particularly in the trucking industry—thought that the fifty-five-mile-per-hour limit struck the wrong balance between such considerations and the interest in quick transport. Presumably agreeing with such claims, Congress raised the speed limit, though not to its earlier high point.

The theses about authority discussed thus far can be illustrated and summarized with reference to this example:

(1) The fifty-five-mile-per-hour speed limit was intended to be observed regardless of individual citizens' views about how best to balance safety and energy concerns against the interest in quick travel (preemption).

(2) The directive was intended to result in a moral obligation to obey the speed limit (correlativity).

(3) This obligation was thought to exist regardless of the accuracy of the legislature's calculation of costs and benefits in weighing safety and fuel conservation concerns against the interest in quick travel (content-independence).

(4) This would be a proper exercise of authority, according to the dependence thesis, if it is based on the same considerations that any citizen should take into account in deciding how fast to drive—national interest in fuel conservation and concern for safety and rapid travel.

(5) Finally, the justification for the legislature's authority to create this obligation depends on the assumption that one is better off following the speed limit than trying to make one's own calculation in each case about how fast to drive in light of the concerns for fuel conservation, safety, and quick transport.

The dependence thesis. Consider the dependence thesis. To say that an authority ought to base its decision on the same reasons that I would normally consider if I were to evaluate the proposed action sounds, on its face, like a fairly strong constraint. It seems to ensure that, even though I may disagree with the authority's calculations about how to weigh the relevant reasons, at least I will not be subjected to directives designed to advance interests completely foreign to mine.

The appearance of constraint is an illusion, for two reasons. First, the dependence thesis, as Raz describes it, does not require that authorities act in the "interests" of their subjects, but only that they act "for reasons which apply also to their subjects."[21] Thus a military commander complies with the thesis, according to Raz, when in the interest of national defense, he orders a soldier to take action that is inconsistent with the soldier's interest in personal safety. That is because soldiers *ought* to put their country above their own interests, whether they do in fact or not. Second, although this is not clear in Raz's account, which reasons apply to a subject its itself a question that the legal authority typically purports to determine. The dependence thesis thus seems to require only that an authority act on reasons that the authority believes its subjects ought to acknowledge, whether or not they do in fact. Under this interpretation, the constraint on the type of reasons that may be considered is jeopardized by the ability of the authority to decide for itself whether it has exceeded the limits.

Some constraint would still remain if the dependence thesis were interpreted to require that the reasons on which the authority relies apply to the subject in fact—that is, as a matter of an objectively correct normative view about what reasons individuals ought to consider, or what areas of individual life authorities can properly control. Thus in the case of the soldier, the military command would be consistent with the dependence thesis only if the commander (and his superiors in turn) were objectively correct in the conclusion that citizens ought to be public-spirited enough to consider the national interests in a particular war. But if this is what is intended by the dependence thesis, it seems at odds with the features of preemption and content-independence. If authority is entitled to prevail regardless of whether it is correct in its evaluation particular actions, why should it not also prevail regardless of whether it is correct in its judgment about the reasons that "ought" to apply to and be considered by its subjects? It seems odd to suggest that the government's authority survives mistakes in its calculation about the legitimacy of a war, for example, but does not survive mistakes in its decision about what reasons individuals ought to consider in deciding whether or not to fight.

In short, the likely response of the state to the suggestion that its authority is limited by the dependence thesis would be, at best, to agree, but to insist that it has the same right to be wrong in deciding what reasons citizens "ought" to consider as it does in determining the content of the law. The government no doubt will claim that its laws are based on reasons that apply to its subjects; but it will insist that its authority is not conditional on a correct determination of what those reasons are or how they apply to particular cases.

I conclude that the dependence thesis should be reformulated to reflect more accurately the extent to which it serves as a normative constraint on the exercise of authority. All that is required, it seems, is that the authority act in good faith in the interests of the general welfare or of justice as it sees it, defending that general pursuit of the public good as broadly based on reasons that all individuals should take into account. Thus reformulated, the thesis is not totally without bite. It rules out, for example, purely self-interested tyrants who "rule" solely in their own interest, as well as rulers who act for nonselfish reasons which, however, they do not believe apply to subjects.[22] It should, however, be recognized that the reformulation is sufficiently vague to include almost any set of reasons and is consistent with almost any substantive goal that can be embodied in legislation. It is also broad enough to cover the spectrum of contested positions within political theory about the range of interests that governments have a right to require individuals to pursue or avoid.

The justification thesis. If the dependence thesis can be satisfied by almost any law, the justification thesis, I suggest, can be satisfied by very few. If that is so, then it means either that assertions of authority by legal systems are frequently illegitimate and impose no obligations, or that we must find an explanation of how to justify authority that more nearly coincides with the claims that legal officials make.

The justification thesis, recall, says that we normally justify the assertion of authority on the ground that correct action is more likely to result if subjects follow authority than if each tries to deliberate directly about what to do. The thesis has several unusual consequences.

First, this view of authority virtually eliminates the traditional distinction between theoretical and practical authority.[23] We typically do justify deferring to theoretical authority on the ground that we are more likely to do the right thing by blindly following the expert's judgment than by trying to make our own direct calculations. And the expert himself, in claiming such authority, would justify it on exactly these grounds (greater expertise). The same does not seem true of the typical assertion of practical authority in law. As mentioned above, practical authority claims complete content-independence (which entails preemption), whereas theoretical authority claims only preemption. We defer our judgment to the expert (preemption), but we would not say that the expert's judgment should bind even if it is mistaken (content-independence). Of course, we act on the expert's judgment without knowing whether it is mistaken and without regard to our own views about its correctness. But the expert himself, for example, could not say that, though he has done his best to calculate the impact of a fifty-five-mile-per-hour speed limit on fuel conservation, we should follow his judgment about the matter even if it turns out that he is wrong.

In this respect the theoretical authority of the expert, testifying for example about the speed limit in a legislative hearing, contrasts markedly with the practical authority of the legislature when the speed limit law is finally passed. The implicit claim of the legislature is precisely the one that the expert cannot make: though the legislature thinks its judgment about the balance to be struck between energy, safety, and rapid transit concerns is correct, it claims that its judgment is to be followed even if it is wrong—indeed, even if it is based on incorrect factual assumptions about the effect on fuel conservation (because the expert, for example, was wrong). In short, the discovery that the expert is wrong always destroys his authority, whereas proof that the law is wrong has no effect (unless the law itself so provides) on the authority of the law. That, at least, is the typical posture of the law.

The collapse of practical into theoretical authority (as respects justification) highlights a second, more general objection to the justification thesis—one that Raz considers but, I think, dismisses too quickly. The objection is that the justification thesis is inconsistent with the preemption and content-independence theses. If authority is to be acknowledged if and only if it is better to follow its directives than to act on one's own, how can one claim that authority continues to bind even if it is wrong? Raz's response recalls the extensive literature on the distinction between rule and act utilitarianism which explains why one should follow a rule designed to promote certain values rather than calculate directly in each case the effect of contemplated action on those values.

But the analogy between the justification for rule-following in moral reasoning and the justification of authority in law seems guaranteed to force a wide divergence between the law's claims and the philosopher's ability to justify them, for several reasons. First, the debate between rule and act utilitarians usually assumes that the rules that are to guide conduct are those that the philosopher or the enlightened individual can justify as most likely to produce optimal conduct. But in law, the rules are designed by legislators or other authorities who are not any better at practical reasoning, by and large, than other individuals.

Second, it would seem to be one consequence of the justification thesis that authority loses its legitimacy whenever a particular legislature is found to be below the average in practical reasoning ability—a situation that, at least in the United States, cannot be ruled out in advance even in high levels of government, let alone local city councils. Moreover, even under the best of governments, there are probably some individual citizens who are better able to judge practical matters than the legislature and who thus, according to the justification thesis, should no longer view law as binding when it affects their particular fields of expertise.

Third, as Christopher McMahon notes, many of the decisions that government embodies in law represent a resolution of controversial moral disputes where "there does not appear to be an independent criterion of success."[24] (Consider abortion.) In these cases, the assumption of superior deliberative ability on the part of the legislature is unwarranted. (We do not think that even the best legislatures resemble Plato's philosopher-kings in moral "expertise.") Thus, the authority claimed by the law in such cases will be illegitimate unless one can find some other explanation for why following the legislature's judgment even in these cases is likely to be better than following one's own.[25]

Finally, even if a particular legislature is more likely to be right in its judgment about the best laws to enact in a particular area, laws by their generality operate far too grossly to allow one to say that second-guessing is always likely to be worse than blindly following the rule. A favorite example of philosophers discussing the obligation to obey the law is the red light in the desert when nobody is around, but the speed limit example also shows that occasions when the law is "clearly wrong" are going to be, by any fair estimate, far more frequent than Raz's example of adding several integers and one fraction and getting an integer as sum suggests.[26] The general solution to the balance of interests involving fuel conservation, safety, and speed represented by the fifty-five-mile-per-hour speed limit will only on the most implausible assumption be the correct balance for all individuals in all circumstances. Even if one adds into the account the expense and energy of making an individual calculation each time, there must surely be many instances when my need to get somewhere fast, coupled with my safety record as a driver and the absence of significant traffic, makes it clear that the legislature's judgment about how fast I should drive is not more reliable than mine.

So far, I am suggesting that the justification thesis has the consequence that many instances of claimed legal authority will in fact be unjustified. That may be a consequence one is prepared to accept. Raz, for example, accepts it, though he admits it seems paradoxical: political officials and legal systems generally make claims of unlimited authority which the justification thesis simply does not support.[27] According to Raz, "[a]n expert pharmacologist may not be subject to the authority of the government in matters of the safety of drugs, an inhabitant of a little village by a river may not be subject to its authority in matters of navigation and conservation of the river by the banks of which he has spent all his life."[28] Motorists who have expert knowledge about the roadworthiness of their cars may not be subject to the authority of laws requiring periodic safety tests, and parents who know their children better than the government (and what parent doesn't?) may not be subject to the authority of laws regulating day-care hours, and so on.[29]

It should now be clear why I expressed doubt about whether the thesis I planned to defend would prove controversial. My thesis is primarily about the concept of authority as it appears from the viewpoint of the law itself. I have been developing that thesis in contrast to the philosophical account provided by Raz. Part of Raz's view—concerning the conceptual features of the claim of authority—coincides with the law's view. Other features—the normative ones—are openly conceded to be inconsistent with the law's view, but nevertheless defended as the appropriate "explanatory-normative" account of the concept of authority. The result is the discrepancy mentioned at the outset between the philosopher's theory and the data for which the theory is intended to account.[30]

Moreover, it is not clear why the insider's viewpoint apparently controls in some of these disputes about the claim of authority but not in others. Recall again the argument over correlativity. Because it was thought that the problem of justification would be eased by concluding that legitimate legal norms do not entail duties to comply, some urged adopting just such a view. The answer in that case was that such a view would simply not be true to the concept of political authority as we know it—as viewed from inside. It is just not plausible to imagine that sanctions would be administered and laws enforced without accompanying claims of moral justification and moral duty. Why is this not also the appropriate response in the case of a dispute about how we typically justify claims of authority? Why not say that the concept of authority implied in the justification thesis is just not our concept of authority?

Imagine a society in which pharmacists who know better than the government what drugs are safe and motorists who are better judges than the legislature of the risk they pose by speeding attempted to challenge the authority of the law as applied to them. Could a society make room for such challenges and still maintain a rule-based system of law? If anything, it seems even harder to imagine how such a system might operate than to imagine a system in which laws and sanctions are viewed as prices to pay or not as one chooses. But whether or not it is conceptually possible to imagine such a system, the empirical point must be conceded: this is not the concept of authority that is at work in any political society that we know of.

At the very least, Raz's view could hardly be called the "normal" justification thesis. It is not clear that it is the normal thesis even within political theory. But it is clear, indeed it is conceded, that it is not the "normal" justification of authority from the viewpoint of the law. If "normality" is related at all to frequency and impact, surely the legal system, as a normative system that routinely affects the lives of all individuals, has a far greater right to claim that its view is the "normal" one and that the inconsistent views of individual moral philosophers, however currently fashionable, are the unusual ones.

The official view about the justification of authority supports an entirely different conception. Consider again the speed limit sign (or the red light in the middle of the desert, or whatever your favorite example is of a law based on reasons that "clearly" do not apply in the particular circumstance). You have been ticketed for exceeding the speed limit and you want to put into issue the question whether, in light of the easing of the fuel shortage, that law still represents the best balance of reasons that apply to the question of how fast to drive. Or you want to introduce your fine, claim-free insurance record, or you want to prove that you are a race car driver, able to travel safely at speeds most people cannot. All such offers of evidence would be inadmissible as irrelevant—not because it is assumed that the law has made the best balance of the underlying reasons, but because the law is binding whether or not it is correct.[31] Indeed, that is the thrust of the preemption and content-independence theses. Of course, one assumes that the legislature thought it was making the best balance when the law was enacted—that is simply the consequence of the dependence thesis, or the requirement of a "good faith" attempt to act in the public interest. But the justification of authority under this alternative conception focuses far more closely on the right to be wrong than on the greater likelihood of getting things right. Unless the law itself has exceptions that allow one to put in issue the justice or wisdom of the law (as in certain constitutional cases), or to raise a necessity defense (as when one is speeding to the hospital), the law's claim is that one has an obligation to obey and that its authority is justified whether or not correct action is more likely to result from following the law. Equally irrelevant, of course, is any attempt to challenge the relative competence of the lawmaker vis-à-vis the average citizen.

In many cases, of course, one may not be able to distinguish between these two conceptions of authority. It will often be true that a legislative body has more time or resources for considering issues and is less biased than most individuals; following its directives in these cases could be consistent with the idea that the legislature's judgment is likely to be better than the individual's.[32] In other cases, notably instances of coordination, the legislature's choice will almost by definition be a better guide to action than *ad hoc* individual decisions (relative legislative competence is not the issue in deciding whether to follow rules of the road). So, too, in the case of prisoners' dilemmas. I may agree to arbitration, not because I think the arbitrator is more likely to decide a dispute correctly, but because I see no other way out of the impasse. If all laws were essentially instances of cases like these (clear deliberative superiority in the legislature, coordination, prisoners' dilemmas), then there would never be occasions that would require us to choose between these alternative conceptions.[33] For reasons discussed above, however, it seems clear that many laws are not of this type: by any fair estimate, the everyday occasions on which the law's assertions of authority will diverge from what is legitimate according to the justification thesis will be numerous indeed.

What then is the justification of authority under the alternative conception? What reasons could one have for acknowledging the right of the law to determine action regardless of the correctness of its judgment about the merits of the action and regardless of the likelihood that following the judgment will better accord with correct action than deliberating oneself? It is not my aim to answer that question here, but we can recall at least the kind of answers that might be and have been given by political theorists whose theories coincide more closely with the data of insider claims. The justification for authority under this conception draws on two persistent ideas: (1) that decisions about the best action to take are often deeply controversial; and (2) that we cannot avoid giving some persons in society the power to resolve these disputes—including disputes about the limits of their own power.

Of course the critical issue for political theory has always been whether one has any reason to follow authority if these reasons for establishing authority in the first place do not seem to bear upon a particular act of disobedience. But there are many attempts within political theory to solve this problem, drawing on ideas about fair play, implicit agreement, or respect for the necessity of compromise. In short, with this alternative conception we are embarked on a journey into the heart of traditional political theory. Unless it is quite clear that no plausible moral theory could crown this quest, we ought not scrap it for a conception that makes it easier to justify submitting to the will of another, but fits the facts—the instances in which we claim authority—far less well.

Raz designates his view the "service conception" of authority: government exists because (and has authority just in case) it does a better job of advancing the aims of the governed (what "ought to be their aims") than they could do on their own. The alternative conception might be called the "leader" conception of authority: government exists because (and has authority just in case) it provides necessary direction in default of agreement about what *are* the aims of the governed.[34]

III. LEGAL THEORY

Modern Positivism

Questions about how to narrow the gap between the view of political theory and the view of the legal system must be left for another occasion. I want instead to consider the implications of what I have called the leader conception of authority for legal, rather than political, theory—in particular for the developments within legal positivism of the last half century.

At least since Kelsen, positivists have insisted on reproducing within their models of law not only the obvious *de facto* power of the law, but the equally persistent *de jure* claims that accompany the exercise of such power. The addition is explicit in Kelsen, even if the basis for it—the explanation for what is wrong with Austin's coercive model of law—is unclear. According to this brand of positivism legal systems share with other normative systems, like morality and religion, the claim or belief that what is done through law is morally justified. This normative model of law, of course, is not meant to reflect the actual beliefs of particular judges. Judges can obviously be cynics about morality in general or skeptics about the morality of the particular laws they enforce and thus have either no beliefs about, or even positive distaste for, what they do. In this respect, the parallel between law and other normative systems, like religion, is maintained: a priest may privately have doubts about or even disbelieve the truth of the religious norms he professes; but he must recognize that the system in which he participates will present him as endorsing the religious propositions that he asserts.

Implications

Consider now the implications of the preceding discussion of authority for this normative model of law. The normative model, like the coercive model, is a positivist theory of law, characterized by the claim that there is no necessary connection between law and morality. But the attempt to maintain this claim and at the same time to reproduce the leadership concept of authority within the model results in the paradox mentioned at the outset: the theory can remain positivist in the normal sense only by rejecting as false the very claim that it must now reproduce.

To appreciate the paradox, compare the positivist's claims about law as a normative system with, once again, an imagined parallel claim about religion. A sociologist or philosopher of religion might develop a model that finds the most important feature of a religion to be the claim of truth or insight that underlies religious "law," rather than the threats about life after death that may or may not accompany the injunction to follow God's law. This model would still preserve the distinction between religious "truths" or norms and actual truth or objective moral norms: what a religion claims to be true is one thing; whether those claims are in fact true is another. In like manner, the normative model of law appears on the surface nonparadoxical and entirely compatible with the positivist's insistence on the distinction between law and morality: what officials claim to be morally obligatory or just is one thing;

whether it *is* just or morally obligatory is another. Legal theory deals with the former; moral theory with the latter.

There is an instructive flaw in the analogy. The claim of justice within law differs strikingly from the claim of "truth" or "moral insight" within a religion. The claim of justice in law, in light of the preceding discussion, is a claim that citizens have moral obligations to comply with legal norms (and officials are morally justified in punishing them if they fail to comply) just because the norms are embraced in the law. Religions make a very different claim. One is "obligated" to heed religious norms, not just because they are religious norms, but because, it is assumed, they are true. Religious authority, in short, resembles theoretical authority in this respect: religious authorities may preempt deliberation, as when a church hierarchy insists on the final say in religious disputes and expects to be followed regardless of the contrary views of members. But such claims of preemption are not also claims of "content-independence." Religious authorities do not suggest that their norms are to be followed regardless of the truth of the underlying religious tenets, but, rather, on the assumption that the content of the religion is correct: it is the right church, the correct religion, the revealed truth.

It is positivism's attempt to reproduce the peculiar, content-independent claim of legal systems that is problematic. Insiders will be portrayed as professing, as a matter of political theory, what positivism denies, namely, that there is a necessary connection between the fact that something is law and a moral conclusion about the duty to obey. Positivism must either falsify the picture of the normative attitude toward law that it has undertaken to include within its legal theory or depict law as entailing a belief in a proposition that positivism claims is false.

Objections

Four possible responses to this alleged paradox can be imagined. First, one might deny that insiders do in fact typically claim that sanctions are morally justified just because the law is broken. The evidence bearing on this question has already been considered: whatever one might think about the true justification for authority, the posture of the legal official seems to be that all that counts is that the law has been broken.[35] Arguments about whether obeying the law solves a coordination problem, or was the best act under the circumstances, or prevents collapse into the state of nature are *legally* irrelevant.

Second, one might respond that the law's claim of justification in punishing just because the law is broken is not really a claim about the connection between the very concept of law and moral obligation, but rather a claim peculiar to the ideology of a particular country. Thus, for example, the reason one excludes evidence about the "justification" of the speeding law might be thought to be connected with the political theory of the society: "this is a democracy, and arguments about the wisdom of the law should be addressed to the legislature," and so on. Legal norms, then, would more closely resemble religious norms, as described above. They would not be completely content-independent, but would depend for their authority on the correctness of the underlying assumption that the ideology of the country is the "true" one.

But this view seems difficult to defend. Undoubtedly, any society thinks its own political theory is best, just as it presumably thinks that the content of its law is correct. But legal officials do not openly suggest that the obligation to obey depends on the correctness—within political theory—of socialist or liberal theories of justice, any more than they would suggest that it depends on the legislature's being right about the content of the law. Attempts to introduce evidence bearing on such issues would be resisted as even more patently irrelevant than attempts to undermine the rationale of the speeding law. Moreover, the recognition that every country makes the same claim of authority for its laws tends to reinforce the view that the insider is asserting a connection between the very concept of law and the obligation to obey—the classical claim of political theory.

A third possible response for the positivist is that the claim that sanctions are justified just because the law is broken is too implausible; nobody could defend it morally, so it is not worth treating as a component of the insider's attitude toward law. The only belief that "counts" is the belief that the content is just; we can ignore the crazy additional idea that, even if the content is wrong, one is still justified in punishing lawbreakers. This response, of course, requires grappling with the issues of political theory that the preceding discussion has uncovered; it also raises again the question of who is out of step—the philosopher or the legal system. If there were absolutely no plausible argument for the legal point of view, then perhaps one would be willing to entertain cynical explanations for the law's stance as the only plausible way to close the gap. But, of course, there are other explanations. From Socrates' impassioned defense of the state's right to put him to death even though he was unjustly accused, to Hobbes's pessimistic claims about the necessity of deferring to whatever sovereign happens to exist, political theory has taken quite seriously the idea that a proper understanding of law brings with it an acknowledgment that its moral authority is not dependent on getting the content right or being a better guide to correct action than individual calculations. It may be that this view about the connection between law and moral obligation is wrong, but it is not so implausible that it can be dismissed out of hand.

A final response for the positivist is this. He might say that, even though many people do claim that sanctions are justified just because the law is broken, and even though that claim is a controversial one within political theory, all that the *meaning* of law requires, for purposes of legal theory, is the belief that the content is just. That belief is sufficient to distinguish law from force, and thus there is no need to investigate the additional claims of political theory, however plausible, that the broader belief entails. This response brings us to the problem of methodology within legal theory. If it is true that the typical insider attitude is that sanctions are justified regardless of the content of the law broken, how does one decide that this attitude is not an "essential" part of the idea of a legal system? If this question of method were more squarely confronted within positivist legal theory, I suspect that whatever reasons justified the departure from the coercive model in the first place would make it difficult to stop short of the full normative claim about the authority of law found in the leader conception.

IV. CONCLUSION

I conclude as I began: the positivist's claim about the separation of law and morality must be presented and defended as a claim of political theory, rather than a conceptual claim about the meaning of "law" and "morality," as has traditionally been the case. It is of course possible that it is the claim of authority within legal systems that should be modified—toned down so that the range of laws that are claimed to impose moral duties (just because they are the law) is narrowed to those that really do result in content-independent moral duties according to a "true" political theory. But if, as I suspect, the law is resistant to suggestions that its claim to authority is unwarranted, we should be cautious about concluding that we have the "true" political theory. At the very least, we should consider just how we could tone down the law's claim and make legal obligations conditional, in unspecified ways, on the kinds of considerations that the political theorist believes are critical to its authority. If we cannot do this, then the breadth of the law's claim of authority and its apparent imperviousness to philosophical doubts about its legitimacy strongly suggest that we just need to work harder at the political theory.

NOTES

Earlier versions of this article were presented at the Centre for Criminology and the Social and Philosophical Study of Law, University of Edinburgh, and at the Jurisprudence Seminar at Cambridge University. I am grateful to the Editors of *Philosophy & Public Affairs* for helpful suggestions. I am also indebted to Joseph Raz, whose gracious comments on an earlier draft prevented some misstatements of his position and corrected errors in the statement of my own.

1. Proponents of such normative models of law include Hans Kelsen, H. L. A. Hart, Joseph Raz, and Neil MacCormick. For further discussion of these "modern positivists," including the differences among them and the nature of their dispute with "classical positivists" like Austin and Bentham, see P. Soper, *A Theory of Law* (Cambridge: Harvard University Press, 1984), chap. 2.

2. See J. Raz, *The Morality of Freedom* (Oxford: Clarendon Press, 1986), p. 66 (defending an "explanatory-normative" account of concepts over earlier "linguistic" accounts).

3. For the strongest assertion to this effect see Raz, ibid., p. 97 (the claim that there is a general obligation to obey the law has "been refuted by various writers in recent years").

4. I put the point in terms of the "belief" of insiders; but it is the posture of the law—the implicit claim of the legal system—that I have in mind, not the actual psychological state of any particular individual or group of individuals. See the discussion in Section III below.

5. See R. Dworkin, *Law's Empire* (Cambridge: Harvard University Press, 1986), pp. 93, 97, 103, 151.

6. For further discussion, see P. Soper, "Dworkin's Domain," *Harvard Law Review* 100 (1987): 1166, 1176, 1183–86.

7. See N. MacCormick, "A Moralistic Case for A-Moralistic Law," *Valparaiso Law Review* 20 (1985): 1, 9–11, passim, and *H. L. A. Hart* (Stanford: Stanford University Press, 1981), pp. 159–62.

8. By analogy, one might think that it would be a good thing if there were no duty to keep promises: we would thereby encourage greater self-reliance and leave individuals free to change their minds. But while these considerations may be relevant in deciding whether there is such a duty, they do not take the place of a moral investigation into the nature of the promising practice that we actually have and the duties that result form participating in that practice. For further discussion see P. Soper, "Choosing a Legal Theory on Moral Grounds," *Social Philosophy and Policy* 4 (1986): 42–48.

9. H. L. A. Hart, *Essays on Bentham* (Oxford: Clarendon Press, 1982), p. 253.

10. J. Raz, "Authority and Justification," *Philosophy & Public Affairs* 14, no. 1 (Winter 1985): 7.

11. Ibid., pp. 7–8.

12. Ibid., p. 8.

13. Hart, *Essays on Bentham*, pp. 254–55.

14. Raz, *The Morality of Freedom*, p. 35.

15. This comparison of requests and commands follows Raz, ibid., pp. 35–37. But other analogies Raz draws seem to me suspect. Consider advice. Raz claims that the typical reason for accepting advice is that it is likely to be good advice—that is, there are reasons for thinking the person giving the advice is correct. Thus a friend who discovered that his advice was judged mistaken but was followed anyway in order not to hurt his feelings would be doubly insulted. Raz finds a parallel here to the normal justification of legal authority. See "Authority and Justification," p. 19.

The parallel is misplaced. The typical person asserting legal authority, unlike the friend offering advice, would not be insulted to discover I had obeyed because of my respect for him or his position, even though I thought his judgment mistaken. Indeed, as the text makes clear, that is exactly the kind of obedience that complete content-independence, as claimed by law, contemplates. (There is no doubt a good deal more to be said about the application of content-independence in various contexts, but this is not the place.)

16. Raz, "Authority and Justification," p. 15.

17. See A. J. Simmons, "Voluntarism and Political Associations," *Virginia Law Review* 67 (1981): 19, 20; see also J. Raz, "Authority and Consent," *Virginia Law Review* 67 (1981): 103.

18. Raz, "Authority and Justification," p. 6.

19. Ibid.

20. Ibid., pp. 18–19.

21. Ibid., p. 15.

22. I discuss the potential constraints of the requirement that governments attempt in good faith to aim at the common good (which is what this reinterpretation of the dependence thesis amounts to) at greater length in *A Theory of Law*, pp. 119–22, 133–43.

23. Raz insists that practical authority differs from theoretical authority by giving subjects new reasons for *action*. Theoretical authority only gives one new reasons to believe that something is the case. Thus the expert can tell me the effect of speed on fuel conservation, but that does not change the proper balance of costs and benefits that determines how fast to drive; it only helps reveal what that balance was all along. (Note that this appears to be another way of saying that theoretical authority preempts but is not content-independent.) Practical authority, in contrast, can make a difference in, for example, coordination cases: when the legislature specifies which side of the road to drive on, I have a reason to *act* differently than I did before there was a rule of the road. See *The Morality of Freedom*, pp. 28–31, 48–53.

Despite this alleged difference in the way theoretical and practical authorities *operate*, it seems clear in Raz's account that there is no difference *in the way one justifies* either kind of authority: in both cases, the claims of authority are justified if and only if one has good reason to think that following the authority is better than acting on one's own lights. See "Authority and Justification," p. 18 (theoretical and practical authority "share the same basic structure").

24. C. McMahon, "Autonomy and Authority," *Philosophy & Public Affairs* 16, no. 4 (Fall 1987): 308.

25. McMahon, ibid., pp. 310–19, develops an intriguing argument to rescue the justification thesis in these cases by suggesting that they may be examples of prisoners' dilemmas: it is better to go along with the legislative determination, however wrong or controversial, because failure to cooperate could lead to the even worse result of the "state of nature." Most theorists have rejected this conclusion as unsound. See Raz, *The Morality of Freedom*, p. 102 ("it is a melodramatic exaggeration to suppose that every breach of law endangers, by however small a degree, the survival of the government, or of law and order"). I shall not evaluate McMahon's attempt to rescue the argument, but only note that it is the kind of argument that would have to be made in order to reduce the gap between the justification thesis and the claim of authority actually made by legal systems.

26. Raz, *The Morality of Freedom*, p. 62.

27. Ibid., pp. 76–78.

28. Ibid., p. 74.

29. Ibid., p. 78.

30. Raz says that one advantage of an "explanatory-normative" account over

linguistic analysis is that the former allows for divergence between the "normative" theory and the actual practice of particular individuals. See *The Morality of Freedom*, pp. 65–66. But surely there must be some limit to the amount of divergence that is allowed. Otherwise, the method is no longer "explanatory-normative" but simply normative—and suspect precisely because the divergence from the data is too large to reflect our understanding of the practice and its point.

31. It is important to recognize that such evidence is not excluded on substantive or administrative grounds—that is, because the "administrative" costs of deciding whether in the circumstances disobedience was best outweigh the gains to be realized. The law's attitude is that this evidence is *legally* irrelevant; that is, one could admit (demur to) the claim that speeding in a particular case was the best thing to do without affecting the legal result.

32. For other factors that bear on establishing the legitimacy of an authority under the justification thesis see Raz, *The Morality of Freedom*, p. 75.

33. As noted, arguments have been made to try to show that all laws are resolutions of these kinds of coordination or prisoner's dilemma problems. See note 25 above. See also W. S. Boardman, "Coordination and the Moral Obligation to Obey the Law," *Ethics* 97 (1987): 546.

34. I should note that Raz tries to respond to the discrepancy between his political theory and the legal view. His attempt to bridge the gap is noteworthy and original. Basically, he suggests that even though law claims far more authority than it has, many individuals may legitimately consent to go along as a way of expressing their identification with a generally just government. See *The Morality of Freedom*, pp. 94–105. This solution, of course, is still unsatisfactory from the law's viewpoint, because the law claims authority regardless of consent and because many individuals may choose not to consent.

Moreover, there is something unappealing about the idea that the way to express one's identification with a system that makes illegitimate demands is to go along with those illegitimate demands—that just encourages the state to continue its overbroad assertion of authority. Since there are other ways of expressing identification with one's community, why would one ever choose this way? If the analogy is with friendship (or social clubs), why not show one's friend the error of his ways, rather than encourage him to think that his overbroad demands are legitimate? Isn't that a double insult rather than an expression of identification? (See note 15 above.)

Note that these problems can be avoided if the respect one owes the state is not a matter of *choice*, as in Raz's theory, but a matter of what the state *deserves* (is morally entitled to) in light of its attempt to carry out a necessary enterprise. See P. Soper, "The Moral Value of Law," *Michigan Law Review* 84 (1985): 301.

35. As Neil MacCormick puts it in a somewhat different context:
it seems inconceivable that it will ever be thought other than virtuous, albeit
at a modest point on the scale of virtue, for a person to be 'law-abiding'—
even when the law by which he or she abides contains much of evil. By the
same token, the law breaker however conscientious will be stigmatized by
the legal officials as a moral wrongdoer and a moral danger. (*H. L. A. Hart*,
p. 161)

Consider: Is MacCormick's claim about "inconceivability" a psychological
point (people can't help making a claim they are not entitled to make) or a
logical one (people can't help connecting lawbreaking with immorality because
that is what the logic of existing concepts of law, morality, authority, and duty
requires)?

11

FREEDOM, RECOGNITION, AND OBLIGATION: A FEMINIST APPROACH TO POLITICAL THEORY

Nancy J. Hirschmann

In the modern liberal state and the liberal doctrines that theorize it, it is fairly well established that obligation is a concept based on voluntarist principles; that is, an obligation is a limitation on behavior, a requirement for action or nonaction, that the actor or nonactor has chosen or agreed to. As opposed to duty—which may be a requirement that exists "naturally" (Rawls 1971) or "positionally" (Simmons 1979) but at any rate is not explicitly chosen—it is central to our understanding of obligations that they arise from our voluntary and free actions.[1] The paradigm for obligations on the liberal model is the promise and contract (Hume 1948; Pateman 1985).

The political paradigm is the social contract, which founded the ideal that political obligations are based on the free choices of citizens, on their "consent" to a government's authority. The reasoning of the social contract theorists was that if people are inherently, naturally, and (most importantly) equally free, how could any limitation on that freedom be imposed on an individual by another individual or a group? The only legitimate limitations are those imposed by the self; for if I am above all else free, a limitation of freedom can be legitimate only if it is simultaneously an expression of my freedom. Thus, the social contract is an expression of human freedom, of our ability to make choices and control our destiny. Of course, all of the social contract theorists imposed limits on people's ability to consent (one could not consent to die or to be a slave or to do evil); but these limits, it was argued, only served to define—rather than further limit—freedom.

This theoretical framework of the priority of liberty carries over into contemporary obligation theory. Many of these theories overtly adopt consent as the basis of obligation but transform how consent is expressed and even its very meaning. For instance, in attempting to reconcile the centrality of consent to obligation in the face of the fact that many people do not even think about their consent, Tussman (1960) suggests assuming that the majority of citizens give their consent like "political child brides," who let others protect and define their best interests. Pitkin (1965), through a creative reading of Locke, develops the notion of "hypothetical" consent: what perfectly free, rational beings would consent to determines what the average unfree, unequal person is obligated to. Flathman (1972) argues for a "good reasons" approach, holding that critical reasoning will reveal that we have (or do not have) good reasons for respecting the authority of a government; while obligation is a "practice" and must operate within the confines of language (this automatically limits what can count as a reason), the final repository is individuals' ability to judge and decide for themselves, one of the main problems that consent theory raises. Even Pateman (1985), who is highly critical of liberal obligation theory, argues for a "fully consistent" consent theory, which can be realized only in a Rousseauist participatory democracy.

Theories ostensibly challenging the idea of consent as the basis for obligation turn around and develop "alternative" theories of obligation that take as their cornerstone the same framework and assumptions that ground consent theory (and indeed, make consent the only possible basis for obligation), namely, the basic priority of individual liberty and the necessity for active and individual choice. For instance, Rawls's "fair play" principle depends on the active acceptance of benefits within a cooperative scheme; while a context of justice is important, passive acceptance or nonavoidance of benefits does not generate obligations. This is juxtaposed to his concept of duty, which is "natural" and not the product of choice. Both duty and obligation involve "schemes" or ends that are just; but obligation, to be such, must be truly voluntary. However, within Rawls's structure, if one does not accept the benefits of a just scheme and hence has no obligation to it, one may still have a natural duty to it by virtue of its "justice." If it is just, one would have agreed to it in the original position. This fact calls into question the usefulness of Rawls's distinction between obligation and duty and highlights a blind acceptance of voluntarism as a prerequisite for obligation even when it does not make theoretical sense.

The problems with voluntarist conceptions of obligation, as numerous theorists have pointed out, are manifold. Since Hume, critics have rejected consent theory on descriptive grounds: When have we ever had a society where the citizens actually were able to give consent and did so? It is also rejected, however, because of internal contradictions and inconsistencies. Some contemporary theorists, such as Simmons (1979), have concluded that obligations simply do not exist. Others, like Pateman (1985), hold that it is not obligation or consent per se but their specifically liberal formulation that is to blame.

None of these critics goes deeply enough to articulate the *reasons* for the problems obligation theory displays. They address themselves to the symptoms, not the causes—with the predictable result that the exact same problems recur, albeit in altered form, in the "new" theories developed to replace the social contract. Even Pateman, who goes farther than many other theorists in tracing the problems of consent to a source, namely, abstract individualism, leaves unasked the question why abstract individualism is so important to these theories.

The answer to this question is extremely important for getting beyond the problems of liberal obligation theory to the creation of a truly new theory, which is my intent here. I assert that the inconsistencies found in voluntarist theories of obligation are inevitable and irresolvable at least in part because of a particular epistemological bias, namely, gender bias. Here I examine one particular avenue of that suggestion, exploring whether a feminist analysis can uncover the deeper roots of the problem of obligation. I will argue that the gender bias found in liberal obligation theory is not merely contingent but structural as well.

By contingent gender bias I mean cultural biases against women, which deny women opportunities for consent and pervert consent theory as a result. Practices of excluding women from standard means of consenting and of denying women the opportunities for choice afforded men present a contradiction to consent theory that it should and can rectify. A fully consistent consent theory would allow women full opportunities to choose their obligations.

This type of argument is not uncommon in political theory and in feminist politics (Jaggar 1983; Pateman 1980). But few have recognized the deeper, structural components of this exclusion. By structural gender bias I mean the bias of the very structure of obligation (its being defined solely in voluntarist terms, and the fact that *nonvoluntary obligation* is an oxymoron) toward a masculinist perspective which automatically excludes women from obligation on an epistemological level. In this light, the provision of "full opportunities" for consent begs, rather than answers, the question of obligation. By declaring that all obligations, to be such, must be taken on voluntarily, consent theory ignores or denies what women's experience reveals, namely, that obligations do in fact exist that are not chosen but stem from the history and character of human relationships. A fully consistent consent theory would have to include (perhaps paradoxically) the recognition that not all obligations are self-assumed.

OBJECT RELATIONS AND THE STANDPOINT APPROACH

To establish this claim, I adopt an approach suggested by Hartsock (1983) called "the feminist standpoint." The feminist standpoint is a variation on the more general conceptualization of Marxian "standpoint epistemology," which was specifically formulated as "the standpoint of the proletariat." A standpoint is the perspective from which one views the world, social relations, and hence reality. It is composed of factors such as race, class, gender, and the kind of work one does; I add psychosexual development. The standpoint approach holds that different people will develop different knowledge frameworks depending on their experiences and circumstances. These experiences form a crucible for perception, interpretation, and understanding by moving many of the unconscious aspects of experience into the realm of consciousness. To the degree that a particular group of people (e.g., women) share socially and politically significant characteristics, they will share a standpoint. Since "epistemology grows in a complex and contradictory way from material life," the standpoint "structures epistemology in a particular way" (Hartsock 1983) that reflects experience.

This does not mean that the feminist standpoint is natural to all women, however; it is not a mere unconscious bias but must be "achieved" or at least acknowledged. This is where political theory is important; it can help translate experience into political meaning or articulate the political significance of women's experience. Feminist standpoint epistemology rejects the idea that epistemology is objective or universal; it holds that epistemology is itself a product of particular social relations. Not just knowledge (*what* we know) is shaped by particular experience and the relations we have to others, but so are *how* we know and how we conceive of knowledge. Thus, if experience differs among groups of people, their epistemological orientations will differ as well.

But it is not just "difference" that is at issue; the standpoint approach further holds that the standpoint of oppressed groups enables them to see more aspects of the social relations that oppress them. Thus, just as the proletariat has a potentially superior vantage point from which to understand the relationship between worker and capitalist, women have greater potential to understand more fully the relationship between men and women. This might suggest that the feminist standpoint is gender-exclusive, but Hartsock would not agree. She specifically uses the term *feminist* rather than *female* to point out both "the achieved character of a standpoint and that a standpoint by definition carries a liberatory potential" (Hartsock 1983, 289). The process of "feminist struggle" welcomes male participants. Other theorists (e.g., Harding [1986]) are very ambivalent about this conclusion—not because they do not want men to be feminists but because they doubt whether the standpoint approach will allow them to participate in "the struggle."

Not surprisingly, there are opponents of the standpoint approach to feminist epistemology, most notably feminist postmodernists. I will not enter the discussion in great detail here (but see DiStefano 1988) except to say that I think the debate is cast in overly dichotomous terms and that I recognize the problems inherent in a concept of *the* feminist standpoint. I will be arguing here for only one of many possible feminist standpoints. The *concept* of a standpoint, no matter how any given standpoint is defined or determined, is philosophically and politically useful and educative in the attempt to understand and analyze mainstream political theory.

The aspect of a possible feminist standpoint that I find most illuminating is offered by object relations theory. This is a school of psychoanalytic theory that maintains that because women, not men, "mother" (that is, have primary if not sole responsibility for the care and nurturance of young children), boys and girls will develop different senses of themselves as gendered subjects as well as different conceptions of their relation to the "object-world," or world outside the self. The power of object relations theory lies in its epistemological implications, for it suggests two very different ways of seeing and "knowing" the world. One fits the dominant discourse of political theory (and political obligation in particular); the other is at odds with it. One speaks the language of rules and rights codified in theory; one challenges that perspective.

Before infants come to have a sense of self (at about six months), their primary identity is subsumed in the one who supplies their needs, who is most generally, across all cultures, female (Rosaldo and Lamphere 1974). Thus, both boys and girls are originally, psychically female. But because gender is culturally an exclusive category, the boy must "become" male. In learning his gender, the boy perceives a fundamental difference between himself and his mother; the girl will learn she is "the same." And because the primary caretaker represents the entire object-world to all infants, the girl comes to see herself as connected to the world: self and other will constitute a continuum for her. In contrast, the boy will come to perceive the self as fundamentally separate and different from the object-world; self and other will be a dichotomy. Becoming male entails making a radical break from primary femininity, represented by the mother, resulting in an overemphasis on separation; a boy defines himself against the mother, as "not-mother."

Such a defensive conceptualization of the self produces what Chodorow (1978) calls "reactive autonomy," a separateness and independence that is a reaction against others. It produces a conception of agency that abstracts individual will (the ability to make choices and act on them) out of the context of the social relationships within which it develops and within which it is exercised, because it sees those relationships as threatening by definition. Furthermore, because the boy's identity is partly formed by the roles that patriarchy dictates for males, the "reaction" is not even to the mother as a person but to what she symbolizes—the boy's primary femininity. Becoming male means becoming "not-female." So while autonomy is defined as independence, its reactive character ensures that others set the terms of one's identity. This contrasts with "relational autonomy" (Bakan 1966), wherein the self derives its strength from its context of relations, not from the absence of others. Thus, "true" autonomy can develop only through a close personal relationship with a mother who is recognized as her own subject

(Flax 1978; Mahler 1968); but in mother-only child rearing, this subjectivity is denied. The resulting concept of autonomy as reactive separation is, like consent theory, mythologizing; for autonomy is a highly relational concept, intrinsically tied up with a qualitatively particular relationship.

These contrasting senses of self and resulting views of the world translate into differing "standpoints" and particular moral perspectives. According to Chodorow, girls' greater sense of connectedness with mother and the world means that they have "a basis for 'empathy' built into their primary definition of self in a way that boys do not" (1978, 167). This is supported empirically by Gilligan (1982), Johnstone (1985), and Lyons (1983), whose studies maintain that female perceive themselves as more connected to others while males tend to see themselves as separate. These contrasting perceptions of the self and its relation to the world result in males who reason more in terms of competing individual rights and rules and females who conceive morality in terms of relationships and overlapping responsibilities. Gilligan in particular argues that women's worldview of connectedness results in a morality of care.[2] Thus, object relations theory suggests that by producing gender-related differences in males' and females' sense of themselves and their relation to the world, exclusively female child rearing provides the material basis for a feminist standpoint, a feminist vision of reality.

I am not suggesting that we take this literature as an essentialist statement about how men and women think. While we can take object relations theory as partly empirical hypothesis, it is also useful to view it as a theory of power. Psychology and psychoanalytic theory—in spite of their misogynist history—gives us a language and vocabulary of power that are very useful for political theory and that *can* transcend gender. After all, men such as Martin Luther King (1969) have expressed the voice of connection and care and have been just as marginalized as women. At the same time, that voice has a history, as does obligation. It is not just coincidence that women have been for the most part powerless and expressed the voice of connection. Indeed, the activities of the private sphere to which they have been assigned—child care, nurturance, affection—have required women to draw on and develop that voice. So while this is not exclusively a "woman's voice," there is a loose gender relationship deriving from history, material experience, and socialization as well as psychology. This grounding in women's experience is the whole point of calling it feminist.

But if we use terms like *the boy* or *the girl* as abstractions that idealize and represent relationships of power, object relations can be seen as a heuristic device for uncovering the epistemological gender bias of Western thought. Most importantly, by identifying individual development as in part the product of created institutions, namely, the social relations of child rearing, object relations can translate individual experience into cultural phenomena or at least explain the institutional and cultural aspects of a supposedly individual experience. If the processes of psychic development produce a view of the self as fundamentally separate or fundamentally connected, this will inform one's view of the world, which in turn will shade one's perception and interpretation of truth, or reality. And of course, if such self-conceptions are gender-related, the accompanying world view will differ by gender as well. Thus, this work suggests that the dominant epistemology that defines political concepts such as obligation, as well as the method of our dominant political theoretical discourses, may themselves be an essential locus of gender bias. So object relations can be an important means of understanding how the problems of liberal democratic theory go beyond the empirical exclusion of women from politics to the fact that the epistemology from which these theories operate is *premised* on that exclusion.

THE PRIORITY OF LIBERTY

Viewing object relations in this way has great potential for challenging many ideals of liberal obligation theory, such as the public-private dichotomy and the inviolability of the individual; for it suggests that what happens in the private relations of child rearing influences how we maintain and define the public. It further reminds us that individuals are not static entities in a state of nature but dynamic beings created and shaped by a variety of factors, particularly relationships with others.

But the strongest link to obligation is through the notion of liberty. As I suggested earlier, liberal voluntarist theories of obligation operate centrally from a notion of what Berlin (1971) has called "negative liberty," consisting of absence of restraints. The individual is free to the extent that she is not restrained by external forces, primarily viewed as law, physical force, and other overt coercion. As anyone familiar with the debate between positive and negative liberty can attest, a central difficulty with the concept of negative liberty is that of determining what exactly constitutes a restraint (Presston 1984). However, Berlin's general concept that restraints come from outside the self is an important basic tenet of negative liberty; specifically, other humans' direct or indirect participation "in frustrating my wishes" is the relevant criterion in determining restraint: "By being free in this sense I mean not being interfered with by others. The wider the area of noninterference, the wider my freedom" (Berlin 1971, 123).

Note the resonance between this concept of liberty and object relations. The quotes selected particularly echo the boy's infantile dilemma. But first I want to look at the term *liberalism*, held by some to be rather amorphous. It may include views ranging from a Hobbesian rational egoism to utilitarianism to Dworkin's and Rawls's concern with the welfare state. Indeed, it is amazing how much liberalism can continually revise itself and still be called liberalism, a privilege generally denied other ideologies. (Could that be testimony to its hegemonic entrenchment?)

The view of liberalism taken by its stronger critics, including a number of feminists, links liberalism inextricably with abstract individualism (Hartsock 1984; Macpherson 1962; Pateman 1985). But I wish to focus on what is less controversial, namely, that one thing common to the various liberal theories is the priority of liberty over other values. Indeed, the very root of the word *liberalism* derives from liberty; as Cranston (1967, 458) says, "By definition, a liberal is a man [*sic*] who believes in liberty, but because different men at different times have meant different things by liberty, 'liberalism' is correspondingly ambiguous." This, of course, is the positive-negative liberty debate; and it can be argued that the welfare state sort of liberalism in fact adopts a positive libertarian view. Yet I maintain that liberalism adopts a consistently negative, not positive, conception of liberty and that positive libertarians like Rousseau are misdescribed as liberals.

For instance, while Rawls ostensibly takes justice as his focus, this is actually subordinate to, and defined in terms of, a real priority of negative liberty. Justice is established through the lexical ordering of principles that give a priority to liberty over equality. Equal worth of liberty—something we might associate with a positive, political liberalism—must take a back seat to liberty per se. Rawls's seemingly innovative ways of addressing inequality, such as the difference principle, serve to justify inequality by veiled appeals to such negative liberty principles as opportunity. Similarly, his theory of the natural duty of justice, as indicated earlier, is unnecessarily complicated by a voluntarist theory of obligation, in an attempt to preserve voluntarism in a nonvoluntarist construct (see Pateman 1985; Simmons 1979).

It can be argued that theorists like Locke are really not so extremely negative as they have been portrayed. Indeed, Locke asserts that "*Law, in its true notion, is not so much the Limitation as the direction of a free and intelligent Agent* to his proper interest" (1964, 347–48), suggesting positive liberty. In this respect Locke may lead the way to a more social view of humans and perhaps of obligation. But he remains firmly in the negative liberty camp. First, Locke also defines liberty as "to follow my own Will in all things, where the Rule prescribes not" (324), emphasizing the necessity of spheres of action not subject to law. Second, what makes law the direction of my will is the fact that I created it, via consent. Of course, laws of nature are to be obeyed because they come from God, not because of consent per se. But because God makes all men rational and coherent with the divine order, they will all naturally want to obey the laws of nature. For example, even if I am too dim or evil to see that the law of nature prohibiting waste is what God wants, I will at least be able to see that violating it is irrational, in that it wastes my labor. So even laws of nature would seem to be legitimized on some level by consent.

The third reason is the most convincing, if most complex; the very fact that Locke felt compelled to develop the doctrine of tacit consent demonstrates his beliefs concerning liberty. Though Locke binds the average unfree, unequal citizen to the state without explicit free choice, he feels compelled to assert that consent is nonetheless given. Through tacit consent he articulates a myth of choice to legitimize coercion through voluntarist language. This is not likely a conscious deception on Locke's part but rather a sincere attempt to reconcile freedom with authority. But it betrays Locke's agenda, for the only justification for the very awkward ideology of tacit consent is the belief in the need for negative liberty. A positive libertarian would not need such a myth (but might need others, as Rousseau demonstrated). A positive libertarian would simply say, "Obey the law because it is in the interest of your higher will, whether you are aware of that yet or not." Thus, the priority of liberty is demonstrated through the assertion that citizens consent even if Locke must use circuitous (if not circular) reasoning to establish it; and the concept of liberty Locke endorses is decidedly negative.

By confining myself to obligation, I hope to establish even more strongly the claim that freedom is central. Social contract theory begins with the assertion of natural freedom and equality; and its more explicitly liberal versions, such as Locke's, further define equality to serve primarily as a means to define and protect freedom. The absolute natural freedom of the state of nature outlined by the social contract theorists entails an absence of restraint except for the restraints imposed by competing and alienated others. The absolute freedom of the state of nature—particularly in Hobbes and Rousseau and to a less obvious degree in Locke—is marked by a lack of control. Fear of ceasing to exist, fear of losing one's possessions, hostility, and suspicion are dominant characteristics (Flax 1983). Even for Locke, the state of war inevitably follows from the state of nature, either because money creates rational reasons to violate the laws of nature concerning hoarding (Macpherson 1962) or because there is no known judge (Dunn 1980). The state of nature is a kind of prison; for within it people cannot realize themselves, they cannot create and control. People in the state of nature seek to escape this chaos by turning to the social contract, thereby trading absolute freedom for "effective freedom," the freedom to act with assurance that one's actions will produce desired results.

Civil society thus seeks to protect the natural freedom that is threatened through war and conflict. It does this in two ways. First, civil society protects possessions and property. By having control over possessions, the individual has control over personal identity. For Locke, for instance, who you are is importantly determined by what you have; and civil society is established first and foremost to protect property. Property is central to freedom. Life, liberty, and property are the basic rights God gives to humans; it can even be argued that property subsumes life and liberty in the liberty to contract one's labor in exchange for wages and in the absolute centrality of property in the social contract. The expansiveness of the term property (Locke uses it alternately to refer to land and the body) also indicates its priority. Similarly, for Hobbes, acquisition and the fulfillment of passions is central to his concept of a person. People must be able to acquire *things* (property) to fulfill their natural passions and perpetuate their motion.

But civil society also exists to ensure that the individual can act rationally. Rules and laws provide predictability, assurance that individuals can act with certainty and hence control their lives. By protecting property and preserving (or making possible) rationality, the social contract not only preserves the citizen from nature but also assists the individual's preservation of autonomy, defined reactively as self-control and self-mastery. From the perspective of this reactive autonomy, obligation necessarily exists only by an act of free will. If I am free above all else (if freedom is what makes me human) I can only be bound (I can only have connections and relationships) by an act of my own free agency.

The logic of the contract thus follows inescapably from the premises of the state of nature. The necessity of consent to obligation must logically derive from the freedom of individuals and from the concept of freedom defined negatively. A positive libertarian like Hegel would force people to be free by forcing them to obey and thus would not necessarily require consent for obligation. Also, by focusing on *individual* consent in the state of nature, these theories make consent to greater or lesser degrees a sufficient condition for obligation. If no relations among people are considered natural,[3] they can only be the product of agreements. As Simmons (1979) argues, the tendency of consent theorists to put limits on consent is not a consistent extension of their theories but a contradiction to the core principles underlying consent. The necessity and sufficiency of consent, in turn, rely on a concept of liberty as absence of restraint, because only such a concept is fully compatible with the extremely individualist view of consent and choice endemic to consent theory.

FREEDOM AND RECOGNITION

If we grant that this negative conception of freedom lies at the heart of voluntarist conceptions of obligation, this gives us a richer perspective on the gender bias of liberalism; for it can be seen in important ways to cohere with the symbolic language of "masculine experience" under mother-only child rearing. According to object relations, the girl, perceiving sameness between herself and her mother, incorporates that sameness into her self-definition and view of the world. She views her relationship with the world as continuous: other is self. For the boy, perceptions of difference cause him to view self and other as totally separate. And these perceptions feed on themselves as the boy actively engages in the conceptualization of the mother as completely other and outside the self.

In dissociating masculine mind-self from the female body–other, restraint is for the boy embodied in the very presence (i.e., the body) of the mother, as the reminder of the boy's primary femaleness and how it is at odds with his masculine gender identity. The mother is viewed as a controlling force that seeks to keep the son imprisoned, that is, merged with her. Her presence thus presents a "barrier" to self-realization of (nonfeminine) masculinity, a limitation and restriction on the boy's ability to become male, to become "himself." Furthermore, this restraint evident in the mother's presence is seen as coming from completely outside the self. Its genesis seems totally other, in spite of the fact that what he is trying to escape—his psychically female identity—is his primary self.

In reaction, the boy "cuts loose" from the (m)other. He detaches, tries to escape her influence and control. By projecting his psychic femaleness onto the mother and by viewing the mother as completely separate, the boy can dissociate himself from his primary femininity. On this reading, a primary goal of the emerging Oedipal boy is to achieve freedom from the constraint of his mother—to excise his femaleness, detach thoroughly from the mother and be free of the female, and thereby "escape the body-female." In short, he seeks absolute freedom from her and from all "others."

But the "freedom" defined by this reactive autonomy further entails domination and contest. Precisely because the deep nature of the boy's psychic femaleness makes it impossible to truly excise, the mother is viewed as a powerful controlling force, inhibitive of self-realization by virtue of her very presence. The search for freedom thus becomes a struggle for control in the boy's subconscious. If he can dominate his mother, who represents his primary identity, he can master that identity. Thus, the boy devalues the mother and his relation to her, belittling all relationship (i.e., "others") in the process. He seeks to deny her subjectivity, her selfhood, and particularly her sexuality. Thus, this "freedom" is viewed as the product of a struggle; the boy achieves freedom only by subordinating the woman.

In reality, however, this freedom is a false abstraction; for in the effort to escape the restraints embodied in the mother-woman, the boy must erect other, artificial barriers; that is, in order to prevent loss of self to the mother, the boy erects barriers to keep her "out" and him "in" his self-identity and gender identity. These barriers range from socially approved institutions of female-exclusive masculinity (from all-boy sports to male-dominated professions) to more pernicious ones, such as widespread belief systems about women's natural inferiority ("the normal male contempt for women" that analysts document in boys from age five on [Brunswick 1940]). These belief systems are partly produced by empirical observation and teaching. The boy can see that women are socially devalued even by observing relations between mother and father. He experiences privileges over his sisters or his friends' sisters. He observes the restraints placed on women by virtue of their sex. But other beliefs develop by extension of these observations because they fill a deep need in the boy to *believe* that women are inferior; for if they are, his mother's power is perhaps not so threatening after all. These belief systems, rules, and practices serve as barriers—restraints—to prevent the boy's return to the mother. Like Locke's "natural law" preventing men from consenting to slavery, these belief systems and rules serve as restraints on action to the end of preserving freedom.

Thus, while this concept of freedom may ostensibly be defined as an "absence of restraint," the conceptual framework afforded by object relations would suggest that it can also be defined as an "absence of the female." Indeed, the notion that freedom in this sense is the hallmark of humanity provides another means of asserting women's nonhuman status. If women were human, they would have a right to freedom. To enact this freedom they would have to seek dominance; and such a search would destroy men, not to mention the fact that it would subvert the very purpose of defining freedom this way in the first place. As long as women are not considered to be human, freedom is not relevant to their existence. They are inhuman and therefore dominatable (like all things in nature) and therefore dominated. But this domination is what asserts women's inhumanity in the first place.

It goes even deeper than this; for if female is "other," freedom entails the absence of the other. This, as Beauvoir and Hegel both brought into our collective intellectual consciousness, constitutes the problem of recognition. Recognition is a key issue to the negative conception of freedom in the masculine psyche; and it is key to the conception of freedom found in liberal voluntarist theories of obligation.

In *The Phenomenology of Spirit*, particularly in the chapter "Self-Consciousness," Hegel argues that the self seeks affirmation by declaring a radical independence. In this, of course, it requires recognition by another being; but self-consciousness seeks to gain recognition from an other without making a simultaneous recognition. Self-consciousness seeks to be perpetually the self, keeping the other perpetually other. Self-consciousness is prepared to die for this recognition. And even though it realizes that death would bring a dubious (if not Pyrrhic) victory, this readiness is what creates masters. Those not so prepared become the slaves, the perpetual objects. The slave is thus "the dependent consciousness whose essential nature is simply to live or to be for another" (Hegel 1977, 116).

This presents a parallel to the "male model" of pre-Oedipal development. For the boy, recognition of the mother as a subject is "dangerous," for it would entail recognizing and accepting his own femininity. Yet because repressing primary identification and excising the female is so difficult (if not impossible), the need to deny the mother as the embodiment of his own femininity becomes intense. And the struggle for recognition becomes, in the boy's unconscious, a life-and-death struggle for dominance. The boy thus resorts to the defensive reaction of taking difference—specifically masculinity as "not-female"—as ostensible validation of his separation or differentiation (Flax 1983). This, however, is an artificial solution with mixed results: it "involves an arbitrary boundary creation and an assertion of hyperseparateness to reinforce a lack of security in a person's sense of their [*sic*] self as a separate person" (Chodorow 1979, 56).

Not prepared to die for the ideal and perhaps even oblivious to the struggle itself, the mother-woman becomes the slave. She is a thing, the perpetual object. Furthermore, because of her perspective—one that values the concrete and real over the abstract and ideal and takes relationship as primary—the mother-woman does not readily perceive this as oppression. She cannot conceive of wishing to die for recognition, which seems to her an inherent contradiction. Her realism and relationship orientation, however, ensure her "enslavement" (objectification, dehumanization, oppression). She, like Hegel's slave, is doomed to "live for another." Yet the reason she does so is not the natural outcome of the dialectic but the result of masculine action. Because of the male's intense need for unidirectional recognition, he creates institutions that solidify woman's role as other.

But in keeping with the standpoint approach, just as the master is in many ways in an inferior position to the slave because he is blind to the importance of material life to self-consciousness, so the boy develops a stance that, while keeping him master, also keeps him from a true realization of his self. For the one-sided recognition he achieves through patriarchy is far from the full recognition required for "relational autonomy," or the full autonomy that can only be achieved through the mutual interaction of subjects and of the location of the self in relationships of mutuality. Rather, we have relationships of domination, which "fail to promote mutual recognition because they prevent individuals from seeing others as anything but totally other; and they accomplish this false othering by promoting differences meant to keep individuals on one level of a hierarchy from being able to recognize individuals on different levels" (Aboulafia 1984, 182–83).

IMPLICATIONS FOR OBLIGATION

What does all this have to do with obligation? I contend that liberal obligation theory has primarily embodied a "reactive" concept of autonomy. The previous discussion has overtly articulated some of the central issues and relevant problems involved in the application of object relations and standpoint epistemology to political theory. It enables us to examine the issue of recognition in a deeper way than liberal obligation theory would at first glance suggest. The themes of the desire for dominance and nonreciprocal recognition have evident parallels in liberal theories, particularly in theories of obligation. They are merely represented more subtly and covertly.

Agency is one of the most important concepts of individualism and consent theory; the individual has the capacity to make choices and thus can assume obligations. But this capacity also carries a moral imperative that obligations can be created *only* by exercising this agency. Agency is the hallmark of independence, autonomy, and adulthood. To be able to make one's own decisions indicates an end to dependence on the will and abilities of another. Hence, agency is what justifies the rejection of divine right and the adoption of the social contract. But because it is a reactive, rather than a relational, autonomy that this agency embodies, it is also what justifies—indeed, creates and perpetuates—the radical and abstract individualism of liberal democratic theory, the market model of society, a theory that obligation can exist only by virtue of voluntary assumption. And these stem in part from the nonrecognition of women.

That is the primary significance of object relations theory for political theory. Because he must become masculine in a world where mother-only child rearing ensures that he is psychically female, where gender is an exclusionary category, and where the female is devalued while the male is elevated, the boy cannot afford to grant recognition to the mother nor, by extension, to any women nor, indeed, to any others. The conception of people as absolutely separate, which the boy develops both from his perception of difference from his mother and from his exaggeration of that difference to bolster his differentiation from her result in a framework in which those separate individuals can resolve conflicts only at discrete and controlled points of contact, only through rule-governed and role-defined structures. This "inability" to grant mutual recognition is the vital seed from which the self-other dichotomy grows, as well as other dualisms that are variations on that theme: subject-object, mind-body, public-private, fact-value, exchange-use. Not coincidentally, these dualisms involve identification of male with the former (the public world of fact, the subject, and the ego) and female with the latter (nature, the id, privatized objects), thus taking as a primary value the denial of women's subjectivity and personhood. On this reading, then, and within this language of symbolization, inequality and dominance serve as a basis for liberal voluntarist obligation. And this suggests important things about its theoretical, ontological, and epistemological grounding and characterization.

If the conception of freedom as negative is premised on the struggle for recognition, particularly on the ability to be recognized without reciprocation—if nonrecognition is (as it is for the Oedipal boy and Hegel's master) a form of power and violence—freedom, too, must be at least in part an expression of that same power and violence. Within a negative conception of freedom, increases to my freedom will come from a lessening of restriction, such as fewer laws; as positive libertarians will point out, however, this may produce less freedom for those not as well off. Thus, freedom becomes zero-sum, a competitive relationship among beings, some of whom seek to win out over others.

Other concepts based on the premises of that freedom will then, likewise, be expressive of power and violence. Thus, "equality," in referring to abstract opportunity and rights, sets the stage for competition and dominance. Opportunity is equal until someone wins the contest, and even then only for those who start off equal in the relevant respects. "Rights" embodies the concept of claims against others, again suggesting competition and dominance; a right further provides a boundary line between various individuals' needs, desires, and wants and hence serves to divide individuals. In the concept of "equal rights," we must respect each other not because we are connected but because of rights, which highlights the line of demarcation between us. Justice Holmes's witticism, "My right to swing my fist ends where the other man's nose begins" is illuminating as much for its articulation of separate and discrete individual spheres of action as it is for its image of violence; the potential for violence lies at the precise point where discrete individuals have contact.

Obligation, as self-assumed, is a particularly significant manifestation of this conception of freedom because, far more than equality, justice, or rights, obligation centrally involves connection, relationship, and bondedness. Yet a completely voluntarist notion of obligation depends on a conception of people as inherently separate and fragmented, and this resonates strongly with the model of male development within mother-only child rearing. The key principle of consent theory is that one has control over one's bonds or connections to others because one creates those bonds. If I do not wish to be obligated to X, I can simply choose not to incur an obligation to X, I simply need not create it. Creation is a form of power in the sense of control and mastery. The act of consent preserves my right to autonomy as self-determination; it thus asserts my separateness and self-control even as I give up some of that control by creating an obligation. By creating bonds through an act of "free will," I maintain control over myself, self-determination, and freedom.

Obligation within the social contract can be seen importantly as a relationship of exchange. Citizens exchange or trade absolute freedom for security, according to Hobbes; for effective and economic freedom, according to Locke; for the moral freedom of self-mastery, according to Rousseau. Humans give up some liberty to the government and agree to obey it; and in return they receive the goods of a "well-ordered society" (to borrow from Rawls).

But underneath the veneer of this exchange relationship is a relationship of power and domination. Within the logic of social contract and consent theory, one potentially puts oneself in another's power when one places oneself under an obligation by giving up part of one's freedom—one's essence—for something else. In this kind of obligation relation, the obligated person must recognize the obliger in performing the obligation, while the obliger need only accept whatever deed is performed in fulfillment and need not recognize the actor. The dangers inherent in this kind of relationship, this formalized connection, are what require the centrality of voluntarism as the legitimator of such a relationship. If obligation is viewed as a power relationship, being placed in such a relationship without active control over one's placement would seem to make such a relationship doubly coercive.

This is certainly most true for Hobbes, but it is also true for more "social" conceptions of consent theory, like Locke's. The purpose of promising as an institution is to ensure that people will keep their word; and the purpose of the social contract is to enforce such contracts with the threat of sanction. Voluntarism would seem to save the individual from nonreciprocated recognition—from connection itself—by giving the individual the power of control over that relationship. Furthermore, since it is an exchange relationship, each self recognizes the other only to the extent that it chooses, that is, to the extent that it is in its interest. Ostensibly, this would seem to pose a solution to the "master's dilemma", for both parties, by expressing their interests, control the degree and form of recognition of the other. Consent thus seems to save us from authoritarian coercion.

But in reality it merely masks it. The seeming reciprocity of exchange is belied by the strict theoretical adherence to consent and voluntarism in face of the fact that such consent is nonexistent for all but a select few. In most of the social contract theories, political obligation is not in fact self-assumed in the full sense by very many people, as critics since Hume have pointed out. Certainly Hobbes's approach to consent, as a "rational fiat," leaves very little to actual human choice. Similarly, Locke's myth of tacit consent served to tell everyone that they had in fact consented when they had not even realized it was an option open to them. Further, those who had not actively (if at all) consented were nonetheless considered obligated to obey the law and government. It is rather widely accepted among modern theorists of obligation (see Flathman 1972; Pateman 1985; Simmons 1979; Tussman 1960) that the conditions for true consent are often absent even today. A large number of people are often not given the opportunity to consent, or they "consent" by performing acts about which they have little choice. Even acts of dissent are interpreted as acts of consent, and unfair bargaining positions belie the freedom implicit in free choice.[4] "Tacit consenters" (usually the nonlanded workers, the poor, not to mention women and people of color) were—and many would say still are—subject to the political decisions of the "express consenters" (the landed and wealthy white men who vote and hold political office). Under a liberal voluntarist conception of obligation, then, the class of "masters" is recognized in every sense (political, social, economic), while the "slaves" are not only denied political voice but are told that their imposed silence is voluntary expression and that they are obligated thereby.

Thus, we are led to the suggestion that voluntarist theories of obligation can be read, at least in part, as theories of power, with power conceived as domination. The "freedom and equality" that supposedly founded all voluntarist theories of obligation are merely a patina that obscures the degree to which the fundamental assumptions guiding our definitions of freedom and equality actually apply to a particular group of people and are at least potentially oppressive to others.

THE FEMINIST STANDPOINT AND FEMINIST OBLIGATION

Why, however, is this a specifically feminist analysis? Women are not the only victims of this conception of obligation; and to that degree there is also a class and race dimension to the problem as well, which will not be analyzed here. Furthermore, it presumes that men will not also use other men of the same race and class in seeking to fulfill the need for dominance.

That the effect is not gender-exclusive, however, does not mean that gender is not an important cause. While object relations theory suggests that the problem of recognition is particularly keen for males, I have also argued that it reflects the experience of the powerful. Since men have power vis-à-vis women, it is to that degree a masculine problem, as well as a white problem and a class, or "bourgeois," problem.

However, the gender dimensions of this problem are particularly powerful because the double-edged exclusiveness of consent theory has special significance for women. The contingent gender bias of voluntarist obligation has portrayed women as incapable of expressing consent and thus of creating their obligations. But even when women's capacity for consent is granted, the structure of voluntarist obligation in fact excludes women by denying the validity of women's experience. Women have been bound historically to an entire series of other obligations— child care most obviously—to which consent is not only often unavailable but often of questionable relevance. Are these "obligations" entirely invalid? Or do they suggest a need to redefine the concept of obligation itself?

The answer is probably a bit of both. Yes, women have been denied opportunities to choose and create their own lives, and these opportunities need to be provided and restored, in part through a "fully consistent" consent theory. Indeed, Enlightenment principles of freedom and equality can be seen as important sources of modern feminism. Many women have left their families, children included, and it can be seen as a form of sexism for us to be horrified by this. But many more women have attempted to carve out choices for themselves without severing relations and responsibilities, for example, by taking their children when they leave a marriage. Many women would balk at the prospect of abandoning their "obligations." One cannot merely blame "false consciousness" or socialization for this. As Gilligan (1982) has argued, "the different voice" engages in moral reasoning from a perspective of relationship and connection, not rights and rules. Such a perspective attunes the reasoner to the needs of others. If a woman takes her children when she leaves her husband, it may well be out of fear for their safety, even though taking them may pose a greater risk to her own safety. Or women might recognize that just as they have been denied choices, so have their children. Should they be the sacrificial lambs to women's realization of their oppression? To say that the women described here have engaged in the process of assessing their options, and have in fact made choices and thus consented, however (even if true consent to their role as mother was not originally given), is disingenuous, for it denies the context within which women are already embedded, a context that places restraints on choice analogous to Locke's tacit consent argument. Rather, the concept of responsibility is the central issue: specifically, responsibility in the positive sense of "responsiveness" (Gilligan 1982).

Obligation needs to be reformulated to account for these values and perspectives, for the very human experience of choicelessness, and for the fact—so adamantly denied by consent and social contract theory—that choices exist in contexts. Indeed, choices are so deeply embedded in contexts of relationship, emotion, value, and taught beliefs—all of which are *social* phenomena, deriving from relations with others and not from a purified or natural self—as to make consent theorists' construal of choice difficult to fit into a realistic picture of human life.

But how would obligation be reformulated along these feminist lines? If the philosophical priority of freedom in part reflects an orientation toward conceiving the self as separate and if women define themselves in relation to others, it follows that a feminist ontology and epistemology would operate from the philosophical priority of obligation. Object relations would then provide us with the basis for suggesting how individual experience at least impinges on institutions like the state as well as on the political philosophy that defines or justifies it.

Accordingly, then, a feminist conceptualization of obligation would operate from a different framework, namely, the givenness of connection and responsiblity. The epistemological perspective of enmeshment in a web of relationships leads to the moral conclusion that freedom—the central element in social contract theory—is, while certainly important to the concept of a person, not necessarily the primary, or central, element. A prior and more central concept would be responsibility in the sense of response, or even obligation itself; that is, from a "feminist standpoint," perhaps obligation needs to be taken as given.

To make sense of this suggestion requires a new framework of inquiry. Working from an assumption of separateness and freedom, consent theorists seek to understand how separate individuals can develop and sustain connections and still be separate, how they can engage in relationships and still remain free. Thus, the central approach involves determining how obligations "arise," how they come into being. But if obligation is given, it does not really make sense to ask how it can arise. Obligation is the standard against which other things, such as the freedom to act as one wishes, are measured. In liberal obligation, the assumption of freedom demands an explanation of any curtailment of that freedom, such as obligations impose. In this feminist conception, such a demand violates the imperative of responsibility and care, and it is the assumption of obligation that demands an explanation of *nonfulfullment*. This different orientation requires inquiry into the contextual conditions surrounding an obligation and obligated person so as to understand the content of an obligation, rather than the process, as well as to understand possible justifications for nonfulfillment. Such an inquiry would examine the concrete particularities of a situation to articulate the conflicting pressures that lead to a particular action as the fulfillment of the obligation, or that provide a possible reason for not fulfilling it. Put rather simplistically, this approach can be seen as more interested in what particular obligations consist of than in how they come to be.

Thus, a feminist method profoundly alters the very terms of the discourse. Beginning with the self as separate, liberal voluntarist obligation seeks to find areas and modes of connection that are safe—that can provide for needs without risking the loss of self. This feminist model, beginning with connection, tries to determine how to carve out a space for the self without violating care. While freedom is certainly achievable in the context of human relationships, it must *be achieved*; it is not a given. Freedom is an entity that must be created, as an individual carves out space for him- or herself. And since freedom is created by a stepping away from, or out of, obligations, freedom must also be justified. Relations cannot be severed by a "mere" desire or act of will. There must be, to borrow from Flathman (1972), "good reasons" for the desire *not* to fulfill obligations.

This does not mean such justification is not possible or even likely for a whole variety of cases. In a century that has seen Hitler, Stalin, and Jim Jones, the concept of a given obligation may make some uneasy. A second source of unease comes specifically from women's experience. Nonconsensual obligations have been imposed on women all their lives. Isn't it time the yoke was shaken off? Should not women be able to choose their obligations, just as men have?

I share these concerns: within the liberal framework, such a construal does not make sense and is indeed nightmarish. But at the same time, these objections miss the depth of the reformulation suggested here. The purpose of a feminist approach to obligation is not to bind us more tightly to the state or to relations, nor am I suggesting that we model political obligations on the relationship between mother and child. Rather, object relations points out that women's experience, which is systematically eliminated from such public ideologies as political theory, can tell us important things about *human* life. It enables us to see the reality that women's lives reveal, that is, that we—men and women alike—are often in fact nonconsensually bound more tightly than our public discourse admits.

Consent theory tells only part of the story of human experience; it presents, therefore, a biased and distorted picture of obligation. The ideology of consent allows us to believe that all obligations are created. We can thus deny the obligatory force of any relations that we do not create or do not wish to maintain. This *we*, however, is largely masculine; for this belief exists, operates, and flourishes in the public realm. In the private realm, women's realm, obligations are often not at all consensual.

At the same time, one cannot merely add women's experience to the dominant discourse because the two utilize different ontological and epistemological frameworks. The problem of women's obligation exists within the context of social institutions and thought that create two different sets of values for men and women—men are naturally free, women are naturally obligated. Within this context, of course, feminists do not wish to maintain the givenness of obligation for women, for that would perpetuate their inferiority. Rather the context must be changed.

But to reverse this order simplistically—to obligate men nonconsensually, as women have been obligated, to "drag them down" to women's oppression—is certainly not a goal. Rather, the point is to call attention to the fact that men already *are* nonconsensually obligated in many ways and that these obligations are appropriate to human relations but that our public ideology will not allow us to recognize this fact. Such a refusal obliterates the hope of a human theory of obligation that recognizes choices *and* givenness. Similarly, women have the capacity to create many of their obligations but are effectively denied the opportunity to do so. This denial, similarly, obliterates the hope of a human theory of obligation.

CONCLUSION

Thus, one must realize that the claim that obligation should be considered as given is an epistemological and methodological claim. It strikes to the heart of how we conduct theoretical inquiry, what sort of questions we ask, and how we formulate them. Certainly, I have provided only a sketch of the positive side of my task, the beginning of an answer to the question of how to reformulate obligation. But the critical dimensions of this feminist theoretical approach are clearly powerful. Through application of the standpoint epistemology method, I have shown how the gender-related experiences that object relations theory articulates can be used to gain a deeper understanding of the epistemological grounding of obligation and of the structural gender bias that voluntarist theories embody. A similar method could be applied to other concepts, like freedom and rights. By asking this very different set of questions, a feminist approach to obligation redefines the issues and problems that political theory needs to address. In doing so, it points new directions for theory to take.

NOTES

A version of this paper was presented at the 1988 annual meeting of the American Political Science Association. Thanks to Richard Flathman and Nancy Hartsock for their comments on an earlier draft.

1. While I will make several remarks on the concept of duty throughout the essay, I will not undertake a detailed discussion of the concept. There are aspects of duty that would prove useful to my analysis, but that is not the project I am engaged in here. My point is that liberal theory places consent at the heart of politics by making it the model for all human relationships. In circular fashion, this is precisely why duty has not been as central to liberal theory, as obligation, justice, rights, and freedom have been. Fishkin's (1979) notion of "general obligation" is also potentially useful to my theory, but I disagree with his claim that nonvoluntary obligation is compatible with liberalism. See Hirschmann, n.d., for a fuller discussion of Fishkin.

2. Gilligan's thesis has bred considerable controversy, for which I refer the reader to other discussions (Kittay and Meyers 1987; Tronto 1987).

3. The obvious, if ambivalent, exception is women's relation to the family. It would bring us into an entirely different discussion, but the family plays a curious and varied role in these theories, as relations between men and women are alternately cast as natural and contractual. But even when the latter prevails, women do not have the same powers and rights as men.

4. I refer here not only to using the roads, which fairly clearly does not correspond to any meaningful interpretation of consent, but also to such liberal demo-

cratic practices as voting and civil disobedience as well. See Hirschmann n.d., Pateman 1985, and Piven and Cloward 1988 for relevant discussions.

REFERENCES

Aboulafia, Mitchel. 1984. "From Domination to Recognition." In *Beyond Domination*, ed. Carol C. Gould. Totowa, NJ: Rowman & Allanheld.

Bakan, David. 1966. *The Duality of Human Existence: Isolation and Communion in Western Man*. Boston: Beacon.

Berlin, Isaiah. 1971. *Four Essays on Liberty*. New York: Oxford University Press.

Brunswick, Ruth Mack. 1940. "The Preoedipal Phase of the Libido Development." In *The Psychoanalytic Reader*, ed. Robert Fleiss. New York: International Universities Press.

Chodorow, Nancy. 1978. *The Reproduction of Mothering: Psychoanalysis and the Sociology of Gender*. Berkeley: University of California Press.

Chodorow, Nancy. 1979. "Feminism and Difference: Gender, Relation, and Difference in Psychoanalytic Perspective." *Socialist Review* 46:51–70.

Cranston, Maurice. 1967. "Liberalism." *Encyclopedia of Philosophy* 3–4:458–61. New York: Macmillan and Free Press.

DiStefano, Christine. 1988. "Dilemmas of Difference: Feminism, Modernity, and Postmodernism," *Women and Politics* 8 (3–4): 1–24.

Dunn, John. 1980. "Consent in the Theory of John Locke." In *Political Obligation in Its Historical Context*. Cambridge: Cambridge University Press.

Fishkin, James. 1979. *The Limits of Obligation*. New Haven: Yale University Press.

Flathman, Richard. 1972. *Political Obligation*. New York: Atheneum.

Flax, Jane. 1978. "The Conflict between Nurturance and Autonomy in Mother-Daughter Relationships and within Feminism." *Feminist Studies* 4 (2): 171–91.

Flax, Jane. 1983. "Political Philosophy and the Patriarchal Unconscious." In *Discovering Reality*, ed. Sandra H. Harding and Merrill B. Hintikka. Dordrecht, Holland: D. Reidel.

Gilligan, Carol. 1982. *In a Different Voice: Psychological Theory and Women's Development*. Cambridge: Harvard University Press.

Harding, Sandra. 1986. *The Science Question in Feminism*. Ithaca: Cornell University Press.

Hartsock, Nancy. 1983. "The Feminist Standpoint: Developing a Specifically Feminist Historical Materialism." In *Discovering Reality*, ed. Sandra Harding and Merrill Hintikka. Dordrecht, Holland: D. Reidel.

Hartsock, Nancy. 1984. *Money, Sex, and Power: Towards a Feminist Historical Materialism*. Boston: Northeastern University Press.

Hegel, Georg W. F. 1977. *The Phenomenology of Spirit*. Trans. Arnold Vincent Miller. Oxford: Clarendon.

Hirschmann, Nancy. Forthcoming. *Rethinking Obligation: A Feminist Method for Political Theory*. Ithaca: Cornell University Press.

Hume, David. 1948. *Hume's Moral and Political Philosophy*, ed. Henry Aiken. New York: Hafner.

Jaggar, Alison. 1983. *Feminist Politics and Human Nature*. Totowa, NJ: Rowman & Allanheld.

Johnstone, Kay. 1985. *Two Moral Orientations—Two Problem Solving Strategies: Adolescents' Solutions to Dilemma in Fables*. Ph.D. diss.: Harvard University Press.

King, Martin Luther. 1969. "Letter from a Birmingham Jail." In *Civil Disobedience*, ed. Hugo Adam Bedau. New York: Pegasus.

Kittay, Eva Feder, and Diana T. Meyers. 1987. *Women and Moral Theory*. Totowa, NJ: Rowman & Littlefield.

Locke, John. 1964. *Second Treatise*. Ed. Peter Laslett. New York: New American Library.

Lyons, Nona. 1983. "Two Perspectives on Self-Relationships, and Morality." *Harvard Educational Review* 53:125–45.

Macpherson, Crawford B. 1962. *The Political Theory of Possessive Individualism: Hobbes to Locke*. London: Oxford University Press.

Mahler, Margaret. 1968. *On Human Symbiosis and the Vicissitudes of Individuation*. New York: International Universities Press.

Pateman, Carole. 1980. "Women and Consent." *Political Theory* 8:149–68.

Pateman, Carole. 1985. *The Problem of Political Obligation: A Critique of Liberal Theory*. Berkeley: University of California Press.

Pitkin, Hannah. 1965. "Obligation and Consent," pt. 1. *American Political Science Review* 59:990–1000.

Piven, Frances Fox, and Richard A. Cloward. 1988. *Why Americans Don't Vote*. New York: Pantheon.

Presston, Larry M. 1984. "Freedom, Markets, and Voluntary Exchange." *American Political Science Review* 78:959–70.

Rawls, John. 1971. *A Theory of Justice*. Cambridge: Harvard University Press.

Rosaldo, Michelle, and Louise Lamphere, eds. 1974. *Woman, Culture, and Society*. Stanford: Stanford University Press.

Simmons, A. John. 1979. *Moral Principles and Political Obligation*. Princeton: Princeton University Press.

Tronto, Joan. 1987. "Beyond Gender Differences to a Theory of Care." *Signs* 12:644–63.

Tussman, Joseph. 1960. *Obligation and the Body Politic*. New York: Oxford University Press.

12

SPECIAL TIES AND NATURAL DUTIES

Jeremy Waldron

I

Philosophical accounts of what we owe the state can be divided into two classes: theories of acquired obligation and theories of natural duty. Theories of acquired obligation are more familiar in political philosophy: our obligation to the state is said to be based on consent[1] or, using the principle of fair play, on the willing receipt of benefits from others' cooperation.[2] The theory that we have a *natural* duty to support the laws and institutions of a just state—the theory that the requirement of obedience is not contingent on anything we have said or done—is less well known and the literature discussing it much less extensive.

This is surprising because, at first glance, the idea of natural duty promises a better account of our moral relation to the law. The law does not predicate its demand for compliance on any contingency such as consent or receipt of benefits. Though few citizens comply with all the laws all the time, those who think there is a moral requirement of obedience usually think so because they believe the laws roughly represent the just demands of life in society.[3] Even those who express their *philosophical* view in terms of acquired obligation tend to push it in the direction of natural duty. Either they assimilate an individual's receipt of benefits from a system (for the purposes of the principle of fair play) to his being treated justly by the system,[4] or if they adopt the consent approach, they turn tacit consent into hypothetical consent, defining a just system as one from which, hypothetically, consent would not be withheld.[5] Philosophers toy with something *like* the theory of natural duty in almost all their thought about what people owe to the state.

It is odd, then, that there has been so little in the way of *direct* discussion of the natural duty idea. A version of it was propounded in John Rawls's book *A Theory of Justice*,[6] but it has not received the discussion that other parts of the book have generated. I suspect this is because the theory is thought to be subject to some rather quick and devastating objections. In this article, I will say what those objections are and show how they can be dealt with. The point is not simply to rebut them. I want to develop an account that responds adequately to philosophical concerns about this way of characterizing what we owe to the state.

II

To understand the objections, we need a formulation of the theory. John Rawls states it in the following terms:

> From the standpoint of justice as fairness, a fundamental natural duty is the duty of justice. This duty requires us to support and to comply with just institutions that exist and apply to us. It also constrains us to further just arrangements not yet established, at least when this can be done without too much cost to ourselves. Thus if the basic structure of society is just, or as just as it is reasonable to expect in the circumstances, everyone has a natural duty to do his part in the existing scheme. Each is bound to these institutions independent of his voluntary acts, performative or otherwise.[7]

Notice that Rawls uses the phrase "just, or as just as it is reasonable to expect in the circumstances." No state in the world is perfectly just; many are egregiously unjust. However, in this article I will discuss only the duties we owe to *just* political institutions. Though this makes the discussion a bit artificial, it is important for the purposes of exposition.[8] Rawls's critics have denied that the natural duty theory would work to bind people even to institutions that *were* perfectly just. If we can rebut these criticisms and develop a plausible account for the ideal case, then—perhaps in subsequent articles—we can see what follows from this theory about duties that are owed to states that fall short of what justice requires.[9]

Let us take the passage from Rawls quoted above as a fair summary of the theory. What are the difficulties that stand in the way of its acceptance? There are, as I see it, two related objections.

The "Special Allegiance" Objection

The first objection is that a theory basing the requirement of obedience simply on the quality of legal and political institutions is unable to explain the special character of a person's allegiance to the particular society in which he lives.[10] I may concede that I am bound to the government of my country insofar as it is just. But what makes it *my* country? Most of us think that is an important aspect of political obligation, for we do not think of ourselves as bound simply to *any* government that happens to be just. The objection is that the natural duty theory cannot explain the moral force of "*my* country" in this regard.

Suppose two countries, say, New Zealand and France, have legal systems that are just.[11] The Rawlsian theory certainly requires the citizens of New Zealand to support New Zealand institutions and requires the citizens of France to support French institutions. So far, so good. However, exactly the same reasoning also requires a Frenchman to support New Zealand institutions and a New Zealander to support French institutions. Since what Rawls postulates is a duty to support just institutions as *as such*, his approach does not establish anything special about the relation between the New Zealander and New Zealand. It seems incapable of capturing the particularity or intimacy of that political relationship.

Theories of consent, by contrast, are in much better shape on this issue. They have no difficulty explaining what is distinctive about a New Zealander's obligations to New Zealand and a Frenchman's obligations to France. In each case, the obligation derives from a promise made to the government or to the other citizens of the country in question. The New Zealander has agreed with his fellow citizens, explicitly or tacitly, to abide by their laws, and he has made no such agreement with the French. That is why his moral situation is special with regard to the laws of New Zealand. The same is true of arguments based on the principle of fairy play. A person living in New Zealand has received the benefits of life lived by others in accordance with New Zealand law; he therefore has an obligation to do his part in the particular scheme of cooperation

from which he has benefited. However, he has received few if any benefits from the law-abidingness of Frenchmen; so he acquires in fairness
no obligation to support or obey their laws.

The objection may seem wrongheaded inasmuch as it neglects an
important phrase in the Rawlsian formula quoted earlier: the duty is "to
support and to comply with just institutions that exist and *apply to us.*"
Maybe French law does not "apply" to New Zealanders, so the difficulty does not really arise. On this account, what is special about my
relation to my own country is that its laws are the only ones that apply
to me. But the insertion of a phrase is not an answer to a philosophical
objection. And anyway, all this maneuver achieves is the opening up of
the Rawlsian theory to a second challenge.

The *"Application"* Objection

The second objection is that the theory fails to explain how a particular
institution comes to be the one to which individuals owe obedience
and support. The theory assumes that in most cases there simply *is* an
institutional structure in society that "applies to us," and that if it is just,
we have a duty to support it. But the notion of an institution's "applying" to a person needs elucidation.

Is "application" simply a matter of the institution's purporting to
address the individual's situation or his claims? If the answer is yes, there
may be all sorts of institutions that "apply" to him. An insurgent movement may appoint "officials" and enact "laws" to "apply" to all the
members of the society whose government they are trying to overthrow.
Do we want to say that the only thing that determines whether people
are bound to such an organization is the justice of its demands? Do we
really want to abandon all interest in whether they have agreed to submit
themselves to its jurisdiction or whether they have brought themselves
under its auspices in some other way, for example, by the acceptance of
benefits?[12]

The Rawlsian theory offers no account, or a plainly inadequate
account, of the existence of political and legal institutions. The problem
is that if we try to articulate a satisfactory account of "application," we
tend to end up abandoning what is distinctive about the natural duty
account. The temptation is to say that an institution "applies" to me
only if I have voluntarily brought myself under its auspices, or to impose

some other similar condition (such as receipt of benefits) on any inference from the justice of the institution to a duty of obedience.[13] But then we are back with *acquired* political obligation. The theory of natural duty fails to provide a real alternative to the traditional Lockean approach. That is the second objection.

III

Though the two objections are connected, I shall answer them one at a time, because I think that is the best way to highlight the neglected strengths as well as the notorious weaknesses of the natural duty approach. I will begin with the objection about special allegiance.

It is not in dispute that the citizens of one country may have *some* duty or obligation to the institutions and laws of another (at least when those institutions and laws are just).

A first example is obvious enough. A New Zealander visiting France is morally bound to obey just provisions of French law, even though they may be different from the provisions of New Zealand law. He should drive on the right side of the road, he should not evade occupancy tax in hotel rooms, he should answer questions put to him by members of the *gendarmerie* even though he might have no obligation to answer such questions if they were posed by a constable in New Zealand.

The idea that two *different* sets of laws might both be just should not require much explanation. For some cases, like the rule of the road, justice does not dictate the particular substance of the rule. The right-hand rule and the left-hand rule are equally just; what matters is that one rule is settled upon. Other cases—for example, those concerning taxes and commercial law—may involve fragments of different systems, each of which, taken as a whole, satisfies the same principles of justice. Thus, for example, a consumption tax may be calibrated to achieve the same distributive effect overall as an earned income tax. A negative income tax may have the same effect as a carefully administered welfare system. Still other cases may involve the application of similar background principles to diverse local conditions, or the integration of local customs, traditions, and ways of doing things into the wider fabric of justice.

It is no objection to the natural duty theory that it requires the New

Zealander visiting France to obey French law and vice versa. However, it is no advantage either. Theories of acquired obligation can explain this as well (if they can explain anything). By choosing to enter France (when he could have gone elsewhere or stayed at home) the New Zealander makes a clear, though implicit, decision to abide by French laws, if only for a short period of time. The New Zealander must know that this is the condition under which his visa was issued, the condition under which the French officials have admitted him, and the condition under which the French people have authorized tourism and immigration arrangements. Or, if the consent theory is rejected, the principle of fair play can explain the tourist's obligation. Sojourning in France, he enjoys the benefits of its social, legal, and economic arrangements, and so for the time being he ought to cooperate in the production of those benefits. This case, then, does not indicate any difference of explanatory power between theories of natural duty and theories of acquired obligation.

A second case is easier for the natural duty theory to explain than its rivals. There are things a Frenchman could do *in France* that would undermine the laws and institutions of New Zealand. We need not play with hypotheticals: a real-life example comes to mind. In 1985, French officials conspired to arrange a terrorist attack by their agents on a ship, the *Rainbow Warrior*, belonging to the Greenpeace organization. The vessel was used by Greenpeace to harass the French in their conduct of nuclear weapons tests in the South Pacific. It was bombed by agents of the French military, operating covertly in New Zealand, while it lay in Auckland harbor. Owing to their Clouseau-like incompetence, the French operatives immediately responsible were apprehended by the New Zealand police and eventually pleaded guilty to charges of manslaughter (for one Greenpeace activist had died in the attack). But it is not the attack itself that is the focus of my example; it is what happened afterwards. During the investigation of the attack, French officials were unhelpful to the New Zealand police, and it is widely believed that they urged their operatives to perjure themselves in the New Zealand courts. Once the saboteurs were convicted, the French persuaded the British and American governments to put economic pressure on New Zealand to secure their release. Thus in various ways officials of the French government living and working in France conspired to undermine the operation of the criminal justice system in New Zealand.[14]

Now we do not need anything like a duty to uphold just institutions to explain the wrongness of the bombing or of the conspiracy to mount the attack. That can be understood quite independently of any duty or obligation to uphold particular laws. It would be wrong whether there were legal institutions in New Zealand or not.[15]

But many would say it was also wrong of the French officials subsequently to obstruct the investigation of the *Rainbow Warrior* affair, to counsel their operatives to perjure themselves, and to interfere with their punishment. That thought *does* seem best captured by the claim that if the criminal justice system of a country is fair, everyone everywhere has a duty not to obstruct it, whether they owe any particular allegiance to that system and live under its laws or not. In this case, obstructing justice in New Zealand was both a possibility and a temptation. The French had a lot to lose if justice were allowed to run its course.

Theories of acquired political obligation cannot explain why it was wrong of them to do this. Not even the most diluted theory of tacit consent is going to yield the conclusion that the officials in Paris had made an implicit promise not to undermine the criminal justice system of a small country on the other side of the world. And no argument from fair play can be made either, for it is unlikely that they ever received benefits from the operation of New Zealand law.[16] The only principle that explains our thought on the matter is one that holds that everyone everywhere has a duty not to undermine just institutions, even when those institutions have nothing directly to do with them.

Let us try a hypothetical example. Suppose a rich playboy with a taste for anarchy contrives to corrupt the judiciary of a foreign country for the sheer fun of it. He bribes the judges to return false verdicts in an array of cases that have nothing to do with him, so that later he can expose yet another legal system as rotten. Surely this action is wrong. But again, the only explanation of its wrongness is that the rich anarchist has violated a duty he has not to undermine the administration of justice—*anywhere*. Neither consent theory nor the principle of fair play can explain what is wrong with his gratuitous interference.

There are two points to be made about the argument so far. First, I assume that proponents of consent and fair play theories share our intuitions about these cases. Since their own theories cannot explain them, they will have to admit that there *is* a duty of the kind Rawls mentions—a duty that applies to everyone with regard to just institutions everywhere. That is not a fatal admission. Their view need not be that consent or fair play is the only principle operating in the area. The first objection is not that there is no such thing as a natural duty to support just institutions, but rather that such a duty cannot by itself account for the special character of political obligation.

Secondly, if there *is* a natural duty that explains why it is wrong for a French official to obstruct justice in New Zealand and wrong for an anarchist to undermine a legal system for the sheer fun of it, presumably the very same duty also holds between an individual and the laws and institutions of his *own* country. Once again, this is not incompatible with theories of consent or fair play. Maybe there are many layers to the moral issue of what one owes to the state.[17]

IV

What can the proponent of natural duty say about the difference between a Frenchman's relation to the just institutions of New Zealand and a New Zealander's relation to those institutions?

I want to develop my account of this difference in several stages: (A) I shall first identify two relations in which an individual may stand to a given principle of justice P_1. (B) Corresponding to that distinction, I shall define two relations in which an individual might stand to an institution administering P_1. Stages (A) and (B) are both abstract: we are to consider the idea of an individual's relation to a principle, and then the idea of an individual's relation to an institution administering that principle. The idea of an institution's administering P_1 includes the idea of certain individuals' being required by further principles—P_2, P_3, and so on—to behave in a certain way with regard to the administration of P_1. For example, if P_1 is "To each according to his need," the other principles may comprise requirements such as "Administer P_1 impartially" (addressed to an official) and "Do not demand more than you need" (addressed to a subject of the institution in question).

At a third stage, (C), I want to shift the discussion from the abstract specification of principles and institutions to their concrete realization.[18] It is all very well to outline the variety of rules that *would* be required for the administration of P_1 by an institution: but we still have to deal with the question of which organizations are *in fact* entitled to occupy that institutional role, that is, which organizations are *in fact* entitled to demand our participation, compliance, and support in their administration of a principle like P_1. As we address this question—as we move from stage (B) to stage (C)—we will also be moving from our attempt to deal with the first objection to our attempt to deal with the second.

(A) Let us begin with a cute example. Hobbes has five children and one cake. He decides that the fair way to divide the cake is to give each child an equal share: "To each an equal amount of cake" is his principle. A neighbor's child, called Calvin, is watching these proceedings from across the fence. Astutely, Calvin points out to Hobbes that the principle "To each an equal amount of cake" entitles him (Calvin) to a slice as well. Hobbes responds that Calvin has misunderstood the principle. The formulation is elliptical, and the principle it abbreviates is not "To each and every one in the world (or even, to each and every one in the neighborhood) an equal amount of cake," but rather "To each *of Hobbes's children* an equal amount of cake." The principle is intended to be limited in its application.

Now Calvin may complain that this is a bad principle to work with inasmuch as it rests on an arbitrary distinction between Hobbes's children and other kids in the neighborhood. Such a complaint may be justified in certain circumstances, but it is not always justified. Hobbes may know for a fact that his neighbor has already served cake to the children on the far side of the fence, so that Calvin does not need any of the cake that Hobbes is now serving to his brood. There may even be a rule in the neighborhood, born out of long experience with incidents like this: "Each parent is to serve his own cake to his own kids."

A principle of distributive justice may thus have a limited application: I shall call such principles "range-limited." In the case we have been discussing, Calvin turns out not to be within the range of Hobbes's principle. He is an *outsider* so far as Hobbes's distribution of cake is concerned. Formally, an individual is within the range of a given principle P_1 (and thus an *insider* with regard to that principle) just in case he figures in the set of persons (or any of the sets of persons), referred to in the fullest statement of P_1, to whose conduct, claims, and/or interests the requirements of P_1 are supposed to apply. Substantively, an individual is within the range of a principle if it is part of the point and justification of the principle to deal with his conduct, claims, and interests along with those of any other persons it deals with.[19]

I hope it is clear where we are heading: I am going to argue that a New Zealander's special relation to the legal institutions of New Zealand is largely captured by the fact that he is an insider with regard to the set of range-limited principles administered by those institutions. However, this account will only work—for Rawls's theory of a natural duty to support *just* institutions—if it is possible for the principles administered by the legal institutions of a country to be both just and limited in their range.

Many recent discussions of social justice presuppose such limitations as a matter of course.[20] John Rawls's theory, for example, is presented as "a reasonable conception of justice for the basic structure of society conceived for the time being as a closed system isolated from other societies."[21] On that approach we could settle what was just for New Zealand and New Zealanders without saying anything about the resources or inhabitants of any other country.

However, the assumption that justice may be confined within the borders of a single society is unsatisfactory. There are vast disparities of wealth between the inhabitants of different countries. The poorest person in New Zealand is considerably better off than most people in Bangladesh, and one feels uneasy about making a passionate case in the name of justice for enhancing the well-being of the former while putting completely to one side all claims that might be made on the Bangladeshis' behalf. Certainly, if we are to use range-limited principles, we must have an argument *justifying* our use of them, and that argument, at least, should not simply treat the Bangladeshis as though they did not exist.

The best candidate in our tradition for such an argument is found in the political theory of Immanuel Kant. Like other contractarians, Kant thought of the state as an arrangement into which people enter for the resolution of conflict and the establishment of a secure system of property. However, Kant believed that morally it was not an open question whether we should enter into such arrangements or not: "If you are so situated as to be unavoidably side by side with others, you ought to abandon the state of nature and enter, with all others, a juridical state of affairs, that is, a state of distributive legal justice."[22] The reason has to do with the avoidance of the "fighting" and "wild violence" that will otherwise ensue among those who find themselves disputing possession of the same resources: "Even if we imagine men to be ever so good natured and righteous before a public lawful state of society is established, individual men, nations, and states can never be certain that they are secure against violence from one another, because each will have his own right to do what *seems just and good to him*, entirely independent of the opinion of the others."[23] The basic principle of morality so far as material resources are concerned is, in Kant's account, that people must act toward one another so that each external object can be used as someone's property.[24] If a stable system of resource use is to be made possible, then a person claiming possession or use of a resource "must also be allowed to compel everyone else with whom he comes into conflict over the question of whether such an object is his to enter, together with him, a society under a civil constitution."[25]

Now, although Kant acknowledges that in principle all humans share the earth,[26] clearly those with whom I come into conflict will in the first instance be my near neighbors. Since no one can afford to wait until all possible conflicts arise so that all can be definitively settled at once, the Kantian approach implies that I should enter quickly into a form of society with those immediately adjacent to me, those with whose interests my resource use is likely to pose the most frequent and dangerous conflicts. These conflicts at any rate must be resolved quickly on the basis of just political and legal institutions, in order to avoid arbitrariness and violence. Throughout the rest of this article, I shall use the notion of "a territory" to refer to any area within which conflicts must be settled if *any* stable system of resource use is to be possible among the inhabitants.

Certainly such resolutions are provisional. As the sphere of human interaction expands, further conflicts may arise, and the scope of the legal framework must be extended and if necessary re-thought, according to the same Kantian principle. But in the meantime, it is important to find a just basis for settling those conflicts that are immediately unavoidable, a basis that is just between the parties to those conflicts.

V

It seems, then, that principles of justice can be limited in their range, at least on a *pro tem* basis. This is sufficient to establish the distinction between insiders and outsiders that I need for the remainder of the argument. I move now to the second stage of the argument, to consider the administration of principles by institutions.

(B) Principles cannot conduct distributions by themselves: they must be administered by working institutions. What would an institution L have to be like in order to administer a range-limited principle of distributive justice P_1? What demands would L have to make on the behavior of those who were insiders and on the behavior of those who were outsiders with regard to P_1?

The first demand made by L would be, of course, the demand of justice embodied in P_1 itself. Suppose P_1 is limited in its range to the interests of A and B: it dictates that a certain fund of resources be divided equally between them. Then P_1 requires of A that he not take more than an equal share. For A to accept P_1 is for A to accept that requirement, and for L to administer P_1 is for L to supervise and enforce it.

Second, L will have to require that A and B *accept* its supervision in this regard. Suppose A and B disagree about the interpretation of P_1 or about what counts as an equal share. A third person, C, may come along and offer an opinion. A or B or both may turn on C and say that it is none of her business; in some contexts that may be an apt reply. Suppose, however, that C is a functionary of L and acting in her official capacity. If A and B accept L's supervision, this changes the picture for them. To accept L's supervision is to say (among other things) that it is for officials of L to arbitrate disputes about the application of P_1. Their determination is to be accepted, if any third party's determination is. No doubt there are also other aspects of A's and B's accepting supervision by L. In general, if P_1 is to be administered by L, then those who are insiders with regard to P_1 are morally required to abide by the following principle, P_2: "Accept the supervision of L with regard to the implementation of P_1."

Like P_1, P_2 will be a range-limited principle. Since it is the point of L to administer P_1 (perhaps among other principles), A and B mark themselves as insiders in relation to L by accepting P_2. In general, a person is an insider in relation to an institution if and only if it is part of the point of that institution to do justice to some claim of his among all the claims with which it deals.[27] So, for example, a New Zealand resident is an insider in relation to the fiscal and welfare institutions of New Zealand, for it is part of the point of those institutions to do justice to his claims to income and assistance along with all the other claims that they address. The aim of the institutions is to determine what burdens it is fair to impose, and what benefits it is fair to confer, on this person and on others in New Zealand in the course of that overall enterprise.[28]

A third demand that will have to be made if P_1 is to be administered effectively by L is this: that both insiders and outsiders refrain from attacking or sabotaging L in its attempts to put P_1 into operation. Even the most just institution is vulnerable to human interference, whether that is motivated by greed or some other antisocial impulse. In order to operate, an institution administering P_1 will have to promulgate or otherwise get accepted a third principle, P_3: "Do not undermine the administration of P_1 by L."

Unlike P_1 and P_2, P_3 will be a principle of unlimited range. It will address anyone and everyone whose actions might possibly affect the administration of P_1. Those whose conduct with regard to L is constrained only by this third principle may be called outsiders in relation to the institution L.[29]

P_3 is entirely consequentialist in conception. The claim made in its behalf will be that everyone should recognize that there is value in justice being done, even when they are not those among whom it is being done in this particular instance. For that reason, they should refrain from interfering with it.[30] Suppose, as before, that L has put into effect a just distribution between A and B regarding a certain fund of resources. A mischievous outsider, C, has it in mind to do something that will undermine or upset that distribution. Why should she refrain? Because her intervention may have an effect that is bad from a moral point of view, namely, that A gets more (or less) of the fund than he is entitled to (as against B). Though B's is the only claim that A's is balanced against in this distribution, the justice of A and B each getting his fair share can be recognized from an impersonal point of view, and the badness of that distribution's being upset can therefore be acknowledged even by someone who does not have a direct stake in the matter.[31] If A were to seize more than his fair share, that would be direct injustice; the moral requirement not to do that is precisely what the initial principle of justice, P_1, amounts to (so far as A is concerned). When C upsets the distribution between A and B, the *result* is injustice even though C's action is not itself a violation of P_1 in the way that a greedy encroachment by A would be. C's act is wrong because of its consequences.

I believe this distinction between insiders and outsiders explains much of the specialness of an individual's relation to the institutions of his own country, at least so far as moral requirement is concerned. It gives a reasonably clear sense to the Rawlsian formulation that a person owes support to just institutions that "apply to him." The laws of New Zealand do not purport to address conflicts involving the ordinary claims and rights of Frenchmen. So, no matter how just those laws are, the relation of most Frenchmen to them is at most an external relation: there are things they can do to undermine the legal system in New Zealand, but they are not bound internally to their determinations of justice.[32] By contrast, a New Zealander *does* have the special insider relation to the laws of his own country. They have been set up precisely to address the question of the rights and duties of someone in his position vis-à-vis his fellow New Zealanders. That is the sense in which they apply to him.

Notice that this answer to the first objection does not make specialness merely contingent. In his original formulation of the "special allegiance" objection, Ronald Dworkin considered the following response: "We can construct a practical contingent argument for the special duty. Britons have more opportunity to aid British institutions than those of other nations whose institutions they also think mainly just."[33] But, he goes on, "this practical argument fails to capture the intimacy of the special duty." Dworkin is right about that. However, the distinction I have developed is a distinction in principle. Though it does not flow from citizenship as such, it depends on the difference between being one of the parties in respect of whose interests a just institution is just, and being a person who is merely capable of interfering with a just institution in some way. It is a difference in the content and structure of the natural duty, not a difference that depends on contingent facts and opportunities.

I concede that there may be other elements of patriotic affect and allegiance that this account does not capture.[34] Though I have lived for years in the United States, I feel a fierce loyalty to New Zealand—and for its institutions as well as its sports teams!—a loyalty that has nothing to do with any special application to my interests of the principles of justice it administers. I suspect that, in the end, these ties must be explained by reference to the idea of *nation* rather than polity, and birth and acculturation rather than any juridical connection. Nation, birth, and allegiance in this sense are matters on which modern political philosophers have had embarrassingly little to say.[35] I am comforted, however, by the thought that theories of acquired obligation—theories based on consent or on the principle of fairness—have even less to say on these matters than theories of natural duty.

VI

An institution will be able to administer a range-limited principle of justice P_1 only if most of the people to whom it applies accept P_2 and only if most others also accept P_3. But how do we establish that a given organization is to fill this role? If an organization simply announces that it wishes to fill the role of institutional administrator of P_1 and shows itself capable of doing so, is this sufficient to establish that insiders and outsiders (with regard to P_1) are actually bound to that organization by principles like P_2 and P_3, respectively? This leads us to stage (C) of the argument and to the hub of our discussion.

(C) The disconcerting thing about the theory of natural duty is that it envisages moral requirements binding us to a political organization (a would-be state) quite apart from our agreement to be so bound, and quite apart from any benefits the organization has conferred on us (not counting those benefits whose conferral follows from its being a just organization). We suddenly find ourselves faced with a body of people purporting to do justice in our territory. In order for them to pursue that aim, they must elicit a certain amount of compliance and support from us. The natural duty theory is that they are entitled to that compliance and support simply by virtue of the quality of organization that they have put together.

Is this acceptable? Are there any other conditions we should stipulate, apart from the requirement that the organization be just—in its own workings and in the principles it proposes to apply?

One obvious additional condition is that the organization be *capable* of doing justice in the territory and over the claims that it purports to address. No one, surely, is morally bound to support a lost cause; or if they are so bound, for example, by personal ties of promise or fealty, they are not bound to an ineffective organization merely by virtue of the just character of what it would do if it were not ineffective. This point applies to collapsing *anciens regimes* as well as to governments-in-exile, hopeless insurgencies, and so on.

Whether an organization is effective will depend partly on whether people are prepared to accept it. In our notation, that includes whether they accept and follow the principles such as P_2 and P_3 that are necessary for its operation. But there is no vicious circle here: I am not saying that one is bound to follow these principles only if the organization L is effective and that L is effective only if one follows these principles. The point is rather that a person must be assured that sufficient others are disposed to comply with the principles before he can reasonably think L is effective and thus before he can reasonably think that he is bound to follow the principles. In some situations, this will generate collective action problems of a type familiar to students of Hobbes.[36] But often it will not. Most of us, when we awake to a consideration of these matters, find ourselves faced with an organization to which the people around us are already lending their support. The effectiveness condition, therefore, is usually already fulfilled for most societies under modern conditions.

But not always. Occasionally there is more than one organization purporting to do justice in a certain territory. I have in mind cases such as Northern Ireland, where in certain Catholic enclaves the IRA purports to administer rules of social conduct (knee-capping muggers, collecting funds to support "law enforcement," distributing welfare assistance, and so on) in a way that rivals the parallel, though much more highly organized, apparatus of the British state. Or consider a situation like that of modern Lebanon, where in certain areas there are several rival and apparently parallel state or proto-state apparatuses. In cases like these, if both rival organizations are in fact just,[37] does either of them have a claim of natural duty on us?

It is no good responding that it does not matter because if both are just their demands will coincide. We have already seen that that need not be the case. The organizations may make different and incompatible demands that nevertheless address all the main issues of justice in society adequately or nearly adequately. And of course each will need to raise money to fund the cost of *its* actually doing what justice requires. If we have a duty to support just institutions, does it follow that we have a duty to support *both* institutions in a case like this? That is a question about the duty of justice owed by insiders, that is, the persons in the territory patrolled by these rival institutions. We can also ask a similar question about the duties of outsiders. If there are two rival states or proto-states in a territory, do outsiders have a duty to refrain from interfering with both of them, or only one (which one?), or neither?

Clearly we need another condition to deal with these issues. I want to suggest that the natural duties come into play only where the organization in question passes not only tests of justice and effectiveness, but also a test of legitimacy. What must be established is that there is a good reason to recognize *this* organization, as opposed to any rival organization, as *the one* to do justice in the given territory or with regard to the claims that are at issue. To the extent that such reasons exist, the organization is "legitimate." Legitimacy, then, is an exclusive characteristic: only one organization may be legitimate with regard to a given set of claims or with regard to the issues of justice arising in a given territory.

The explication of the legitimacy requirement has three parts to it: (i) We must recall why it is important for there to be institutions doing justice. (ii) We must show why it is important for there to be only *one* such institution in a territory. (iii) We must indicate grounds on which it might be appropriate to favor the claims of one particular organization over those of its rivals.

(i) The first step takes us back to the Kantian theory we noted in Section IV. The setting up of political institutions, Kant argued, is the way to avoid or mitigate the disagreements and conflicts that will otherwise inevitably arise even among people attempting in good faith to follow the dictates of justice. Because the stakes are high, these conflicts always threaten to issue in violence. Such violence will involve death and suffering, and, as Thomas Hobbes famously pointed out, the anxiety and unpredictability that accompany it will make it difficult for anyone to pursue a decent life.[38] Political institutions are capable of making things better in this regard: they can mediate and arbitrate disputes, they can develop practices of impartiality, and they can collect together sufficient force to uphold their determinations. There is therefore a clear moral interest in their establishment.

(ii) The reasons for having political institutions are also reasons for ensuring, if possible, that there is just *one* in each territory. In *Anarchy, State and Utopia*, Robert Nozick imagined that some of the inhabitants of a territory might join one enforcement-and-arbitration organization and some might join another. The reasons that led people to join these organizations would, he said, also lead to fighting between them.[39] If anything, such violence will be worse than that of the Hobbesian "war of all against all," because the battles will be better organized. The moral interest in reducing such fighting provides a reason for all of us to join and support the same organization, and that gives each of us a reason to join and support whatever organization others are joining and supporting. Once again, this may involve collective action problems: but it need not, and even if it does, the problems are not necessarily intractable.[40]

There are other reasons too. Justice is partly a matter of cooperation. Though in most human situations (even those in which institutions are lacking) individuals can distinguish between just and unjust courses of action, they will often feel that things would go better from the point of view of justice, and that their own actions would make more of a difference, if they could be sure that others were following the same goals as they were. A single person contributing to charity, for example, may see his own donation as a drop in the ocean—worthwhile in itself, no doubt, but in the long run essentially futile in comparison to the magnitude of the problem. He may think that a problem like world poverty is adequately addressed only if all or almost all well-off people make an organized effort to do something about it. In other words, it may make a difference to what it is just for me to do whether I have the assurance that others are cooperating with me.[41] An institution with authority over a large number of people may help to provide this assurance. But usually that assurance can be provided only if the number of institutions addressing the problem that concerns me is limited (perhaps to one). Too great a plurality of institutions may dissolve the advantages of an assured scheme of cooperation and reintroduce the chaos of a number of cross-cutting initiatives, each of which seems futile in itself.

For some cases, the importance of singling out one organization to do justice in a given area stems paradoxically from the plurality of possible just schemes. The point is clearest in the case of simple coordination problems. A scheme that required motorists to drive on the left would be just. And so would a scheme that required motorists to drive on the right. But this plurality does not mean we can allow rival schemes to operate in the same territory. The problem of coordination here will not be solved unless one and only one is chosen. Though either would be just and though either would be better than no solution at all, common sense requires that one of them be rejected.

Now we cannot use coordination problems as a model for all issues of justice and political obligation.[42] But many of the issues of choice with regard to just institutions do have this character. Suppose we establish something like a Rawlsian difference principle as a fundamental criterion of economic justice.[43] There may still be choices to be made about the best institutional structures for achieving this: a negative income tax, for example, or some more familiar scheme of welfare support. Some of these choices are made on the basis of which structure is more likely to be just, given the contingent circumstances and history of each society. But some of them may simply be arbitrary: welfare scheme W together with fiscal scheme X may be every bit as just as welfare scheme Y together with fiscal scheme Z. It will matter that we settle on one combination, but it may not particularly matter which.

The example also illustrates another point about the need for a single scheme of justice. As Rawls has stressed, the institutions of a society operate as a single structure and, for the purposes of a theory of justice, have to be assessed as a whole.[44] It may not be possible to say that the taxation scheme of a society is just until we consider how it fits with the property system, the education system, the welfare system, and so on. Because justice is in this sense systematic, and because systematicity may depend on there being a unique set of interrelated institutions, it seems that any claim that justice can make on us presupposes the identification of one set of organized institutions as *the system* that makes a claim on us, if any system does.

(iii) The reasons for having a single scheme of justice in a society give us our best grip on the criteria for political legitimacy. To the extent that the underlying reason has to do with strategic choice in something like a coordination game, anything that establishes the salience of one system over others will be a reason for preferring it. In most cases, the fact that there *is* a state and that it is, for all practical purposes, dominant and unchallenged in a territory will be sufficient. This is the organization that deserves our support in the enterprise of doing justice if any organization does.

What if there is competition between two or more plausible contenders? How should we choose which to support? Since effectiveness is one of the conditions we have imposed, there may be reason to choose the more powerful contender. Alternatively (if this does not amount to the same thing), we may have reason to choose the organization with the greater popular support.

This criterion might seem to reintroduce the idea of government by consent—the very idea that natural duty theories are trying to replace. The idea seems to be that if most people in a territory agree that some organization L is *the* system to keep order and mete out justice in that territory, then their consent confers legitimacy on L and provides *me* with a basis for identifying L as the institution deserving of my support and allegiance.

However, this does not amount to a reintroduction of the consent theory of obligation (though it may help to explain why consent is so often appealed to in this context). For one thing, consent is being suggested here as one possible ground for legitimacy; it is not the only possible ground. The sheer existence of an institution as dominant and unchallenged may suffice to establish its salience, whether it is popularly supported or not. For another thing, the consent that establishes legitimacy in this sense affects the duties not only of those who give their consent but of outsiders too. Once a Frenchman has identified the institutions that are supported by the people of New Zealand, he is bound (as a matter of natural duty) to regard those institutions as the ones he must not attempt to subvert or undermine even though he himself has never agreed to support them.

In general, the use of consent in relation to legitimacy is quite different in its logic from its use as a direct ground of obligation.[45] In the latter case, consent is represented as a promise; in the former case, it is more like a permission or nomination. Few of us think that hypothetical promises can create real obligations; but we do often believe that hypothetical consent can confer real permissibility on what would otherwise be wrongful intrusions. A surgeon pondering whether to operate on an unconscious accident victim does not have to wait for actual consent; she can proceed on the basis of her best sense of what the accident victim would have agreed to if he had been conscious.

Also, consent in this context is not incompatible with majoritarianism, as it is in classic theories of social contract. One cannot be voted into a social contract, because there the image of consent is being used to explain individualized obligation and it is part of the logic of that image that one's own obligations can be generated only by one's own agreement. But if the consent of a community is being used to establish institutional salience, or to provide the assurance one needs for cooperative action, then the agreement of a majority of the inhabitants of a country may suffice. The advantage of the natural duty approach is that the *obligatoriness* of respecting an institution's demands of justice is secured independently of consent, as a matter of moral background. Consent is used here simply to establish which institutions may appropriately embody those demands.[46]

Indeed, for this latter purpose, propositions about *hypothetical* consent (even hypothetical majority consent) might be sufficient (though again they are not sufficient as direct grounds of obligation).[47] If a pair of rival institutional systems, L_1 and L_2, in a territory T are such that most of the people of T would clearly agree to be governed by L_1 rather than by L_2 if they were asked, and if almost everyone in T knows this about the two systems, then it seems that L_1 is clearly the salient choice as *the* system to which allegiance is owed on grounds of justice, if such allegiance is owed to any institutional system. That the people of T have not *actually* consented to L_1 is neither here nor there. They have a natural duty to support whatever institution can be identified as the appropriate one to do justice in their territory; and these hypothetical propositions about their consent (or the consent of most of them) are sufficient basis for that identification.

Popular consent may, finally, be relevant to institutional choice as an aspect of justice. In our models so far, we have imagined institutions administering substantive principles of social justice; we imagined that P_1 was something like "To each according to his need" or "To each equally" and that it applied to the distribution of material resources. But institutions will also have to address the distribution of political power. Most of us think that, in this regard, an institution is just only if it is democratic: that is, only if it proposes to settle disagreements about what justice requires by some form of voting among all the people who are subject to its jurisdiction. The idea of a natural duty to support just institutions may therefore involve the idea of a natural duty to support democratic institutions, institutions that embody regular appeals to popular consent. Even so, the requirement to support such a regime is based on the justice of its political system: it is not based directly on consent.

VII

The position we have reached is that an organization that is just, effective, and legitimate (in the sense of being singled out as *the* salient organization for this territory) has *eo ipso* a claim on our allegiance. Though popular consent may be implicated in its justice, its effectiveness, or its legitimacy, the moral requirement that we support and obey such an organization is not itself based on any promise that we have made.

Despite the conditions we have imposed, someone might still balk at the general idea behind this position. Can an organization simply *impose* itself on us, morally, in this way?

There comes a point when the theorist of natural duty must stop treating this question as an objection and simply insist that the answer is yes. His affirmative answer is, after all, what distinguishes a theory of natural duty from theories of acquired political obligation.

To defend the answer, he will emphasize two considerations: first, the moral importance of justice, and second, the moral significance of the difficulties that attend the pursuit of justice without political institutions. We have rehearsed the second consideration already. The pursuit of justice often requires coordination, among those who are attempting to do justice and among the various spheres in which they are attempting to do it. Institutions are necessary for that coordination. Without them, there will be more injustice. So to the extent that the avoidance of injustice is a moral imperative, the establishment of coordinating institutions is a moral imperative.[48] In addition, there are the considerations about conflict that were also discussed earlier. The pursuit of justice in an institutional vacuum leads to conflict among persons who have different views about what justice requires, and that in turn issues in violence, suffering, and anxiety. These things are worth avoiding in themselves: they are additional evils (that is, evils over and above injustice itself) attendant on the conflicting efforts of a number of people to avoid the primary evils of injustice.

In all of this, the assumption of the natural duty approach is that the pursuit of justice is a moral imperative. This proposition is one that needs to be understood carefully. At the beginning of *A Theory of Justice*, Rawls writes: "Justice is the first virtue of social institutions, as truth is of systems of thought. A theory however elegant and economical must be rejected or revised if it is untrue; likewise laws and institutions no matter how efficient and well-arranged must be reformed or abolished if they are are unjust."[49] But the analogy is misleading. To say that *if* I propound a theory it is important that the theory be true is not the same as saying that it is important that I propound a true theory. From the point of view of truth, there may be no problem with silence or theoretical reticence. Analogously, Rawls seems to be saying in this passage that *if* we have social and political institutions, it is important that they be just. In fact, the importance of justice goes beyond this. It is morally imperative that the demands of justice be pursued *period*. If institutions are necessary for their pursuit, then it is morally imperative that such institutions be established. Our duty of justice is not satisfied by ensuring that whatever institutions we happen to have are just: it is satisfied only by our doing our part to establish just institutions. The point, once again, is the Kantian one. Because we are not to regard remaining in the state of nature as a permissible option, we may not say that whether we are bound to legal institutions is a matter of whether we happen to promise our cooperation. Our cooperation in establishing and sustaining political institutions that promote justice is morally required. That is the backbone of the natural duty position.

Once we see this, we see how to deal with an alleged counterexample put forward by A. John Simmons in articulating the second of our original objections—the "application" objection. Simmons asked us to imagine an organization simply arriving on the scene and announcing that it proposes to do justice.

> Imagine . . . that a group a benighted souls off in Montana organizes an "Institute for the Advancement of Philosophers," designed to help philosophers by disseminating papers, creating new job opportunities, offering special unemployment benefits, etc. Moreover, these benefits are distributed strictly according to the demands of justice; and they are made possible by the philosophers who pay "dues" to the Institute. . . . One day the Institute . . . decides to expand its operations eastward, and I receive in the mail a request that I pay my dues. Does this institution "apply to me"? There is a very weak sense in which we might say that it does; it is an institution for philosophers and I am a philosopher (of sorts). I may even stand to benefit from its operations in the future. But am I *duty-bound* to pay my dues, in accordance with the "rules" of the Institute?[50]

Simmons thinks the answer is no, irrespective of the justice of the Institute: "People cannot simply force institutions on me, no matter how just, and force on me a moral bond to do my part."[51]

The example is ambiguous, so far as the justice of the Institute is concerned. An institution can be just in two ways: (a) it can be just in the way it operates; and (b) it can be just in the sense that it is doing something that justice requires. Simmons stipulates that the Institute is just in sense (a): comparing the charges it levies with the benefits it distributes, it deals fairly with the revenues it raises. But to establish that it is a just institution in a sense that would engage the Rawlsian principle, one has to show more than that. One has to show that it is just in raising the levy in the first place. That involves considering both the benefits it offers and the other purposes on which philosophers might want to spend their money. It involves showing that, as a matter of justice, it is imperative that people do what they can to support philosophers (over and above the general schemes of social support to which they are already contributing). Our readiness to agree with Simmons' verdict on the hypothetical stems, I suspect, from the belief that this cannot be shown. We think that a philosopher may fairly resist the Institute's demands by saying, "I concede that your organization is just so far as its internal workings are concerned. I even concede that helping philosophers is a nice thing to do. But I deny that it is important from the point of view of justice to offer philosophers this assistance, so I don't see that I am doing anything wrong in refusing your request for my support, at least so far as the natural duty theory is concerned."

Suppose the case were different. Suppose the benighted souls off in Montana were to set up an institute to give aid to the homeless. Suppose, moreover, that the founders of this institute were right in thinking that their organization is not only just in sense (a)—that is, with regard to its internal workings—but just also in sense (b). They believe that the homeless are entitled, as a matter of justice not charity, to much more than they are currently receiving under state welfare arrangements. If they were right about that—if it really *were* a demand of *justice* that they were responding to—then, assuming their institute was effective and not competing with any other organization to address this problem, the theory of natural duty *might* yield the conclusion that we are morally bound to support it. As soon as we became aware of the organization, of the true nature of the problem it was addressing, and of its position as the only organization in the country proposing to deal justly with homelessness, maybe we *would* be bound to send off our check for the amount it determined we should contribute. That conclusion might seem counterintuitive and certainly uncomfortable. But I wonder how much of this discomfort is due to our bad faith about justice, rather than to any specific difficulty about the duties that we owe to institutions.

NOTES

I am grateful to Leslie Green, Kenneth Kress, Michael Moore, and Eric Rakowski for earlier discussion of these ideas. A first draft of this article was prepared under the auspices of the Program in Ethics and Public Life, Cornell University. I am particularly grateful to Henry Shue for his support and his comments. A later draft was presented to a Philosophy Department seminar at Princeton University; comments and criticisms received on that occasion are also much appreciated. I am also indebted to the editors of *Philosophy & Public Affairs* for their criticisms.

1. Arguments basing political obligation on agreement are of course as old as the *Crito*. The classic exposition of the theory of tacit consent is John Locke, *Two Treatises of Government*, ed. Peter Laslett (Cambridge: Cambridge University Press, 1988), II, pars. 87–89, 119–22 (pp. 323–25, 347–49). For a modern discussion, see Leslie Green, *The Authority of the State* (Oxford: Clarendon Press, 1988), chap. 6.

2. The principle of fair play is defended in H. L. A. Hart, "Are There Any Natural Rights?" in *Theories of Rights*, ed. Jeremy Waldron (Oxford: Oxford University Press, 1984), p. 85. See also John Rawls, *A Theory of Justice* (Cambridge, Mass.: Harvard University Press, 1971), pp. 108–14, 342–50; and George Klosko, "The Obligation to Contribute to Discretionary Public Goods," *Political Studies* 37 (1990): 196–214.

3. See Tom Tyler, *Why People Obey the Law* (New Haven: Yale University Press, 1990).

4. See A. John Simmons, *Moral Principles and Political Obligations*: Princeton: Princeton University Press, 1979), pp. 109–14.

5. See Hanna Pitkin, "Obligation and Consent," *American Political Science Review* 59 (1965): 996 and 60 (1966): 39, 44.

6. Rawls, *A Theory of Justice*, pp. 114–17, 333–37.

7. Ibid., p. 115.

8. See ibid., pp. 8–9, for this order of exposition.

9. One important topic that Rawls does address concerns the tension be-

tween social justice as a substantive standard and justice in the distribution of political power. If people disagree in good faith about what justice requires, then their operation of a just system of political choice may require some of them to put up with policies whose justice they dispute. See ibid., pp. 195–201, 221–34.

10. See, for example, Ronald Dworkin, *Law's Empire* (Cambridge, Mass.: Harvard University Press, 1986), p. 193: "That duty . . . does not provide a good explanation of legitimacy, because it does not tie political obligation sufficiently tightly to the particular community to which those who have the obligation belong; it does not show why Britons have a special duty to support the institutions of Britain."

11. I shall use New Zealand and France as examples throughout this article because they satisfy the following conditions: (1) neither society is so egregiously unjust that it would strain credibility to use it as a paradigm for the purposes of this argument; (2) they are distant enough from one another that there is no question of their really being part of one big society (as France and Britain are part of the European Community); (3) there are relatively few cases where New Zealand courts have to make decisions about the rights of people living in France and vice versa; but (4) there are things that the citizens of the one country can do to promote or undermine justice in the institutions of the other. If France and New Zealand are thought bad examples, any other pair of countries satisfying these conditions will do, though condition (4) was dramatically illustrated for this pair in the *Rainbow Warrior* affair, when operatives of the French state blew up and destroyed a vessel lying at anchor in Auckland harbor in July 1985.

12. The objection is put forward by A. John Simmons. See Simmons, *Moral Principles*, pp. 147–52. I will discuss Simmons' version of the objection in more detail in Section VII.

13. See ibid., p. 151, for Simmons' notion of "strong" application.

14. There are excellent accounts in Richard Shears and Isobelle Gidley, *The Rainbow Warrior Affair* (London: Unwin, 1986); and John Dyson, *Sink the Rainbow: An Enquiry into the "Greenpeace Affair"* (London: Victor Gollancz, 1986).

15. To put it another way, the idea of natural law suffices to explain why it is wrong to blow up a ship with the danger of loss of life. See Locke, *Two Treatises*, II, par. 9 (pp. 272–73), for the claim that the magistrates of one country may rely on natural law if they wish to punish aliens.

16. However, the French police would have received normal cooperation from the New Zealand police in the past in homicide and antiterrorist inquiries, so that the withdrawal of cooperation in the *Rainbow Warrior* case might be seen as a failure of reciprocity.

17. Rawls argues that at least some citizens and officials have an obligation to the laws and institutions of their society based on the principle of fairness in addition to the normal bond of natural duty: see Rawls, *A Theory of Justice*, pp.

336–50. For a critique of this "two-tier" approach, see Green, *The Authority of the State*, pp. 244–46.

18. Rawls notes that an institution may be thought of in two ways: "first as an abstract object, that is as a possible form of conduct expressed by a system of rules; and second, as the realization in the thought and conduct of certain persons at a certain time and place of the actions specified by those rules" (Rawls, *A Theory of Justice*, p. 55).

19. I am simplifying a bit here. Of course P_1 need not refer to an individual A by name in order for him to be within its range. Usually what it will do is use some phrase like "every citizen" and A will be within the range of the principle just in case he satisfies that description.

20. Some even *define* justice meta-ethically in terms of *local* understandings. This, I take it, is Michael Walzer's approach in *Spheres of Justice: A Defense of Pluralism and Equality* (Oxford: Basil Blackwell, 1983): "Every substantive account of distributive justice is a local account" (p. 314) and "The very phrase 'communal wealth' would lose its meaning if all resources and all products were globally common."

21. Rawls, *A Theory of Justice*, p. 8.

22. Immanuel Kant, *The Metaphysical Elements of Justice*, trans. John Ladd (Indianapolis: Bobbs-Merrill, 1965), sec. 42, p. 71.

23. Ibid., sec. 44, p. 76.

24. Ibid., sec. 6, p. 60.

25. Ibid., sec. 8, p. 65.

26. Kant writes elsewhere of "that *right to the earth's surface* which the human race shares in common," a cosmopolitan right that establishes the basis of a "universal community": Immanuel Kant, *Perpetual Peace: A Philosophical Sketch*, in *Kant's Political Writings*, ed. Hans Reiss (Cambridge: Cambridge University Press, 1970), pp. 106–8.

27. See note 19 above.

28. What about the situation where a French company is temporarily doing business in New Zealand, or where a New Zealander has a claim against some property or person in France? We develop rules of private international law to determine (sometimes arbitrarily but not unjustifiably) which forum is competent to determine such issues. If it is a New Zealand court and it makes its determination justly, then the French party *is* bound in justice to accept the determination, and that is a requirement—like P_2—on a par with a New Zealander's duty to accept the just determinations of local courts. The only thing that distinguishes the French party from a New Zealander in this respect is that special circumstances have to arise before French claims are adjudicated in New Zealand courts, whereas for New Zealanders such adjudications are (properly) a matter of course.

29. Insiders are of course also subject to P_1. Apart from grabbing more than he is entitled to under P_1, an insider might try to obstruct or undermine its administration in other ways for purely malicious reasons.

30. The situation is complicated somewhat by the fact that outsiders may sometimes justly demand to be treated as insiders. Suppose an outsider interferes with the local administration of P_1 because he wants to promote a principle of wider range—principle $P_1{}^\star$—that deals justly with his claims as well as those previously dealt with under P_1. The outsider in question may be a Bangladeshi and $P_1{}^\star$ may be a principle of global redistribution. Perhaps in this case there is no moral basis for condemning his interference. Who, after all, is entitled to object if his interference is calculated to bring about the administration of $P_1{}^\star$? Certainly not those who are insiders with regard to P_1, for they have claims of justice only against one another, not against those whose interests are neglected in the administration of that principle. Still, P_2 applies to *some* acts of interference by such outsiders, namely, those that do not enhance the prospects for P_1's being replaced by $P_1{}^\star$. And it certainly applies to the actions of outsiders such as Frenchmen who do not have this special interest in the replacement of P_1 by a principle of wider range. (I assume here that both Frenchmen and New Zealanders are better off under the range-limited principles that are already being administered in their respective societies than they would be under any just principle of wider range.)

31. This helps to explain torts of interference with contractual relations. Though a contract between A and B creates purely *in personam* rights, C can wrong B by inciting A to violate these rights.

32. Except, that is, in the extraordinary case in which some property of his is governed by New Zealand courts for the purposes of some dispute, under private international law. See note 28 above.

33. Dworkin, *Law's Empire*, p. 193.

34. This paragraph is in response to a criticism by Mark Johnson.

35. Recent communitarian discussions of patriotism and loyalty are all predicated on the idea that I owe something to the community that is currently making my life and the exercise of my rights possible. See, for example, Alasdair MacIntyre, *Is Patriotism a Virtue? The Lindley Lecture* (Lawrence: University of Kansas, 1984); and Charles Taylor, "Atomism" in his *Philosophy and the Human Sciences: Philosophical Papers* 2 (Cambridge: Cambridge University Press, 1985). These accounts do not explore the idea of an allegiance that is more atavistic and that stands quite independently of the communal attachments I currently enjoy. The best recent account is Neil MacCormick, "Nation and Nationalism," in his *Legal Right and Social Democracy: Essays in Legal and Social Philosophy* (Oxford: Clarendon Press, 1982).

36. See the excellent discussion in Jean Hampton, *Hobbes and the Social Con-*

tract Tradition (Cambridge: Cambridge University Press, 1986), chap. 6. Hampton shows that these collective action problems are not prisoners' dilemmas.

37. I do not mean to suggest the truth of this hypothesis (about justice) in either the Irish or the Lebanese case, but simply to consider what would follow if it *were* true (and what does follow to the extent that it *is* true).

38. Thomas Hobbes, *Leviathan*, ed. Richard Tuck (Cambridge: Cambridge University Press, 1991), chap. 13, pp. 89–90.

39. Robert Nozick, *Anarchy, State and Utopia* (New York: Basic Books, 1984), pp. 12–17.

40. See Hampton, *Hobbes and the Social Contract Tradition*.

41. See Don Regan, *Utilitarianism and Cooperation* (Oxford: Clarendon Press, 1980) for an excellent detailed argument to this effect.

42. See Leslie Green, "Law, Co-ordination and the Common Good," *Oxford Journal of Legal Studies* 3 (1983): 299–324.

43. The difference principle holds that inequalities of wealth and power are acceptable only if they redound to the benefit of the least favored group in society; see Rawls, *A Theory of Justice*, pp. 75–79.

44. Ibid., pp. 7, 170–71. See also John Rawls, "The Basic Structure as Subject," *American Philosophical Quarterly* 14 (1977): 159–65.

45. There is a more expansive discussion of this in Jeremy Waldron, "Theoretical Foundations of Liberalism," *Philosophical Quarterly* 37 (1987): 135–40.

46. This use of consent is different again from its use within Rawlsian-style contractarianism. There the image of consent is deployed as a model-theoretic device for establishing what justice actually amounts to; it has no political or institutional significance, either with regard to obligation or with regard to legitimacy (in the sense I am discussing).

47. For the argument that hypothetical consent cannot generate actual obligation, see Ronald Dworkin, *Taking Rights Seriously* (London: Duckworth, 1977), pp. 150–59.

48. For a dissenting view, see Nozick, *Anarchy, State and Utopia*, chaps. 2–6. It is Nozick's contention in this part of the book that the moral force of constraints of right and justice does not translate automatically into a moral imperative of submission to and cooperation with whatever organization seems best positioned to uphold and enforce such rights. Nozick's position is based partly on his particular conception of rights as agent-relative side-constraints: that A has a right against B that B not attack him does not, on Nozick's account, provide any third party C with either a duty or a moral justification for restraining or helping to restrain B from attacking A. I am grateful to the editors of *Philosophy & Public Affairs* for pressing this point.

49. Rawls, *A Theory of Justice*, p. 3.

50. Simmons, *Moral Principles*, p. 148.

51. Ibid.

13

WHO BELIEVES IN POLITICAL OBLIGATION?

Leslie Green

I s there a general obligation to obey the law, at least in a reasonably just state? Increasingly, political theorists deny that proposition. Of course, anarchists, marxists, and many theologians have denied it all along—their allegiance is to things higher than, or at any rate different from, the state. Now, however, a number of writers within the liberal tradition are denying it too.[1] To call this an emerging consensus would be more performative than descriptive; but it is, shall we say, a significant coalescence of opinion. Here, I want to explore one particular reaction to this skeptical thrust.

The issue arises this way. Theorists are denying the existence of an obligation to obey the law while most other people are said to endorse such an obligation. The skeptical position thus appears to be at variance with what most people in fact believe; so, quite apart from any internal difficulties in the skeptical argument itself, it fails to meet an external test: reasonable correspondence with our considered judgments. George Klosko, for instance, calls the belief in political obligation one of "our deepest intuitions about political matters": "[T]he existence of strong general feelings that we have political obligations . . . is supported by our most basic feelings about politics. I take it as obviously true that most people believe they have obligations to their governments."[2]

Is the claim that most people believe this, as Klosko supposes, "obviously true," and, if it is, does it matter? Those are the questions I try to answer here, taking the second first.

COHERENCE AND COMMON OPINION

Whether it is significant that there is a widespread belief in political obligation depends on one's account of the nature of justificatory argument in political theory. One popular view, advocated by Klosko, is that we should strive for a certain kind of coherence, or what Rawls calls a "reflective equilibrium," between our considered judgments about cases and a systematizing normative theory.[3] An acceptable theory should therefore normally account for our most basic pretheoretical judgments, what Rawls calls our "provisional fixed points" in argument: fixed because we are not to abandon them lightly, but provisional because they might, in principle, yield to a compelling theory that had enough other merits.

Is the method of coherence circular, or does it involve some other kind of cheating? That is a common enough charge, and one often brought by those whose model of justification is patterned after one view of natural science: data are to be explained, not altered. It is in fact, however, the naive view of scientific justification that is wrong: the theory-ladenness of observation statements means that a recalcitrant observation can always be explained away. The process should be quite familiar to empirical social scientists who regularly remove "outliers" from their data plots before drawing a regression line through the remainder. It is only confidence in an attractive theory that lets us identify outliers in the first place. Because all data may include outliers, our fixed points are always provisional.

In moral and political theory, it is true, there is often more willingness to mess with the data, but even here there are points that most would agree must be explained and not just explained away. Consider a familiar example. Utilitarianism offers a coherent and elegant justification for punishment. It says that punishment is justified when, but only when, it brings about the greatest social good. The difficulty for the theory is notorious. It needs somehow to explain our view that the innocent ought never to be punished; yet one can construct a variety of scenarios in which it would be optimal to do just that. Very few utilitarians are willing simply to bite the bullet and say, "Well, that just proves that we may sometimes punish the innocent." On the contrary, they go to great lengths to show that their theory does not commit them to the repugnant conclusion. As much as their opponents, they regard the case of punishing the innocent as a fixed point.

Some political theorists treat the belief in political obligation that way. Klosko, for example, is willing to reject consent theory because it cannot explain the general belief in an obligation to obey.

> If legitimate political power can be derived only from the consent of (a high but oftentimes unspecified percentage of) the governed, then most, if not all, existing governments are illegitimate. Moreover, if we were to argue that individuals—including those who have consented—can be obligated to obey only legitimate governments, then the implication would be that very few citizens have political obligations.[4]

His point is that consent theory is incompatible with one of our deeply entrenched judgments. And this is just a special case of the general complaint against skepticism: it gives insufficient weight to one of the provisionally fixed points of political consciousness.

Is this a good argument? I do not wish to challenge the coherence method in the example of theories of punishment, but I do want to examine the putative analogy with those arguments. I think that a Klosko-type response ignores an important distinction. In the case of punishing the innocent, the conflict is between a general theory of punishment and our "intuitive" judgment about a particular case. The problem is one of casuistry: can the utilitarian get the right answer in this circumstance? The objection to skeptical theories of obligation is not like that, however. It is not a conflict between a theory and a judgment about a *case*, but between a theory and another *theory*, namely, the "theory of political obligation." The claim is that the skeptic's theory is not widely held, not that the skeptic has failed to deliver the correct judgment about a certain case, for instance, a case in which a useless or unjust law should nonetheless be obeyed. What is claimed to need explanation is not such a judgment, but rather the fact that a competing theory, the doctrine of political obligation, is widely accepted.

The distinction between particular casuistic judgments and theoretical beliefs at a high level of abstraction is an important one. To get a good analogy with the dispute about punishment, we need to consider instead the conflict between utilitarianism and the popular view that the guilty deserve to suffer or that offenders should always be paid back. In philosophical argument about punishment, however, antiutilitarian theorists rarely appeal directly to the supposed popularity of retributivism. The method of coherence does not take as its provisional fixed points popular theories—and for good reason, for in this case they recognize a need to distinguish retributive sentiments from mere vengeance. That is why, against the utilitarians, the retributivists appeal to our judgment about a particular case. They recognize that that case has more probative force than does the abstract statement of their theory.

The belief in political obligation, however, is more like the belief in the propriety of retribution than it is like the belief that a particular innocent person ought not to be punished. Political obligation is not a fixed point of moral consciousness, but a popular though controversial theory. That it is widely held might be relevant to its credibility, but if it is, it cannot be for the reason suggested by coherentist justifications.

There is, however, a different argument to which one might turn, one found in Hume's criticism of Locke. This is the argument from the authority of common opinion in moral matters.

The distinction between the two is this. In the argument from coherence we draw on the authority of a deeply held, intuitive belief about the morally correct disposition of a certain case. To know that this belief is among our considered judgments, we do not normally need to survey opinion. The armchair reflection of a single, fairminded person will do. In this respect, casuistic judgments claim an authority analogous to the judgments of grammaticality that a single native speaker is competent to make about his or her mother tongue. In the case of punishment of the innocent, the fixity of that judgment rests not on its certification by social science, but in the security of our armchair. The argument from common opinion is different. It inherently relies on knowledge of public opinion. To know whether some theoretical proposition is widely held, we need to go and find out. It is not part of the surface grammar of our judgments; we must put it to people and see how they react.

I thus want to draw a distinction between the nature and methods of the casuistic argument from coherence and the more general argument from common opinion. The distinction is not specific to political theory. Do people believe that they have bodies? Armchair reflection about the logical grammar of terms such as "my hand" will suffice to tell us the answer. Do they generally believe that comet impact was responsible for the extinction of the dinosaurs? We would need to find out.

Hume does not clearly distinguish this second form of argument from the first, though he relies on its distinctive power whenever he contends that historical evidence refutes consent theory.[5] Whether the argument from common opinion is a sound justificatory procedure in political theory is a matter I have disputed elsewhere.[6] I think the strongest case that might be made for it is the one that Hume invokes, namely, that to the extent that morality rests on sentiment, there can be no higher court than public opinion, and that competing, more rationalistic, theories are philosophically suspect. The cogency of these arguments cannot be addressed here. Suffice it to say that the significance of the common belief in political obligation would have to rest on something like this, rather than on the standing of "provisional fixed points" of casuistry that figure in the argument from coherence.

EXPLAINING AWAY

Interpreted in this second way, as an appeal to common opinion, a widespread belief in political obligation may or may not be threatening to skeptical theories. The argument from common opinion must always allow for the possibility that some opinions are formed in circumstances that make them likely to be false or misleading. In some cases it is therefore proper to explain away a consensus.

A belief, however well entrenched, might nonetheless be false. John Mackie introduces the idea of an "error theory" in ethics to describe the deeply ingrained but (he thinks) false view that moral judgments are objective.[7] Ordinary moral thought, he concedes, incorporates the belief in objective values, so subjectivism cannot be sustained on the strength of any sort of "linguistic" or "conceptual" analysis of moral discourse. But the belief is nonetheless a false one, and Mackie thinks that its falsity can be adequately established by empirical and theoretical considerations.

We might, in a similar way, adopt an error theory of political obligation. We might concede that the theory is ingrained in ordinary political discourse but reject it as false or even incoherent. It is true that this will involve refuting or at least weakening the argument from common opinion, but perhaps that can be done. An error theory depends on the positive strength of the skeptical argument.

A different, though overlapping, approach is to reject the widespread belief in political obligation as being ideological, or grounded in false consciousness.[8] Antonio Gramsci properly recognized that the deliverances of "common sense," our everyday theoretical beliefs, are often deeply ideological. Here, one emphasizes the negative case by calling into question the grounds on which the belief is held. In particular, beliefs that result from manipulation or indoctrination or which would be abandoned if their causal origins were known are suspect. If one is to avoid the genetic fallacy, specifying the conditions under which such beliefs may be dismissed will be a delicate matter; but if the argument from common opinion is attractive, the counterargument from ideology may be too.

This is, in part, John Simmons's move in addressing the consequences of his own skeptical position:

> If it [skepticism] runs counter to normal feelings about the citizen-state relationship, I think there are better explanations for this fact than the falsity of my conclusion. For what belief can better serve the interests of one's political leaders than the belief that all are specially bound to support their government and obey the law?[9]

Of course, this is a very compressed statement of the argument. Practically all interesting political beliefs serve someone's interests. The important point is that this particular belief is, in most political societies, the normal outcome of a complex system of formal and informal processes that foster such beliefs. This means not merely that it is unsurprising that many people believe in political obligation, but also—and this is a different point—that many people will avow the belief who do not in fact hold it, because it is both socially expected and often advantageous to do so.

Klosko objects to Simmons's argument. He says that Simmons proceeds on the basis of the coherence method, relying freely on our considered judgments about cases, but then, when he gets to the feeling that we have special bonds to our own states, he inexplicably shifts gears and becomes more rationalistic. Klosko objects:

Unless Simmons can distinguish aspects of our consciousness that result from indoctrination from aspects that do not, his appeal to indoctrination in regard to this one aspect of our political beliefs undermines
his use of the coherence method throughout his book.[10]

This is an objection targeted at someone thought to endorse the
method of coherence in justification; it would have no purchase against
a more thorough-going rationalist. That is not, however, the most important point; rather, it is this: the belief in political obligation is not, as
I have said, a provisional fixed point in judgment; it is not a particular
judgment at all. It is a piece of low-level, commonsense political theory
like, for example, the widely held view that majority rule is democratic.
A coherentist thus can distinguish our commonsense theories from our
casuistic judgments and with good reason set a higher threshold of the
credibility of the former than for the latter. Commonsense theories are
at one remove from our practical experience. Being taught as doctrines,
insisted on by officials, inculcated in schools, and so on, they are more
susceptible to ideological distortion than are casuistic judgments thrown
up by the unstructured experiences of life.

This particular theory is, moreover, right at the center of the power
structures of the modern state. Historically, its career has paralleled that
of the state. It emerged in the conflict between the normative order of
the state and the claims of a universal church. Now, as the state trans-
forms itself under the pressure of the globalization of market economies,
the doctrine of political obligation is losing some of its appeal. The idea
that we are all, first and foremost, citizens of particular states to which
we owe particular duties of allegiance is under strain, just at the moment
those states are themselves under strain. Political obligation is thus a
doctrine that is peculiarly sensitive to the ideological context in which
it functions.

This is not, of course, a decisive argument in favor of explaining
away political obligation as a piece of ideological detritus. It is not decisive, in part because ideological beliefs should be self-effacing under the
scrutiny of reason. Once their social roots are exposed, the weed should
wither away; yet that does not seem to be the case here. The belief in
political obligation has proved remarkably resilient; it is endorsed even
by those who are perfectly aware of its ideological functions. That suggests that the case against it is not proven, but at the same time I do not
see how one can doubt that there is a serious case here to answer.

THE CONTENT OF THE BELIEF

I turn now from the question of the significance and standing of the claim to its truth. Klosko says that it is "obviously true" that there is a widespread belief in political obligation. I want to begin with some general reasons for doubting that and then, in the next section, consider briefly some empirical evidence that purports to bear on it.

What does one have to believe before one can properly be said to believe in political obligation? This is the crux of the issue. Let me begin with an analogy. Suppose that an adherent of the Roman Catholic church says that he believes in the authority of the pope. What would make it correct to say that he has this belief? To begin, we need to distinguish the claim that he has the belief from the claim that he avows the belief. All sorts of Catholics avow this belief who do not in fact accept it. They avow it because, theology aside, it is part of Roman Catholic religious culture to do so; thus, there are reasons for Catholics to avow it whether or not they actually hold it.

To get behind the avowals, one therefore needs to know more. Because it is papal authority that is in issue, one needs to know what that amounts to before one knows whether our subject believes in it. How do we identify the character of such authority? By recourse to the authoritative sources and traditions of Catholic theology. Suppose we find, to simplify things, that one essential element of papal authority is the claim to infallibility in certain matters of faith when the pope speaks ex cathedra. Believing in that is thus part of what it is to believe in papal authority. If, like many North American Catholics, our subject avows the belief in papal authority but wholly rejects the doctrine of infallibility, then it would be wrong, in fact, to say that he believes in the authority of the pope. What he believes just does not amount to that.

Political obligation is similar. One believes in an obligation to obey the law only if one accepts, on certain terms, the authority of the state. How does one determine what the terms are? We may consult the tradition of argument within political theory to see what it is that people are arguing about when they dispute political obligation, and we may consult the authoritative voices of the state to see what it is that the state actually claims for itself. These are, of course, matters for discussion, and they do implicate, indirectly, a variety of different evaluative standards, but they are not matters for first-order moral or political argument; they are part of the abstract but descriptive part of political theory.[11]

By either route, one comes to the following conclusion.[12] Political obligation is the doctrine that everyone has a moral reason to obey all the laws of his or her own state and that this reason binds independently of the content of the law. This does not imply that the obligation to obey is absolute, nor that it applies in fundamentally unjust circumstances. The doctrine of political obligation is supposed to explain the character of allegiance, prima facie, in reasonably just states. One believes in political obligation only if one thinks that states have the authority they claim, and what they claim is supreme power to determine our rights, obligations, and powers and to have our compliance with their requirements independent of our assessment of the merits of what is required.

Like any other descriptive proposition, this one is disputable; but it is not in fact much disputed. It is the image of the state that is presented in the Western tradition of political theory as well as in the works of contemporary writers.[13] Most important, it is also what the officials of states have in mind as they issue orders and expect compliance.

Although it is fairly general, this characterization of the authority of the state nonetheless has theoretical bite, for it entails that a belief in political obligation differs from a variety of other beliefs that people may hold. For example:

(1) We ought never lightly to disobey the law.

This is not political obligation. One who believes this need not concede the authority of the state at all. This belief can be supported just by the (important) truism that the state regulates matters of vital concern in which the moral stakes are high. In a reasonably just state, officials act in good faith to promote the public interest, and citizens make plans based on the expectation that people will give serious weight to what the law requires.

(2) We ought, most of the time, to comply with most of the laws.

This is entailed by a belief in political obligation, but it is not equivalent to it. It is not equivalent because, for one thing, it acknowledges a commitment to comply only most of the time and, for another, it says nothing about the nature of the reason for complying. It might, for instance, have nothing to do with the fact that the requirements are laws or are the laws of our own states. After all, (2) is, on plausible factual assumptions, entailed also by (3).

> (3) There is an obligation to do what the law requires, but not because the law requires it. The only reason for compliance is that there is normally a coincidence of moral and political obligations.

This is not political obligation, because the fact that the behavior in question is required by law is immaterial to the duty to comply. This duty rests instead on a content-dependent reason for compliance. Even an anarchist can believe that it is wrong to murder people and thus that there is a moral reason for complying with the law against murder. In a reasonably just state, most of the laws will be coincident with, or at least not objectionably discordant with, what we ought to do anyway.

> (4) With respect to some laws there is a strict obligation of obedience: here, we ought to take the law at its word. There are other laws, however, with respect to which it is appropriate to assess one's compliance on a case-by-case basis.

This is not political obligation, though it is on the margins of it. This view allows that there is a certain range over which the appropriate attitude to the law is to regard it as authoritative, and another range where this is inappropriate, and that it is a mater of individual discretion where to draw the line. This is not political obligation because the state does not itself share this view: it claims authority wherever it purports to regulate.

I think the four statements above are fairly common attitudes toward law, and there are many other similar examples; moreover, they are politically important attitudes, for they help support valuable institutions such as governments and they contribute to a shared conception of justice and so on. What is relevant here, however, is that they all stop short of acknowledging the authority that a reasonably just state claims. They do not amount, severally or jointly, to the belief in an obligation to obey the law as it claims to be obeyed.

Which of these or other related attitudes are most prevalent in our societies is a factual question. I am not sure of the answer, but bearing in mind these distinctions, it does seem hasty, to say the least, to claim that it is "obviously true" that most people believe in political obligation. All that is obviously true is that most people have pro-attitudes toward their own governments—but that truth is no threat at all to the skeptical position about political obligation.

SOME EMPIRICAL EVIDENCE

To the best of my knowledge, no one has yet designed a satisfactory study to test the extent to which people believe in the theory of political obligation. There are, however, a number of studies that bear on it indirectly, studies of things such as compliance with law, support for governments, willingness to pay taxes, and so forth. One of the very few to make an explicit effort to estimate the popularity of belief in political obligation is Tom R. Tyler's *Why People Obey the Law*.[14] A brief review of its methods and findings shows how hard it is to come to firm conclusions even here.

Tyler surveyed people in Chicago to investigate the extent to which compliance with law is based on normative as opposed to instrumental reasons. He finds, unsurprisingly, that people obey because they think it is proper to do so and that this belief has roots in things other than the consequences of compliance, such as the perceived legitimacy of the system. In particular, he claims, "The extent to which respondents endorsed the obligation to obey is striking."[15]

His account of the normative grounds of compliance draws an important distinction between what he calls "personal morality"—the view that the law corresponds with what the agents regard as right behavior—and "legitimacy"—the view that the legal system has a right to dictate their behavior whether or not it corresponds with their own view of what is right. The theoretical significance of legitimacy is evident, for personal morality may require resistance as well as compliance.

Tyler is rightly critical of those social scientists who, following David Easton, have assimilated a belief in the legitimacy of the system to a diffuse sort of support for it. Merely feeling positive about one's state does not amount to accepting its authority.[16] Tyler writes:

The fundamental difference between obligation and support lies in the clarity of the motivation underlying compliance. Theories that measure legitimacy assume that support for the government leads to the type of discretionary authority directly tapped by measuring the perceived obligation to obey.[17]

That assumption is plainly a fragile one. If a person agrees with the laws, he or she will be supportive of the government but need not feel any obligation at all, and might even withdraw support following a policy change. What is needed, then, is a direct measure of the perceived obligation to obey. In service of this, Tyler asked respondents whether they agreed with the following statements and got the following results:[18]

(1) People should obey the law even if it goes against what they think is right. (82 percent agreement)
(2) I always try to follow the law even if I think it is wrong. (82 percent agreement)
(3) Disobeying the law is seldom justified. (79 percent agreement)
(4) It is difficult to break the law and keep one's self-respect. (69 percent agreement)
(5) If a person is doing something and a police officer tells them to stop, they should stop even if they feel that what they are doing is legal. (84 percent agreement)
(6) If a person goes to court because of a dispute with another person, and the judge orders them to pay the other person money, they should pay that person money, even if they think that the judge is wrong. (74 percent agreement)
(7) A person who refuses to obey the law is a menace to society. (74 percent agreement)
(8) Obedience and respect for authority are the most important virtues children should learn. (82 percent agreement)

Items (5) and (6) were ultimately dropped from the scale, since a first test suggested that some respondents had trouble understanding the questions, and items (7) and (8) were introduced because there was little variance in the other answers and thus not much to explain.

A number of methodological questions are worth pursuing here, but I want instead to focus on the conceptual ones, and here I am reminded of Wittgenstein's remark about psychology enjoying both experimental methods and conceptual confusions.

Do these questions, in the first place, accurately track the distinction between obligation and support? They do not. Items (3), (4), (7), and (8) may all elicit agreement from a person who rejects the obligation to obey the law and complies instead on grounds of prudence or personal morality. I, for example, do not believe that there is an obligation to obey the law, but I do think that those who make a point of refusing to obey it are generally a menace, and I think that disobeying it, at least in a reasonably just state, is seldom justified. All those questions are thus just irrelevant to the perceived obligation to obey.

The only items that might capture the attitude in question are (1), (2), (5), and (6). These do probe the binding and content-independent character that political obligation purports to have, though none of them conclusively eliminates the possibility of a purely prudential attitude. (Consider (5): Most people are aware that even a cop in the wrong can cause them big trouble.) Still, it is true that only these items ask whether a person would comply even in cases where he or she feels that compliance is wrong, and thus only they measure a noncoincidental connection between legal requirements and obedience, one that does not depend on the content of what is required.

How then should we interpret the overwhelmingly affirmative (and nearly invariant) responses to these items? Does it indicate a broad consensus, or is it perhaps a warning that respondents know what they are expected to say? Is it significant that items (5) and (6), the two that give the clearest test, are also the questions that gave some respondents trouble? They do not seem conceptually or linguistically challenging. Could it be that, in a concrete application, people become more hesitant about avowing an obligation to obey when it is made plain that this means obeying even when the police and judges are wrong?

All this is so much speculation: the difficulties in assessing the sincerity of sample survey responses are well known. There is, however, a more urgent conceptual point. Even if sincere, these avowals are insufficient to establish the belief in an obligation to obey. The point is simply that they do not reveal why these avowals were made. They do not tell us enough about the structure of the views they express.

Let us return to the religion analogy, this time in more general form. If we ask respondents, "Do you believe in God?" we will find, particularly in America, an overwhelming majority who say yes. Can we therefore conclude that Americans overwhelmingly believe in God? Well, some of those who agree to that question might, if asked to elaborate what their belief in God amounts to, say things such as, "Well, I believe there really is meaning to life," or, "I believe there is a basic principle of order in the universe," or "There are truths about the universe we cannot explain." Some of these may or may not fall within the margins of religious belief, and, of course, just what one has to believe in order to be said properly to believe in God is a controversial matter, but many of these avowals extend well beyond the hazy boundaries of that controversy, and some of them are compatible with atheism. If all one means by "God" is "some principle of order in the universe," then any atheistic naturalist believes in God.

This is not a fanciful analogy. Many people who say they believe in God do not really do so, and the fact that they do not can be shown by investigating what their supposed belief commits them to. They may nonetheless avow the belief because they believe it is socially acceptable to do so or because they are unsure about the most appropriate terms of denial (am I an atheist? an agnostic?) or just because they want to avoid argument.

What then of people who are willing to agree with the proposition, "People should obey the law even if it goes against what they think is right"? Might they be committed to something other than a belief in political obligation and yet honestly make such an avowal? Plainly, they might. The question does not ask them whether this is something people should always or even normally do. It does not ask whether it makes any difference to them if the law in question is the law of their own state or whether they owe similar allegiance to any state that exercises de facto control over their behavior. It does not even ask whether the "should" is a moral "should" as opposed to a purely conventional or prudential "should." (One valid reason for obeying the law, especially in a foreign country, is that it is rude not to.) As it stands, we have no evidence about what the eighty-two percent who agreed with this proposition thought they were agreeing to, nor even whether they all took it in the same way.

The same objections apply also to the other relevant items. I am not saying that it is impossible to design a survey instrument that could tell us who believes in political obligation, and I am certainly not saying that no one believes in it—some citizens, many officials, most judges, and certain political theorists plainly do. My only point is that complex, abstract beliefs such as the belief in God or the belief in political obligation need to be approached in a more subtle way than is normally done and that the casual empiricism on which the argument from common opinion rests is in fact too lax for the confidence that theorists place in it. To isolate the true believers we will need a tighter marriage of normative and empirical political theory than we have yet had.

CONCLUSION

Theorists are inclined to believe that abstract philosophical ideas are more influential than they are. This is usually a harmless enough piece of self-deception. It is frequently said, for example, that Western liberal culture is founded epistemologically on a Cartesian notion of reason or morally on a Kantian notion of the person. These ideas, however, are difficult—in the case of Cartesian reason, probably unintelligible—and they are certainly not as deeply entrenched as some suppose. To the extent that nonphilosophers have any view about reason or the person, what they believe is usually indecisive among competing accounts.

Some political theorists hold that there is a belief in political obligation that is of wide enough currency and deep enough root to be taken as a datum that any competent theory of allegiance needs to explain. I have argued to the contrary: first, that even if there is such a belief, its importance cannot be certified by the method of coherence and that it requires instead confidence in the authority of common opinion. Even if such confidence is in general well placed, I have claimed also that with respect to this particular theory there are reasons to want to explain away the opinion. Second, I suggested that it is far from obvious how widely held the belief in political obligation actually is and that the best empirical evidence we have is deeply equivocal. The skeptics' positive case remains unanswered, and its incompatibility with common beliefs remains unestablished. The doctrine of political obligation is an implausible view of what we owe the state.

NOTES

An earlier version of this paper was presented to the North American Society for Social Philosophy panel at the American Philosophical Association, Eastern Division Meeting, Washington, D.C., December 1992. I am grateful to the participants and especially to George Klosko, John T. Sanders, John Simmons, and Jeremy Waldron for their helpful comments.

1. See M. B. E. Smith, "Is There a Prima Facie Obligation to Obey the Law?" *Yale Law Journal* 82 (1973): 950–76; J. Raz, *The Authority of Law* (Oxford: Clarendon Press, 1979); A. J. Simmons, *Moral Principles and Political Obligations* (Princeton, N.J.: Princeton University Press, 1979); J. Feinberg, "Civil Disobedience in the Modern World," *Humanities in Society* 2 (1979): 37–60; R. Sartorius, "Political Authority and Political Obligation," *Virginia Law Review* 67 (1981): 3–17; L. Green, *The Authority of the State* (Oxford: Clarendon Press, 1990).

2. George Klosko, *The Principle of Fairness and Political Obligation* (Lanham, Md.: Rowman & Littlefield, 1992), 22. See also p. 68: "I take it as intuitively obvious that most individuals believe they have political obligations. As a corollary of this belief, most individuals believe that their governments are legitimate and so, by implication, acceptably fair."

3. See J. Rawls, *A Theory of Justice* (Cambridge, Mass.: Harvard University Press, 1971), 19–21, 46–53, 578–86. *Cf.* N. Daniels, "Wide Reflective Equilibrium and Theory Acceptance in Ethics," *Journal of Philosophy* 76 (1979): 256–82.

4. Klosko, 142–43.

5. For example, I take this passage in the *Treatise* as an appeal to the argument from common opinion: "[A] man living under an absolute government, wou'd owe it no allegiance; since, by its very nature, it depends not on consent. But as that is as natural and common a government as any, it must certainly occasion some obligation; and 'tis plain from experience, that men, who are subjected to it, do always think so" (L. A. Selby-Bigge, ed., *A Treatise of Human Nature* [Oxford: Clarendon Press, 1967], 529). In contrast, Edmund Burke's remark is an appeal to our judgment about a case: "[I]f popular representation, or choice, is necessary to the legitimacy of all government, the house of lords is, at one strike, bastardized and corrupted in blood. That house is no representative of the people at all . . ." (C. C. O'Brien, ed., *Reflections on the Revolution in France* [Harmondsworth, Middlesex: Penguin, 1969], 147).

6. L. Green, "Against Hume on Allegiance," a paper delivered at the 1991 Annual Meeting of the American Political Science Association, Washington, D.C.

7. J. L. Mackie, *Ethics: Inventing Right and Wrong* (Harmondsworth, Middlesex: Penguin, 1977), 35, 48–49.

8. For a good account, see R. Geuss, *The Idea of a Critical Theory: Habermas and the Frankfurt School* (Cambridge; Cambridge University Press, 1981).

9. Simmons, 195. For my own, slightly different, response, see Green, *The Authority of the State*, 263–67.

10. Klosko, 25–26.

11. I should reiterate that I am *not* arguing that this is a matter of value-free science. I am claiming that it is a descriptive rather than a moral question. For the distinction I have in mind, see L. Green, "The Political Content of Legal Theory," *Philosophy of the Social Sciences* 17 (1987): 1–20.

12. Green, *The Authority of the State*, 220–34.

13. Simmons endorses a similar view in *Moral Principles and Political Obligations*, 7–38, as does Klosko in *The Principle of Fairness and Political Obligation*, 2–16. It may be that Ronald Dworkin rejects parts of the view: see his *Law's Empire* (Cambridge, Mass.: Harvard University Press, 1986), 190–215, and especially 429–30 n. 3. For criticism of Dworkin on obligation, see L. Green, "Associative Obligations and the State," in A. Hutchinson and L. Green, eds., *Law and the Community: The End of Individualism?* (Toronto: Carswell, 1989), 93–118. Apparently, Bikhu Parekh also disputes what political obligation amounts to in his "A Misconceived Discourse on Political Obligation," *Political Studies* 41 (1993): 236–51. He says that I and other skeptics confuse the narrow duty to obey the law with a wider sense of political obligation that also includes things such as an obligation to participate in politics, take an interest in public affairs, and so on. If this is true, it is irrelevant, for the skeptical argument shows that there is no narrow obligation to obey the law: it follows therefore that there is also no combination of this and wider, more exigent obligations—if p is false, then the conjunction of p and q is also false, and nothing substantial turns on whether we call p or $(p\&q)$ "political obligation."

14. T. R. Tyler, *Why People Obey the Law* (New Haven: Yale University Press, 1990).

15. Tyler, *Why People Obey the Law*, 45.

16. I have argued the same point against Easton in my "Support for the System," *British Journal of Political Science* 15 (1985): 127–42.

17. Tyler, 28.

18. Combining Tables 4.3 and 4.4. Tyler, 46–47.

14

SURRENDER OF JUDGMENT AND THE CONSENT THEORY OF POLITICAL AUTHORITY

Mark C. Murphy

I t is a widely held thesis that being subject to a political authority involves in some way a surrender of one's own judgment to the judgment of the political authority. Thus, H. L. A. Hart writes that "The commander characteristically intends his hearer to take the commander's will instead of his own as a guide to action and so to take it in place of any deliberation or reasoning of his own"; Richard Friedman holds that "The man who accepts authority is thus said to surrender his private or individual judgment because he does not insist that reasons be given that he can grasp and that satisfy him, as a condition of his obedience"; and Joseph Raz, even while suspicious of this notion, takes the metaphor of surrender of judgment to be a way of getting at a fundamental truth about authority.[1] Both those sympathetic to the notion that political institutions possess genuine practical authority and those hostile to that idea seem to agree that there is some connection between authority and the substitution of judgment.

Now, it seems also to be a common assumption that any requirement to surrender one's judgment comes from whatever makes political institutions genuinely authoritative in the first place; the requirement to substitute the judgment of one's governing institutions for one's own is logically posterior to whatever grounds the political authority in question. Consider, for example, Hobbes' view. Hobbes insists that citizens are bound to surrender their judgment to the sovereign's: while in "the condition of meer Nature" "every private man is Judge of Good and Evill actions," within a commonwealth the law is the "publique Conscience" that dictates how subjects are to act.[2] But Hobbes is equally clear that it is what makes the sovereign a practical authority—the covenant that institutes sovereignty, together with the third law of nature requiring conformity with one's covenants—that generates this requirement to surrender one's judgment to the judgment of the sovereign.

In this paper I want to take the first steps toward providing a refurbished consent theory of political authority, one that rests in part on a reconception of the relationship between the surrender of judgment and the authoritativeness of political institutions. On the standard view, whatever grounds political authority implies that one ought to surrender one's judgment to that of one's political institutions. On the refurbished view, it is the surrender of one's judgment—which, I shall argue, can plausibly be considered a form of consent—that makes political institutions practically authoritative.

The reason why this sort of consent is important is this. Recall that the reason why consent theories of political authority are almost universally rejected as explanations for any practical authority that political institutions possess is that the standard principle of consent requires the performance of a certain sort of speech-act for that principle to apply; but, as many philosophers have noted, it is simply a "brute fact"[3] that very few citizens have performed a speech-act by which they consent to be governed.[4] Thus, while there might be nothing incoherent about the idea of a political society whose citizens are bound to their government by ties of consent, it simply is not the case in political societies as presently constituted. As I shall argue, though, surrender of judgment is a kind of consent, and this type of consent requires no speech-act. It follows that if I am right that surrender of judgment can be the basis of rather than a consequence of the existence of genuinely authoritative political institutions, then the brute fact that there are very few speech-acts of consent would not entail that consent does not provide the practical basis for political authority.

AGENT-DEPENDENT MORAL REQUIREMENTS

Standard accounts of political authority rely on a moral principle which, if it were to apply in actual political conditions, would suffice to show that the dictates issued by political authority are authoritative over citizens.[5] Consider, for example, the following:

(A) If one has performed an act by which one consents to obey one's governing institutions, then one is morally required to obey the dictates issued by those institutions.

(B) If one's political society is "a mutually beneficial and just scheme of social cooperation"[6] in which cooperation is necessary to achieve its advantages but in which free riding is possible, then one who accepts the benefits yielded by the legal order is morally required to obey the rules of that legal order.

(C) If one owes a debt of gratitude to the governing institutions under which one lives, then one is morally required to obey the dictates issued by those institutions.

(D) If the institutions of a just legal system "apply"[7] to one, then one is morally required to obey the rules of that system.

The first of these principles is the principle upon which standard consent theory rests; the second is the principle of fair play advocated by Hart[8] and (the earlier) Rawls;[9] the third is the principle of gratitude, the classic formulation of which is in the *Crito*;[10] and the fourth is (the later) Rawls' natural duty of justice.[11] Now, while the moral principles to which these writers have appealed are a rather disparate bunch, they do have at least one feature in common. All of these principles are what I will call agent-independent moral requirements. By 'agent-independent moral requirement' I mean a moral requirement that dictates how agents ought to act in certain situations, regardless of the judgments that those agents have made with regard to what the morally relevant features of the situation are and with regard to what moral principles apply. Such moral principles contrast with 'agent-dependent' moral requirements, which dictate how agents ought to act given the judgments that those agents have made with regard to what the relevant features of their situation are and with regard to what principles of good and right are at stake.[12]

The importance of making this distinction is that while the typical consent theory of political authority (like all other standard accounts of political authority) rests on an agent-independent moral requirement, the refurbished consent theory offered here will rest on an agent-dependent moral requirement. Now, it might be thought that any attempt to ground the authoritativeness of political institutions on an agent-dependent moral requirement is bound to be a non-starter. Any agent-dependent moral requirement requires the performance of an act that is either required by agent-independent moral requirements or not required by agent-independent moral requirements. If the proposed agent-dependent moral requirement is in accord with the relevant agent-independent moral requirements, then we may simply appeal to those agent-independent moral requirements as the basis for political authority; appeal to the agent-dependent moral requirement is redundant. If, on the other hand, it is not in accord with agent-independent moral requirements, then the agent must have made a mistake of some sort in his or her judgment concerning what is to be done in the circumstances, that is, the agent has misperceived the situation or has made an error in moral reasoning. In such a situation, although it might be correct to say that political institutions possess authority over that agent, that agent is in a sad, deluded state, bound to a political authority only through his or her confusion. To be bound to one's political institutions only through errors of this sort is not, I think, what those that seek a moral basis for political authority are looking for.[13]

This dilemma is, however, a false one. It assumes that agent-dependent moral requirements must either merely reflect agent-independent moral requirements or rest on mistakes about how agent-independent moral requirements apply in a particular case. But these alternatives are not exhaustive. For one might hold that moral principles that state agent-independent moral requirements are, in many cases, too general to yield concrete answers to the question of what is to be done in specific cases. When one judges that such-and-such is the way to go about fulfilling a general moral requirement, and such-and-such is not implied by that general moral requirement, one need not be making any error; one is merely concretizing, for the sake of action, that general moral requirement. If there were some sort of agent-dependent moral principle for one to act in accordance with one's concrete specifications of general agent-independent moral principles, then a moral requirement arising from this agent-dependent moral principle could escape the dilemma. For in some cases it might be neither redundant nor the outcome of any error in moral reasoning.

In order to state and defend the agent-dependent moral requirement on which the refurbished consent theory of political authority will rely, I will need the following definitions: that of a *determination* and that of a *minimally acceptable determination-candidate*. What it is to be a minimally acceptable determination-candidate can be characterized without reference to the judgment of any agent. With regard to a set of moral requirements M, an agent S, and a set of circumstances C, d is a minimally acceptable determination-candidate of M for S in C if d is a plan of action such that if S successfully followed d in C then it would be false that S violated any member of M in C. By contrast, the notion of a determination essentially makes reference to an agent's judgment. With regard to a set of moral requirements M, an agent S, and a set of circumstances C, d is S's determination of M for C if S judges that adhering to d is the way for S to fulfill M in C. In short, minimally acceptable determination-candidates are ways for an agent to fulfill a set of moral principles; determinations are agent's judgments concerning the way to fulfill a set of moral principles.

It is perhaps worth elaborating a bit on the idea that determinations and determination-candidates specify the 'way' for agents to fulfill moral requirements. For determinations and determination-candidates to specify ways for agents to fulfill moral requirements is for them to indicate means to the satisfaction of those requirements. In saying this, though, I do not aim to discriminate between two kinds of means, one of which may be called 'instrumental' and the other of which may be called 'constitutive.' A determination-candidate specifies instrumental means to the fulfillment of a set of moral principles to the extent that acting in accordance with that plan brings about the fulfillment of the members of that set, yet what it is to fulfill that set of moral principles can be characterized independently of that determination-candidate; a determination-candidate specifies constitutive means to the fulfillment of a set of moral principles to the extent that acting in accordance with that determination-candidate brings about the fulfillment of the members of that set and what it is to fulfill the moral principles in that set cannot be characterized independently of acting in accordance with that determination-candidate. The same distinction applied, *mutatis mutandis*, to determinations. With regard to both determination-candidates and determinations, those plans of action may include specifications of how to bring about efficiently the end stated in the moral requirements and of what counts as the fulfillment of those moral requirements.

Given these definitions and clarifications, the agent-dependent moral requirement upon which I will rely in providing a refurbished consent account of political authority can be stated as follows: given set of moral requirements M, agent S, and set of circumstances C, then if d is S's determination of M for C, and d is a minimally acceptable determination-candidate of M for S in C, then S is morally required to act in accordance with d. If S judges that d is the plan of action to be followed in satisfying the requirements of M, and following that plan of action is at least one way of satisfying the requirements of M, then S is bound to adhere to the plan of action laid out in d.

Now, it seems to me that this principle cannot be rejected on the grounds that it is normatively superfluous, that is, that other moral principles cover all of the normative ground that this proposed principle covers. For, so far as I can tell, the only way to show its normative superfluity would be to show that for any agent attempting to act on a set of moral principles in concrete circumstances, there is only one minimally acceptable determination-candidate. If that were the case, then by the necessary-means principle (if S is morally required to ϕ, and S's ψ-ing is necessary in order for S to ϕ, then S is morally required to ψ), one would be morally required to act on every minimally acceptable determination-candidate. But that would make the proposed agent-dependent moral requirement normatively superfluous: for in all cases in which S's determination of M in C is identical with the minimally acceptable determination-candidate of M, S would already be bound to that determination-candidate by the necessary-means principle; and in all cases in which S's determination of M in C is distinct from the minimally acceptable determination-candidate of M, the proposed agent-dependent moral principle would not apply, for that principle only applies when S's determination is minimally acceptable. Thus, if moral principles always uniquely determine a single minimally acceptable determination-candidate for an agent in concrete circumstances, then there is reason to reject the proposed agent-dependent moral requirement on account of its normative superfluity.

It is therefore important for the defense of this principle that there be cases in which moral principles do not determine a single minimally acceptable determination-candidate. But it is highly implausible to deny this. Even on moral views that would yield extremely precise dictates given perfect empirical information, like utilitarianism, it seems that in some cases there would be more than one plan of action that one could perform while remaining faithful to every relevant moral principle. If the idea that moral principles always generate single minimally acceptable determination-candidates in each situation is highly implausible in the case of utilitarianism, it seems even more implausible for those moral views that affirm either a plurality of moral principles or less precise moral principles.

It thus appears that on any plausible normative view, the proposed agent-dependent moral requirement would not be normatively super-fluous. It is important to recognize, though, that the fact that the moral principles relevant to a given case need not pick out a unique minimally acceptable determination-candidate does not imply that all judgments among eligible determination-candidates will be completely arbitrary, matters of moral indifference. For there are two different ways that a set of moral principles might generate indeterminacy with regard to how one ought to fulfill those principles in a given case. One way is that of mere indifference: if, given the set of moral principles M, there is no reason to prefer minimally acceptable determination-candidate d to minimally acceptable determination-candidate e, and no reason to prefer e to d, then it is a matter of indifference whether d or e is selected; choosing d or e is of necessity a morally arbitrary matter. But not all cases of indeterminacy need be cases of moral indifference. Instead of there being no reason to prefer d to e or e to d, there could be a reason to take d to be superior to e and a reason to take e to be superior to d. This result seems particularly likely to occur in cases in which one is attempting to satisfy distinct moral requirements. Suppose, for example, that I am under a moral requirement to my employer to put in time doing philosophical research, and that I am under a moral requirement to my family to spend time with them. While it seems to me highly improbable that these principles jointly specify a unique determination-candidate, it does not seem to me that the choice among members of the class of determination-candidates that would satisfy both principles is a matter of indifference. Consider, for example, a determination-candidate that has me spending 60 percent of my available time at research and 40 percent with my family and a determination-candidate that has me spending 40 percent of my available time at research and 60 percent with my family. It is not an arbitrary matter which one of these I judge to be the way to fulfill the moral requirements binding upon me, for there is a reason to judge the former better (it better fulfills the requirement to devote myself to research) and a distinct reason to judge the latter better (it better fulfills the requirement to spend time with my family). This is a case of indeterminacy without indifference.[14]

There is, then, no reason to reject the proposed agent-dependent moral requirement on the basis of normative superfluity. What positive grounds do we have, though, for affirming it? Aside from any intuitive appeal that the principle might have, support for it can be offered only indirectly. First, it seems that we have reason to hold that we are bound to come to at least minimally acceptable determinations of general moral principles, even where those principles do not, together with the empirically given facts of the situation, imply a unique minimally acceptable determination-candidate for that situation. Since moral principles are general, one will need to render determinations of them in order to act on those principles; no one fulfills a moral requirement in the abstract. And because the only way that one will genuinely satisfy those principles is to render determinations of them that fall into the class of minimally acceptable determination-candidates, the determinations that one ought to reach should belong to that class. Since forming minimally acceptable determinations is necessary in order to act on general moral principles, one is required to come to determinations of those principles.

Now, the requirement to come to determinations of general moral principles is not identical to a requirement to act in accordance with them. But I claim that the existence of this moral requirement to come to minimally acceptable determinations gives us reason to affirm the proposed moral requirement to act in accordance with one's determinations, at least those that are minimally acceptable. The basis for this claim is that if one affirms a moral requirement to ϕ, and ψ-ing is necessary to give point to ϕ-ing, then one ought to affirm a moral requirement to ψ. It seems, though, that forming a determination d of a set of moral principles M would be a pointless activity if one did not go on to act in accordance with d in attempting to satisfy M. Since acting on one's determinations gives point to the forming of them, and one is morally required to come to minimally acceptable determinations of general moral principles, then one is bound to act in accordance with one's minimally acceptable determinations.

I shall therefore rely on this agent-dependent moral requirement in the sequel in showing how a surrender of judgment can play a part in explaining how political authority is generated. What makes this moral requirement especially important for our purposes is that it has its practical relevance not by way of conflict with agent-independent moral requirements—conflict that has as a prerequisite the confusion or ignorance of the moral agent—but by way of the underdetermination of the principles stating agent-independent moral requirements. Determinations can go beyond general moral principles without conflicting with them: indeed, such determinations are necessary if one is to act on general moral principles.

MORALLY CHOICEWORTHY GOALS AND CONSENT IN THE ACCEPTANCE SENSE

Let us consider next a certain kind of morally desirable goal, one that can be realized in varying degrees, and that is best brought about by collective, coordinated action. Further, the goal is such that its being choiceworthy is not reducible to its being constituted by or being an instrumental means to the satisfaction of the wants or desires of the agent that attempts to realize this goal, nor is its choiceworthiness reducible to its being constituted by or being an instrumental means to the satisfaction of the desires and wants of the several persons that take part in a cooperative scheme to realize it. Among such goals would be, for example, the feeding and sheltering of the homeless. One person can do something toward feeding and sheltering the homeless, but the feeding and sheltering of the homeless is best brought about by cooperative action. And obviously, the choiceworthiness of feeding and sheltering the homeless is not solely the result of one person's desiring to feed and shelter the homeless, or several persons' desiring to feed and shelter the homeless. On some views, the choiceworthiness of this project might be wholly reducible to the preferences of the homeless that they be fed and sheltered; although I do not think that this is true, nothing that I have said here rules out their preferences as the sole source of the value of the project of feeding and sheltering the homeless. All that is required for my discussion here is that the choiceworthiness of the project is not reducible to the desires of any particular person or group of persons taking part in the project.

Suppose that an agent determines that attempting to realize such a goal is the proper means to fulfill one or another of his or her agent-independent moral requirements. One might, for example, determine that acting to feed and shelter the homeless is the means to fulfilling the agent-independent moral requirement that one assist those who are in great need. Further determinations will, of course, be needed. No one ever feeds and shelters the homeless *simpliciter*. One feeds and shelters the homeless in a particular way, after deliberating about the proper way to go about doing so. Perhaps one decides that, due to the relative mildness of the weather this time of year, it would be better to concentrate on the feeding of the homeless, and that the way to go about feeding the homeless is to spend Saturday morning putting meals into boxes and to spend Sunday afternoon distributing them. This judgment seems to me to be a paradigm of the sort of judgment that is not determined uniquely by the moral principle at stake and the facts of the situation. What is needed is the sort of determination that must go beyond what is strictly implied by conjunction of the moral requirement and the circumstances at hand.

It is important, though, that many morally choiceworthy goals are such that although one may do something to realize these goals acting alone, one's efforts would be better spent engaging in coordinated action with others. Attempting to act in such a coordinated fashion, though, brings with it a difficulty. Presumably those who are attempting to engage in coordinated action to feed and shelter the homeless are united insofar as they are aiming to realize a common goal, and insofar as they aim to realize this action at least in part due to its being a fulfillment of an agent-independent moral requirement they have determined their moral principles in the same way. Unfortunately, though, in order to act in a coordinated fashion they will have to possess more determinations than that one in common: they will have to determine the means to their common goal in the same way. If persons determine the means to their common goal in different ways, then coordinated action is frustrated. To some extent, of course, the problem of differing determinations is ameliorated due to the fact, mentioned above, that there are some determinations that are so far off the mark that they do not even bear consideration. The fact that the problem of differing determinations is partially assuaged by elimination of these silly solutions, though, is not sufficient to ensure the possibility of coordinated action. For there will in many cases remain a class of determinations that are not silly, the class of which we called minimally acceptable determinations.

How do persons engaged in such common projects solve the problem posed by differing minimally acceptable determinations? What often occurs is that there comes into existence a set of rules about how things are to be done *or* a person is recognized who decides how things are to be done *or* there comes into existence a set of rules about how it is decided who the person is that decides how things are to be done. When several persons are forming a group for the first time to carry out a common project, this adoption of a set of rules of action, recognition of a person to act as decision-maker, or adoption of a set of rules to decide who is the decision-maker is often explicit—a constitution is voted on, perhaps, or a person becomes by unanimous acclaim the decision-maker. But this need not be the case, and when one person comes to an already formed well-coordinated group he or she rarely takes part in any overt act whereby he or she agrees to the rules or recognizes a person as the decision-maker. In either case, there emerges some set of rules that are the determinations that the members of the group can act upon, or some person who determines what precepts the members of the group will act upon, or some set of rules that specifies who the person is that determines what precepts the members of the group will act upon.

Now, there are at least two different ways that agents involved in such a scheme could treat the rules of that scheme that are laid down to solve the problem of differing minimally acceptable determinations. Consider two persons, A and B, who take part in a cooperative scheme to realize a morally choiceworthy goal. Person A treats the rules of the scheme in the following way. She knows that other persons in the cooperative scheme are likely to comply with the rules, for whatever reason. Given that other persons in the scheme are following the rules, the course of action that would be most likely to be effective in achieving the morally choiceworthy goal would be to follow the rules. Person A therefore follows the rules.[15] Person B, on the other hand, treats the rules in a different way. Instead of calculating each time the effect that her obeying the rule would have, given others' compliance, she has accepted the rules of the scheme as her own determinations. Instead of treating them as determinations issued by an outsider, to be obeyed or disobeyed as her calculations dictate, she treats them *as her own*, in the same way that she would treat them if they were the products of her own deliberation about how general moral principles should be specified for the situation at hand.

I shall call 'consent in the acceptance sense' the manner in which B (but not A) treats the rules of the cooperative scheme.[16] Now, since B need not undertake any speech-act whereby she declares herself bound to do what the rules or the decision-maker say—as I said, recognition of the rules or the decision-maker as authoritative need not be explicit—this consent cannot be identified with the speech-act version of consent, what Simmons calls the "occurrence" sense of consent.[17] Neither, though, is B's consent to be identified with a mere feeling of approval toward the rules or the decision-maker, what Simmons calls the "attitudinal" sense of consent.[18] Rather, B consents in the acceptance sense. One consents to another in a certain sphere of conduct in the acceptance sense of consent when one allows the other's practical judgments to take the place of his or her own with regard to that sphere of conduct. (This consent may be either to a person or to a set of rules:[19] both of these can be authoritative.) It is important to be clear, though, about what acceptance of another's determinations as one's own does and does not entail. It does not entail that one accepts the other's judgments into one's theoretical as well as one's practical reasoning. When not reasoning with an eye to action, one who has consented to another in the acceptance sense need not believe that the authoritative judgment that has been rendered is the best judgment, or the judgment that the agent would make if rendering a determination on his or her own. It is during practical reasoning that such judgments must be accepted. On the other hand, when one accepts another's judgments as his or her own for the purposes of practical reasoning, one does not merely act *as if* these judgments were his or her own. At some level or other—this level will vary with what the correct account of practical reasoning is—these judgments must enter as premises in practical reasoning; they must be used, not mentioned. That is to say, if authority L has rendered determination p, then p must enter into the practical reasoning of the agent that accepts L's authority, not merely "L says 'p'." Even this condition, though, is not quite strong enough. For if one has promised to obey L, then one may deduce from the fact that L told one to ϕ that one ought to ϕ; but this is not a case of consent in the acceptance sense. On the acceptance sense of consent, there is no intervening logical step.[20] It is simply true that the authority's determinations enter one's practical reasoning as one's own; the determinations do not enter one's practical reasoning as conclusions from other premises.

Before we examine how agent-dependent moral requirements might be generated as a result of consent in the acceptance sense, we should pause to consider why one would consent to another in the acceptance sense of consent.[21] There are at least two sorts of reasons why one would do so. The most straightforward reason is familiar from elaboration of rule-egoism and rule-utilitarianism. One might rightly believe that he or she would succeed better in fulfilling his or her agent-independent moral requirements if he or she were to consent to the authority of the rules of a cooperative scheme rather than to calculate for each performance whether he or she should obey the rules. The straightforward reason for consenting provides, that is, an instrumental justification for accepting another's determinations as one's own: consenting may be the best means to achieve an independently specifiable end. That there may be a reason of another kind for consenting becomes apparent, though, by attending once again to the distinction between instrumental and constitutive means; for in addition to the instrumental justification for consent in the acceptance sense, there may be justification for such consent that is based on the constitutive means to achieving a morally choiceworthy goal. It might be the case, that is, that the morally choiceworthy end that brings persons together into a cooperative scheme cannot be adequately specified independently of the rules of the scheme, rules that are themselves determinations.[22] Although persons entering the scheme do so because they wish to secure a morally choiceworthy goal, this goal cannot be characterized independently of these determinations. Hence, in order that the end that is sought may be concrete enough for common action, it may be necessary that persons consent to an authority to provide the specifications of the common goal.[23]

It is clear that if there are cases of consent in the acceptance sense, those are cases that we would describe as surrenders or substitutions of judgment: one gives up one's own private judgment, the determinations that one would have made, and instead accepts the determinations rendered by some other party. But while it is obvious that this sort of surrender of judgment might be implicated in a merely descriptive account of what it is for one person to treat another as authoritative (we might say, that is, that Jack treats Jane as authoritative because he allows her judgments to replace his own in some sphere of conduct), we have yet to see how this surrender of judgment has normative implications, so that it could serve as part of an account of the basis of practical authority. Consider, though, the following. There are morally choiceworthy goals the realization of which is best achieved by coordinated action, where coordination can be achieved only by appeal to some set of rules determining the general moral principles or to some person who determines those principles. Now, suppose that it is the case with regard to one such scheme that those who participate in it do consent to the rules or to the decision-maker in the acceptance sense described: they accept the determinations stated in the rules or issued by the decision-maker as their own determinations for the purpose of practical reasoning. Note, though, what would follow from this acceptance. If one is under an agent-dependent moral requirement to act according to one's minimally acceptable determinations of agent-independent moral requirements, as I claimed earlier, and by consenting to the rules or to the authoritative decision-maker one accepts their determinations as one's own, then one is under an agent-dependent moral requirement to act according to those minimally acceptable determinations stated in those rules or issued by the authoritative decision-maker—*and without the occurrence of any speech-act of consent.* If, for example, B were to consent to a certain person's authority within the group organized to feed and shelter the homeless, and this person were to tell B to spend both Saturday and Sunday distributing food rather than to split B's weekend up into production and distribution, B would be acting contrary to an agent-dependent moral requirement if B were not to act on the former of these determinations.

If it is granted that B would in some way be acting wrongly by not acting according to this person's determination, yet it is denied that the wrongness of B's action derives from its being contrary to an agent-dependent moral requirement of the sort described, it would seem that some rival explanation for the wrongness of that action must be provided. But note that many of the standard explanations for the presence of obligations do not apply here. B need not have performed a speech-act of consent in becoming a part of this cooperative scheme, so the moral requirement does not result from consent in the occurrence sense. Obligations of fair play, as typically understood, do not apply either, for

B has received no benefits from the group that would bind her to the rules of the cooperative scheme. Since there has been no such benefit, neither can there be an obligation of gratitude. If it is claimed that others' reliance upon B is the source of the obligation, the rejoinder must be that one can have moral reasons to act according to such determinations even when others do not rely upon him or her and that most explanations of why inducing reliance generates obligations are grounded in the detriment that will fall on the person in whom reliance has been induced if the person who has induced reliance does not perform. It is difficult to see what agent-independent moral requirement would apply in such a case.

Before we turn to the application of this notion of consent to the problem of political authority, an objection to the idea that we accept others' determinations of moral principles as our own needs to be considered. The idea that by consenting in the acceptance sense we allow others to render determinations for us has an unsavory air about it. First, it seems to make us excessively vulnerable: accepting others' practical judgments would allow those others to use us for their own, perhaps disreputable, ends rather than for the realization of a morally choiceworthy goal. Second, it seems to undercut the value of our agency, implying a kind of mindless, blind obedience to authority.[24]

Consenting to others' authority in the acceptance sense, though, need not bring with it such pernicious consequences. First, consenting to another in the acceptance sense does not imply that one accept every command that the other issues. For the scope of one's acceptance might be limited. One might, that is, accept only those determinations issued that are relevant to a certain coordination problem. Or, to place an even sharper limit on the scope of acceptance, one might accept only those determinations issued that are both relevant to a certain coordination problem and minimally acceptable as solutions to it. (Note that this limited acceptance does not unduly weaken the authority in question: since the need for authority arises from the multiplicity of minimally acceptable yet incompatible determinations, acceptance of only those determinations that are minimally acceptable would be sufficient to solve the coordination problem.) Second, even if the scope of one's acceptance goes beyond accepting minimally acceptable determinations, the scope of the other's authority can go no further than that: since the authority results from the application of the agent-dependent moral principle that one is to act in accordance with one's own minimally acceptable determinations, one could be bound to only those determinations that are themselves minimally acceptable. Third, it is often the case that rules to which members of such schemes consent often impose limits on what determinations the person in authority can or cannot make, such as in the case of constitutions that describe what authority is conferred on persons who make decisions for other members of the scheme. Fourth, although the precepts expressed in the rules of the scheme or issued by an authoritative person are more specific than the general principles of which they are determinations, the members of the group will often have to exercise some of their own practical reasoning in attempting to perform the requisite actions. And, fifth, it needs to be remembered that nothing has been said here about how the authority in question reaches its determinations. It could be the case that the rules of the scheme specify that the determinations to be acted upon are decided by a vote of the members of the scheme after each member has had an opportunity to propose a common set of determinations and to defend that proposal. The picture of a member of a cooperative scheme who has a chance to defend a proposal, has that proposal voted ultimately rejected, but nevertheless accepts the group's decision *qua* minimally acceptable set of determinations for carrying out the group's project hardly seems to fit the description of blind acceptance of authority. It is therefore clear that consent in the acceptance sense does not bring with it implications of vulnerability or practical mindlessness.

THE REFURBISHED CONSENT ACCOUNT OF POLITICAL AUTHORITY

Thus far I have argued for the existence of moral requirements that result from one's determinations of general principles stating agent-independent moral requirements, and have argued that there is a notion of consent in which one consents to another if one accepts the other's determinations of general principles as his or her own. We may now turn to the importance these conclusions have for the possibility of a refurbished consent account of political authority.

Suppose that at least one of the reasons that political authority is instituted is that there is a morally choiceworthy goal, resulting from an agent-independent moral requirement, means to which must be determined if that goal is to be achieved by cooperative action.[25] If it is true, then, that persons consent to their political institutions in the acceptance sense, then they have surrendered their judgment in these matters, instead allowing the determinations issued by those institutions to take the place of their own for the purpose of practical reasoning. As each person is under an agent-dependent moral requirement to act according to one's minimally acceptable determinations of general moral principles, then one is under an agent-dependent moral requirement to act according to those minimally acceptable determinations issued by the political authority to whom one consents.

Now, I do not deny that there are a number of morally choiceworthy goals that governing institutions can help to promote. But on the consent account of political authority defended here, the goal of the institution of government in terms of which that institution has authority is the promotion of a just order. By 'justice' I mean more than distributive justice. I mean, rather, a state of affairs in which persons and groups of persons act properly with regard to what they owe to one another and the political community as a whole; that is, they act in ways consonant with the legitimate claims that the good of others and the common good make upon them. Now, it does seem that rules of justice in this broad sense are incomplete in that if one is given the rules of justice and the empirically given facts of the situation to which the rules of justice are to be applied, it will not always be the case that the just thing to do can be deduced. This is not to say, though, that in such cases it is inevitably an arbitrary matter whether one action is performed rather than another. I take it that while the exercise of logical acuity will not be sufficient to determine what one ought to do, there are reasons that can be advanced for rendering one determination rather than another, even if these reasons are not sufficient to characterize one determination as ultimately the only minimally acceptable determination-candidate.

Even among persons that are committed to just action, then, there will arise the problem of numerous incompatible yet at least minimally acceptable determinations that can serve as the basis for common action. Indeed, the problem of differing determinations would seem to be far more severe in this case than in the case of those who aim to feed and shelter the homeless, and not just because of the far greater scope of the goal in question. Although there may be great divergence within a group with regard to what instrumental means should be taken in order to feed and shelter the homeless, what constitutes the completed goal of fed and sheltered homeless persons is relatively straightforward. It seems, though, that the problem of differing determinations is exacerbated in the case of the securing of a just order, for not only are determinations regarding instrumental means at stake, but determinations about what constitutes just action have to be made. And this is, I take it, one of the tasks that belong to governing institutions: that of providing determinations of rules regarding justice. Legislatures, in passing laws, lay down guidelines that determine what citizens owe to one another and to the political community as a whole; the judiciary serves a subsidiary role by producing authoritative accounts of how legislative determinations are to be interpreted, and, on some jurisprudential views, producing determinations of their own in the underdetermined space left by legislators.

I have argued thus far for a refurbished consent account of political authority that places the source of such authority in citizens' surrender of judgment regarding determinations of principles of justice. Now, two different types of objection might be raised with regard to the emphasis placed here on determinations of justice. First, one might object that not all of a governing institution's dictates that we would take to be authoritative can be explained in terms of a principle of justice. Second, one might object that since the agent-dependent moral principle invoked only binds one to act in accordance with one's minimally acceptable determinations, the scope of authority possessed by political institutions would be unduly limited.

The first of these objections claims that the appeal to a single type of moral principle—that pertaining to justice—is insufficient to ground political authority. For, as I already admitted, governing institutions have a number of purposes, and aim at a number of worthwhile goals. Consider, for example, that many take one of the aims of government to be to maintain an environment for citizens that is not aesthetically horrible; in light of this aim, many governments pass laws pertaining to the beautification of the areas in which citizens dwell. How could laws regarding (e.g.) city beautification be viewed as embodying determinations of justice? If this objection is sound, then I would be forced to either reject the authoritativeness of all such laws or expand my account of the type of moral principles determinations of which are relevant to political authority. But it seems to me that the objection is not sound, for it underestimates the extent to which the exercise of political authority, even if aiming to secure some other desirable goal, is bound up with justice. For such laws aim to specify, to make concrete, what citizens *owe* to one another or to the state with regard to the securing of this other socially desirable goal, thus providing an authoritative pronouncement regarding what is *due* from each citizen in our common pursuit of a multiplicity of socially desirable ends.[26] Hence, although political authority undoubtedly aims at promoting a variety of social goods (which may as a class be referred to as 'the common good'), it functions to promote these goods by specifying what each citizen is bound by justice to do to secure them.[27]

The second of these objections functions by contrasting a certain conception of what an account of political authority should achieve with what the refurbished consent theory of political authority in fact achieves. The view that I have presented implies that any pronouncement issued by political institutions that is not a minimally acceptable determination does not fall within the scope of any political institution's authority. If this is an objection, though, I fail to see why. Perhaps it would be an objection if I were purporting to provide an account of a general obligation to obey the law *and* it were the case that a condition of adequacy for such accounts is that for each law that a political authority could issue there must be at least a *prima facie* reason to obey it. But granting that to offer an account of political authority is by implication to offer an account of the obligation to obey the law, I would not take it to be a condition of adequacy for a theory of political obligation that it imply that every law generate a reason for action—only that we can specify which do and which do not, and of those that do, we can explain why an appeal to their status as law is necessary to explaining why subjects have reason to perform the action required by those laws.[28] If consent in the acceptance sense were a thoroughly general phenomenon within a political community, and law were to be characterized as the dictates issued by governing institutions, it would follow not that there is a general reason to obey any law that might be laid down but rather that there is reason to adhere to any law that is a minimally acceptable determination of principles of justice. It would not strike me as at all implausible that our political obligations are limited in this way. And it is clear that such an account, if correct, would make clear how the existence of law functions in generating that type of reason for action:

what laws actually exist settles the issue of which of the wide range of possible minimally acceptable determinations the citizens are to act upon.[29]

PROSPECTS FOR THE REFURBISHED CONSENT ACCOUNT

The refurbished consent model of political authority preserves the authority-generating character of consent without relying on the claim that a citizen must perform a certain sort of speech-act in order to be bound. This model therefore escapes the objection that the paucity of speech-acts of consent is simply a brute fact that renders such theories inapplicable to present political conditions. I take it that the greatest advance offered to consent theory by this sort of view is that critics of consent theory cannot remain content with versions of the arguments that Hume employed in 'Of the Original Contract' to show that consent theory is irremediably flawed.[30] The scarcity of express acts of consent is sufficient to show that if consent theory is to succeed, some other sort of consent must be the source of the moral requirement to obey the law. Advocates of consent theory, while recognizing the dearth of express consent, have unfortunately modeled their accounts of tacit consent on express consent, and thus fall prey to the same objections that have been successfully pressed against express consent theories. By placing no reliance at all on these sorts of consent, the refurbished consent theory takes these critics out of familiar territory—accounts that rely on consent in the occurrence sense—to unfamiliar territory—accounts that rely on consent in an acceptance sense.

It is open to these critics, of course, to argue that the type of consent theory offered here either falls prey to the same sort of worries about application that the standard consent theory does or somehow loses part of the appeal of the standard consent view. Consider first the worry about application. It is of course true that nowhere have I offered evidence for the claim that there is at present general consent within political communities either to a set of rules that determine the principles of justice or to some person that is the authoritative determiner of those principles. As critics of consent theory generally rest their criticisms on empirical grounds, not on the rejection of the principle of consent, it would be crucial to present arguments that show that there is such general acceptance. The presenting of such arguments would necessarily involve an investigation into how the dictates issued by political authorities function in the practical reasoning of citizens. But even if I have not yet presented such arguments, there are at least two reasons to believe that the refurbished argument from consent is a genuine advance on earlier consent theories. First, the refurbished argument from consent is a genuine advance because the absence of consent in the acceptance sense is at least not a glaringly obvious brute fact, as is the absence of consent in the occurrence sense. The political behavior of many citizens presents evidence that the existence of laws does play some role in their moral reasoning, and it is at least initially plausible that this role in moral reasoning is due to consent in the acceptance sense. Consider drunk-driving laws, for example. It does seem that such laws are determinations of principles of justice, and are determinations that could not be reached by any wholly-rule-governed decision procedure. Those who think that the maximum blood alcohol level that drivers should be permitted should be 0.08 and those who think it should be 0.10 have no knock-down arguments for their positions. Neither is this a purely arbitrary matter: it makes a difference whether 0.08 or 0.10 is the legal limit. Do many people accept their government's authority on this matter? Most people that I know seem to, anyway: even if they think that they would not be overly impaired by having a blood alcohol level slightly above 0.10, they accept their government's determination that anything over 0.10 is out of bounds. Other examples might be produced: laws regarding what taxes are due, laws regarding the fair use of copyrighted material, laws regarding speed limits. It is quite likely, it seems, that for most people there are at least a few governmental determinations that they accept as authoritative. And it may very well be the case that further investigation into the structure of citizens' practical reasoning may reveal consent to authority in the acceptance sense that is more thoroughgoing than that manifested in these admittedly few and inadequate examples.

Second, the refurbished consent theory, even if it were ultimately to fail as an account of political authority in present conditions, may succeed as part of an account of why citizens *ought* to surrender their judgment in this way and thereby make their political institutions authoritative. Consider in this regard Jeremy Waldron's attempt to provide an account of the moral requirement to comply with one's governing institutions in terms of the natural duty of justice, an argument that refuses to make any recourse to consent, acceptance of benefits, or any other voluntary act.[31] Waldron argues that (i) all of us are under a moral requirement to promote justice; (ii) justice cannot be secured unless institutions function to ensure that the principles of justice are satisfied; (iii) those institutions cannot function in this way unless those to whom those institutions apply accept the supervision of those institutions; and therefore (iv) those to whom such institutions apply are bound to comply with them.[32] Now, as I have argued elsewhere,[33] Waldron's argument fails: it is the transition from (iii) to (iv) that is problematic, for the mere fact that we are bound to accept the supervision of those institutions does not imply that we are bound to comply with them; it could be the case that our being bound to comply with those institutions *depends* on our acceptance, so that if we fail to accept those institutions' supervision we are under no requirement to comply with them. What is illuminating about Waldron's view, though, is that even if it fails as a natural duty account of political authority it may succeed as an account of why we ought to place ourselves under the supervision of a political authority with respect to the implementation of justice. It seems highly unlikely that we could, without placing ourselves under such institutions, come to sufficient agreement in determinations of justice in order to promote it through cooperative action. Thus, the refurbished consent theory presented here can be viewed as building upon Waldron's account in the following ways: it incorporates his account of the importance of justice in explaining the authority of governing institutions; it explains how 'acceptance'—a term undefined in Waldron's paper—is to be understood; and it provides an account of how that acceptance makes governing institutions practically authoritative over us.

Consider next the worry that somewhere in the move from the standard to the refurbished consent account something has been lost. Certainly it is not that the state of being under an authority is a self-imposed one: in both views, it is oneself that ultimately determines whether one is subject to a political authority, and the extent of one's consent determines the extent to which one is bound. But perhaps what is worrisome is that while the standard consent view can account for the endurance of political authority, the refurbished consent view cannot. What I have in mind is this. One who consents in the speech-act sense is bound until released from his or her obligation; one who consents in the acceptance sense, on the one hand, can escape obligation by simply ceasing to accept as one's own the determination issued by the political authorities. This is why the refurbished view cannot account for the endurance of political authority.

I recognize the implication that on this view one's subjection to a political authority ceases if one no longer accepts as one's own the determinations issued by that political authority, but I deny that this is an objection to the account. Why is it that an account of political authority would have to show that the status of political institutions as authoritative is independent of one's continuing acceptance of authority? Perhaps the worry is that if there is not such independence, one could too easily remove oneself from the ranks of those subject to authority: one could simply decide not to accept particular determinations whenever one is dissatisfied with them, or might decide for some trivial reason not to accept any such determinations. And I grant that one can remove oneself in this way. But I do not think that this is a worry, for even if it is *practically possible* to cease to accept determinations as one's own, it does not follow that it is *morally permissible*: one might be acting wrongly in refusing to accept determinations in certain matters, or in ceasing to accept authority at all. If the securing of a just order requires common determination of principles of justice, and common determination is only practically possible by acceptance of authority, one could be acting wrongly in ceasing to accept these determinations. If, then, one ceases to accept his or her government's determinations in order to avoid being subject to authority, one may be acting wrongly in doing so; and it does not seem to me to be an untoward result that one can become free of political authority only by acting wrongly.

The upshot is this: if it were morally neutral whether one consented in the acceptance sense to one's political authorities, it might be objectionable that one can avoid obligation by ceasing to accept that authority. But it is not morally neutral whether one has accepted the dictates of one's political authorities as one's own. Thus it is not clear why it is an objection to this consent account that one can avoid being subject to political authority by ceasing to accept the dictates issued by the political authorities as one's own.

Of course, there is more that is controversial about the view that is presented here than claims about the scope of consent in the acceptance sense to political institutions and about the extent to which the refurbished consent theory preserves what is attractive about standard consent views. The refurbished consent theory requires a certain view of the incompleteness of moral rules, of the agent-dependent moral requirements that can arise through the rendering of determinations, of the possibility of accepting another's determinations as one's own, and of dictates issued by political authorities as determinations of principles of justice. These are substantive theses of moral and political theory, and it cannot be pretended that I have offered anything resembling a complete defense of them here. Critics of consent theory could reject these claims, and thus eliminate the threat presented by the refurbished consent theory. But while these claims are controversial, they are not implausible. Previously, critics of consent theory could remain content merely showing that present political conditions are such that the principle of consent fails to apply. If they are compelled to deal with these substantive moral and political premises, then they must themselves affirm a controversial position, thus increasing substantially their argumentative burden.

NOTES

I owe a debt of gratitude to David Schmidtz, Henry Richardson, M. B. E. Smith, and a referee at *Law and Philosophy* for criticism of earlier drafts of this article.

1. H. L. A. Hart, *Essays on Bentham* (Oxford: Oxford University Press, 1982), p. 253; Richard Friedman, "On the Concept of Authority in Political Philosophy," in Richard Flathman, ed., *Concepts in Social and Political Philosophy* (New York: Macmillan, 1973), p. 129; Joseph Raz, *The Morality of Freedom* (Oxford: Oxford University Press, 1986), pp. 38–69. The quotations from Hart and Friedman are cited in Raz 1986, p. 39.

2. Thomas Hobbes, *Leviathan*, pp. 168–69 of the 'Head' edition.

3. M. B. E. Smith, "Is There a Prima Facie Obligation to Obey the Law?" *Yale Law Journal* 82 (1973): 950–976, p. 960. For some other recent criticisms of consent theory, see Joseph Raz, *The Authority of Law: Essays on Law and Morality* (Oxford: Oxford University Press, 1979); A. John Simmons, *Moral Principles and Political Obligations* (Princeton: Princeton University Press, 1979), pp. 57–100; Kent Greenawalt, *Conflicts of Law and Morality* (Oxford: Oxford University Press, 1987), pp. 62–88; and Leslie Green, *The Authority of the State* (Oxford: Oxford University Press, 1990), pp. 158–187.

4. What of arguments from tacit consent? Aren't they a prominent exception to the claim that consent accounts of political authority require one to

perform a speech-act in order to be bound? They are not an exception, for insofar as such arguments are genuinely arguments from consent (rather than from fair play, or gratitude, or justice) they function by holding that an act such as remaining in residence or voting is as significant a speech-act as uttering "I consent to be governed." Critics of consent theory argue convincingly, however, that neither residence nor voting constitutes a speech-act of consent. See Simmons 1979, pp. 79–83, and Smith 1973, pp. 960–964.

5. I assume that an institution's possessing political authority over some persons involves those persons' having reason to comply with its dictates. For accounts of political authority that do not carry this implication see (e.g.) Rolf Sartorius, "Political Authority and Political Obligation," *Virginia Law Review* 67 (1981): 3–17, and Greenawalt 1987, pp. 50–58; for criticism of this rival conception, see Raz 1986, pp. 23–26.

6. John Rawls, "Legal Obligation and the Duty of Fair Play," in Sidney Hook, ed., *Law and Philosophy* (New York: New York University Press, 1964), p. 9.

7. John Rawls, *A Theory of Justice* (Cambridge, Mass.: Harvard University Press, 1971), p. 334.

8. H. L. A. Hart, "Are There Any Natural Rights?" *Philosophical Review* 64 (1955): 175–191, p. 185.

9. Rawls 1964.

10. Plato, *Crito*, trans. G. M. A. Grube (Indianapolis: Hackett, 1981), 50d–51c.

11. Rawls 1971, pp. 334–336.

12. What I call 'agent-independent' and 'agent-dependent' moral requirements have been called by other writers 'material' and 'formal' moral requirements, respectively, as well as 'objective' and 'subjective' moral requirements, respectively. See Alan Donagan, *The Theory of Morality* (Chicago: University of Chicago Press, 1977), pp. 136–137. I decline to employ the former pair of alternative terms because they don't strike me as informative; I decline to employ the latter because of the unhealthy connotations with which the term 'subjective' is infected, at least in discussions of ethics. I choose the terms 'agent-independent' and 'agent-dependent,' with some reservations, in order to highlight the distinction between those moral requirements that do not arise from the agent's deliberation with regard to how to act and those moral requirements that arise from the agent's deliberation with regard to how to act.

13. In treating of agent-dependent moral requirements, recent writers have focused exclusively on the cases in which there is conflict between what is required by an agent-independent moral requirement and what is required by an agent-dependent moral requirement. See Donagan 1977, pp. 131–142, and John Finnis, *Natural Law and Natural Rights* (Oxford: Clarendon Press, 1980), pp. 125–126.

14. It is decidedly unlike typical cases of arbitrariness—the classic example being the judgment of which side of the road we ought to drive on—in which there is every reason to choose one option as to choose the other.

15. Joseph Raz considers the function of law as coordinating action to achieve common goals to be one way in which it is causally effective in producing moral requirements. But he argues that no moral requirements derive from the existence of the law itself; rather, it is the existence of the social practice of cooperation that generates the moral reasons for action. See Raz 1979, pp. 247–248; see also "The Obligation to Obey: Revision and Tradition," *Notre Dame Journal of Law, Ethics, and Public Policy* 1 (1984): 139–155, pp. 151–152. If the only stance one could take with regard to the rules were that of person A, then Raz's argument would be successful. As I shall argue, though, the stance that B takes with regard to the rules generates moral reasons that do not derive from the social practice alone.

16. Some have suggested to me that there is no reason to call this sort of practical stance with regard to the rules of the scheme a case of consent. But, so far as I can see, there is support in ordinary language for calling this a case of consent and no good philosophical reason against it. The ordinary notion of consent is just that of agreement or acceptance; and accepting the rules in place of one's own judgments seems to fit this idea well enough. It seems to me that the reason that philosophers have fixed on the speech-act sense of consent, rejecting other senses of it as spurious, is that they want to reserve the term 'consent' to those cases in which moral requirements are generated. But even under this rationale, as I shall shortly argue, consent in the acceptance sense is not ruled out.

17. Simmons 1979, p. 93.

18. Simmons 1979, p. 93.

19. There are some similarities between the acceptance notion of consent employed with regard to a set of rules and H. L. A. Hart's notion of the "internal point of view" with regard to rules. See Hart, *The Concept of Law* (Oxford: Clarendon Press, 1961), pp. 55–56.

20. This does not exclude the possibility of a filter-type mechanism at work in specifying which determinations I accept and which I do not. A filter-type mechanism would prevent certain determinations from being allowed into one's practical reasoning to be treated as one's own. Such a device might filter out determinations that are logically incompatible with the moral principle of which they are supposed to be determinations, or determinations that are outside of the scope of the ruler's authority. To say that some determinations can be filtered, though, does not imply that the determination appears in one's practical reasoning as a conclusion from some independent basis of authority, such as a promise.

21. In ascribing reasons to persons who consent in the acceptance sense, I do not mean to say that all persons who consent do so deliberately. It seems to me that some persons just do consent in that sometimes ineffable process by which one becomes a member of a rule-governed scheme. For many, their consenting can be explained retrospectively by appeal to certain reasons, even if such reasons were not at the front of their minds; or we might consider these reasons as reasons not to attempt to extricate oneself from consent in the acceptance sense. Indeed, I imagine that very few persons consent in the acceptance sense in a totally deliberate fashion.

22. On John Finnis' view, the law's authority is grounded in its capacity to coordinate action for the common good. See Finnis 1980, pp. 231–254; see also "The Authority of Law in the Predicament of Contemporary Social Theory," *Notre Dame Journal of Law, Ethics, and Public Policy* 1 (1984): 114–137, and "Law as Coordination," *Ratio Juris* 2 (1989): 97–104. Finnis' argument is an argument from hypothetical necessity: if a certain end is to be secured, then certain means are necessary. Finnis holds that the common good is an end that it would be practically unreasonable not to foster and promote, and that obedience to law is necessary for that end. Consent is therefore unnecessary on his view. But although Finnis recognizes that the content of the common good is to some extent constituted by the determinations rendered by political authority, he fails to see how this undermines his argument. For if the judgment of the citizens concerning the content of the common good conflicts with the judgment of the political authorities, citizens will have no reason to believe that obedience to law is necessary for the securing of the common good. If, on the other hand, Finnis were to attempt his argument based on the concept of the common good as it exists prior to determination, the end given would be much too diffuse to yield the conclusion that obedience to law is necessary for securing the common good.

23. There is another possibility within the realm of constitutive means for consenting: it could be the case that consenting itself contributes to the common goal. This is not just an abstract possibility: it is part of Aquinas' view of political authority. For Aquinas, the common good consists in "justice and peace" (*Summa Theologiae* IaIIae 96, 3), where peace is not just absence of conflict but a proper ordering (*Summa Theologiae* IIaIIae 29, 2). Within a political community (of humans that are, by nature, equal—see *Summa Theologiae* Ia 109, 2 and 3), this order is produced (in part) by consent. Thus consent itself helps to constitute the common good on Aquinas' account. For further discussion of Aquinas' view, see my "Consent, Custom, and the Common Good in Aquinas's Account of Political Authority," *Review of Politics* 59 (1997): 323–350.

24. That such considerations show that we ought not consent to authority is part of Wolff's defense of anarchism. See Robert Paul Wolff, *A Defense of Anarchism* (New York: Harper and Row, 1970).

25. Tony Honoré has recently presented a careful and persuasive argument that morality depends on law for its determination. See Honoré, "The Dependence of Morality on Law," *Oxford Journal of Legal Studies* 13 (1993): 1–17.

26. Raz imagines a case in which the government has issued certain safety regulations regarding the use of dangerous tools. He holds that those who have knowledge of the use of those tools superior to those who drafted the regulations are not bound to comply with them. See Raz 1984, pp. 146–148. If all that were at stake in such a case were the socially desirable goal of safety, then Raz would clearly be right: noncompliance with the law by experts may not hinder pursuit of that goal. But the laws in question aim to dictate what is *owed* by each person in pursuit of the goal of safety. Hence, even if the aim of safety is not damaged by noncompliance, the noncomplying expert may go afoul of the demands of justice.

27. This adds a further dimension to the difficulties involved in determining principles of justice. For if the following highly abstract principle of justice is correct—"each citizen is bound to do his or her part in promoting the common good"—determinations may be needed not only to specify what counts as doing's one's part but also to determine the content of the common good.

28. It would not suffice, that is, to say that there is an obligation to obey certain laws, those laws that happen to require what is independently required by objective morality. For it genuinely to be an account of the obligation to obey the law, it must appeal to the fact of a law's existence to account for the reasons for action that an agent has.

29. A natural law theorist of civil law could claim that there could be a perfectly general requirement to obey the law on this view, holding that a law that is not even a minimally acceptable determination of correct general practical principles is not to be counted part of the civil law. Taking into consideration the qualification noted in Finnis 1980 (pp. 364–365) this is essentially Aquinas' view (*Summa Theologiae* IaIIae 96, 4).

30. David Hume, "Of the Original Contract," in *Essays Moral, Political, and Literary*, ed. Eugene F. Miller (Indianapolis: Liberty Classics, 1985).

31. See Jeremy Waldron, "Special Ties and Natural Duties," *Philosophy & Public Affairs* 22 (1993): 3–30.

32. All of these claims are explicitly assumed or argued for in Waldron 1993; for (i), see p. 28; for (ii) see p. 15; for (iii) see pp. 15–16; for (iv) see pp. 20, 21.

33. Mark C. Murphy, "Acceptance of Authority and the Duty to Comply with Just Institutions: A Comment on Waldron," *Philosophy & Public Affairs* 23 (1994): 271–277.

INDEX

agent-dependent moral requirements, 321–26, 331, 332, 333–42, 343n12
agent-independent moral requirements, 321–22, 327–28, 332, 334–35
anarchism. *See* philosophical anarchism
anarchy, 26–29, 62
Anscombe, Elizabeth, 144, 146–47, 149, 178, 187
associative obligations, 14, 173
Austin, John, 1, 234
authority, 3, 7, 14, 63–66, 86–87, 213, 309–11; "dependence" thesis, 224–27; justification of. *See* legitimacy; "leader" conception of, 233–34, 237; military, 219–20, 225–26; "normal justification" thesis, 225, 227–33; and obedience, correlated, 5, 6, 8–9, 12–14, 64, 66, 86, 99–100, 160, 222–23, 225, 234–38; and obedience, not correlated, 6, 7, 143–47, 177–88, 215; parental, 145–46, 147, 182–83, 221, 230; practical, 4, 14, 181–82, 222, 227–29, 240n23, 319–20; religious, 234–35, 308; and right to be wrong, 9, 217, 231, 313; and right to rule, 6, 64–65, 66–67, 72,

147; "service" conception of, 233; and surrender of judgment, 219, 319–20, 327, 331; theoretical or scientific, 14, 222, 227–28, 235, 240n23. *See also* preemption, content-independence
autonomy, individual, 3, 68–72; conflict with authority, 72–73, 219; "reactive" and "relational," contrasted, 248–49, 255–56, 258

Beavoir, Simone de, 256–57
benefits: acceptance of, 5, 112, 129–34, 144, 198–99; open, 6, 78, 130–32, 137. *See also* goods
Berlin, Isaiah, 250–51
Brandt, R. B., 92–93
burden of proof, 61, 179, 198, 206–8

Chodorow, Nancy, 248–49
civil disobedience, 1–2, 3, 49, 54–56; justification of, 56–62, 95–96
claim right, 145–47, 184
classical-music example. *See* Nozick's PA system example
coercion, 6, 144–45, 155–56, 178–82, 184, 196, 217, 234, 237, 251
coherence, method of. *See* reflective equilibrium

347

consent, 5–7, 10, 11, 107, 118, 146–51, 172, 180, 243, 258, 262, 266, 271, 320–42; acceptance of benefits contrasted, 127–28; acceptance sense of, 12, 330–42; advantages of consent theory, 273, 276; express, 151–52, 262, 338; hypothetical, 149–50, 271–72, 290–91; implicit, 84–88; indirect, 86; occurrence sense of, 330, 332, 338–39; roles in legitimacy and obedience contrasted, 290–91; tacit, 144, 150, 152, 261–62, 264, 271, 277, 342n4

consequences, argument from, 26–28, 31, 41

content-independence, 9, 94–95, 97–98, 152, 220–22, 225, 231, 235, 238, 309–10, 313

coordination problems, 7, 171, 232, 235–36, 286, 288–89, 292, 328–29, 332

correlativity, of right to rule and duty to obey. *See* authority

Cranston, Maurice, 251

determinations of moral principles, 11, 323–42

Devlin, Lord Patrick, 97

duty: absolute, 2, 19–21, 100n3, 309; of fair play. *See* fair play, principle of; general or generic, 4, 76–77, 162, 167; natural. *See* natural duty; and obligation contrasted, 3, 140n14, 210n23, 243, 267n1, 271; prima facie, 2, 4, 20–21, 26, 76–77, 100nn3,5, 143, 149, 200, 309; and remorse, 98; to take responsibility, 68–70, 72; weight of, 93–95, 97–98, 160

Dworkin, Ronald, 8, 13, 14, 217–18, 284

Easton, David, 311

fair play, principle of, 3, 5, 8, 38–40, 47n23, 52–53, 79–83, 96, 101n10, 107–39, 152–55, 172, 193–208, 244, 271, 321, 333; acceptance-of-benefits condition, 112–13, 126, 129–35, 136–38, 198–99, 202; advantages of, 119–20, 139, 201–2, 273–74, 276; compliance condition, 111; consent not a condition, 125–28, 153–54, 210n23; cooperative-scheme condition, 138–39; justice condition, 110, 113–17, 153, 203, 204–6, 211n33; net-value-of-benefits condition, 121–22, 133, 137, 154, 201, 204–7; participation condition, 122–27, 202; rule-governedness condition, 110–11

fairness, duty of. *See* fair play, principle of

feminist standpoint. *See* standpoint epistemology

Finnis, John, 8, 169–71

Flathman, Richard, 178, 244, 265

free riders, 132–34, 150, 196, 197, 199–200

Friedman, Richard, 319

gender bias of voluntaristic theories, 10, 245, 250–62

generalization argument, 29–32, 34, 90–92, 103n32

Gewirth, Alan, 85, 87–88

Gilligan, Carol, 249, 263

goods: discretionary, 8, 198, 203–8; excludable, 194–95, 199, 209n6; nonexcludable, 194–96, 199, 202, 209n6; presumptive public, 8, 197–

201, 203, 204, 210n22; primary, 8, 197; public, 194, 198, 209n7
Gramsci, Antonio, 306
gratitude, argument from, 78–79, 321, 333
Green, Leslie, 11, 14
Greenawalt, Kent, 7–8, 13

Hardin, Russell, 196
Hart, H. L. A., 1, 3, 5, 79–80, 107–13, 135–36, 138, 147–48, 151, 153–54, 193–94, 218, 220, 319, 321
Hartsock, Nancy, 246, 247
Hegel, G. W. F., 254, 256–58
Hirschmann, Nancy, 10, 13
Hobbes, Thomas, 7, 10, 172, 216, 220, 237, 253, 260–61, 287–88, 319–20
Holmes, Oliver Wendell, Jr., 223, 260
Hume, David, 1, 51, 150–51, 245, 261, 304–5, 338

Jackson, Shirley, 202
justification right, 145–47, 184

Kant, Immanuel, 51, 66, 216, 280–81, 287
Kelsen, Hans, 233
Kennedy, John F., 19–20, 33
King, Martin Luther, Jr., 249
Klosko, George, 8, 13–14, 301–3, 306–7, 308

Ladd, John, 118–19
Ladenson, Robert, 6, 145, 148
law, motivational function of, 163–64
legitimacy, 4–8, 13, 66–68, 73, 99–100, 148, 178–81, 186–88, 219–20, 222, 227, 229, 243, 311–12
Locke, John, 1, 7, 10, 65, 84–85, 107,

139, 147–48, 150, 172, 244, 252–53, 256, 261–62
Louis XIV, 63
Lyons, David, 194, 201

MacCormick, Neil, 217–18
Mackie, John, 305
MacMahon, Christopher, 229
majority rule, 34–35, 53–54, 56, 290–91
malum in se, 76, 95, 138
malum prohibitum, 97
Marx, Karl, 184
Murphy, Mark, 11–12, 13

natural duty 10–11, 271–95; advantages of natural duty account, 271–72, 276–78, 284–85; "application" objection to, 274–75, 293–95; of civility, 3; consent not a condition, 290; effectiveness condition, 285–86; fairness obligation contrasted, 296n17; legitimacy requirement, 286–91; "special allegiance" objection, 273–74, 275–95; to support just institutions, 3, 50, 52–53, 83–84, 244, 272–95, 321, 339–40
natural law, 8, 22–26, 188
necessary-means principle, 324
necessity as ground of political obligation, 146–47, 187
neutral principles, 37
nonexcludable benefits. *See* benefits, open
Nozick, Robert, 5, 120–34, 148, 153, 196, 202, 203, 287
Nozick's PA system example, 5, 8, 121–26, 129, 136, 196–98, 204

obedience: conformity contrasted, 4, 7, 65, 71, 160–62, 166, 309–11. *See also* authority

object relations theory, 247–50, 254–58, 262–63, 264, 266
obligation: voluntarist theories of, 245, 250–62, 271. *See also* duty, and obligation contrasted
original position, 50–52

participation, 33–36, 86–87, 119, 124–26, 198
Pateman, Carole, 244, 245
philosophical anarchism, 13, 73, 143, 301
Pitkin, Hannah, 178, 244
Plamenatz, John, 85–87
Plato, 84–85, 216, 229
positivism, legal, 8–9, 44n10, 147–48, 213, 215, 233–37
preemption, 9, 218–22, 225, 227, 231, 235
presumption. *See* burden of proof
Prichard, H. A., 75
prima facie obligation. *See* duty, prima facie
prisoners' dilemma, 196, 232
promise, 35–36, 45n20, 84–85, 331
public goods. *See* benefits, open

range-limited principles, 10, 279–84, 285
Rawls, John, 2–4, 75, 79–80, 83–84, 96, 109–17, 124, 126, 129, 134, 135–36, 138, 152–54, 195, 244–45, 251–52, 272–73, 280, 289, 292–93, 302, 321
Raz, Joseph, 6–7, 9, 14, 178, 218–19, 222–31, 319
receipt of benefits, 37–38, 271
reflective equilibrium, 11, 215–17, 302–4, 315; argument from common opinion contrasted, 304–7;

and error theory, 305–7; provisional fixed points and theories contrasted, 302–7
Ross, W. D., 2, 85
Rousseau, Jean-Jacques, 64–65, 139, 172, 251–53

Sartorius, Rolf, 6, 13
Simmons, John, 5–6, 13, 153–54, 198–99, 245, 254, 293–94, 306–7, 330
Singer, Marcus, 29–32
Smith, M. B. E., 4–5, 13
social contract, 50–52, 64, 85, 172, 178, 180, 188, 243–44, 253, 261, 290–91
Socrates, 1, 17, 33, 237
Soper, Philip, 8–10, 14
standpoint epistemology, 246–70
stop-sign examples, 4, 82, 94, 229, 231

taxation, 30–31, 38–39, 57–58, 137, 155, 223
Thucydides, 201
tragedy of the commons, 196
Tussman, Joseph, 244
Tyler, Tom R., 311–12

universalization argument. *See* generalization argument
utilitarian arguments, 88–93

Waldron, Jeremy, 10–11, 13, 339–40
Wasserstrom, Richard, 1–2
Weber, Max, 66
Wechsler, Herbert, 87
Wellman, Christopher, 13
Wittgenstein, Ludwig, 313
Wolff, Robert Paul, 4, 6, 13, 143, 159, 179

ABOUT THE CONTRIBUTORS

William A. Edmundson is professor at Georgia State University College of Law. He is the author of *Three Anarchical Fallacies: An Essay on Political Authority* (Cambridge University Press).

Leslie Green is professor of philosophy at York University, where he also teaches at the Osgoode Hall Law School. He is the author of *The Authority of the State* (1988).

Kent Greenawalt is Benjamin N. Cardozo Professor of Jurisprudence at Columbia University. His books include *Conflicts of Law and Morality* (1989) and *Law and Objectivity* (1992).

Nancy J. Hirschmann is associate professor of government at Cornell University. She is the author of *Rethinking Obligation: A Feminist Method for Political Theory* (1992).

George Klosko is professor of government and foreign affairs at the University of Virginia. He is the author of *The Principle of Fairness and Political Obligation* (1992).

Mark C. Murphy is assistant professor of philosophy at Georgetown University.

John Rawls is professor of philosophy, emeritus, at Harvard University. He is the author of *A Theory of Justice* (1971) and *Political Liberalism* (1993).

Joseph Raz is professor of the philosophy of law at the University of Oxford and a regular visitor at Columbia University. His books include *Practical Reason and Norms* (1975) and *The Morality of Freedom* (1986).

Rolf Sartorius is professor of philosophy, emeritus, at the University of Minnesota. He is the author of *Individual Conduct and Social Norms* (1975).

A. John Simmons is professor of philosophy at the University of Virginia. His books include *Moral Principles and Political Obligations* (1979) and *On the Edge of Anarchy* (1993).

M. B. E. Smith is professor of philosophy at Smith College.

Philip Soper is James V. Campbell Professor at the University of Michigan Law School. He is the author of *A Theory of Law* (1984).

Jeremy Waldron has taught at Berkeley and Princeton, and is now professor of law and philosophy at Columbia University. He is the author of *Liberal Rights* (1993).

Richard A. Wasserstrom is professor of philosophy at the University of California at Santa Cruz. His books include *The Judicial Decision* (1961).

Robert Paul Wolff is professor of philosophy and African-American studies at the University of Massachusetts at Amherst. His books include *The Poverty of Liberalism* (1968) and *In Defense of Anarchism* (1970, reissued with a new preface, 1998).